playing with paints

watercolor

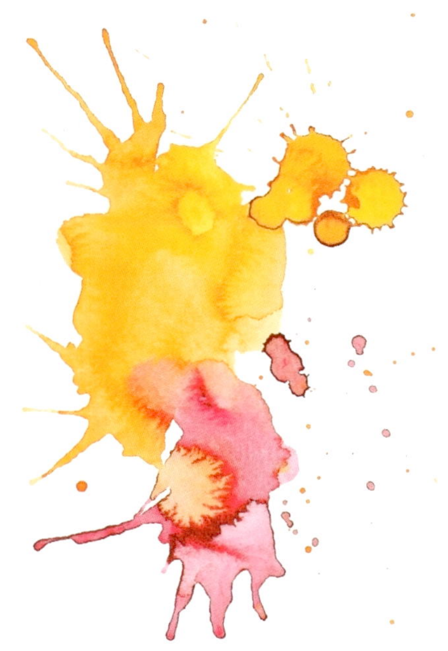

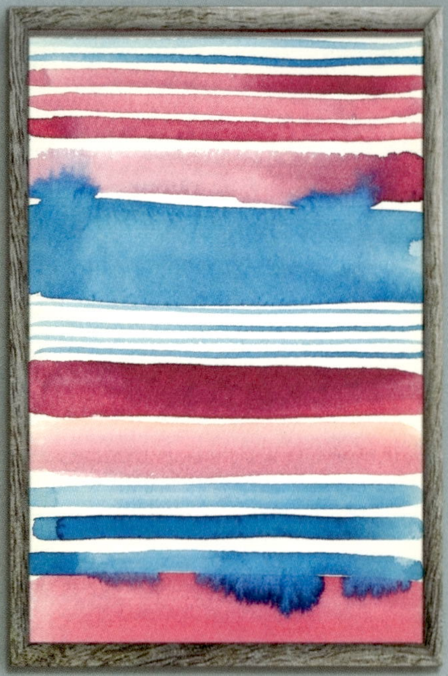

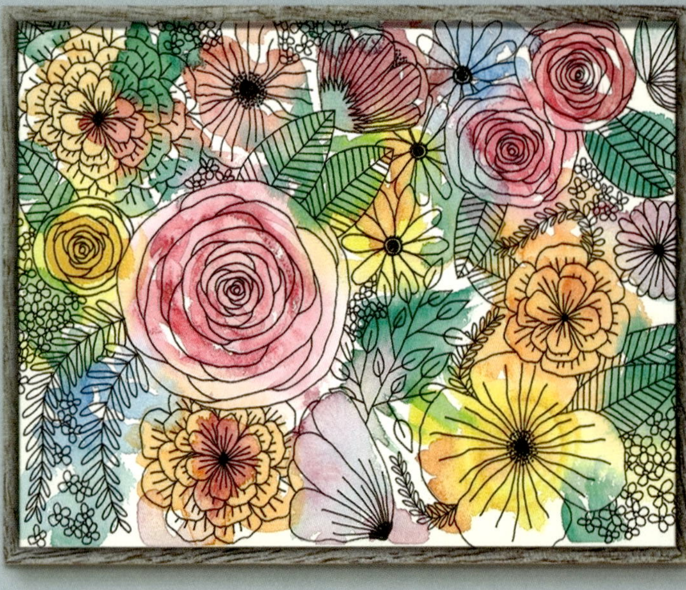

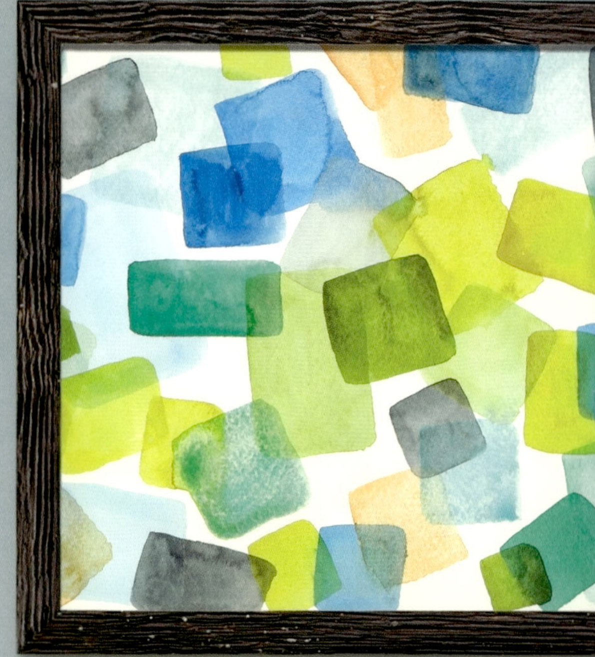

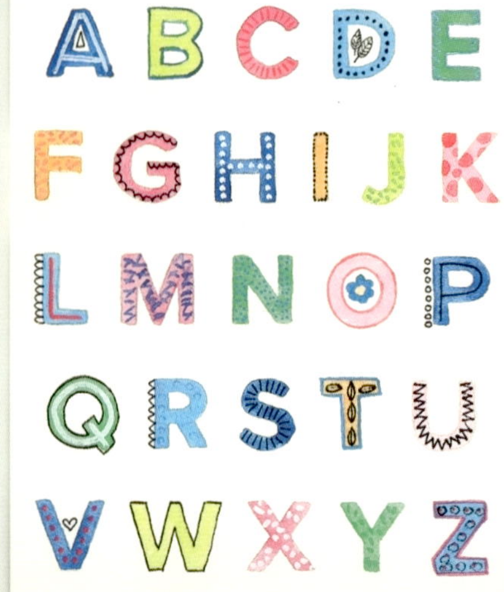
A B C D E
F G H I J K
L M N O P
Q R S T U
V W X Y Z

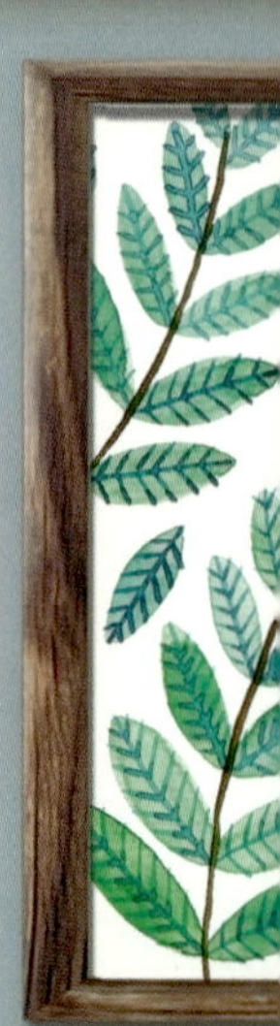

playing with paints

watercolor

100 PROMPTS, PROJECTS AND PLAYFUL ACTIVITIES

SARA FUNDUK

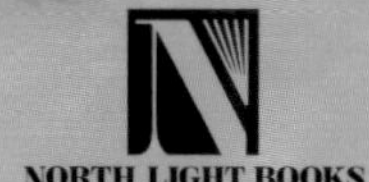

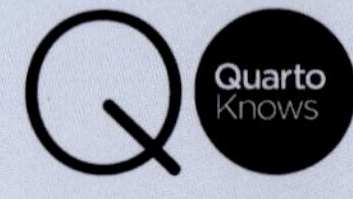

Inspiring | Educating | Creating | Entertaining

Brimming with creative inspiration, how-to projects, and useful information to enrich your everyday life, Quarto Knows is a favorite destination for those pursuing their interests and passions. Visit our site and dig deeper with our books into your area of interest: Quarto Creates, Quarto Cooks, Quarto Homes, Quarto Lives, Quarto Drives, Quarto Explores, Quarto Gifts, or Quarto Kids.

Published by North Light Books, an imprint of Penguin Random House LLC

First Edition.

penguinrandomhouse.com

10 9 8 7 6 5 4 3 2 1

ISBN: 978-1-4403-0092-9

Conceived, edited, and designed by Quarto Publishing plc, an imprint of The Quarto Group, 6 Blundell Street, London N7 9BH

QUAR.326687

Senior editor: Kate Burkett
Senior art editor: Emma Clayton
Designer: Rachel Cross
Photographer: Phil Wilkins, Michelle Gibson, and Sara Funduk
Art director: Gemma Wilson
Publisher: Samantha Warrington

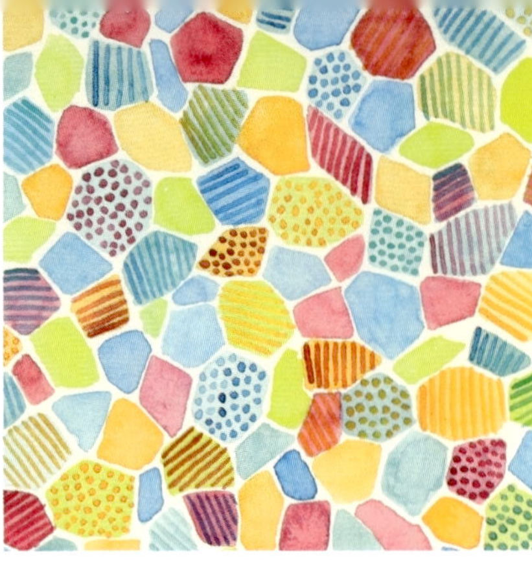

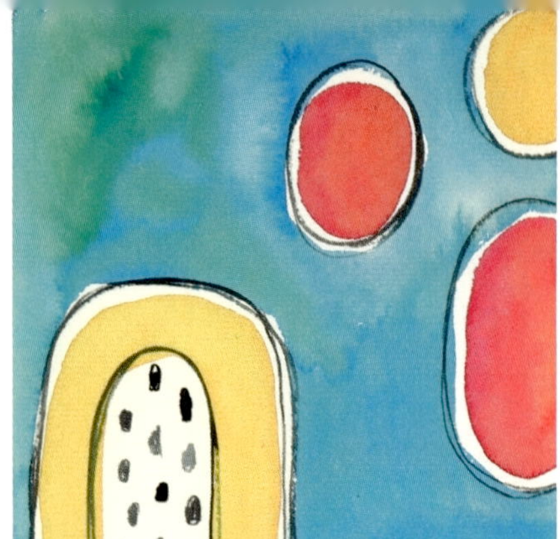

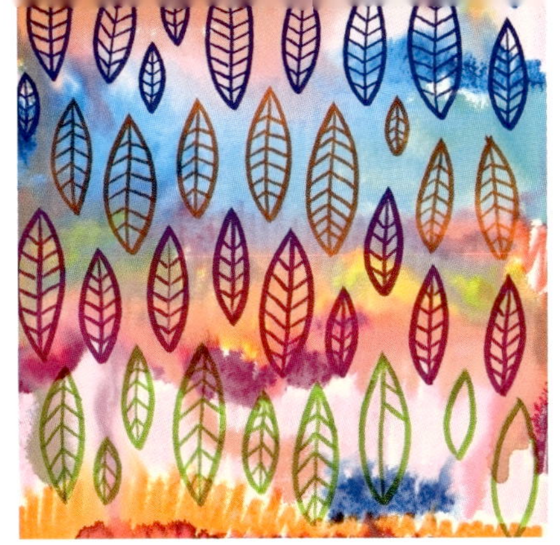

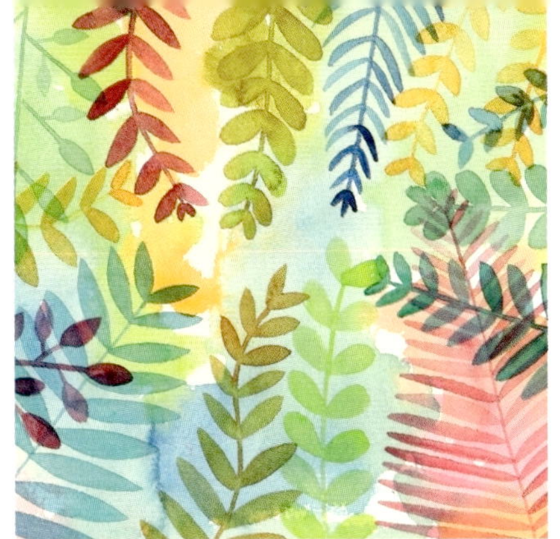

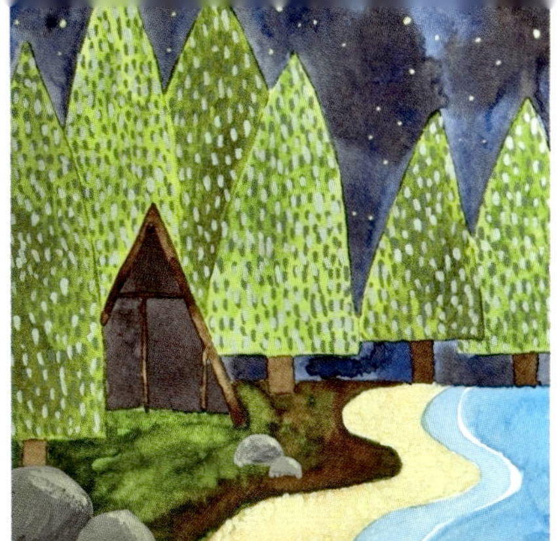

Chapter 3

Chapter 4

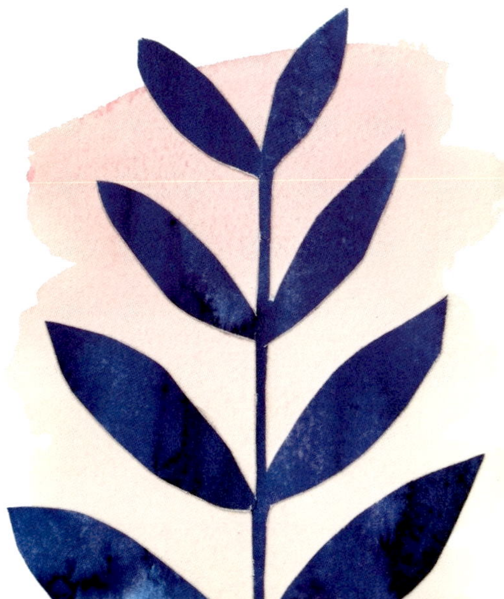

Meet Sara

Hey you! I'm so happy you picked up this book!
Are you ready to create some art with me?

My name is Sara Funduk and I live in Ontario, Canada, with my husband Ryan, my son Stanley, and our two grumpy old cats. I am an art-supply hoarder; I use all the colors when I paint; and I am completely obsessed with patterns. I have been making art since I was old enough to hold a crayon, but it took me a long time to discover watercolor.

When my son was born, I almost let my creativity dry up. I felt like I had no time to paint and I definitely didn't have time for all the setup and cleanup work that went with it. One day, during nap time, I pulled out a barely used watercolor palette from my stash and it all clicked.

This medium is wonderful for so many reasons, but I especially love that it is so approachable and affordable. All the supplies you need to create a beautiful watercolor painting can fit in your back pocket. With my tiny watercolor palette and small sketchbook, I painted whenever I found a spare moment and completely fell in love with art all over again.

Watercolor has a reputation for being unpredictable and hard to control. But, if you ask me, that's exactly what makes it so much fun to work with. If you learn to let go, beautiful and unexpected things will happen on the page. Quite often my "mistakes" turn out to be the most exciting part of a painting!

In this book, I'm not going to teach a list of specific rules to follow. Instead, you'll find plays, prompts, and projects designed to show you just what this beautiful medium is capable of. I hope these exercises will show you how to paint with joy and take pleasure in the process. Incorporating art into your life is something anyone can do even if you've never picked up a paintbrush before! And if you're more experienced, I hope I can teach you to use your watercolor skills in new and exciting ways.

So, get ready to have some fun, make mistakes, surprise yourself, and fall in love with watercolor!

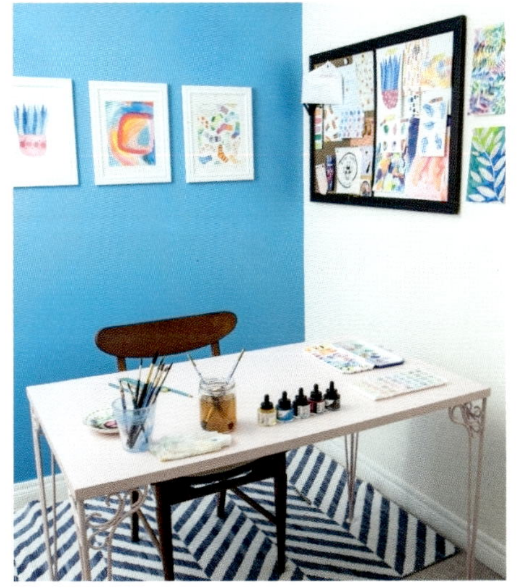
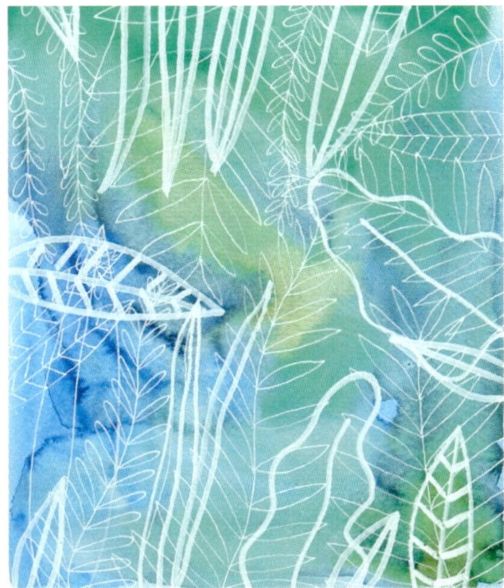
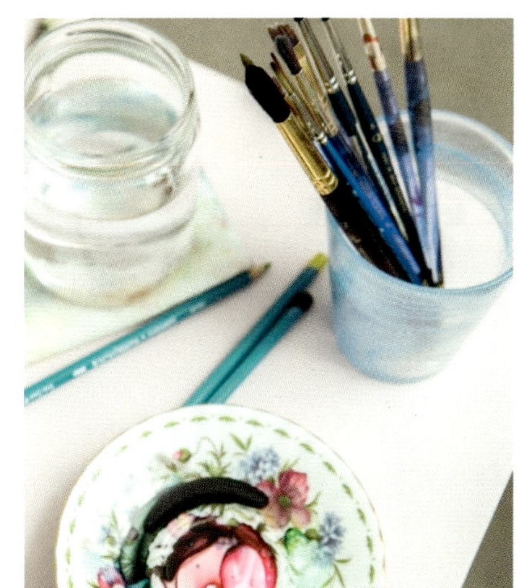
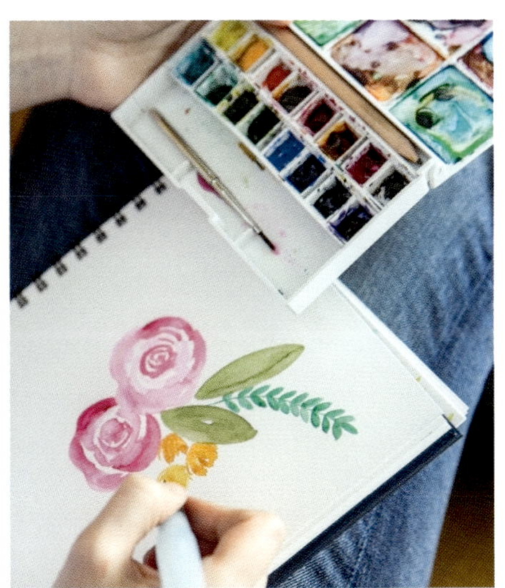
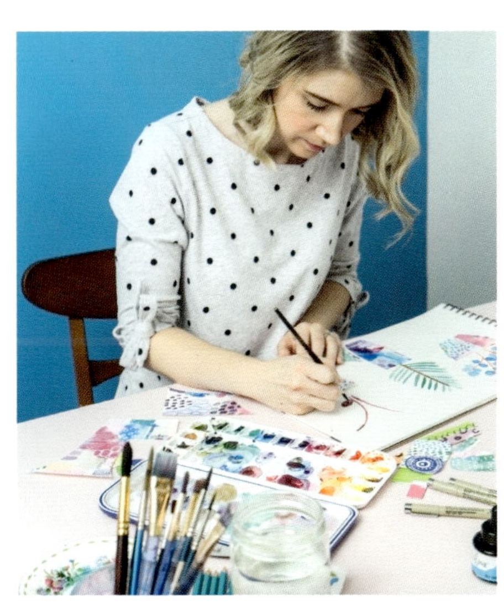
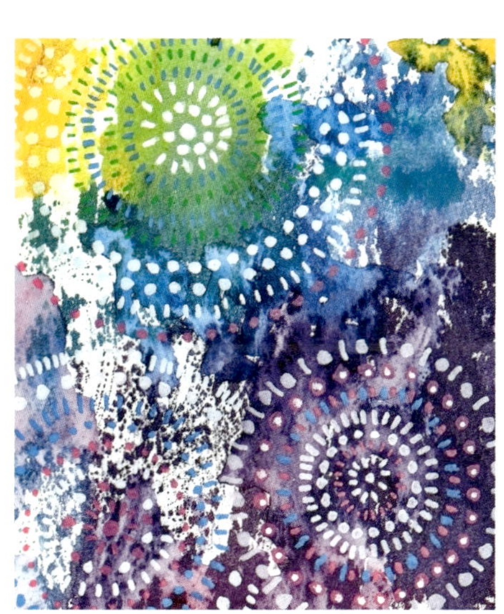
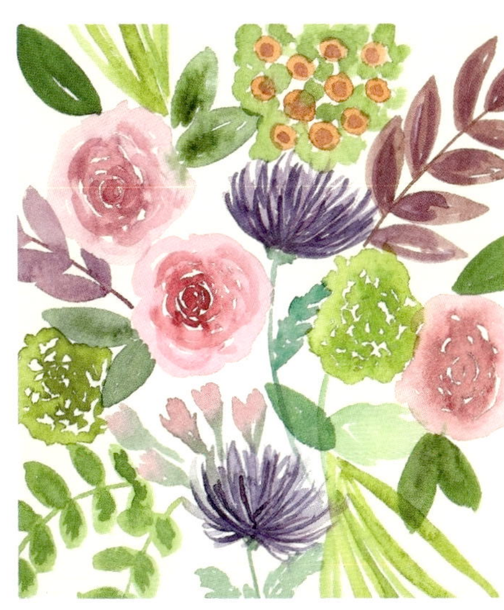
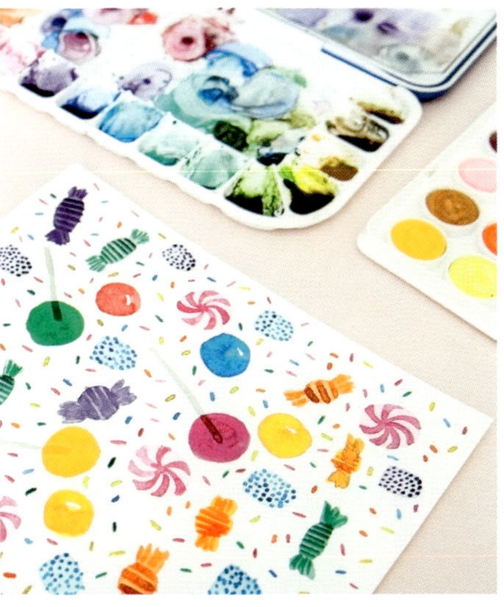
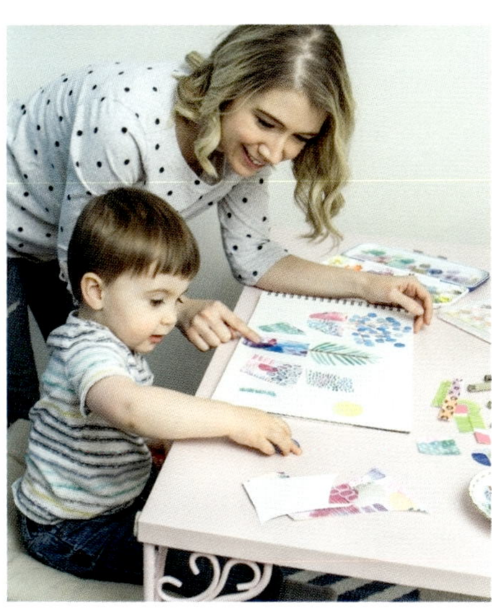

1

Jump right in

In this chapter you will learn how to put together a beginner's watercolor kit to suit any budget and start experimenting right away. Don't worry too much about the rules! The first few exercises will show how this surprising medium behaves and how easy it can be to achieve beautiful results. You will learn all about color and how it blends and works together. Then jump right in by exploring your brushes and making some marks. These simple brushstrokes will come together to form some lovely pieces of art. I will guide you through a few beginner techniques and you can take off from there.

Basic watercolor supplies

Getting started with watercolor painting does not require a ton of supplies. Any watercolor set you can get your hands on will teach you how to work with the paint. As you fall in love with the medium (and you will!), you can upgrade your supplies as you go.

Paint

Watercolor paint generally comes in two forms: tubes (1) and pans (2). Paint from a tube is wonderfully vibrant and beautiful to work with, but can get a bit pricey. Watercolor pan sets are generally more affordable and can vary in quality. For most of the exercises in this book, I use tube paint, but use whatever you have at hand, or can afford, and work up from there. You can make lovely art even with a children's set of paints!

Brushes

A round brush with a good point is definitely the brush I reach for the most. You can complete almost every exercise in this book with just a medium round brush (3). I also love water brushes (4) that have a handle which can be filled with water. They are great for painting on the go. When you are ready to expand your collection, you will probably need a large flat brush (5) for washes and a small liner brush (6) for detail. Be sure to buy brushes specifically made for watercolor because they will hold the most paint.

Palettes

The best things about a set of pan paints are that it comes with its own storage case and the lid doubles as a mixing palette. If you are using tube paints, you'll want to get a palette (7) too. I use a plastic one with a lid so I can take my paint with me anywhere. I almost never clean my palette, because the paint can always be reactivated.

Paper

Thick, good-quality watercolor paper is important for achieving that signature watercolor look. Watercolor paper (8) comes in bound books, sheets, and blocks that are gummed on every side to prevent wrinkling. I tend to practice on cheaper paper and save he more expensive paper for finished projects. Not all watercolor paper is created equal. You will notice a big difference in your finished artwork when you use high-quality paper.

Water

It might seem obvious, but clean water is an important tool! I like to keep two jars of water when I paint: one for cleaning my brush (9); the other for mixing with the paint (10). If your water gets too muddy, it will start to affect the color of your paint, so clean water is essential.

Tape

Tape the paper to a hard work surface with painter's tape or washi tape (11). It prevents wrinkling and gives a nice clean edge. But be sure to wait until your painting is completely dry before pulling up the tape.

Pens and pencils

A black waterproof pen (12) is a great way to add some linework and detail. I also love to add accents with a white gel pen (13). You'll see pens used a lot in this book as a finishing touch. And be sure to always have a light pencil (14) at hand for making initial sketches.

Other useful tools

Masking fluid (15); Watercolor markers (16); Watercolor pencils (17); Salt (18); Rubbing alcohol; Gouache (19); Paint pens (20); Props and photos for reference.

PRO TIPS

- Be sure to always rinse your brushes well after each painting session and store them pointing upward, to ensure they keep their shape.
- Watercolor paint can always be reactivated after it dries on the palette, so there is never any waste. Even paint from a tube can still be used after it has dried.
- Keep a spray bottle of water at hand to quickly mist your whole paint palette before you start.
- For paint that is especially old and dry, warm water will resurrect even the crustiest of palettes! Just spray and let it sit for a few minutes.
- If you are covering the page with paint, be sure to use a watercolor block, or tape the paper to a hard surface. Let the painting dry completely before removing the tape.

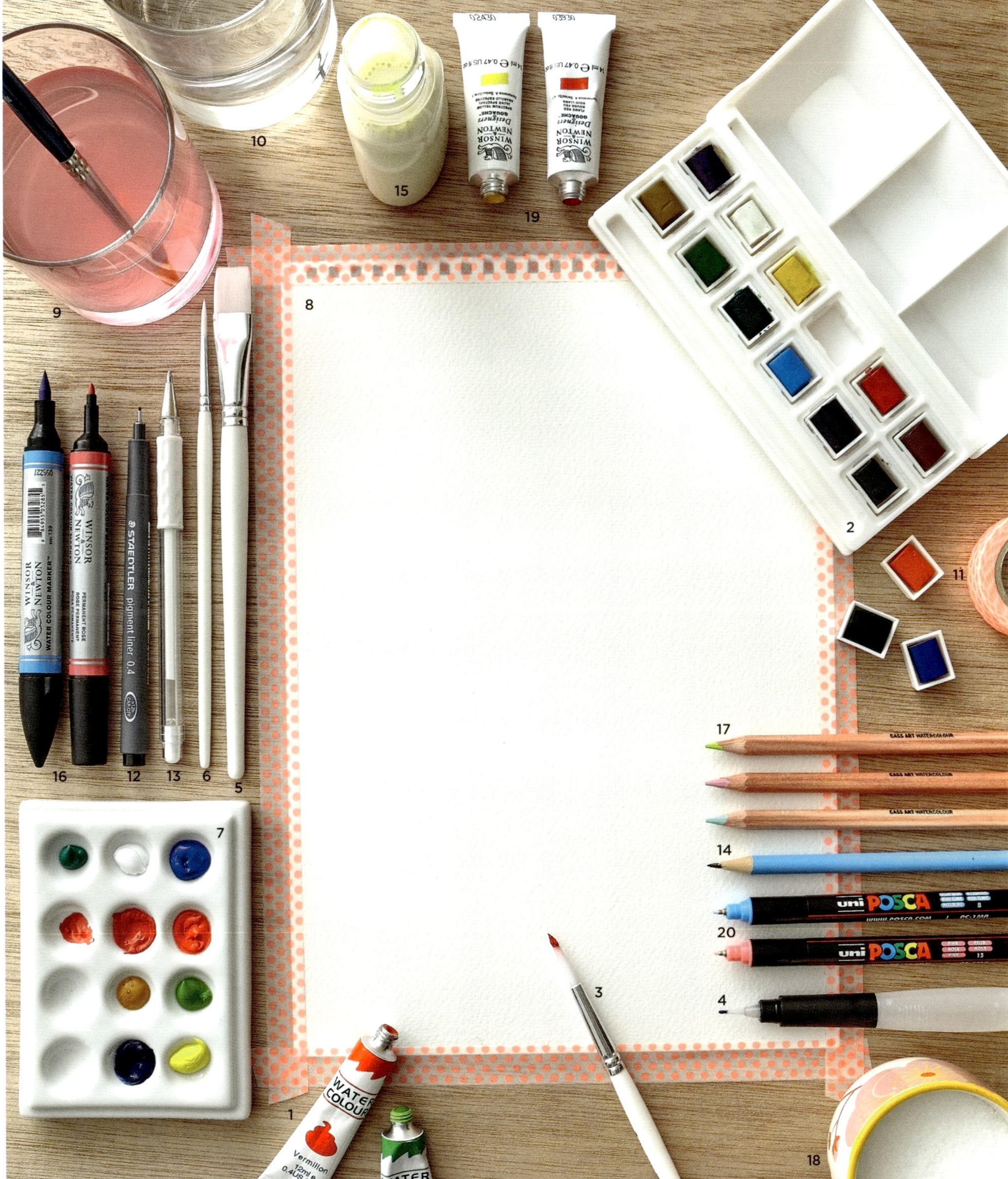
10
15
19
9
8
2
11
16
12
13
6
5
7
17
14
20
3
4
1
18
WINSOR & NEWTON
Designers GOUACHE
WINSOR & NEWTON WATER COLOUR MARKER
STAEDTLER pigment liner 0.4
uni POSCA
CASS ART WATERCOLOUR
WATER COLOUR
Vermillion

Play Get to know your paint

In this exercise you'll get a feel for your paints, the colors, and how they behave on paper. It seems so simple, but sampling all the colors is a great way to break the tension when you are faced with a brand new palette and a perfect, blank sketchbook.

The first thing I do when I get a new set of paints is create a swatch chart of all the colors. Watercolor paints are notorious for looking completely different on paper than they do in the palette. This is especially true for the kind that comes in tubes. So grab your paintbrush and create a little chart of all your beautiful paints. Swatch the color at full strength or create a gradient by pulling the paint across the paper and adding a bit more water as you go.

If you paint a little gradient, you will be able to see what each color looks like at different strengths. This can be very handy when searching for the perfect shade of green, for example. Swatch your paints in the front of your sketchbook or on a little scrap of paper that you slip into your palette. You will find yourself consulting this chart all the time. And now that you've tried every color you have, you're ready for more experimentation!

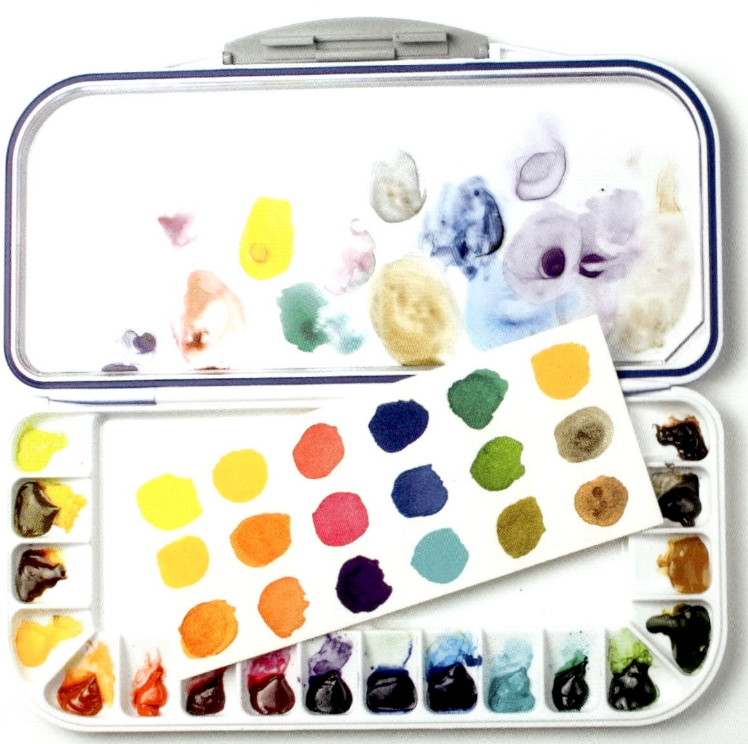

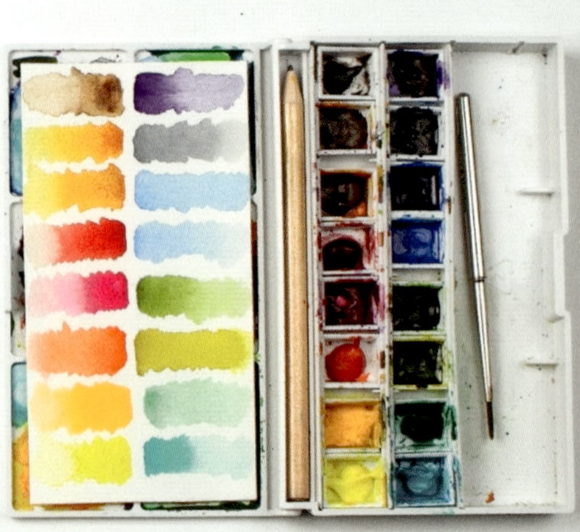

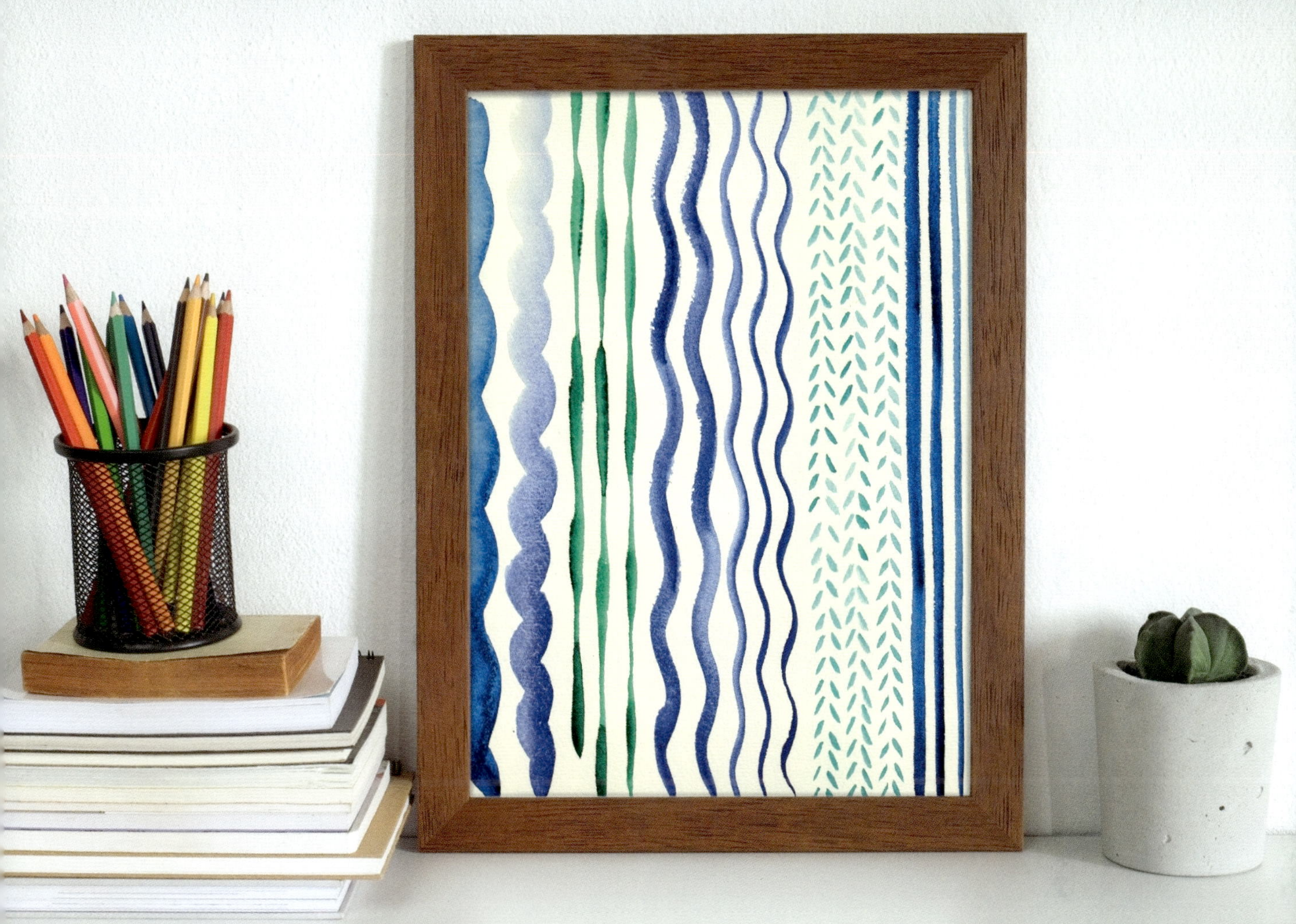

Play Exploring lines

It is time to take your brushes out for a test drive to see what they are capable of. Get a feel for the type of lines and marks that each brush can create.

If you have a medium-sized round brush (I like a 6 or 8) and maybe a larger brush, you are good to go. You might be surprised at how many lines you can create with just one brush by varying the pressure. First, start with a really thin line. Barely graze the paper with your brush and see how fine you can get the line. For the next few lines, gradually increase the pressure and watch the lines grow thicker. Now press down on the brush so the bristles are almost completely flat against the page. Next you can experiment with long wavy lines, short little dashes, and big fat squiggles. You can even vary the pressure in one continuous line to get a neat bumpy effect. Not only is this a great way to get to know your brushes, it is also a wonderful warm-up for your hand. If I am not sure what to paint, I sometimes just fill a page with lines to limber up. It almost always results in a new idea.

Play Create a color wheel

Mixing your own colors is easy to do, but it can take a bit of practice to get just right. The best first step is to create a color wheel for practice and to use as a reference later. Painting a color wheel is a fun exercise that will teach you a lot about color and how each color is made.

You can divide a circle into 12 sections for a traditional color wheel, or you can do something a little more fun. I sketched out a flower with three large petals for the primary colors, three slightly smaller petals for the secondary colors, and six even smaller petals for the tertiary colors.

When mixing, if your colors are looking a little dull or muddy, make sure to mix two colors with the same temperature. A warm blue and a cool yellow together will make a dull green; a cool blue and cool yellow will mix to create a bright green. That is why I like to keep a few different versions of the primary colors around.

After you are done with your color wheel, try mixing a little black with each color to make a darker shade and add more water to make a lighter tint. There is white watercolor paint on the market, if you would like to try that out, too. You can also tone down a color by mixing in a bit of the color that is directly across from it on the wheel. So, if your blue is too bright, add a little orange to tone the brightness down.

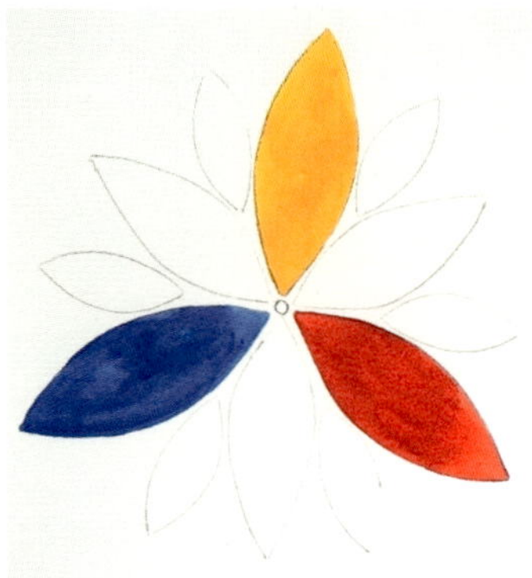

Primary colors
Begin with the three primary colors, which are red, blue, and yellow. You can't mix these colors yourself, so use them straight from the pan or tube. These colors are the building blocks for creating all the others.

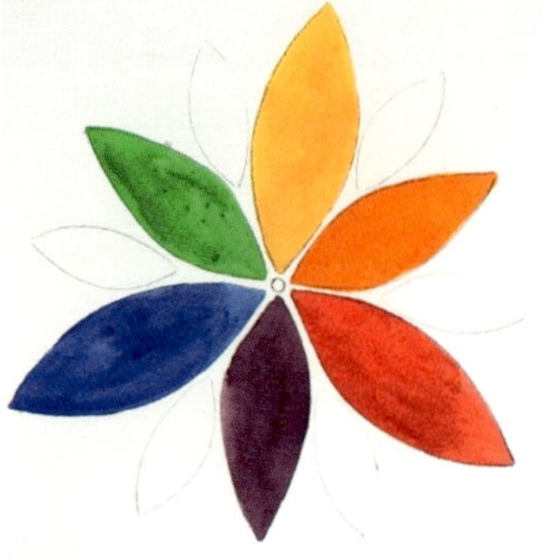

Secondary colors
These colors are created by mixing each primary color with its neighbor. Mix red with yellow to create orange, yellow with blue to create green, and blue with red to create violet.

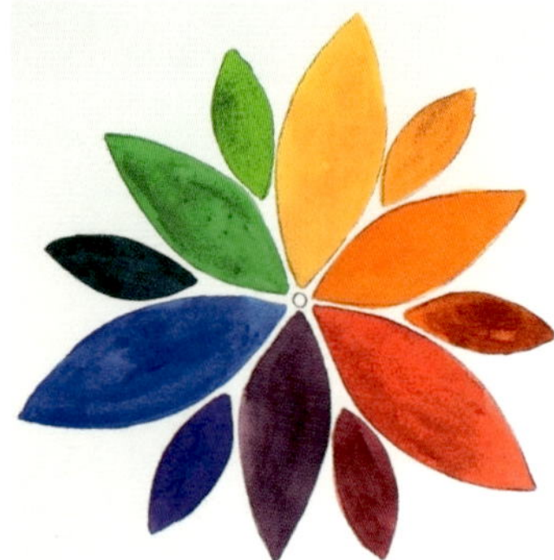

Tertiary colors
These colors are made by mixing each primary color with the secondary color next to it. There are six tertiary colors: red-orange, yellow-orange, yellow-green, blue-green, blue-violet, and red-violet.

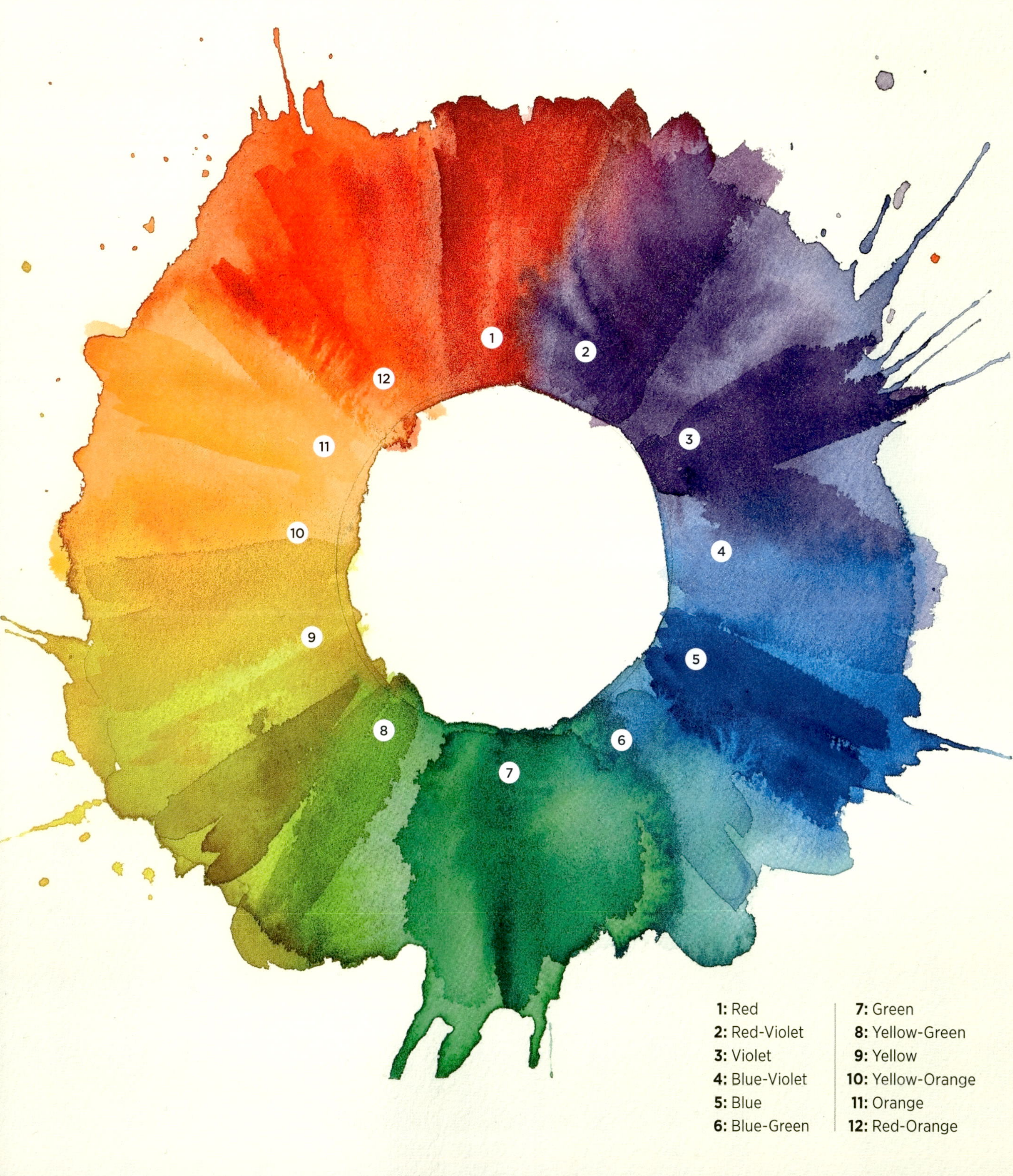
1
2
3
4
5
6
7
8
9
10
11
12
1: Red
2: Red-Violet
3: Violet
4: Blue-Violet
5: Blue
6: Blue-Green
7: Green
8: Yellow-Green
9: Yellow
10: Yellow-Orange
11: Orange
12: Red-Orange

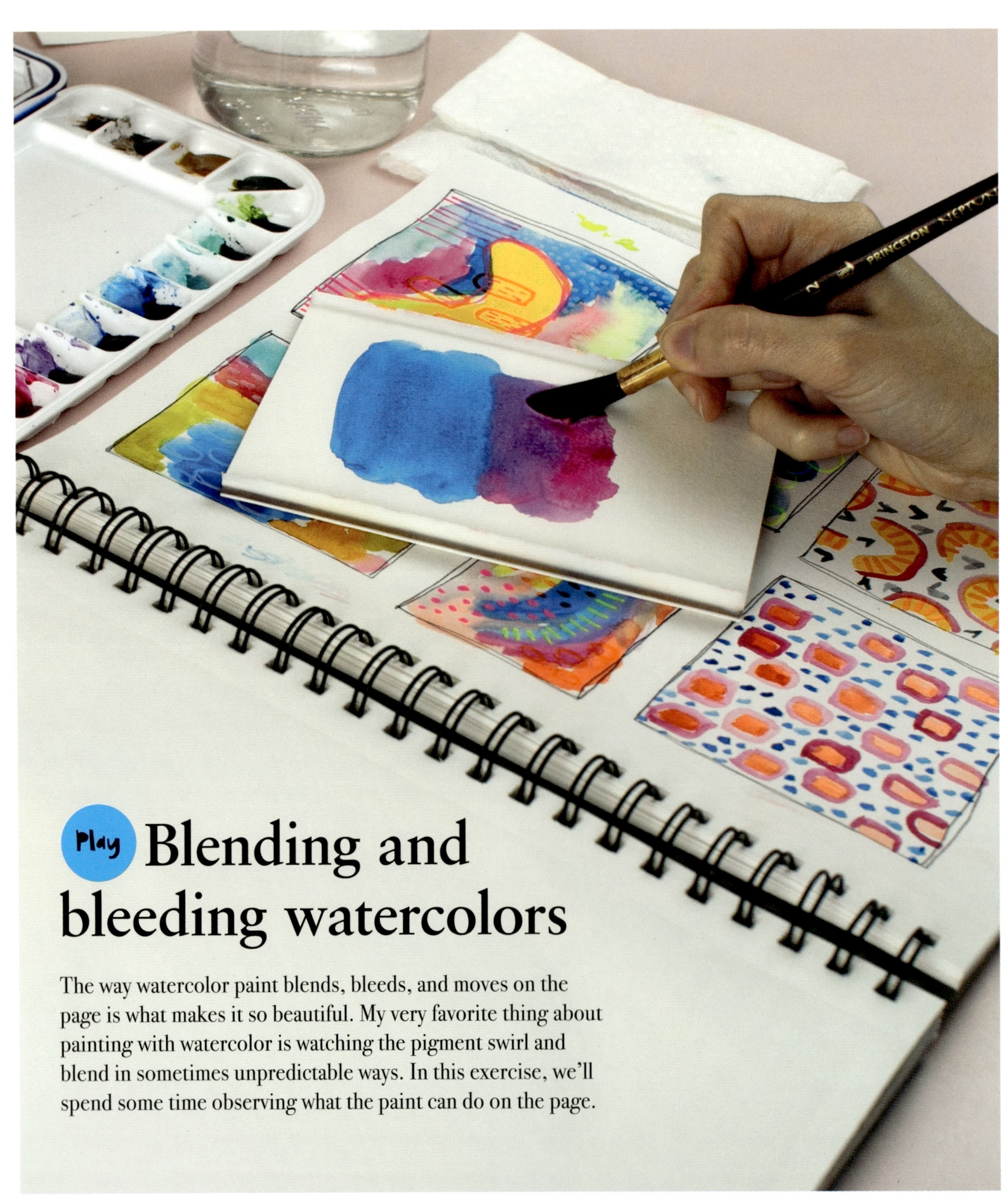

Play Blending and bleeding watercolors

The way watercolor paint blends, bleeds, and moves on the page is what makes it so beautiful. My very favorite thing about painting with watercolor is watching the pigment swirl and blend in sometimes unpredictable ways. In this exercise, we'll spend some time observing what the paint can do on the page.

Creating a gradient Grab your favorite color and paint a thick line down the page. While it is still wet, rinse your brush and pick up some clean water. Touch your brush to the pigment and pull it down the page. You can rinse and add more water again to create even more transparency. If you want the beginning of the gradient to be more opaque, you can always go back and add more pigment.

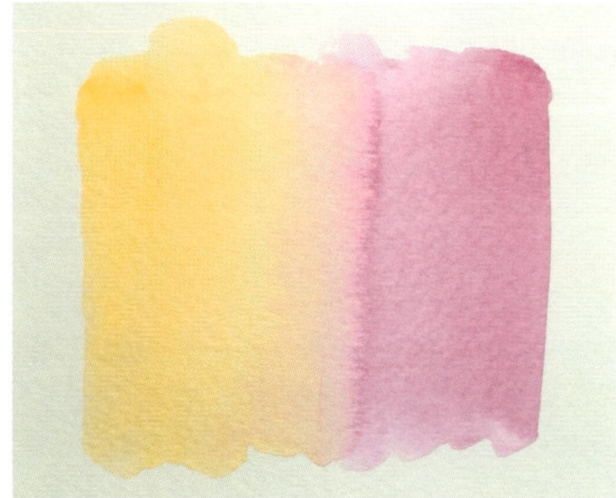

Blending two colors Pick two colors that are close to each other on the color wheel, so they will blend easily. Paint a swatch with your first color. Clean your brush and pick up the second color. Paint a swatch beside the first, dragging the paint into the first color. The colors will bleed together naturally. For a smoother gradient, blend out with a clean, almost dry brush.

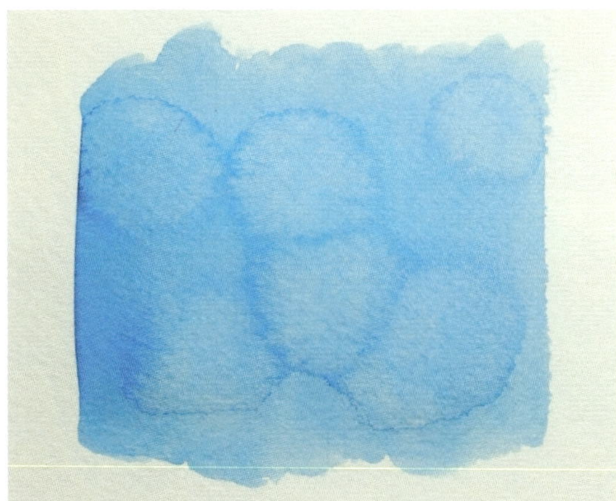

Adding water for blooms Some traditional watercolor artists consider these "blooms" mistakes, but I think they are beautiful. Start with a swatch of any color you like. While the paint is still wet, but not soaking wet, use your brush to drop some clean water onto the pigment—it will create little blooms of light. Wait until the whole thing dries before you make your judgment—this effect tends to look very different when dry.

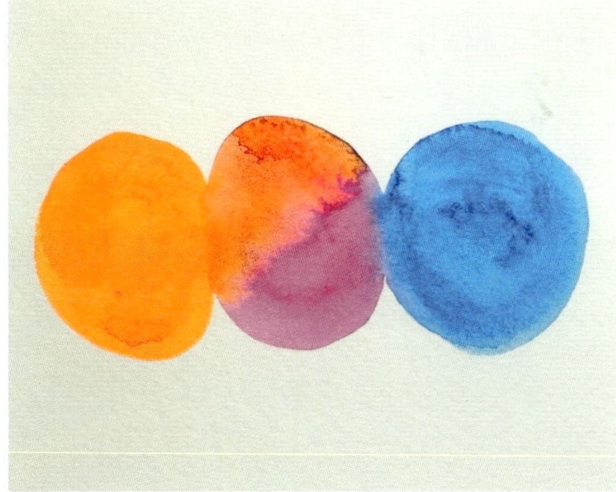

Happy accidents This bleeding effect tends to happen accidentally for me when I am too impatient to let the paint fully dry. But I always love it, and if you keep it in mind, you can use this effect purposefully in your work with beautiful results. Paint two shapes right next to each other. Now don't touch anything! Just let the two colors mingle and bleed together. This is another effect that looks quite different once dry.

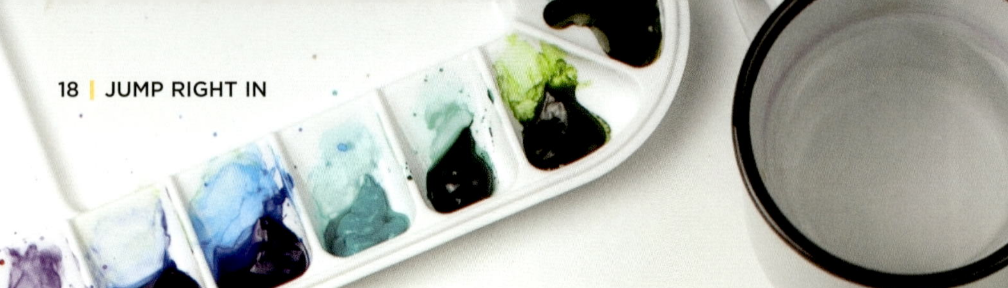

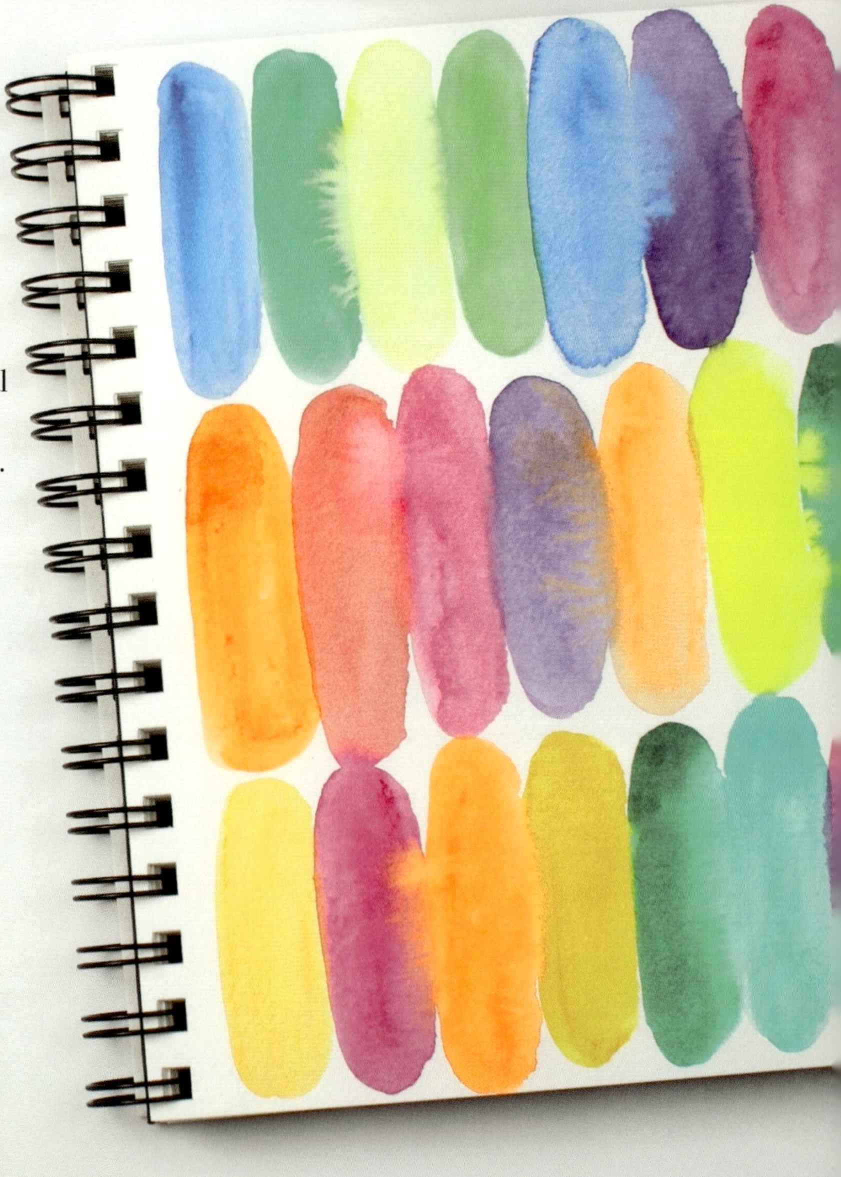

prompt Your first pattern

Patterns are my absolute favorite thing to paint. I love how you can start with a very simple shape and create something beautiful by filling the page with that shape. Patterns are easy and fun, and can make a big impact.

This pattern is so easy to paint and I guarantee you will love the result. Pick a simple shape, such as a circle, line, or oval, and repeat it across the page. That's it! Don't think about an overall color scheme. Instead, choose colors as you go based on the one you just laid down. For example, if you start with a pink shape, think of which color you would like to see next to that pink. Maybe choose something that contrasts with it, such as a dark green. Or pick a color that provides a soft transition, such as an orange or purple. It is all about experimentation. I like it when some of my shapes bump up against each other, so the colors bleed together.

Don't let the simplicity of this exercise fool you. This is a great way to learn which colors you like to see together and which colors blend in an interesting way. It is also a fabulous way to get to know your brushes—I use a round brush, size 6 or 8—and learn how much water you need to use to achieve different shades. Feel free to repeat this exercise as many times as you like. I love to curl up with my sketchbook and paint some meditative patterns. These simple spreads can often lead to bigger ideas.

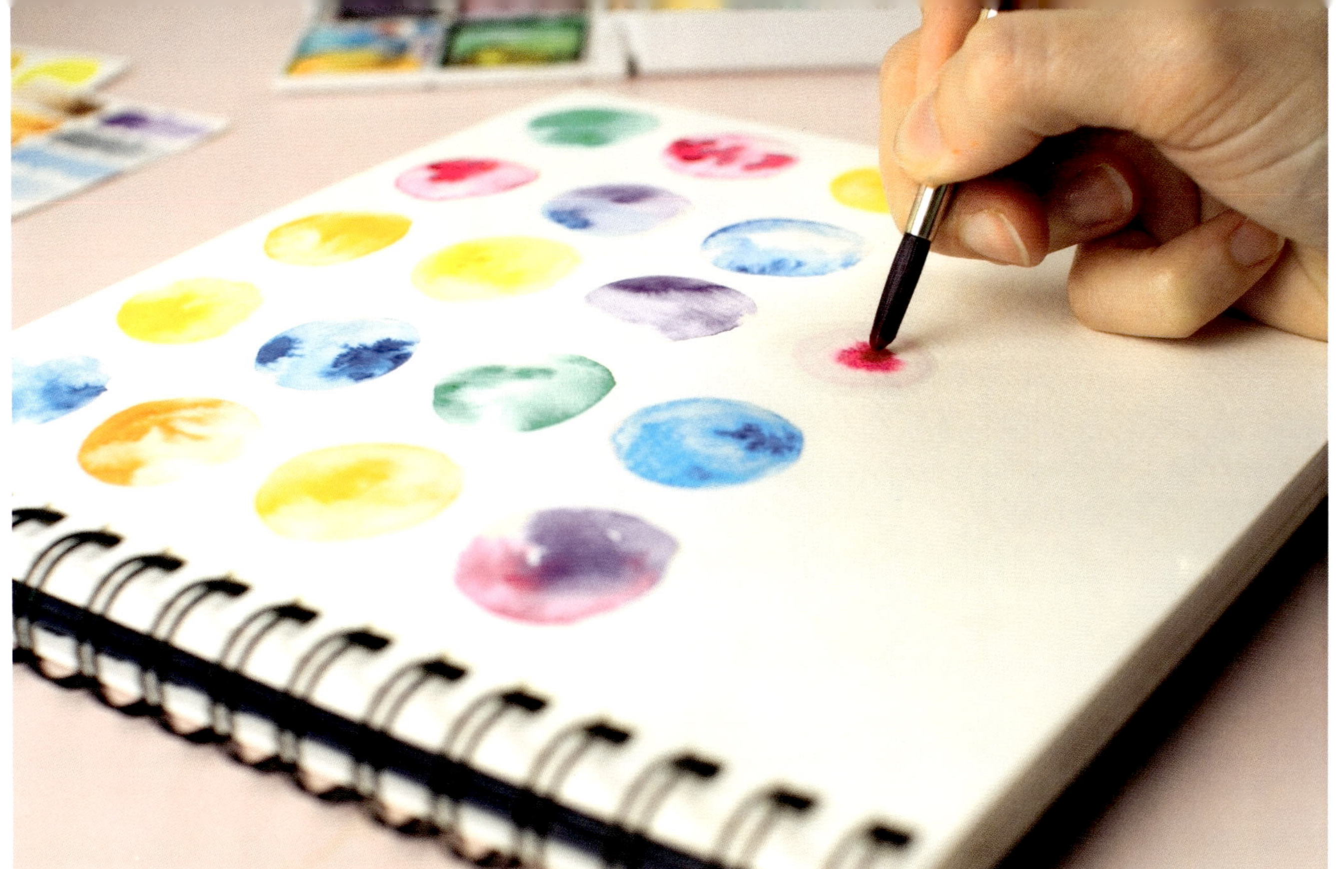

Play Making moons

This fun exercise is going to teach you a lot about working wet-on-wet, which is a term used for painting onto a wet surface. It can take some practice to use the right touch, so have fun filling the whole page with swirly watercolor moons.

Working wet-on-wet can take some practice, so don't be upset if your first couple of moons don't turn out quite right. Start by painting a small circle on the paper with clean water using a small round brush. It might help to keep two jars of water: one in which to rinse your brush and another for painting your shapes, so you are always using sparkling-clean water.

The trick here is to put down just the right amount of water. If the water is pooling on the page, or if it is sitting in a dome on top of the paper, you have too much. If the circle is drying before you get a chance to add color, then you have too little. You will need to experiment to learn exactly how much water you need. Once you have the perfect amount of water, dry off your brush a little and pick up some paint. Drying your brush a bit will ensure you don't dilute the pigment too much. With a light touch, dab the brush onto the circle and watch what happens. When you have the technique down, you can play around. See what happens when you place two blobs of color on opposite ends. What happens if you lightly paint around the edge of the circle? What about adding a second color? Have fun and play around until you have filled the whole page.

Layered abstract piece

Abstract art doesn't have to be intimidating. This exercise will teach you how to use your intuition to create a beautiful layered painting. And once you get the hang of it, you will be filling page after page of your sketchbook with unique abstract work.

YOU WILL NEED

- Watercolor paper
- Watercolor paint in 4 or 5 colors
- Medium round brush
- Small round brush

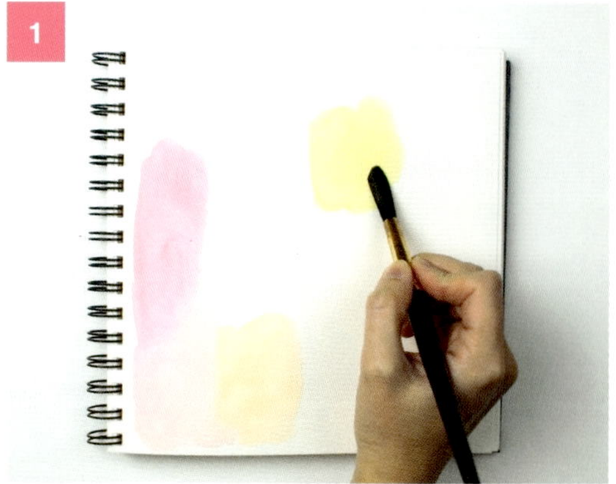

Start with a few light colors and lay down some messy blobs randomly on the page. Think about which colors might blend well together and which colors you would like to see next to each other.

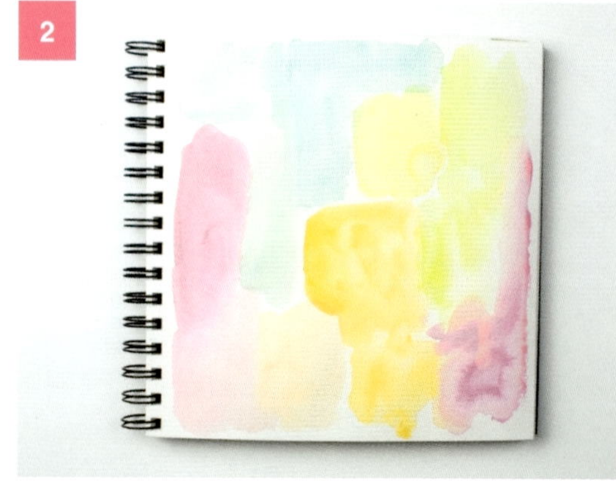

Have fun filling the page with color. Paint some shapes close together so the colors bleed and leave some white space between other shapes. Try to keep your palette to four or five different colors.

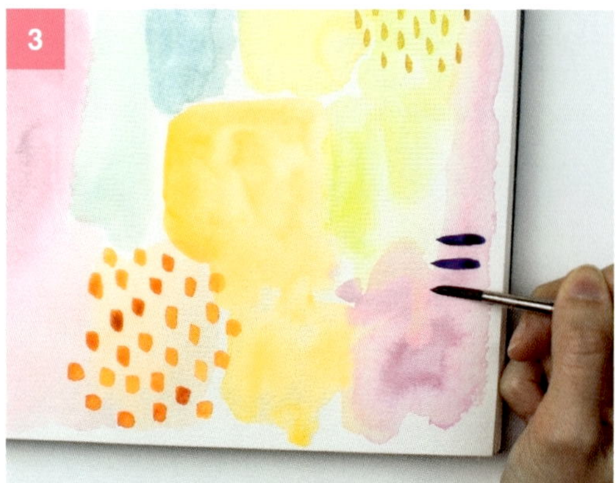

Once the first layer is completely dry, it is time to add some pattern. Paint dashes, marks, and dots over your shapes using darker colors that stand out over the light washes in the first layer.

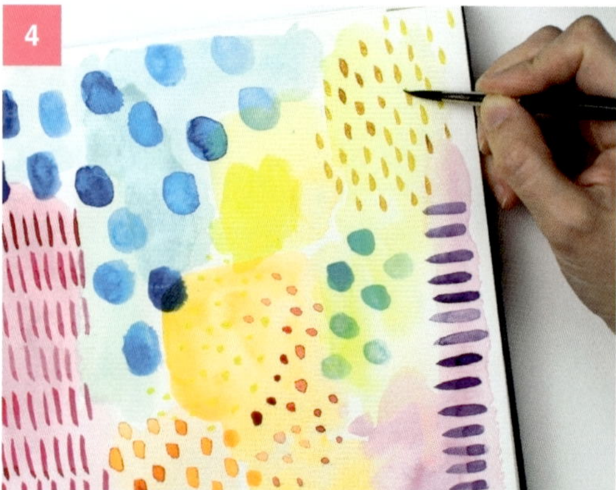

Keep filling in the page with as much or as little pattern as you like. Varying the size of your marks (tiny dots versus big fat dashes) will add interest to your piece.

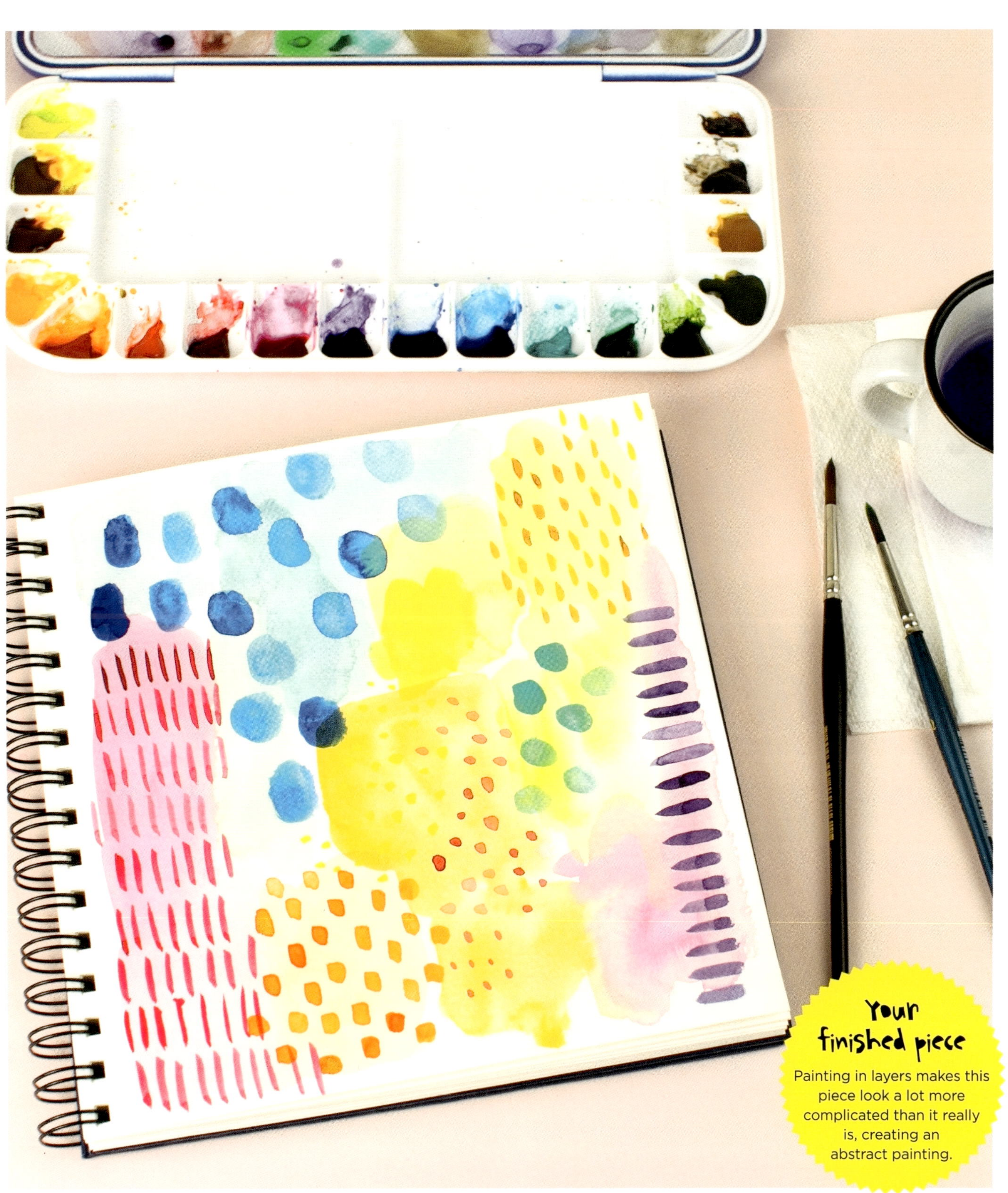

Your finished piece

Painting in layers makes this piece look a lot more complicated than it really is, creating an abstract painting.

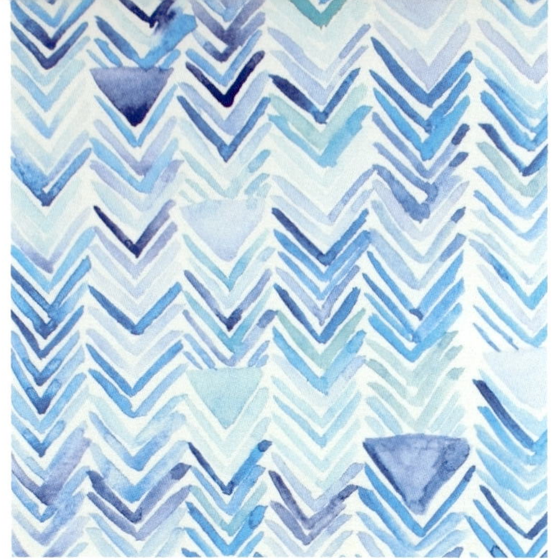

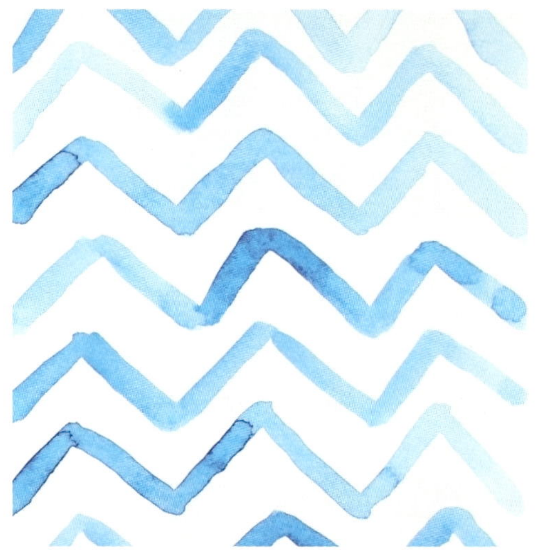

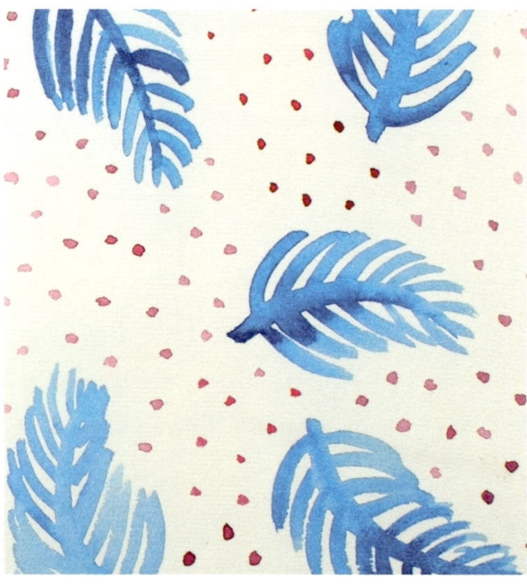

prompt Monochrome doesn't mean boring

Have you ever been stuck on a color choice? Monochrome could be the answer! By working with a single color, you can take your mind off choosing a color scheme and instead focus on the painting itself.

You can create a monochrome color scheme by using shades, tones, and tints of a color. Shades are made by adding black to a base color; tones are made by adding gray to a base color; and tints are made by adding white to a base color. In the case of watercolors, though, we add water to mix a tint instead of white paint and create gray paint by adding water to black.

So all you need to create a beautiful monochromatic color scheme is your favorite color, some black paint, and water. You don't need every color in the rainbow to make a beautiful painting. This can be a great way to slowly invest in better-quality paints.

Monochrome designs let you focus on the process of painting instead of fretting over color choice. Being able to mix your own colors is a great skill to learn and creating those shades, tones, and tints will be good practice. Besides, single-color patterns look super-sophisticated, so what starts out as a choice driven by your lack of supplies can end up being some of your favorite work.

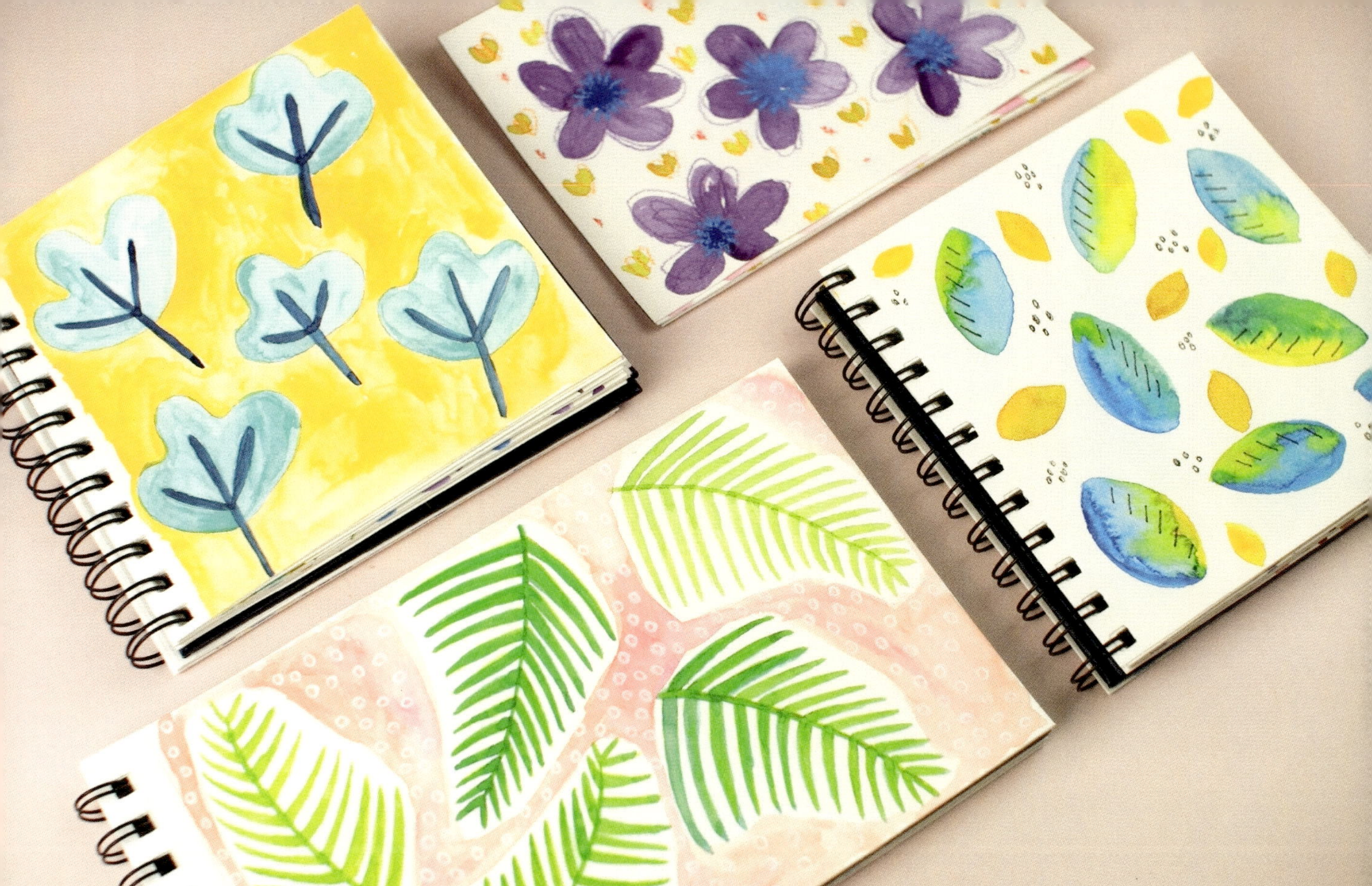

prompt Frenemies: complementary colors

Complementary color schemes are iconic. They are often used by sports teams for visibility, on corporate logos, and in many areas of design. They can be bold and even a bit jarring–but there are a few tricks you can learn to tone down these duos and make them work.

Complementary colors are found directly across from each other on the color wheel. You will know you have found a complementary pair because they tend to vibrate against each other. Some people will even say they clash and shouldn't be used together, but I think this type of color scheme can add interesting contrast to your art and draw the eye in.

Subduing a complementary color scheme is done by using shades, tones, or tints of those colors. So, instead of using a vibrant red and green full strength, shift those colors to a salmon-pink and teal. Instead of bright blue and orange, go with a light sky-blue and warm sunny yellow.

Another way to soften things up is to use a split complementary palette. Start with any color you like, then follow it across the wheel to find its complementary friend. Instead of using the complementary color, though, pick the two colors on either side of it.

Of course, I am not a big fan of rules, so if you love the way two colors clash and vibrate against each other, then you should definitely use them in your art. Those colors that really zing when placed next to each other can be eye-catching and dramatic.

Prompt Soothing analogous colors

An analogous color palette is so easy to create and pleasing to the eye. Just walk through the woods on a fall day and you will see a gorgeous analogous color scheme at work. Take a lesson from nature and incorporate these wonderful palettes into your artwork.

An analogous color harmony is created by using three or four colors that are found next to each other on the color wheel. Using colors that are neighbors will give your painting a serene and calming look. I particularly love to use this combination with patterns, because it ties all the motifs and shapes together to give a cohesive look. It is a surefire way to make a sophisticated and modern painting.

A word of caution: Analogous color palettes don't have much contrast and can look washed-out. To avoid giving your painting a dull look, pick one color to dominate the page and use the other two as accents. You can also add more pop by introducing white, black, or another neutral into your painting. It can help break up the monotony that an analogous palette sometimes creates. Even just incorporating lots of white space into your work will make a big difference, as it will keep the colors from blending together too much.

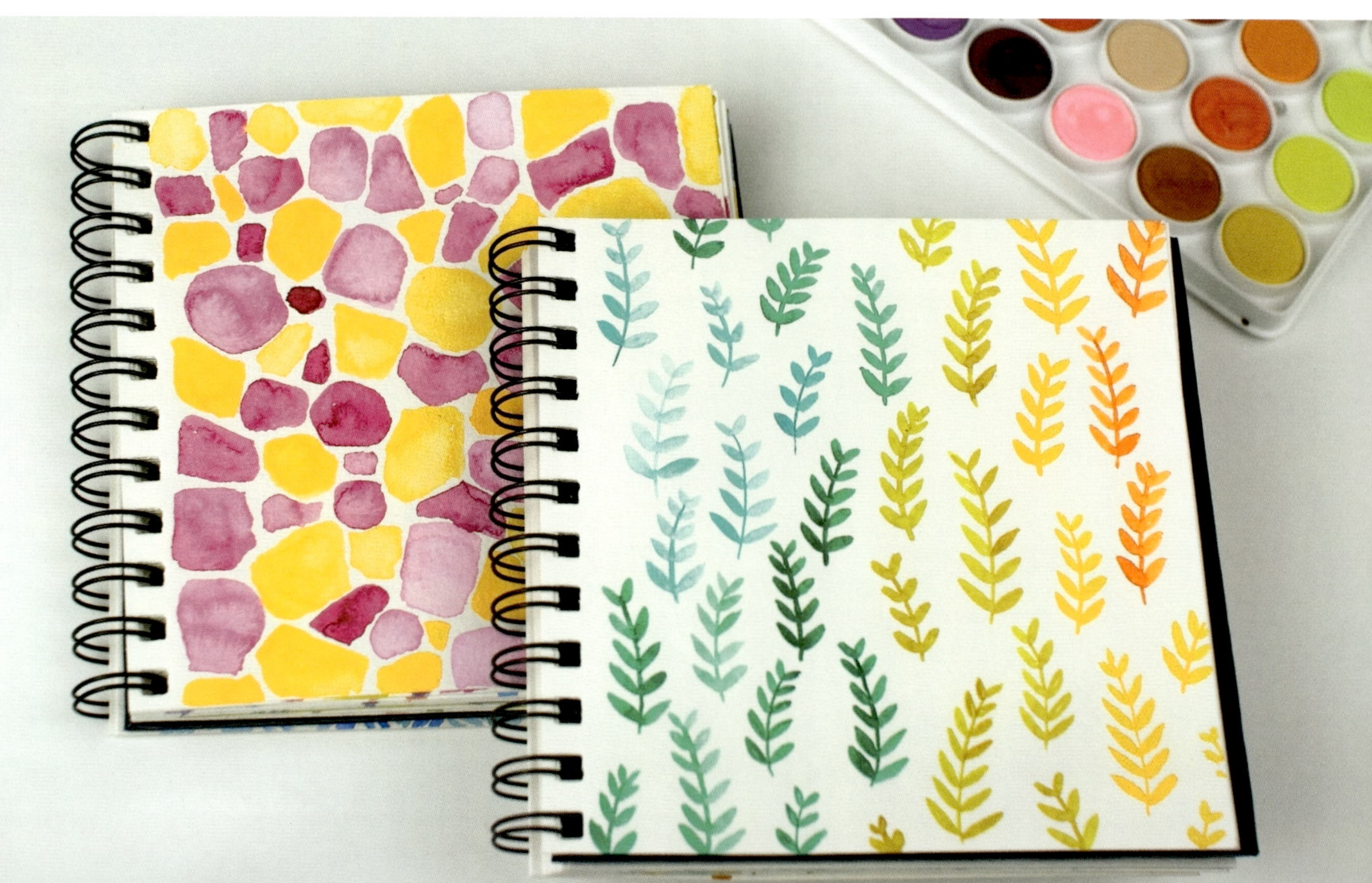

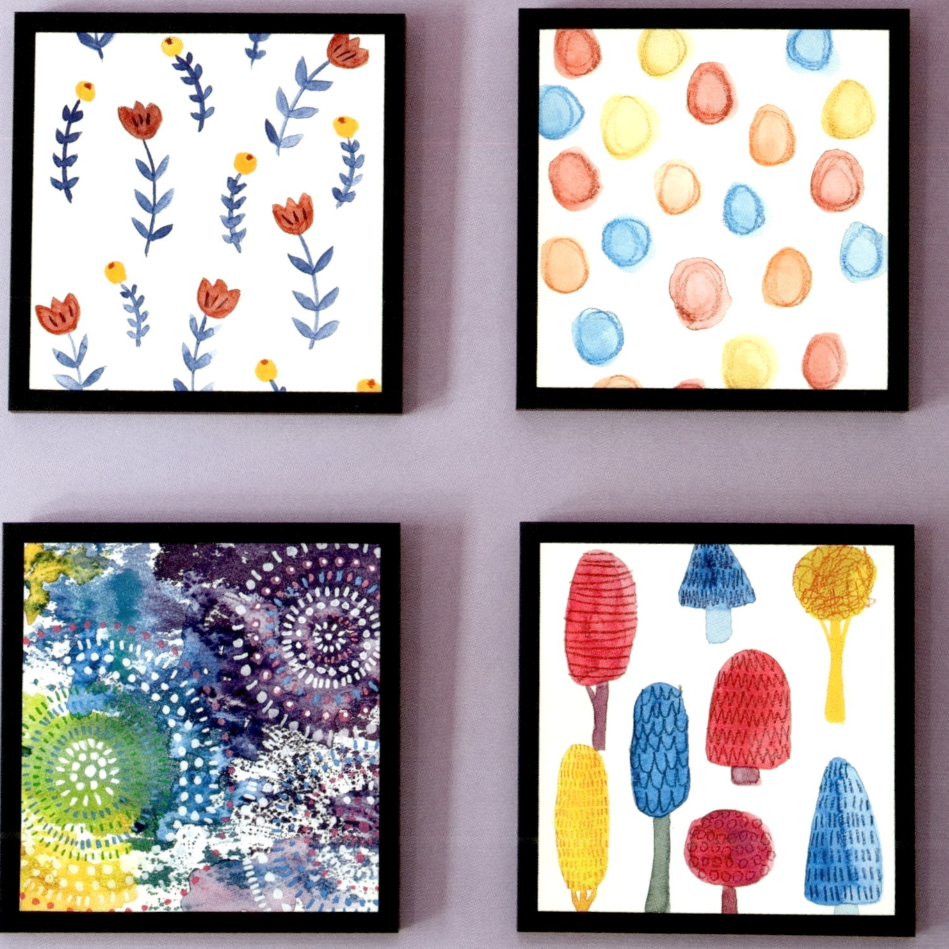

Prompt The fun triadic palettes

Triadic color schemes are fun, bright, bold, and exciting. I love color so much and I really have to hold myself back from using every color I own in a single painting. Sticking with a triadic palette helps me reign things in while still showcasing my love of the rainbow.

A triadic scheme is created by using three colors that are evenly spaced around the wheel. These harmonies tend to be very vibrant, even if you are using desaturated or toned-down versions of the colors. But I love bright, colorful artwork so I gravitate toward this palette often.

A word of warning, though: These combinations can look a little childlike, especially if you are using red, blue, and yellow. Primary colors such as these could make your painting look like it belongs in a kid's room, which is great if that's what you are going for. If not, you can make this palette look more mature by tweaking one or two of the colors. Instead of using full strength red, blue, and yellow, try switching out the red for hot pink. Even by changing up one color you can make a big difference.

Getting the triadic palette right can take a bit of experimentation. So play around with different shades, tones, and tints until you get something you love.

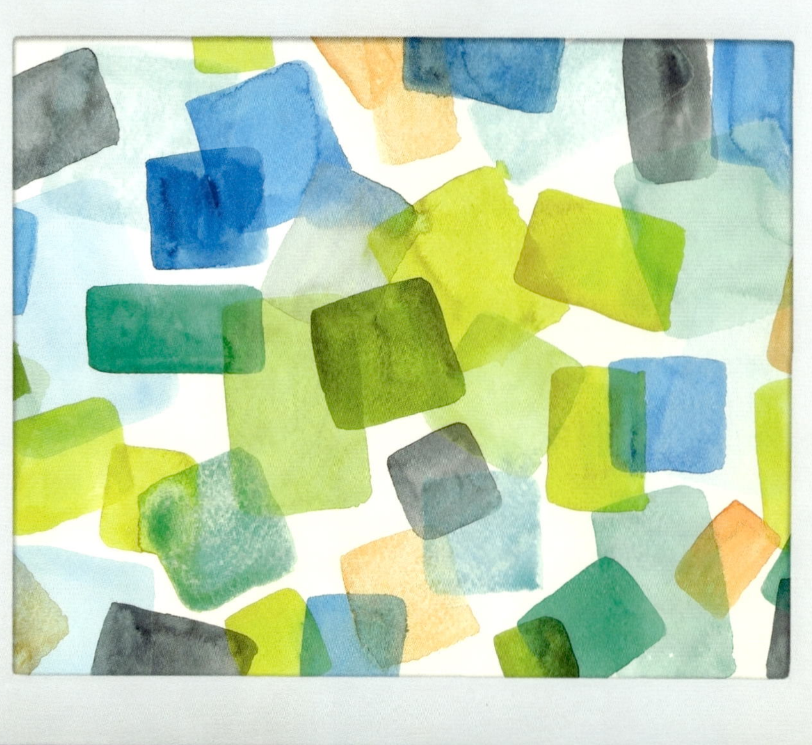

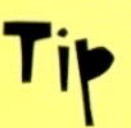

Try this prompt using only one color. You will create so much depth just by continuing to build layers.

Prompt Light, dreamy layers

Watercolor painting is all about layering. If you have already created a color chart (see page 12), you will know that a color can have a huge range in opacity depending on how much water you add. Here, we will use lots of water to create light, translucent layers.

Grab your favorite colors and create some light washes by adding lots of water to your paint. For layering, it is probably best to stick with colors that are close to each other on the wheel (see Soothing analogous colors, page 24). If you stick with similar colors, you can be sure they will look pretty in layers. You can definitely experiment with other palettes, but more colors mean a greater chance the layers will look muddy.

In this piece, I painted rounded rectangles in a few different sizes and started building layers. Let each layer dry completely before adding more paint, if you want those nice crisp edges. Of course, I am always impatient and accidentally end up with a few shapes bleeding together, but I think this adds some personality.

Keep building and building layers until you are happy with the look. It is interesting to see how the colors look laid on top of one another—prepare for some unexpected results.

Prompt Adding special details

Layering colors wet-on-dry is a perfect way to add interesting details to your work. Those small touches can quickly take your painting from boring to beautiful, so don't overlook this important step. When I think a piece is finished, I like to step back, let it dry, and see if I can add more interest with another layer.

If you have tried watercolor in the past and got frustrated, chances are part of that frustration came from trying to add too much paint while the page was still wet. It is tempting to keep adding to the painting if you are not happy with it, but watercolor works best in layers and it can take some patience to let everything dry completely.

Another thing I have learned while playing with watercolor is that using only one layer of paint can tend to look a little flat. If you have done your first layer and you're not happy with it, you can almost always save it by adding more detail later. The best way to add dimension and interest to a painting is to go in with some detail and shading once the first layer is dry.

In this pattern, the simple leaf shape would have looked a little plain had I left it after one layer. But I went back after everything was totally dry and added dark brown stems and dark green veins to the leaves, which make the colors pop and give the pattern a more polished look.

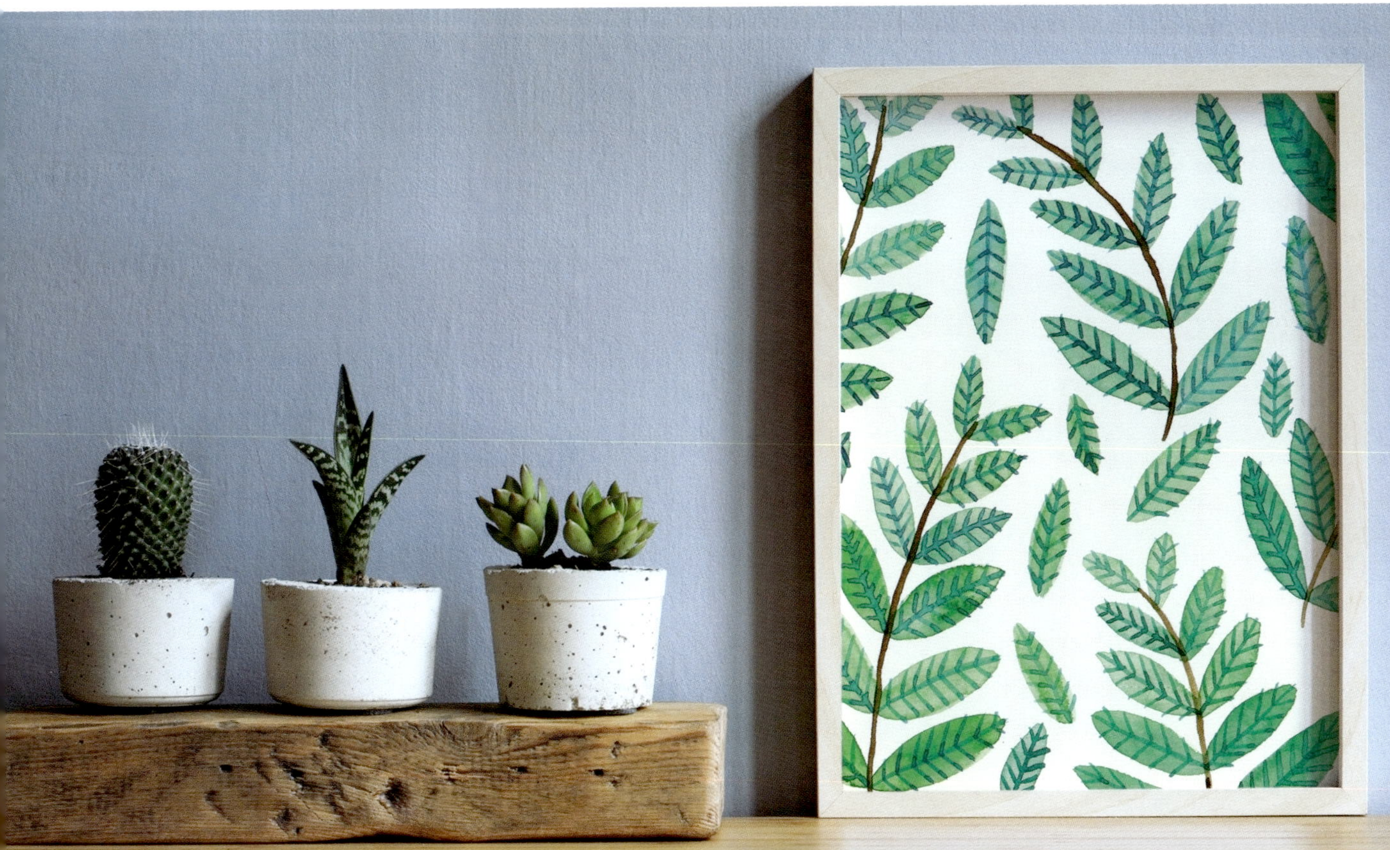

Create a pebbles pattern

This exercise is all about brush control and detail. Practice using a small brush by painting little lines and dots on your pebbles. Creating these details can be meditative, so grab a big sheet of watercolor paper and fill it with pattern!

YOU WILL NEED

- Watercolor paper
- Watercolor paint in 4 or 5 colors
- Medium round brush
- Small liner brush

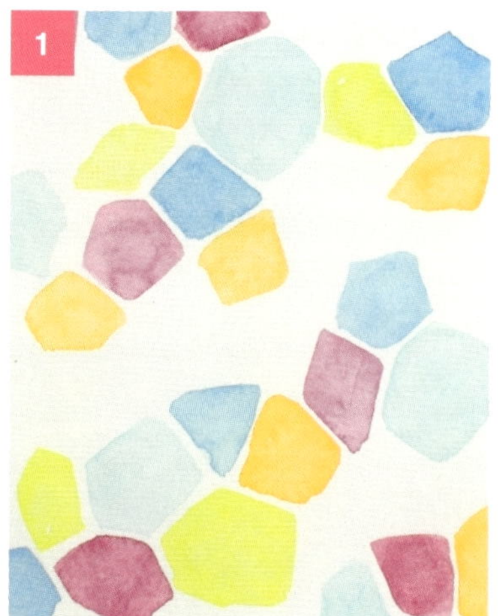

Start with lighter colors, or water down your paint to create translucent shades. I would recommend four or five different colors in total. Begin by creating some random geometric shapes, scattered across the page, with the medium round brush.

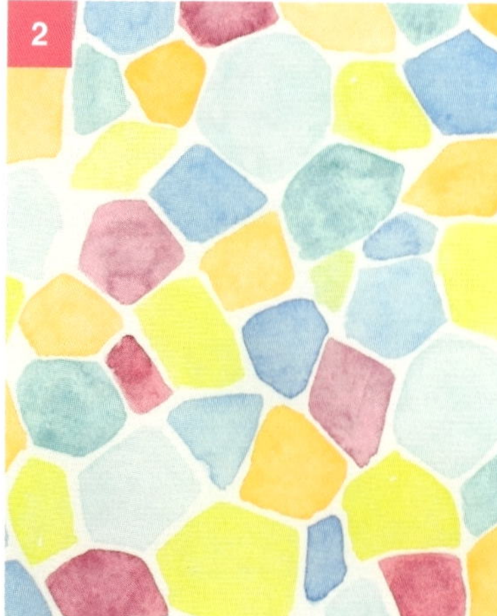

Continue adding more pebble shapes and fill in the empty spaces. To make sure I don't have too many of the same color clustered together, I rotate through the colors several times.

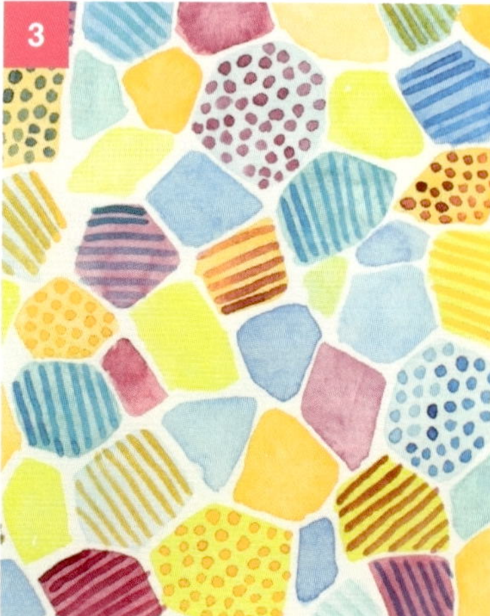

Once your pebbles are completely dry, go in with more pigmented versions of your pebble colors and add some detail with a small liner brush. I think it looks interesting when you leave some pebbles plain, too.

Your finished piece

This pattern looks complicated, but when you break it down you'll see how easy it is. Switch up the colors for a different look.

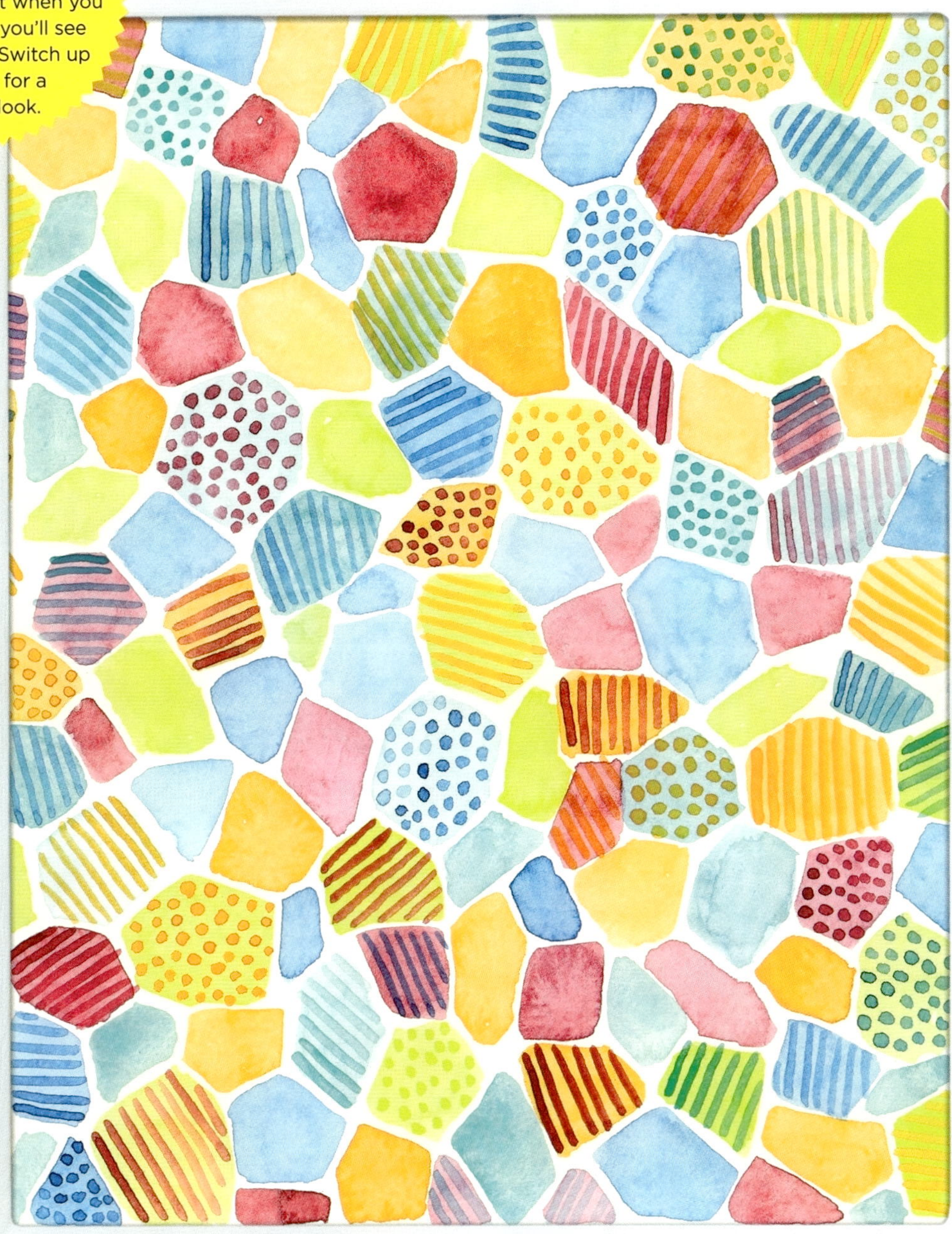

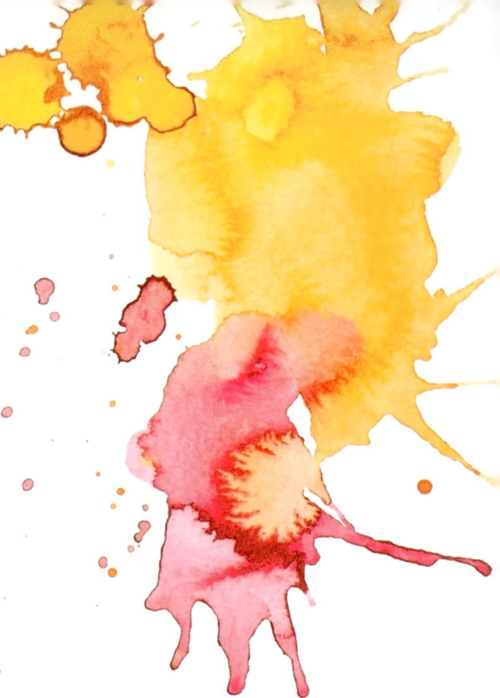

Play Spatters and drips

As watercolor paints are fluid, there are all sorts of fun, splashy effects you can only enjoy with this medium. It is unpredictable and takes a little practice, but when you see those spatters and drips, you know it is, unmistakably, watercolor.

There are a few different ways you can achieve these splatter effects with watercolors. Each one gives a distinct result, so it is fun to experiment with all of them. The first step is always to load your brush with lots of paint and water. Tube paints work best for this because they are very pigmented and won't get too watered down, but you can still achieve some nice results with pan paints—you will just need to use a bit more paint to create the same vibrancy.

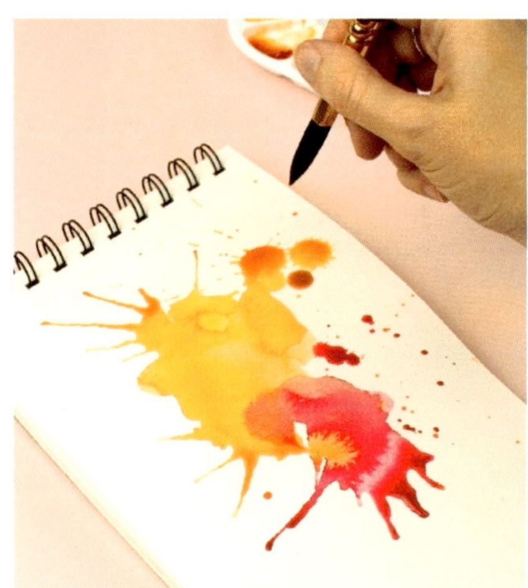

Tapping brushes
Pick up some color on a brush, hold it over the paper horizontally, and lightly tap another brush on top of it. This will leave directional spatters, so be sure to vary the angle of the brush to make them look random.

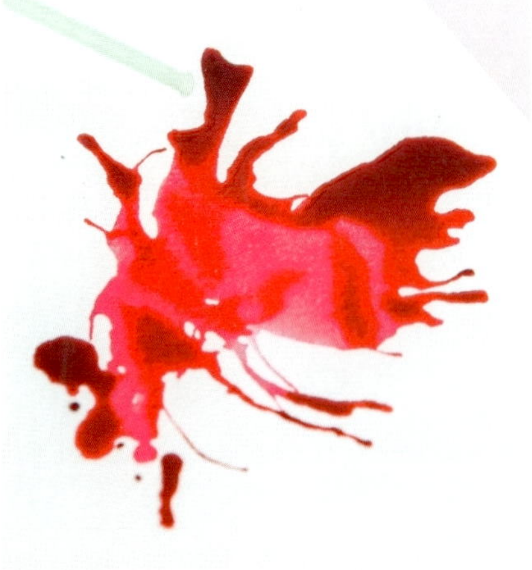

Blow on the paint
Lay down some really wet paint on the paper, in any shape you want. Then get close to the page and blow the paint out toward the edges. This technique gives you a fun splat mark.

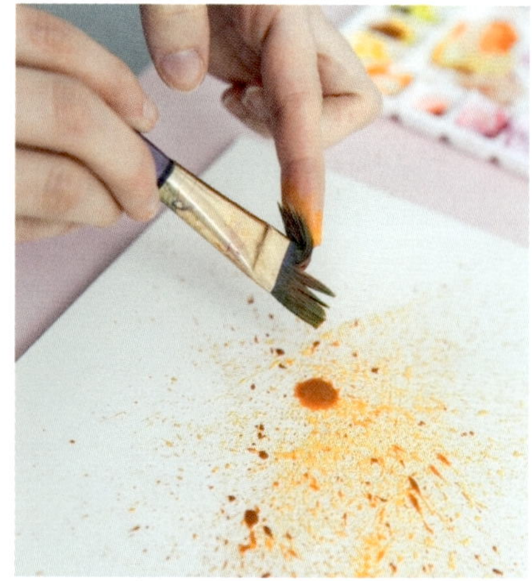

Use a frayed brush
This is a great way to put to use those old brushes that you might otherwise throw away. Load up a frayed brush with some paint and use your fingers to flick the paint. This can get messy, but it looks great!

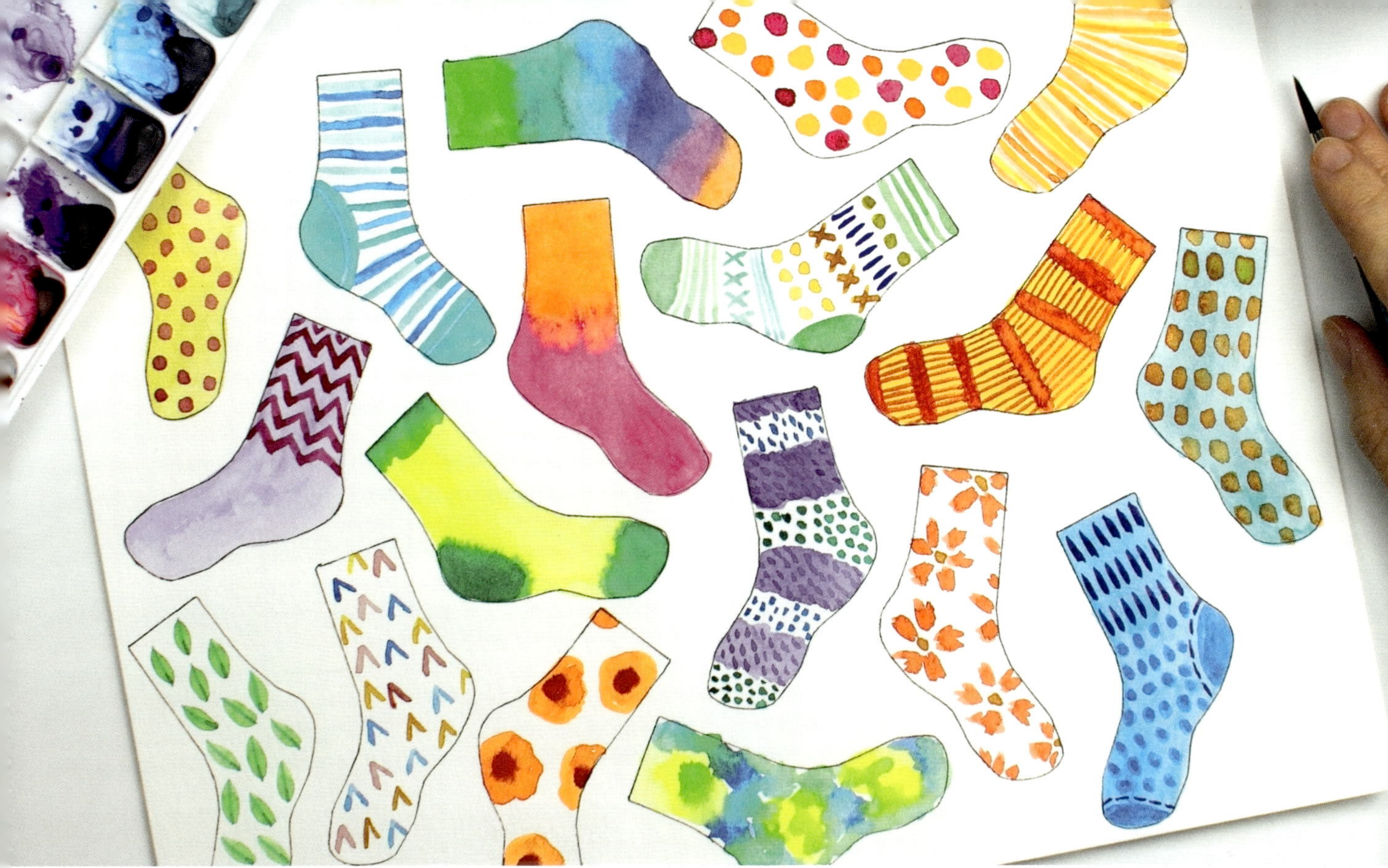

prompt Design some crazy socks

This is the kind of thing I can do all day long. Not only is this exercise fun, but it is also a great way to work out some new ideas and techniques. So grab a brush and get creative!

This activity is the absolute best way to play with pattern, new techniques, and color. There is something about confining myself to a certain shape, in this case, a sock, that helps me let loose. There is no pressure to make a masterpiece—experiment within the lines of each sock shape and see what happens. When you have filled the space, move on to the next one. Once you have finished, you may be surprised how much you love this crazy page in your sketchbook.

I started by drawing a sock shape on a scrap of paper and cutting it out to create a little stencil. You don't have to use socks though! Try doing this pattern with shirts, vases, hats, or anything else that you want to fill with color. Once you have your stencil, fill the entire page. I used a black waterproof pen to trace my socks, to give them a bold outline. It is important to use something waterproof here so the pen does not bleed in to your pattern.

Now to design your socks! Use your imagination or anything around you for inspiration. Don't be concerned about making each one perfect—have fun playing with different colors and techniques. If you don't like one of the socks, forget it, and move on to the next one. This exercise is guaranteed to spark an idea for a new piece of art.

Project Showcase a special date

If you have been itching to try out hand-lettering but feel a little intimidated, this project is for you. Numbers are so much more forgiving and easier to paint than letters. You can be as fancy as you like with this, but it will still look amazing if you stick to a clean style for your numbers. Combined with a super-simple frame around your special date, this is a project worthy of display.

YOU WILL NEED

- Watercolor paper
- Watercolor paint
- Pencil
- Small round brush
- Medium round brush

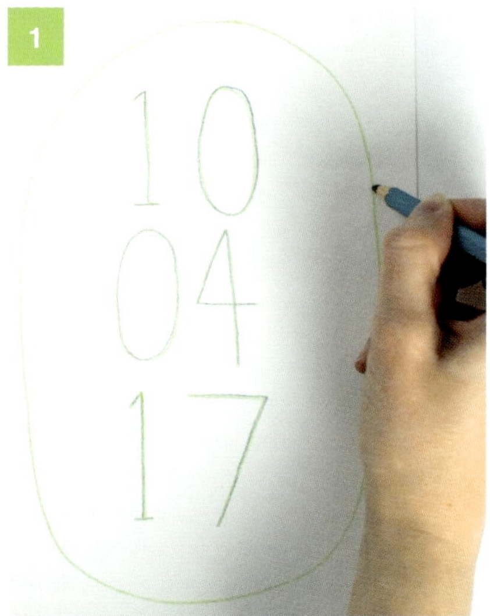

Very lightly sketch your date and a loose oval shape around the numbers. You can use a graphite or watercolor pencil for this. Remember to keep the sketch light, so you can barely see it.

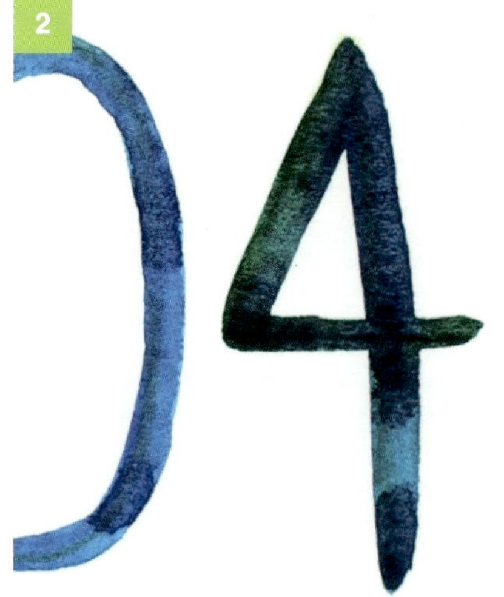

Begin painting over the numbers with a steady hand and a small round brush. I dipped into two colors for my text to give it more gradient.

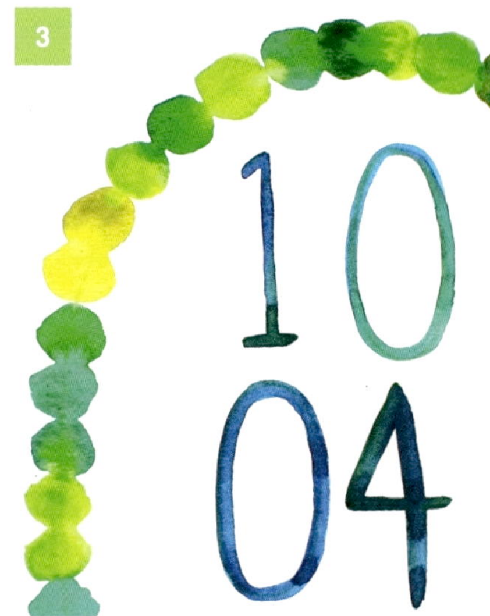

Once the date is dry, paint your frame using a medium round brush. You can do polka dots, dashes, triangles, or anything else you can think of. Get creative with color here!

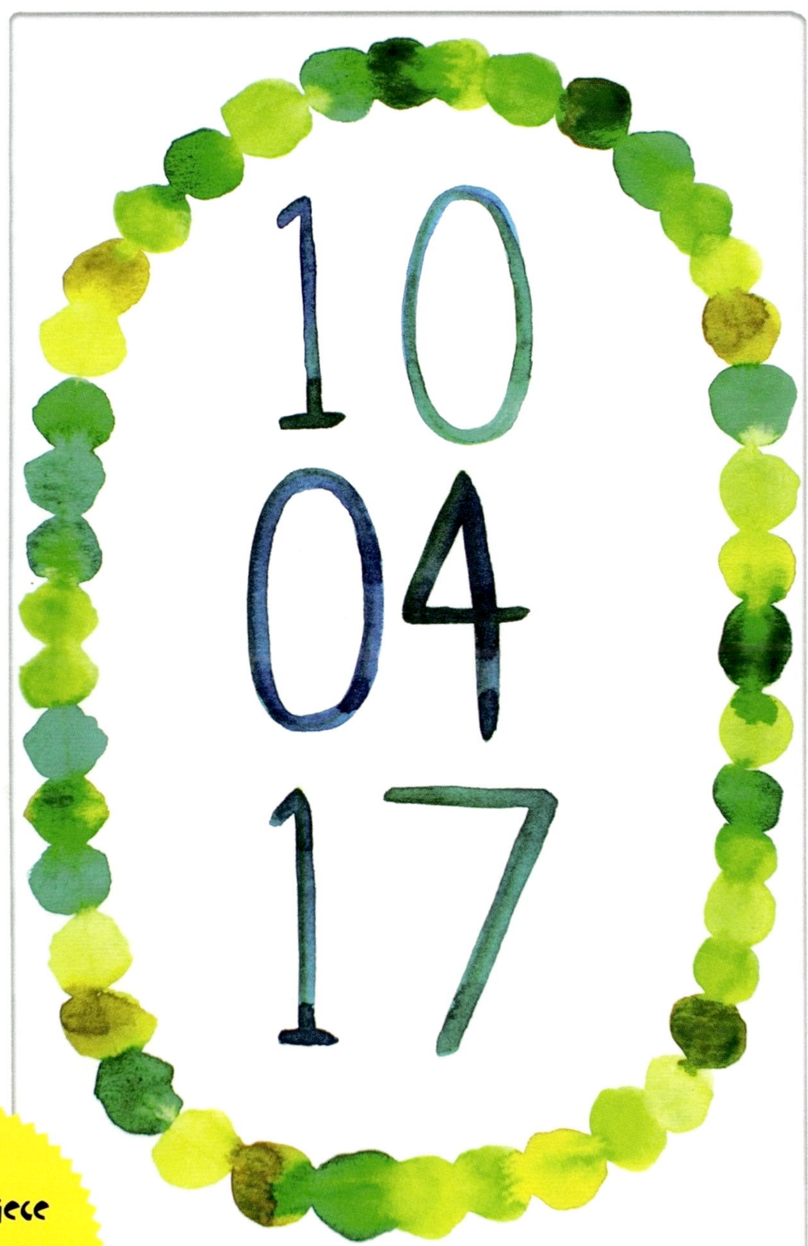

Your finished piece

This project is perfect for a baby shower, wedding, or house warming—there are so many special dates to remember.

2

Surprise yourself

Now that you are getting a feel for the paint, let's take things to the next level. One of my favorite things to paint is pattern. I love pattern because you can take something as simple as a dot and create a striking painting just by repeating it. The repetition also gives you a chance to practice painting the same thing over and over. Along with pattern, you will use nature as your inspiration, paint what you see around you, learn to layer, and even recreate a favorite photo. This chapter will build your confidence and encourage you to enjoy the process. Don't worry if you are a total beginner or are feeling rusty–these exercises will get you excited about filling those blank pages.

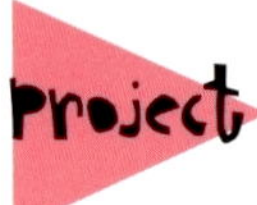

Explore a piece of fruit

When I think about something as common as a piece of fruit, I often fixate on a certain picture in my head of what I think that fruit should look like. That is why learning to paint from real references is so valuable. For this project, grab any piece of fruit. Start by painting the uncut fruit, then slice it in half, cut it into wedges and slices, and paint those, too. Start by laying down a light layer in the basic shape and then building details on top of that.

YOU WILL NEED

- Watercolor paper
- Watercolor paint
- Medium round brush
- Small round brush

1

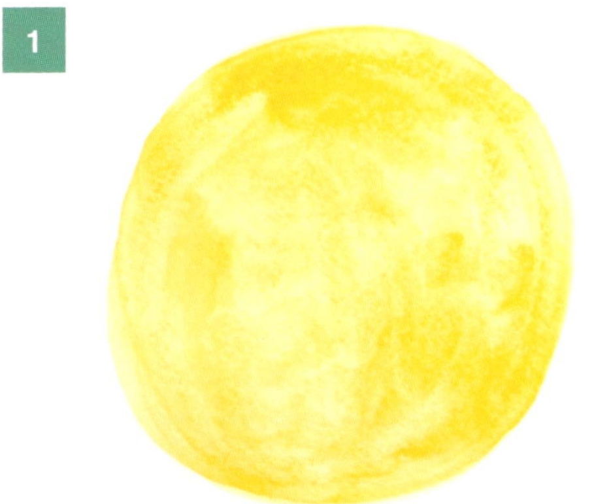

Always start with the lightest color first. For this orange slice, begin by painting a light orange circle as a base.

2

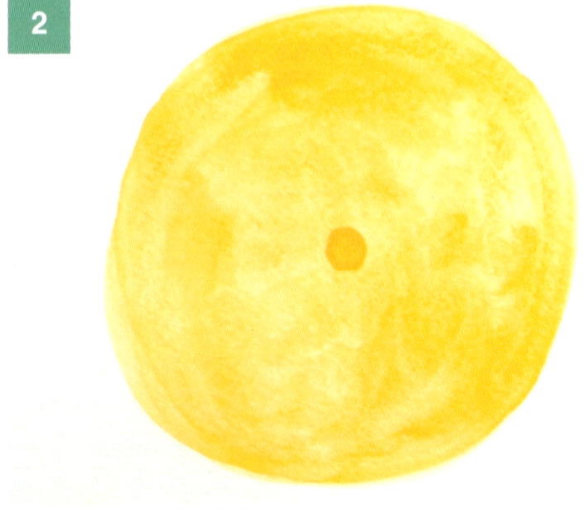

After the circle is completely dry, use the same color orange to make a little dot in the center of the fruit. This dot acts as an anchor and will stop the next step from going wrong.

3

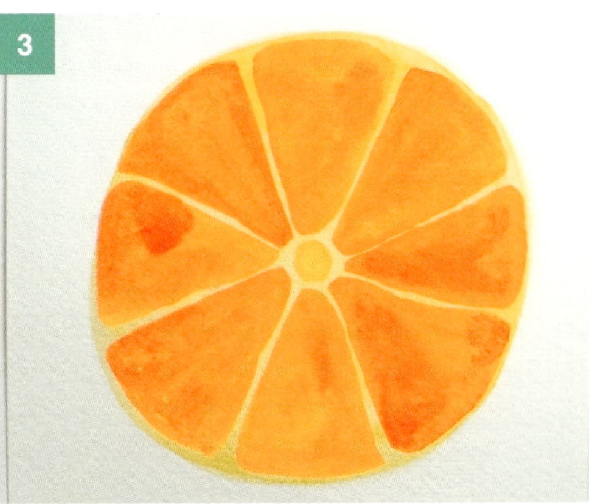

When the base layer is completely dry, start to add in the basic shapes of your fruit. Use darker orange in two different shades to give dimension.

4

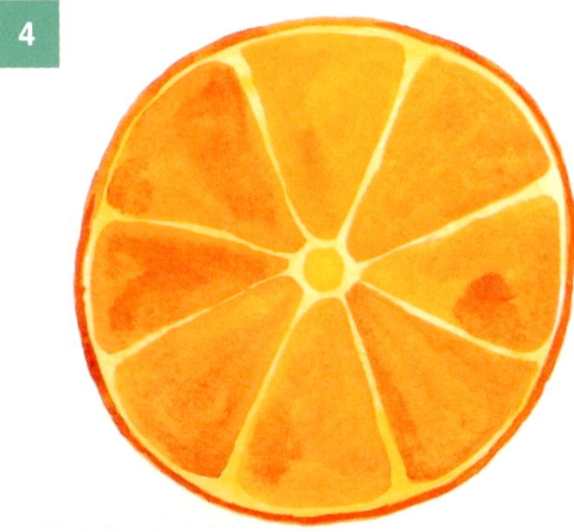

Waiting until everything is dry again (ugh I know, so much waiting!), you can then go in again and add some finer detail, texture, or even some fun pattern.

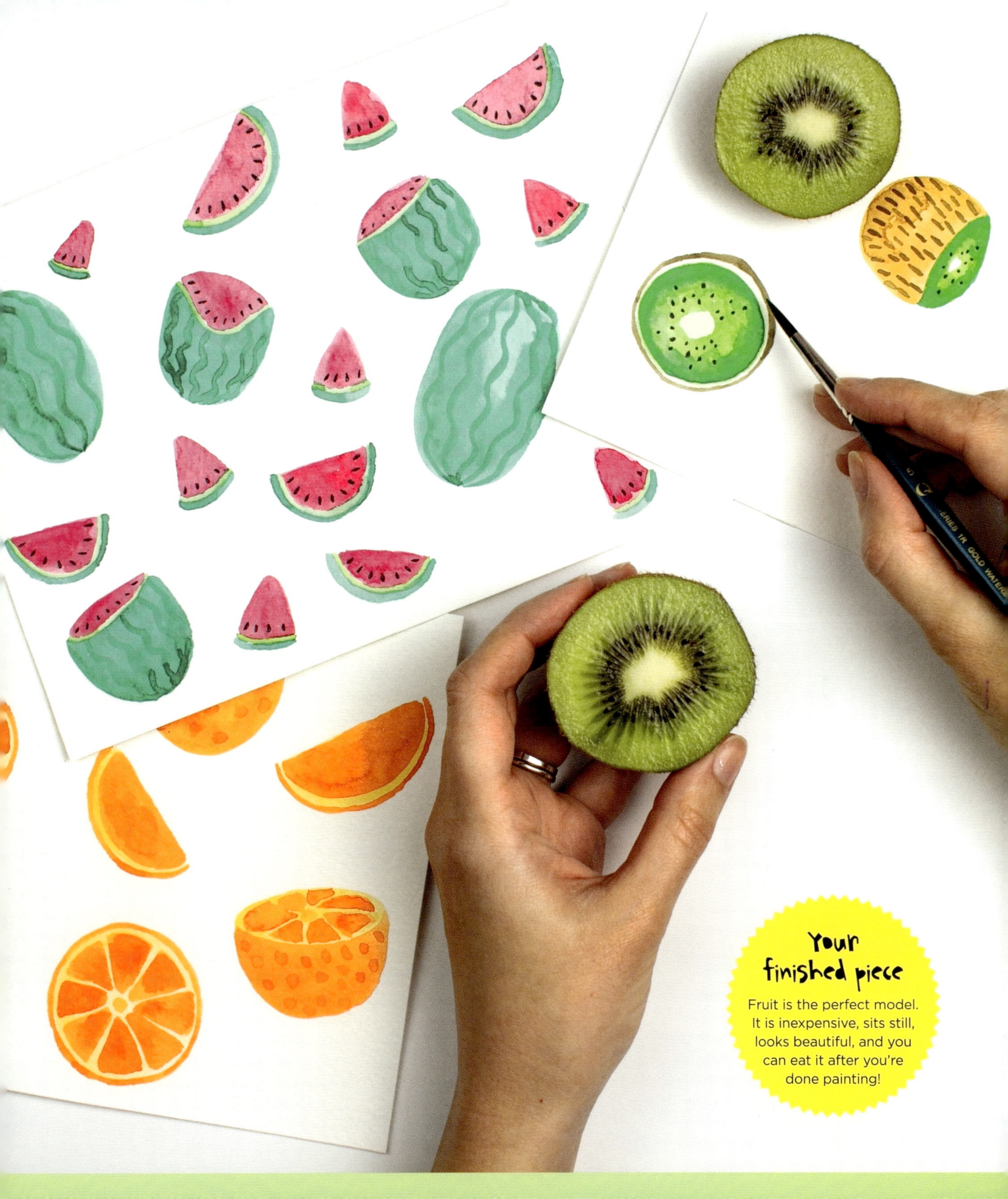

Your finished piece

Fruit is the perfect model. It is inexpensive, sits still, looks beautiful, and you can eat it after you're done painting!

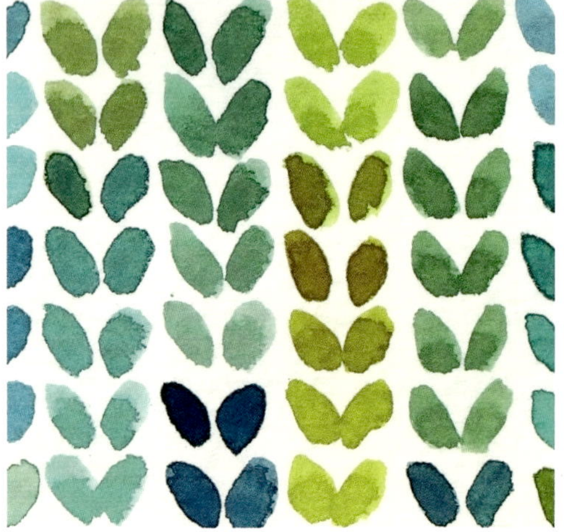

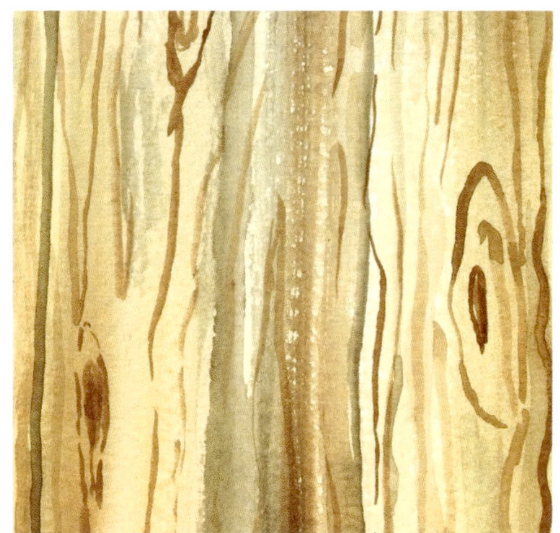

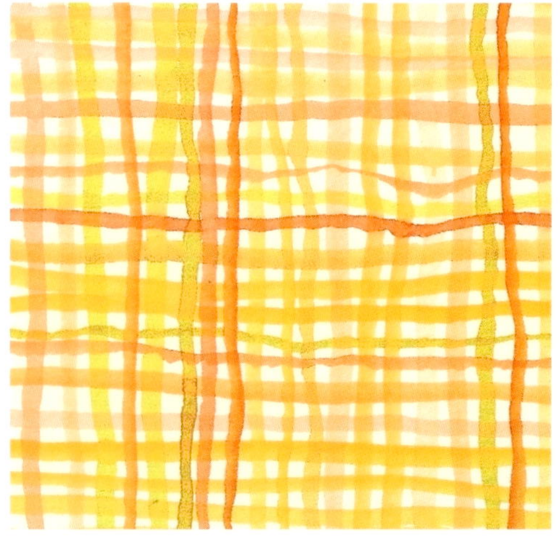

Prompt Replicate textures with paint

You are probably surrounded with beautiful textures that usually go unnoticed—the grain of a wood table, the texture of your knit sweater, or the weave of a piece of fabric. The textures around you can provide endless inspiration.

If you haven't noticed already, I don't paint with a whole lot of realism. One of my favorite parts about making art is interpreting what I see on paper in a way that I find interesting. I especially like finding something boring or even ugly and trying to turn it into an unusual pattern. So, with this exercise, don't worry about replicating your texture with perfect photo realism. The main thing to take away is to learn how to get better at seeing details and translating them using your brush and paint.

Look around you wherever you are and see if you can spot a few interesting textures. Natural textures are my favorite, but you can even find beauty in something as lowly as a brick wall. Everyday inspiration is all around us; all you need to do is look for it. And don't forget that you are the artist, you can interpret what you see however you want. You can even switch up the colors to something that better reflects your style.

If you like this prompt, challenge yourself and go big! It might take a while to complete, but the result will be worth it.

Prompt Weird, wonderful animals

Painting subjects such as animals can be intimidating. You feel like you need to get all the proportions and colors just right. So, for this prompt, we're throwing all the rules out the window and dreaming up our own weird and wonderful animal.

Let's face it, painting animals is hard. I am always striving to improve as an artist, but sometimes I just want to play around and have some fun in my sketchbook without any pressure to paint something realistic. So, what is my solution? To forget about all the rules and come up with my own wacky animal to paint.

Don't worry about getting the anatomy correct, or the colors even remotely sane. Use your imagination to create an interesting fantasy creature. Your real favorite animal could be a starting point if you like, or you could come up with something completely new.

I started off by lightly sketching a cat shape with pencil on watercolor paper and then filled it in with a wash of orange. Once that was dry, I added patterns such as spots, stripes, and other colorful accents. Then I painted big facial features to give it some personality. You can even paint a whole scene for your creature to live in!

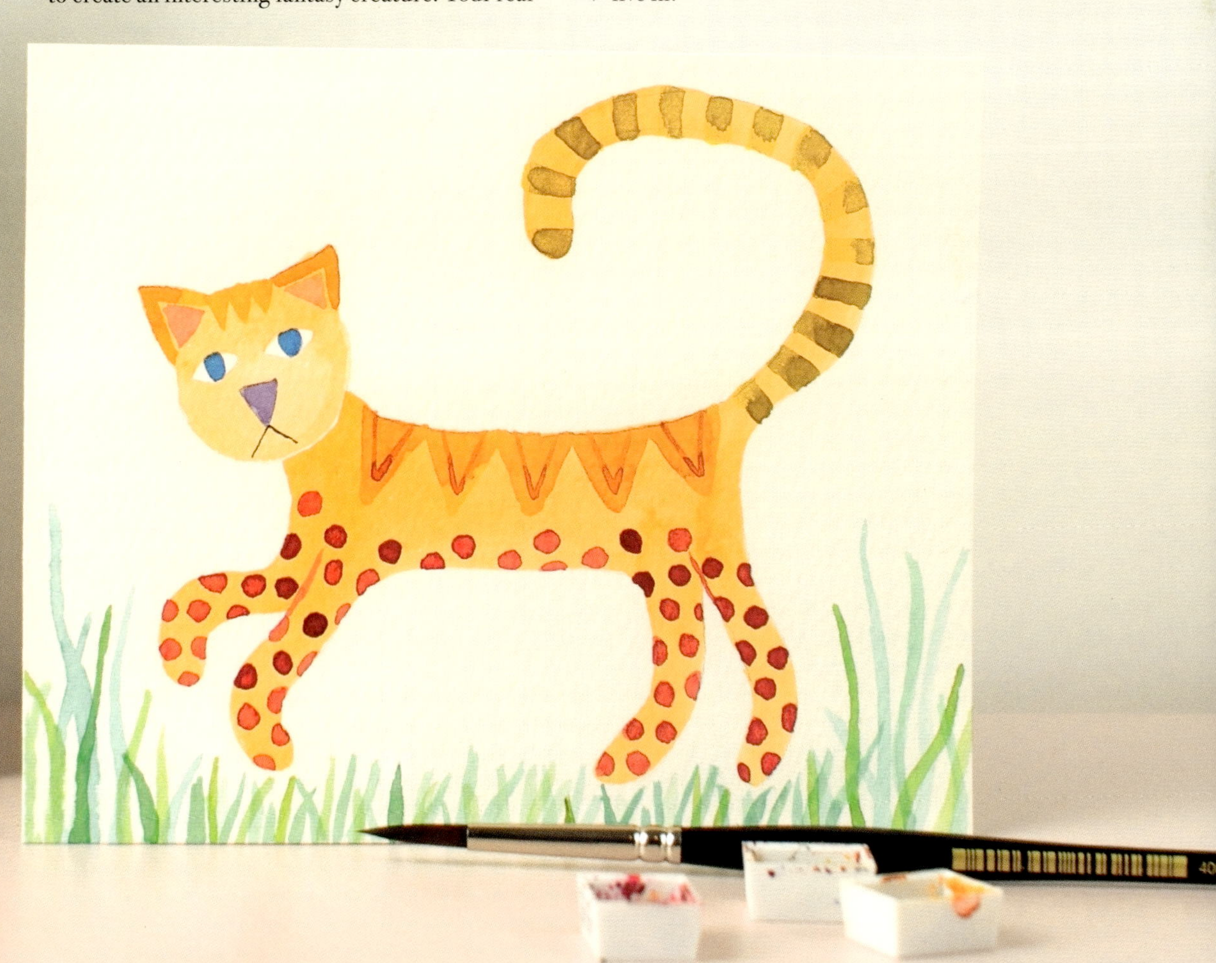

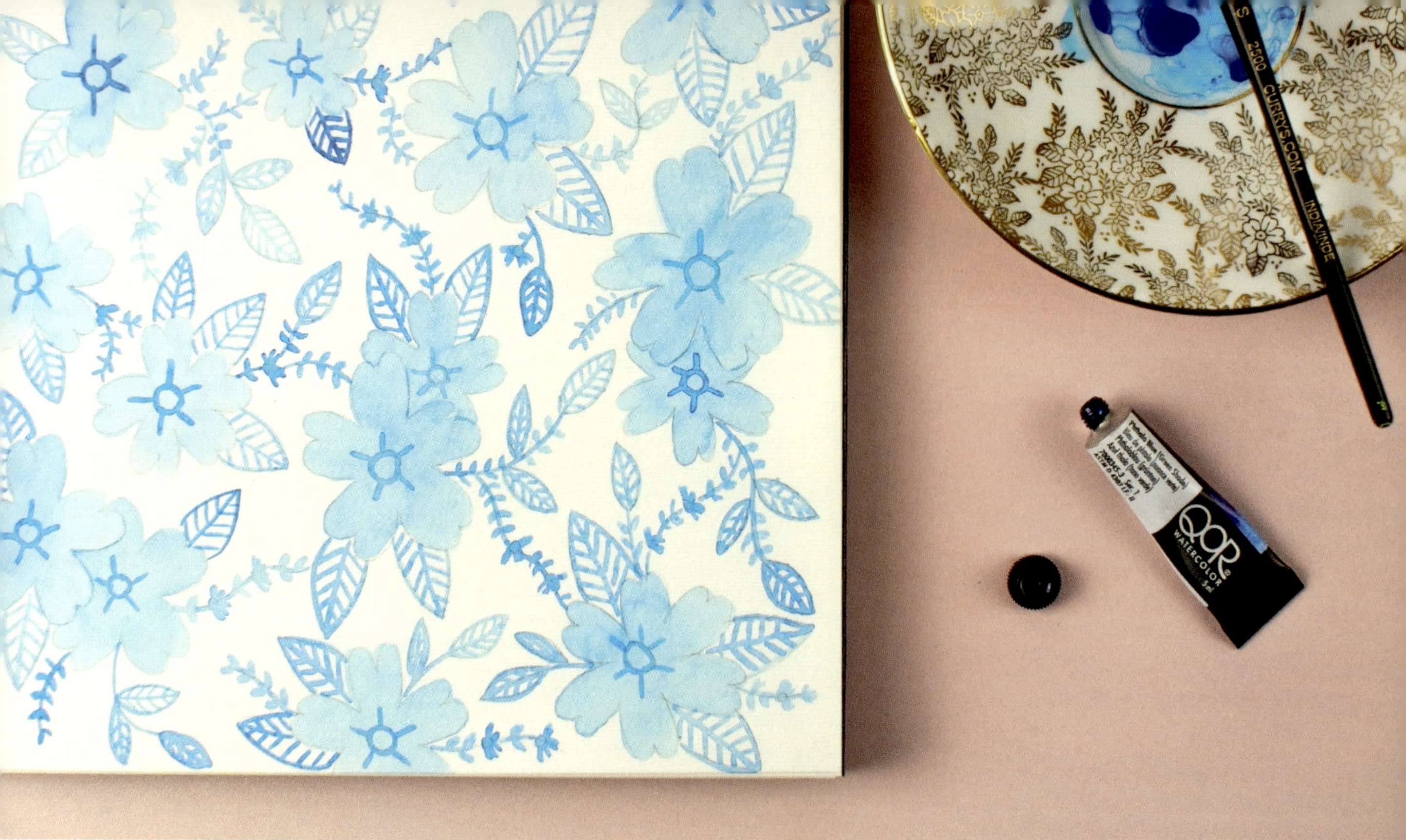

Prompt Look for inspiration in vintage china

The Internet is an amazing place for creative inspiration, but I find the best way to test my skills is to look for ideas in the real world. When you use a found object as a starting point for a painting, you start to develop your own style and point of view, instead of trying to paint like your favorite online artist.

Yard sales, vintage stores, thrift stores, and Grandma's closet are all great places to hunt for old china. These tiny, delicate works of art lend themselves so well to watercolor.

I picked up a few old tea cups and saucers at a thrift store. Using the designs as inspiration, I tried to interpret the pattern into something that fits with my own style. You don't have to paint a replica; in fact, it is even better if you can come up with something unique based on the vintage design.

Pick something from the artwork that first demanded your attention. For me, it was the intricacy of this gold floral pattern. I also love how it is painted all in one color to simplify the complicated tangle of flowers and leaves. Doing my best to capture those aspects of the design, I tried to recreate it in my own style. And did you know that vintage plates and saucers make excellent watercolor palettes? It is such a beautiful way to use your paints.

Play Paint the white space

This is a fun play to get you thinking a little differently by painting the space around the objects instead of the objects themselves. It's also a great skill to practice because with watercolor you usually paint the background first.

For this play, you will want to start by lightly sketching out some simple shapes on the page. Try to keep the shapes fairly large and plain. It is a lot easier to paint around smooth edges without too much intricate detail. Loose leaves and flowers are always some of my favorite shapes to paint because they are easy to draw and very recognizable.

You will want to work quickly with lots of water to keep the page wet. If you let a section dry, it will be harder to blend it into the rest of the background and it could end up looking a little patchy. In this example, I used two colors and let them bleed and blend together for a cool effect. You can use just one color if that is easier.

When working with watercolor, people tend to paint the background first. This is because it is easier to achieve crisp lines on the objects in the foreground if you work on them last. Keeping the background separate from the foreground is also very helpful when your background color is too dark to paint another layer on top. I think it looks unexpected and interesting when the shapes are left plain white, too.

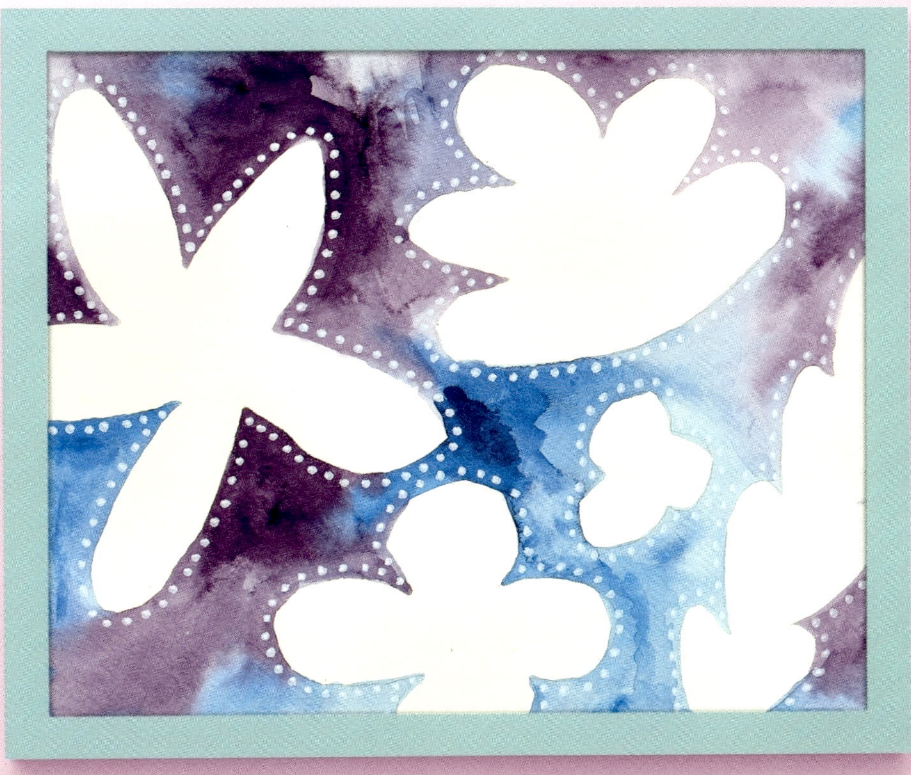

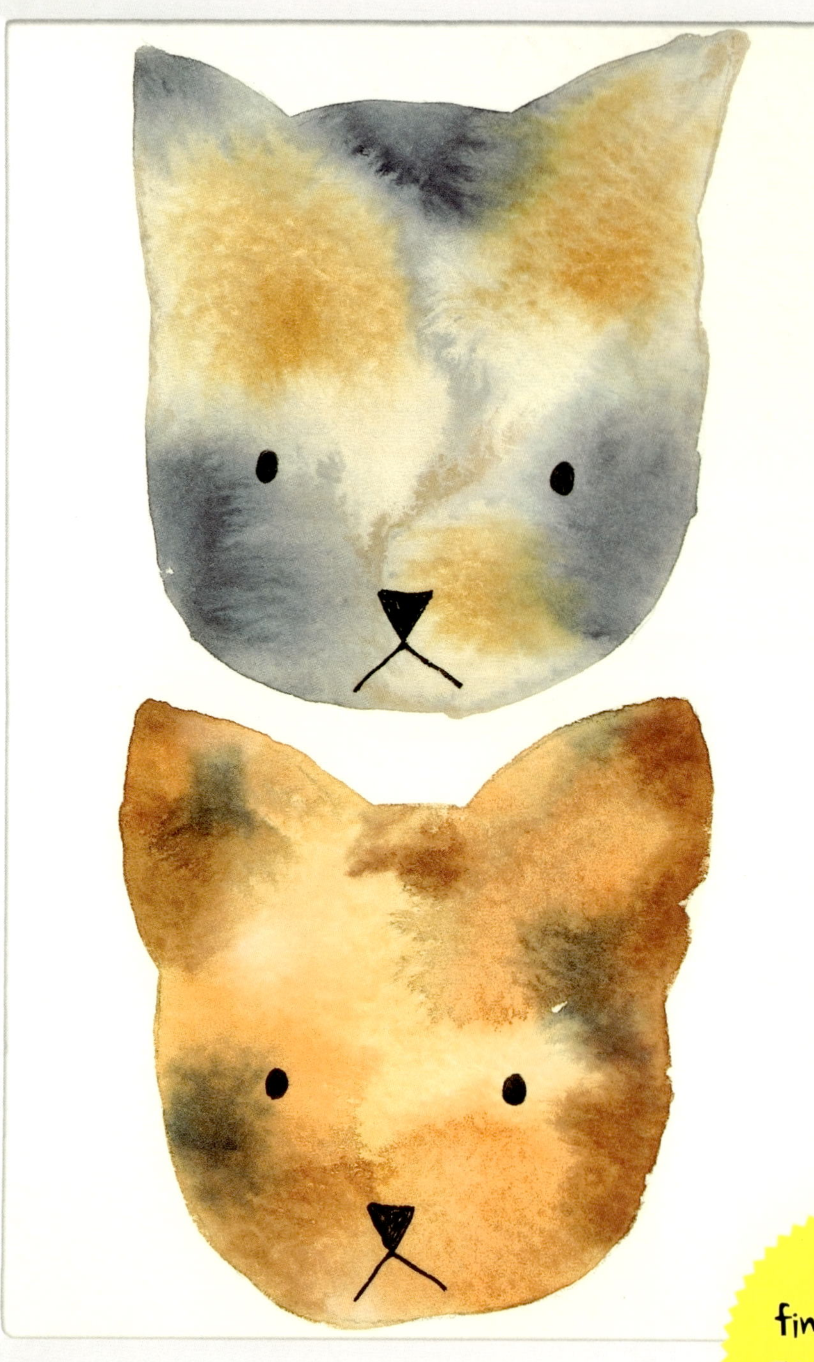

Your finished piece

This technique always produces different results, meaning no two cats will turn out the same!

Project Fuzzy kitty faces

Proud cat lady here! One day, I was experimenting in my sketchbook and noticed that the way watercolor bleeds together can resemble fur. I was so excited I just had to try painting my favorite animal. The fuzzy effect of wet-on-wet makes such great fur and the markings on each painted cat are all totally unique, just like in real life!

YOU WILL NEED

- Watercolor paper
- Watercolor paint
- Pencil
- Large round brush
- Black waterproof pen

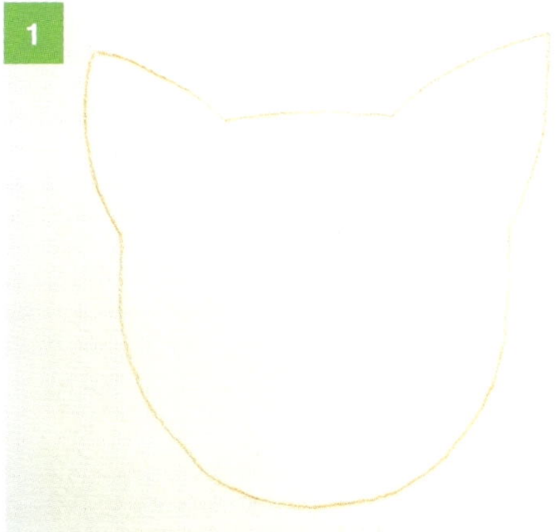

1 Begin by sketching out a simple cat-face shape—a circle with two triangles on top for ears.

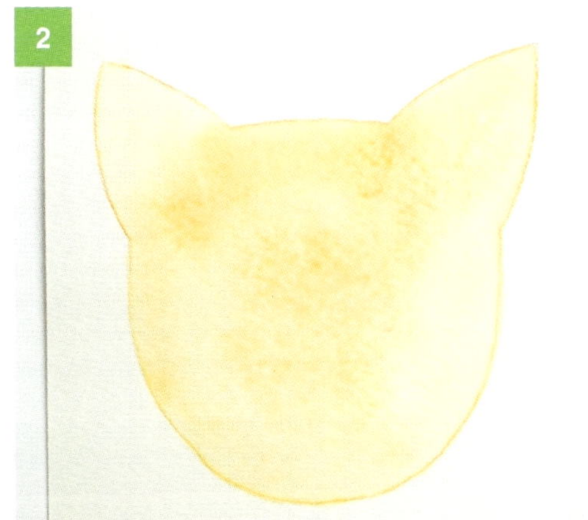

2 Choose a light color and fill in the face with a watery wash. I used a large, fluffy round brush because it holds lots of water.

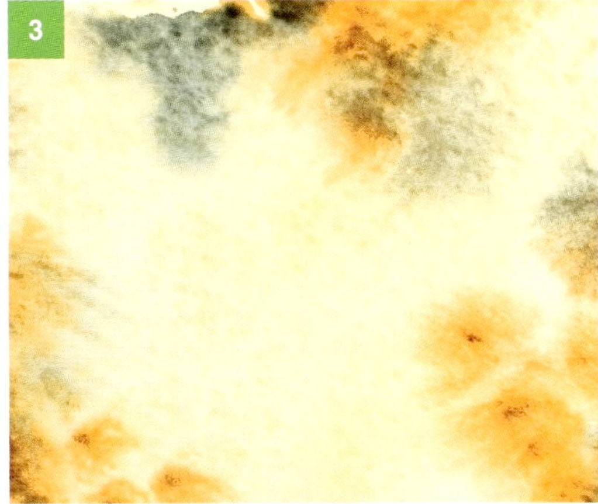

3 When the first layer is still quite wet, pick up some other colors and drop them onto the wash. They will move and blend on their own.

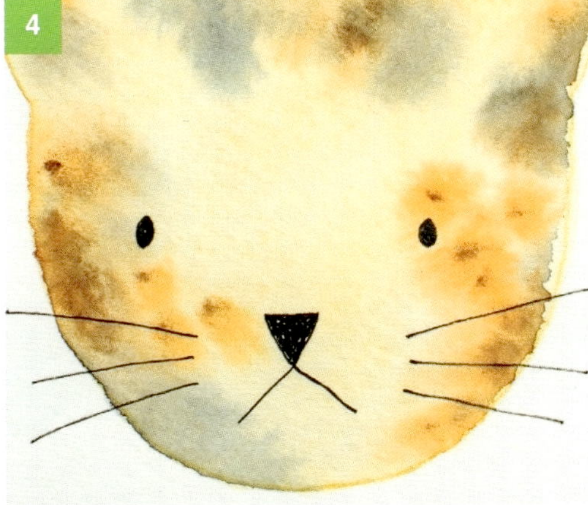

4 Once everything is completely dry, you can use a black waterproof pen to add some eyes, a nose, a mouth, and whiskers.

prompt Exploring leaf shapes

Leaves and flowers are my favorite things to paint. There is endless variety to the shapes, sizes, and colors. Using your imagination is fun but there is no substitute for painting from the real thing. Go for a walk, and no matter where you live, you will find lots of interesting leafy inspiration.

When it is warm out, I like to take home pretty-looking leaves whenever I find them and press them in between pages in a book. That way, when the weather turns cooler and the branches outside are bare, I have lots of ideas to draw from.

All it takes is a short stroll around the block and you will be able to spot so many interesting and unusual shapes. If you don't want to take the leaves home, snap a quick picture for reference.

Begin by studying the leaf. What is the basic shape? Are there vein patterns or small details around the edges? How many leaves are attached to the stem? Once you take a really good look, you can figure out how you will use the shape in a painting.

It is fun to experiment by playing with the size, colors, and proportions. The leaf may be green, but your version could be purple or yellow. If your leaf is tiny, try painting a giant version of it; if your leaf is large, try shrinking it down and repeating it across the page.

You can make your leaf paintings even more interesting by adding stripes, dots, and other marks. Nature is such great inspiration!

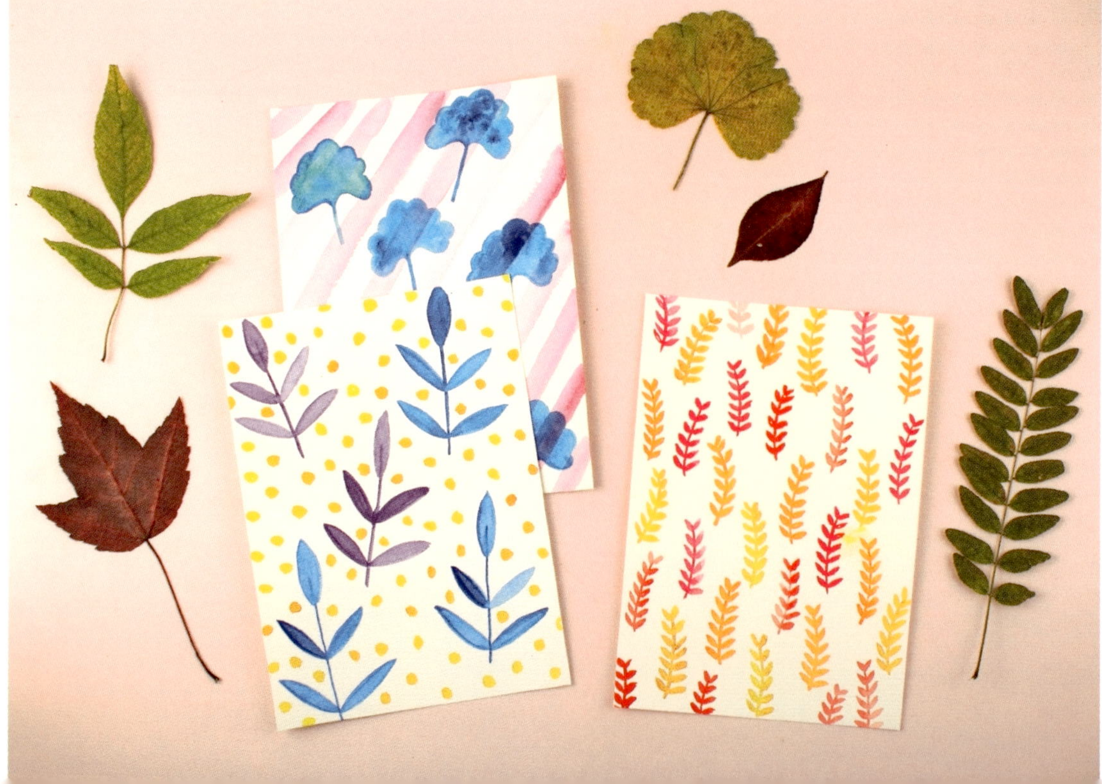

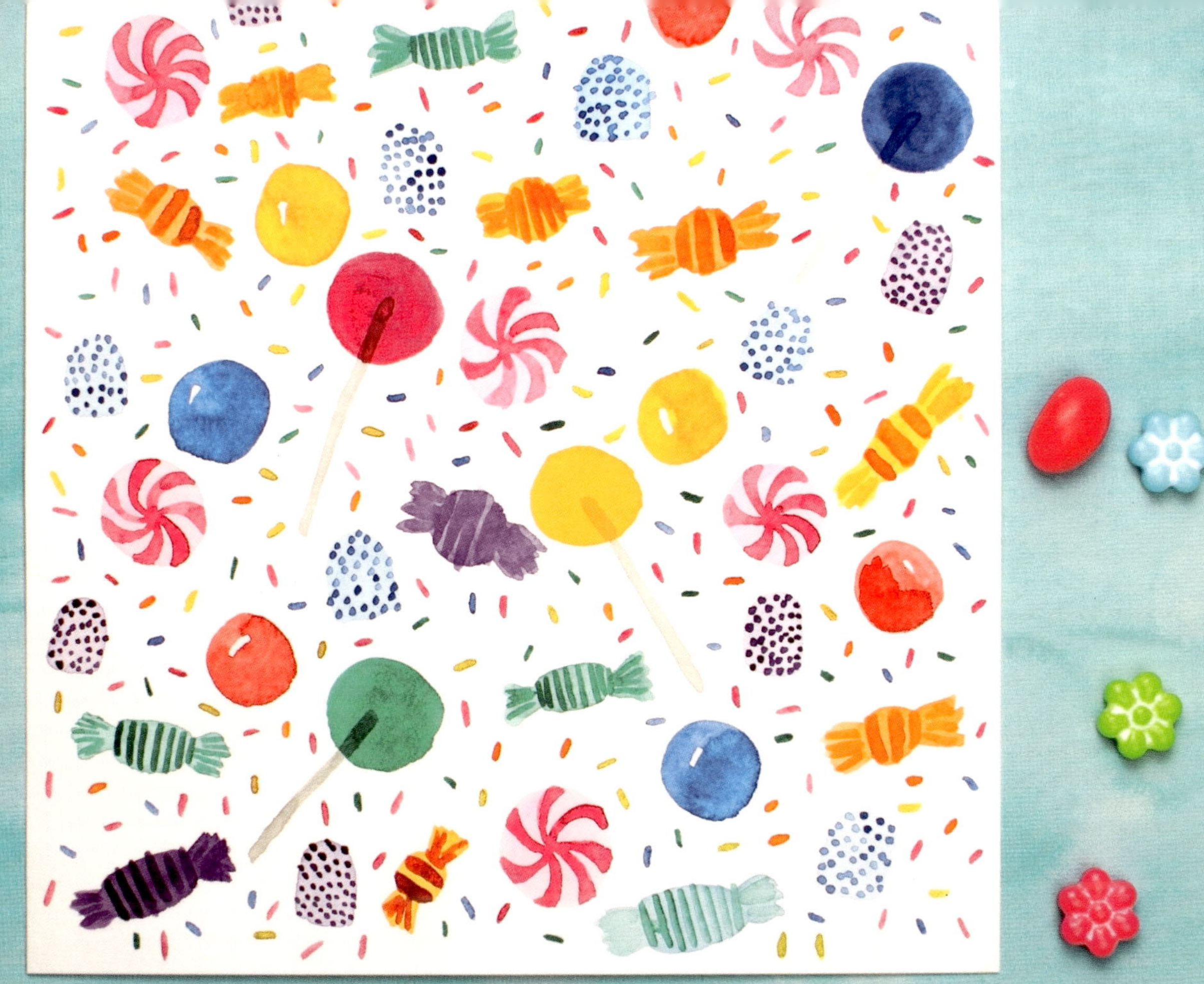

prompt Yum! Paint a sweet treat

When sugar cravings hit, give in to your sweet tooth and paint a colorful candy page in your sketchbook. You can use your imagination or real candy as a reference. And the best part is you can eat your reference material when you are done!

Candies and baked goods look so lovely painted in watercolor. They come in such a variety of shapes and colors that there is endless sweet inspiration. It is fun to use your imagination and dream up something decadent, but it can also be great practice to paint what you see on your own plate. What a great excuse for dessert!

To make this scattered pattern, I started with one piece of candy and painted it randomly across the page. Then I came up with another motif and scattered it evenly across the page too. I kept working like that, filling in the white space and switching colors, until the whole page was filled with treats.

I chose bright, bold colors so the candy would stand out against the white of the page, but this pattern would look tantalizing in pretty pastels too. To add some interest: vary the size of your motifs; paint some large candies and some small; find candies with fun shapes and interesting textures. As a finishing touch, I went in with rainbow colors and added sprinkles all around the candy.

Play Pattern hunting on the go

One of the things I love about watercolor is how portable it is. You can easily build a travel watercolor set that will fit neatly in your pocket or bag, so you are ready to paint anywhere.

My travel watercolor supplies are so small they can fit in the palm of my hand. I have got a small set of paints in a case and the lid doubles as a paint palette for mixing colors. I also use the case to store a small pencil and a scrap of towel or sponge to clean my brush. My smallest sketchbook is only 3 by 5 inches (7.5 by 12.5 cm), with an elastic band around it to keep it secure. The set is completed with my beloved water brush—a paintbrush that can be filled with water!

All of these supplies are very affordable and easy to find. You can even make your own travel palette by squeezing some tube paints into a small tin. By always having art supplies in my bag, I know I will never be bored in a waiting room. It also reminds me to keep my eyes open for beautiful things when I am out.

One of my favorite activities is pattern hunting. I head out with my travel set and see how many patterns I can find on my walk. It can be a neighbor's garden fence, a scattering of leaves on the ground, or an interesting architectural detail. These tiny patterns often lead me to bigger ideas and influence other paintings.

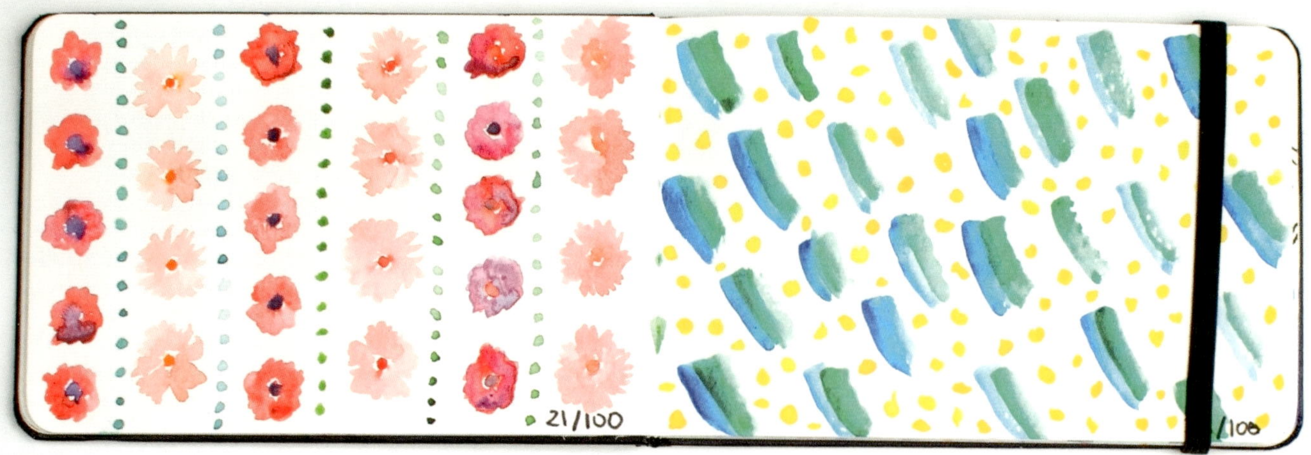

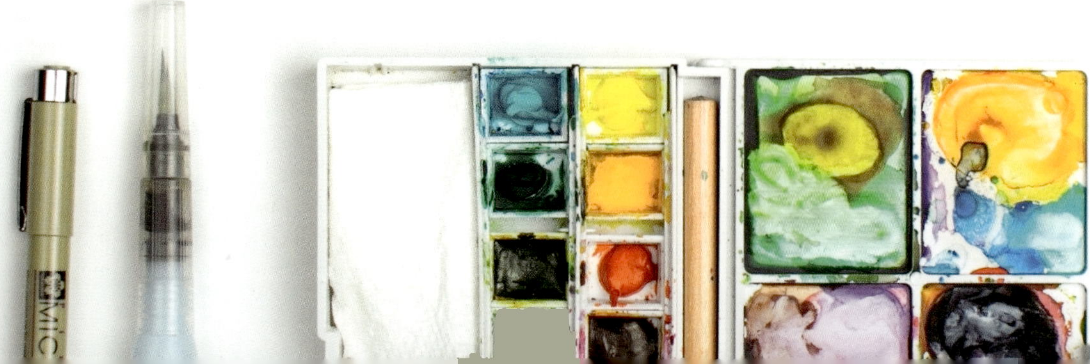

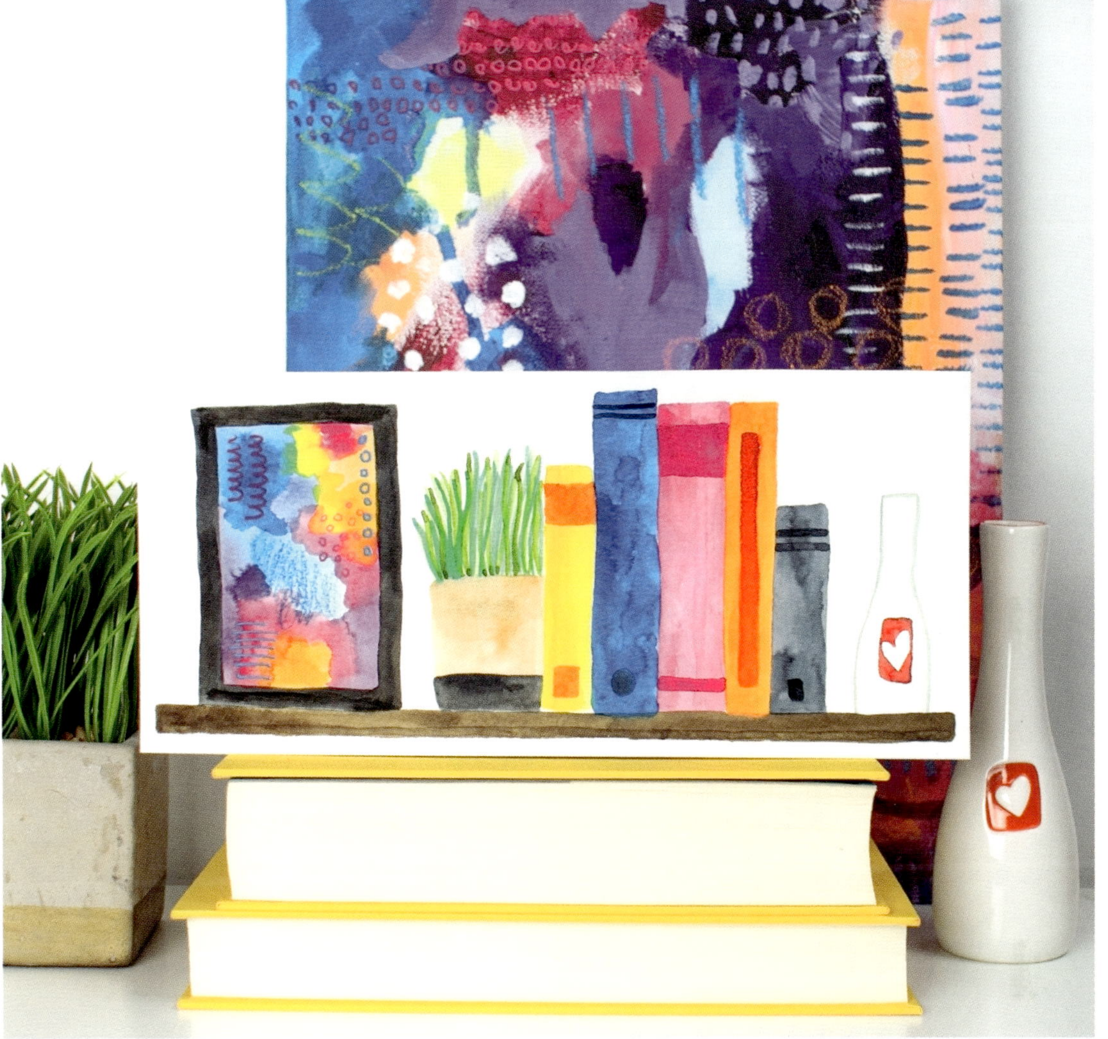

Prompt Take a shelfie

You know what a selfie is, but have you ever heard of a *shelfie*? Most of us have at least one shelf where we keep our most interesting and special items. These little displays can tell you a lot about a person, sometimes just as much as a selfie.

The little objects you keep on display in your home are such fun to paint. These items are likely arranged with care and represent your interests and hobbies. Whether you have a huge collection of objects you want to show off or you have just a few important mementos, this painting will be personal and specific to you—it is almost like painting a self-portrait.

Grab a chair, your sketchbook, and paints, and sit down in front of a shelf. Arrange your items so you have an assortment of sizes, colors, and textures to make the painting interesting. As always, I use what I see only as a starting point and make changes where desired. I started off with a quick pencil sketch to put everything in place, then painted a rainbow of books and a miniaturized version of one of my favorite pieces of art. Now I have a snapshot of my life as it looks today.

Project

Layered confetti

These easy but colorful projects are my favorite. You can take something as simple as a dot and just keep repeating it across the page to make something beautiful. I love how the confetti is concentrated at the bottom of the page, as if it has collected there after a big party. You can try other shapes, too!

YOU WILL NEED

- Watercolor paper
- Watercolor paint in 3 colors
- Medium round brush

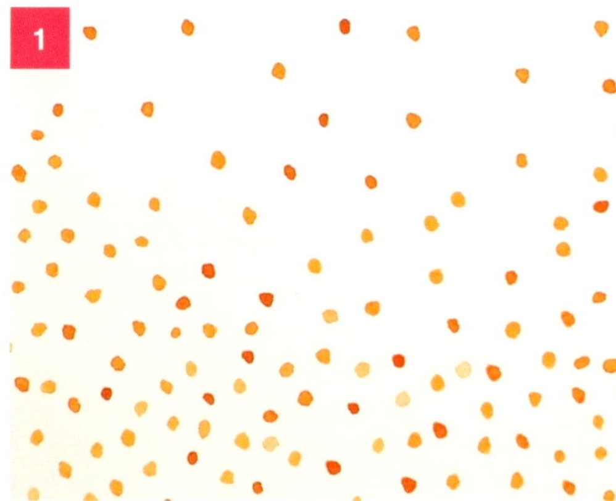

With your first color, paint some randomly placed dots on the page. Start loosely forming them into a shape where the confetti will be more concentrated.

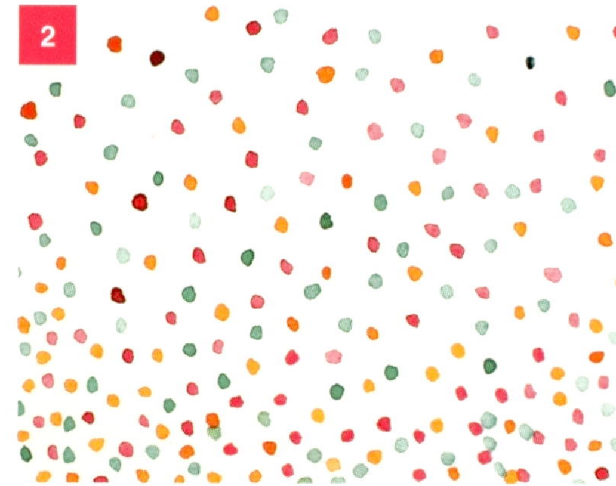

Add in two or three more colors of confetti. Let each color dry before moving on to the next layer.

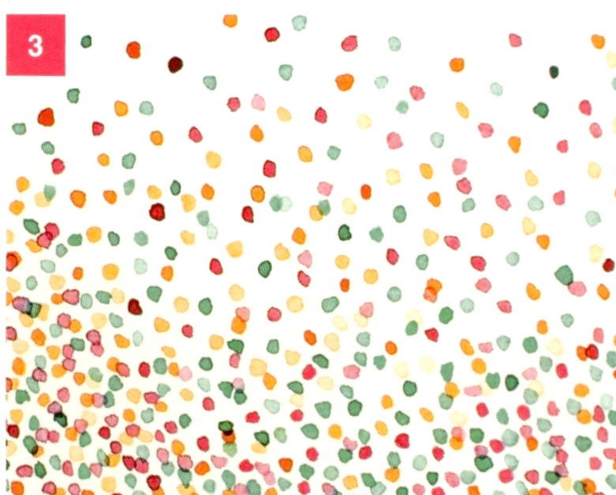

Keep rotating through the colors and start focusing on filling the bottom part of the page.

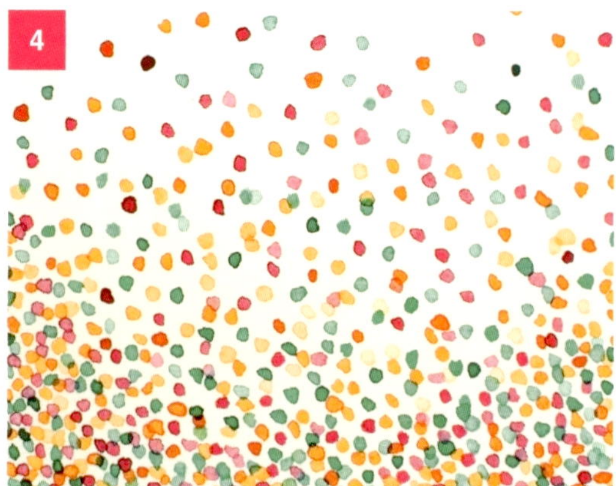

Continue to add dots and overlap the confetti. When you have very little white space left at the bottom part of the page, you're done.

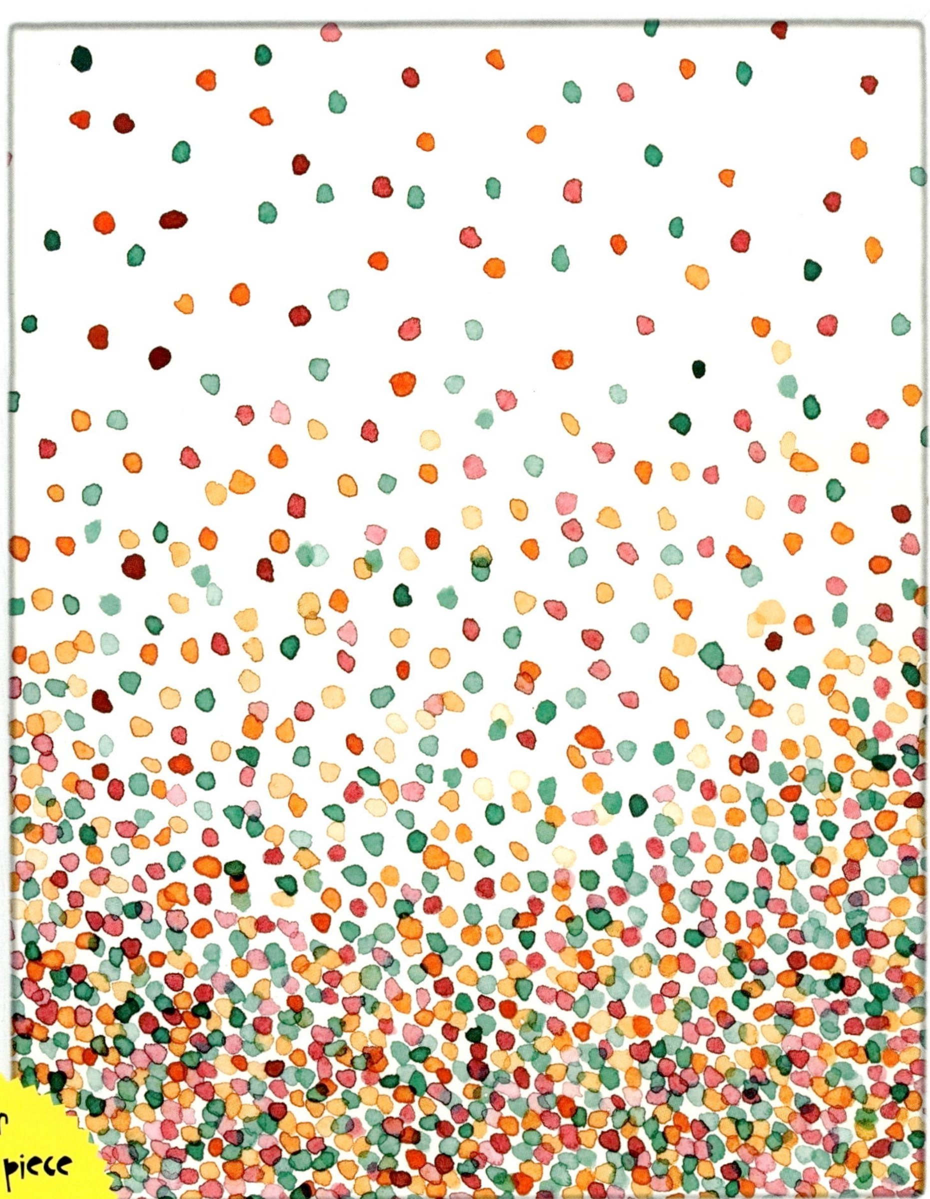

Your finished piece

This art project is oh-so-simple to create but looks like a party on paper. Try it in different color combinations and shapes.

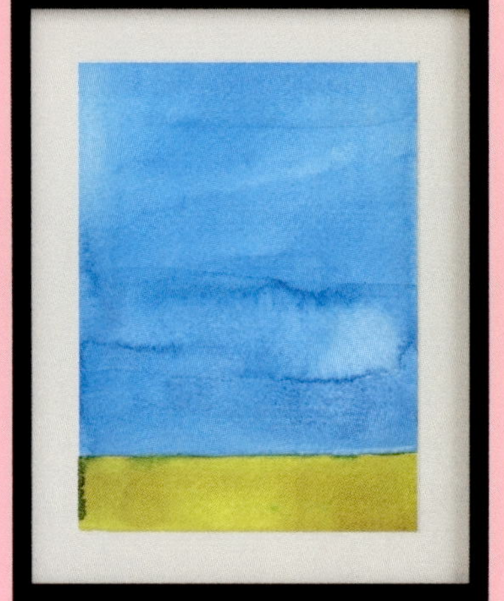

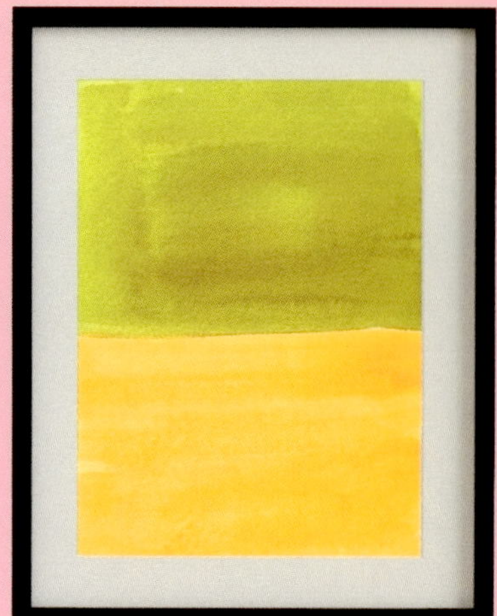

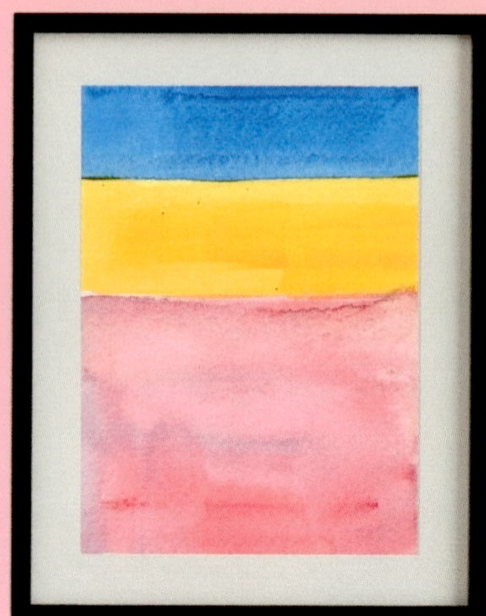

Tip

Play with size: instead of a series, create one extra-large painting.

prompt Color blocking

In this prompt, you're going to create your very own series of bold, modern paintings. I love to do groupings of paintings like this because you can take a simple concept and really tell a story with it.

For these paintings, I first sketched the general layout of each one on a scrap piece of paper. I decided where each of the colors would go, sticking to two or three large sections for each painting. Then I chose four strong colors to go with my bold design.

Before I started painting, I created a small border on each piece of paper with masking tape, for a clean edge. You can let each color dry before moving on to the next to get a crisp, clean line; or you can apply the next color immediately for a fuzzier line.

I love creating paintings in a series like this. A piece such as this on its own might look a little uninteresting, but when you place it next to some friends, it comes to life. It is a quick and easy way to make some bold artwork for your home.

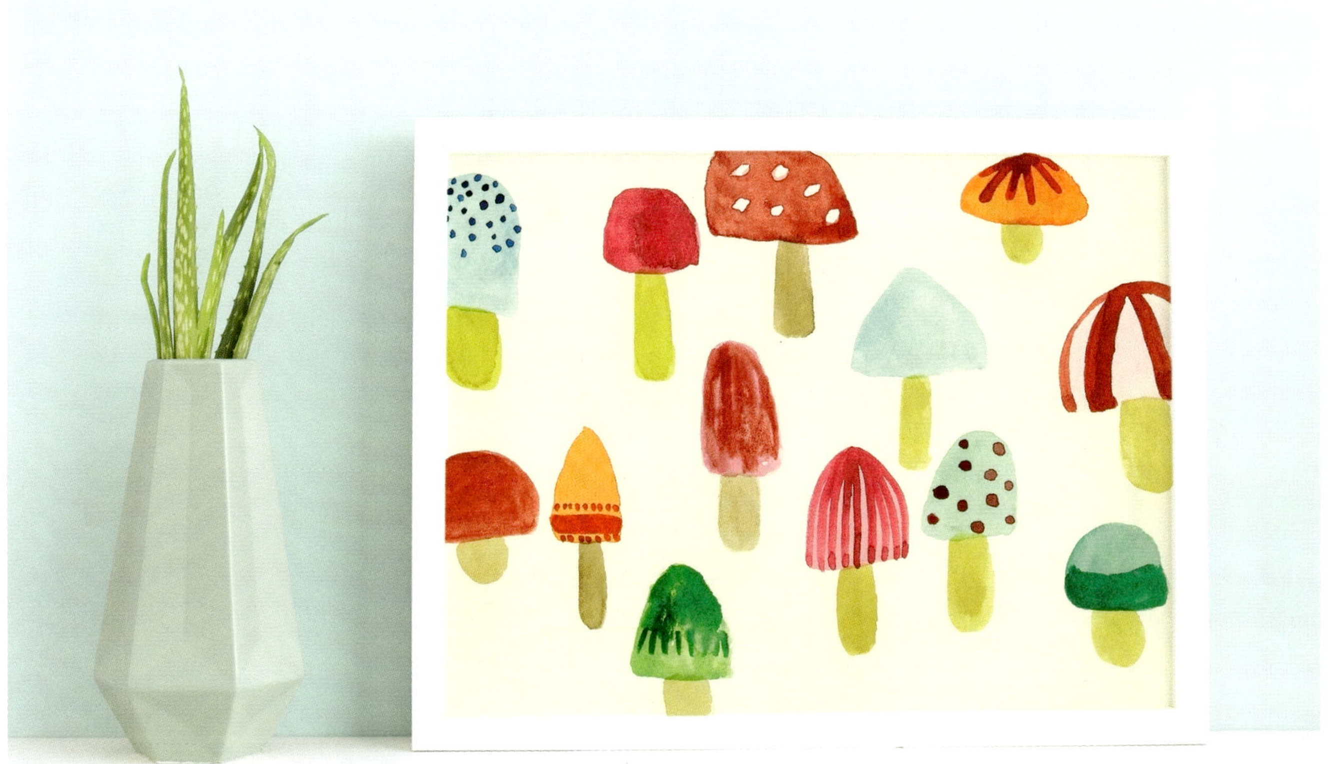

prompt Paint a mushroom garden

This is another excellent chance to play with pattern and color. In this exercise, we will paint a whimsical mushroom garden from a fairy-tale. Grab all your favorite colors and start dreaming up some fantastical mushrooms.

Watercolor artists tend to gravitate toward florals for their paintings because flowers come in so many different shapes, sizes, and colors. A mushroom garden is a wonderful alternative to the standard floral painting. The mushrooms I paint might not be found in nature, but they sure are fun to look at, and they remind me of a colorful fairy garden.

Painting your mushrooms is an opportunity to experiment with different patterns, textures, and colors. Try out new color combinations, and layering, and see what marks your brushes can make. Remember that no two mushrooms will look exactly the same, so paint some that are tall, skinny, wide, flat, short, fat, and every combination you can think of. You might feel like you run out of ideas after painting two or three but keep pushing yourself to come up with new designs.

Work in layers by painting the stem first. Once the stem is dry, paint the mushroom cap in a solid color. After that layer is dry, go back and add some details such as stripes, dots, and lines. Keep going until you fill the whole page.

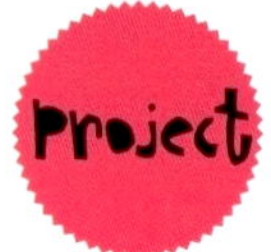

Growing a floral pattern

There are so many different ways to build a floral pattern, but I want to show you my tried-and-true method, in case this is something you are struggling with. When it comes to floral patterns, you want balance, interest, and variety. You want the viewer's eye to move freely across the page and take it all in. Once you perfect the basic floral pattern, you are free to experiment with proportions and the mix of motifs.

YOU WILL NEED

- Watercolor paper
- Watercolor paint
- Variety of brushes

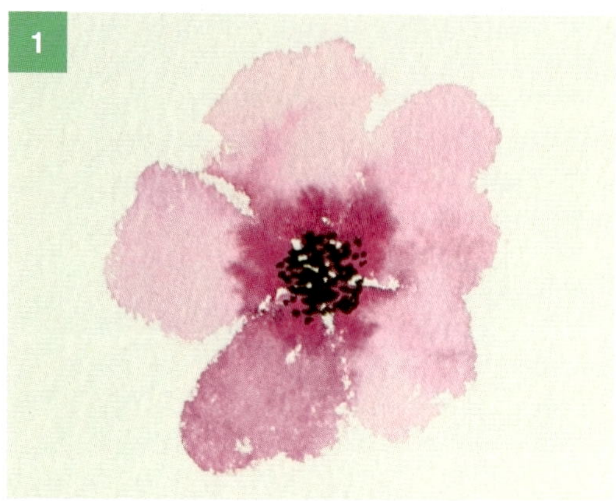

I always start with a big feature flower. This will be the focus of the pattern. Try to choose an eye-catching color.

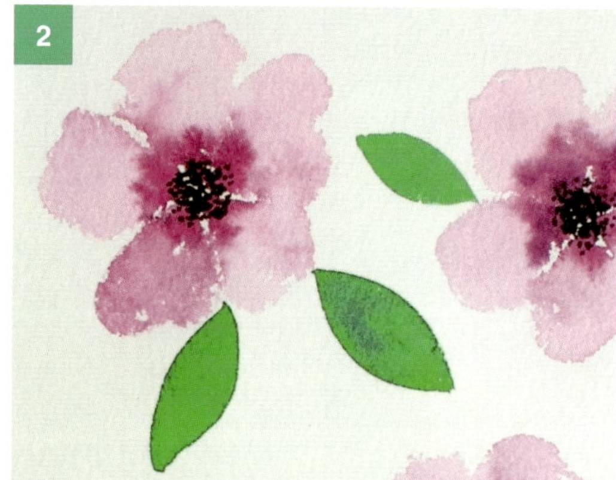

All floral patterns need a little green—let's add in some large leaves around the flowers.

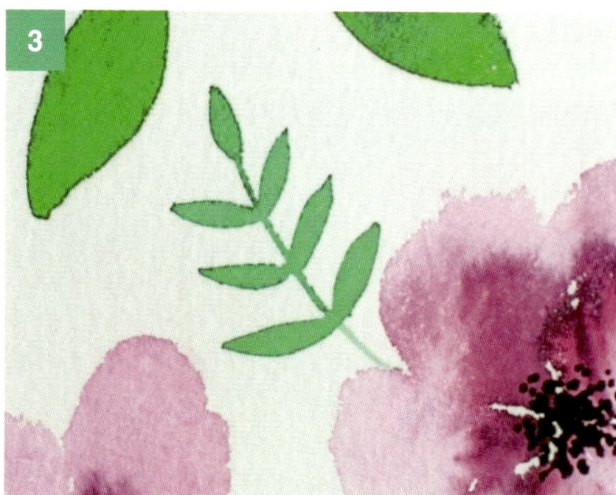

Next, add in a bit more green with a delicate stem of leaves. I painted these in a slightly different green to the large leaves.

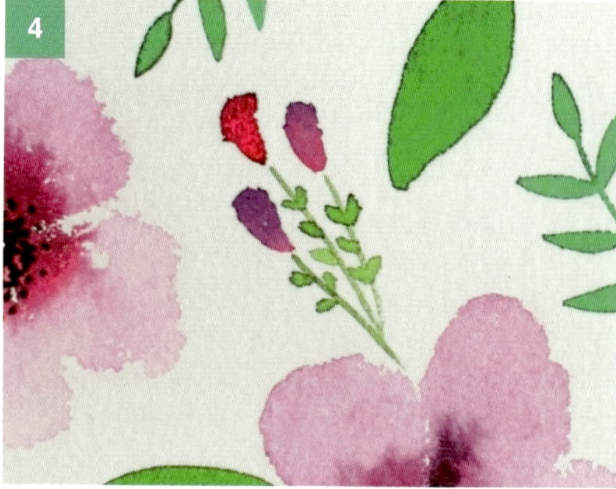

Then paint some accent foliage, such as a small flower bud. Paint the bud as if it is coming out from the flower's hidden stem.

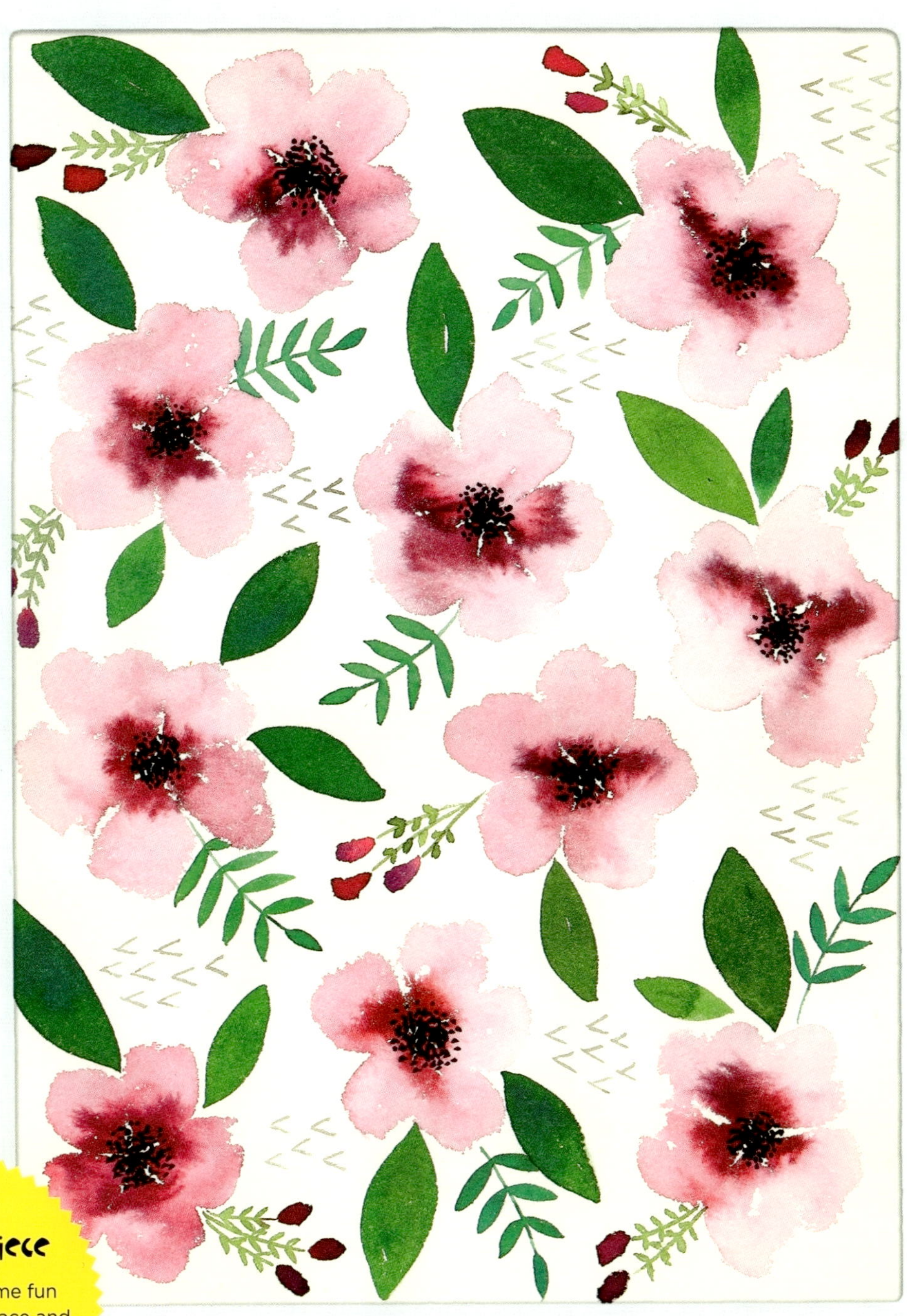

Your finished piece

I like to paint some fun marks to fill up space and give a little variety. These can be anything from polka dots to little "V" shapes.

Play Fixing and embracing mistakes

Watercolor is known for being an unforgiving media. Once the paint is on the page, there aren't too many ways to cover up a mistake. Combine this with the fact that watercolor paints are often unpredictable and things can get tricky. But don't despair! There are a few ways you can salvage your hard work.

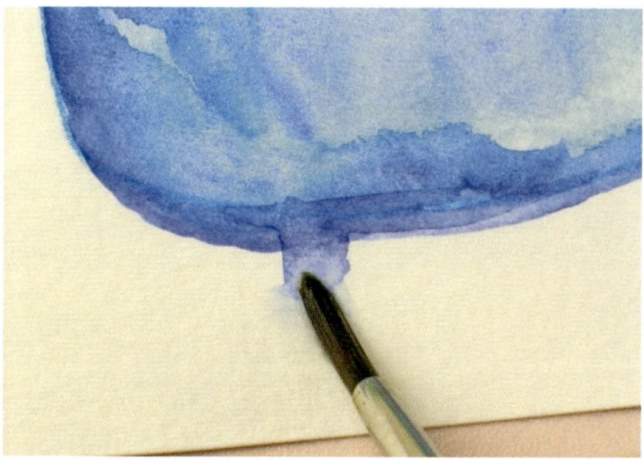

Clean up

If you have one little spot of paint to remove, try lightly scrubbing at it with a damp, clean brush. The water will reactivate the paint and the brush will soak up what you don't want.

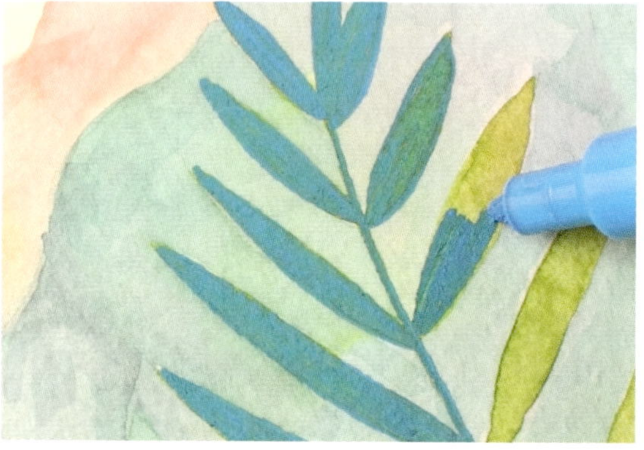

Cover up

If you can't get your painting to look right, try adding an opaque medium such as gouache, acrylic, or paint markers. Sometimes the best thing to do is cover up the mistake and move on.

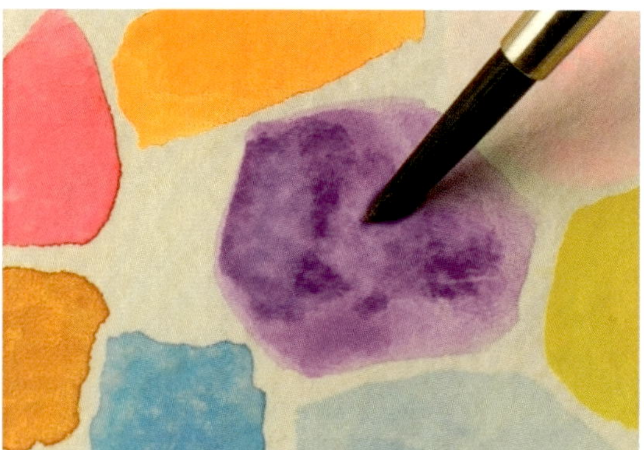

Second coat

When your painting dries and the colors look uneven or blotchy, try going over it with another coat. A second coat will often smooth out any unwanted textures.

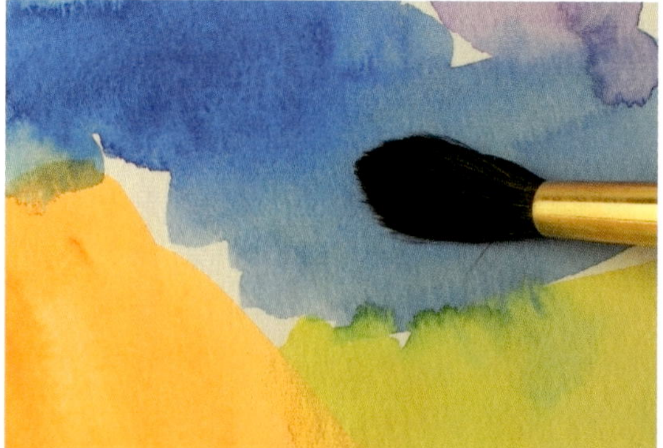

Live with it

This is my favorite way to deal with mistakes: learn to love them! Those color bleeds, blooms, and textures make your painting unique and interesting.

prompt Paint a cloudy sky

Sometimes it is less about the paint you put down and more about the paint you take away. In this prompt, you will learn a lifting technique using paper towel to create a cloudy sky. This is also a great technique to use if you have laid down too much color and want to pare it back.

Secure your paper to your work surface with some painter's tape. You will be saturating the page with paint, so if you don't tape it down, the paper will curl. Take a medium flat brush and paint a light wash of water over the entire piece of paper.

Next, mix up some paint for the sky. I used blue mixed with a tiny bit of black, but this would also be lovely with warm sunset colors. Use your flat brush to paint a wash of blue across the whole page. Don't worry too much about where the ground will be; you will be adding that later. The sky tends to be darker toward the horizon, so concentrate more of the color toward the bottom of the page.

Before the sky dries, grab a paper towel and scrunch it up. Use it to carefully lift some of the paint off the paper. Be sure to rotate the towel as you work, and apply different amounts of pressure to vary the shape of the clouds.

If you like, you can wait for the paint to dry, add another coat of sky color, and blot more cloud shapes. This will create more depth. Once it is all dry, go back and add some ground and scenery.

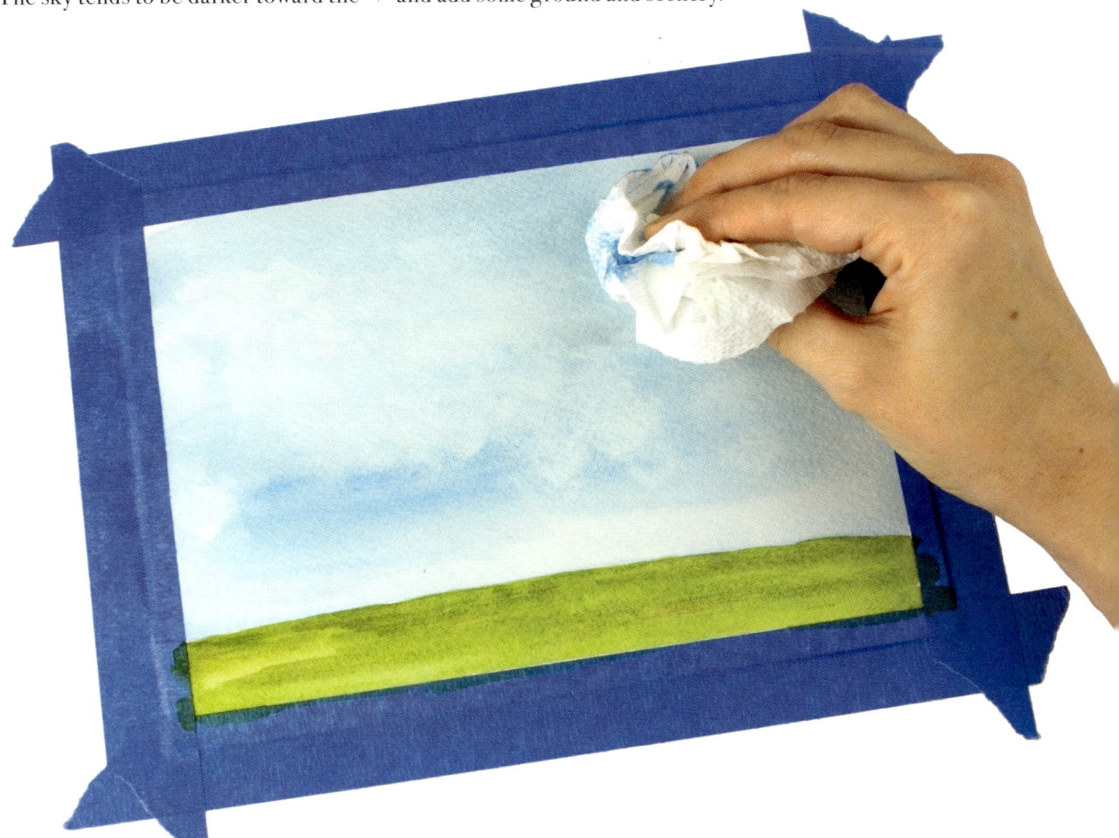

Play Expressive brushstrokes

Practicing expressive brushstrokes is one of my favorite painting warmups, and learning to be freer with your strokes will help you with any type of painting.

This play is meant to be fun and carefree, so put on your favorite music and let loose with your paints. You can start with a scrap piece of paper first to get a feel for things or just dive right into a painting.

Start with big, bold brushstrokes using your largest brushes. Loosely map out a shape on the page with those first strokes. I like to start with lighter colors, making it easier to layer. Once your first layer is dry, grab more colors and keep working. Try not to overthink things; let your music guide you and use your whole arm to paint, even your whole body!

When the second layer is dry, start adding some smaller strokes. Try dabbing the brush on the page and flicking it lightly. Vary the pressure and see the different marks you make. Every so often, step back to take a good look at your painting, to decide if you have finished.

Tip

Work on two or three paintings at once to keep your momentum during drying time.

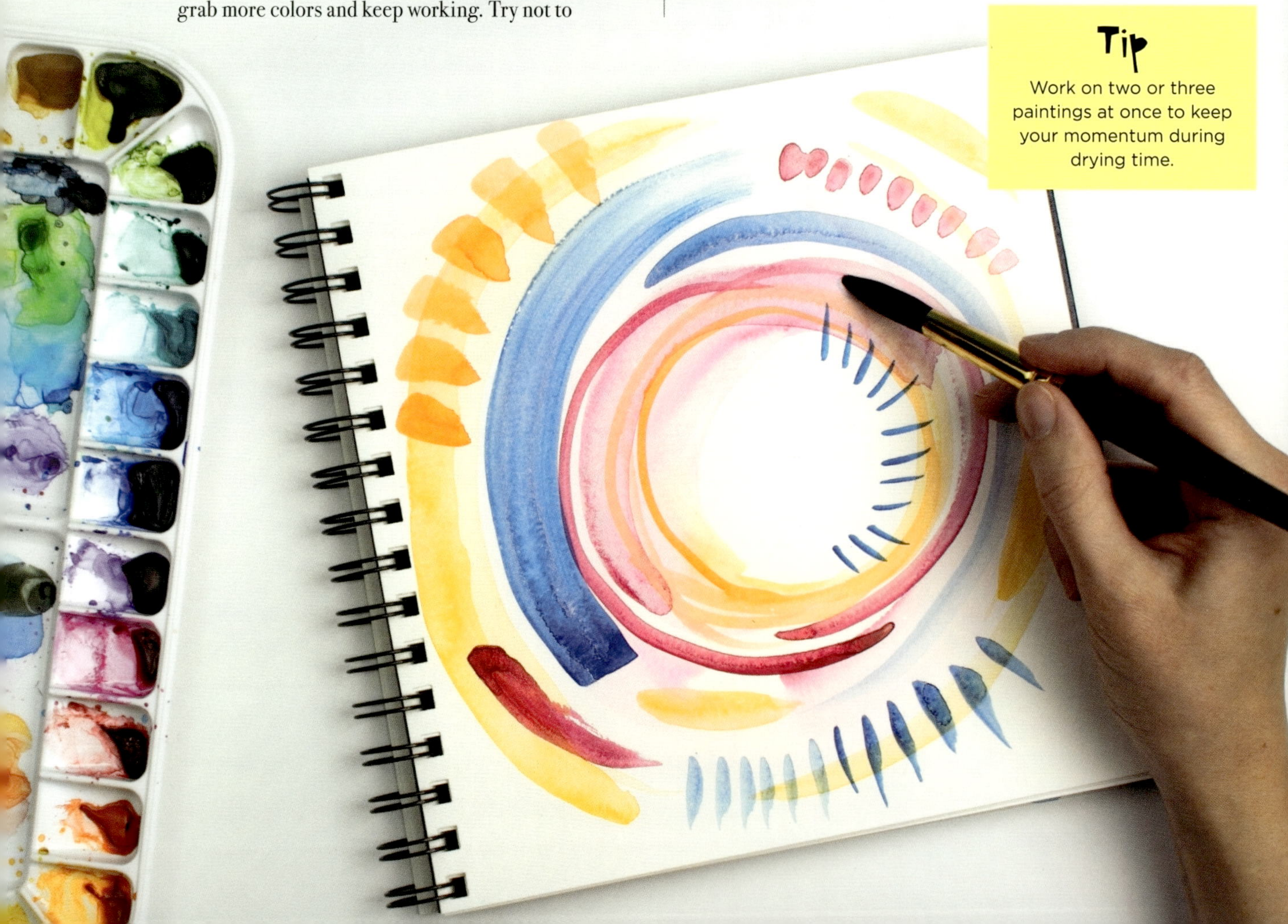

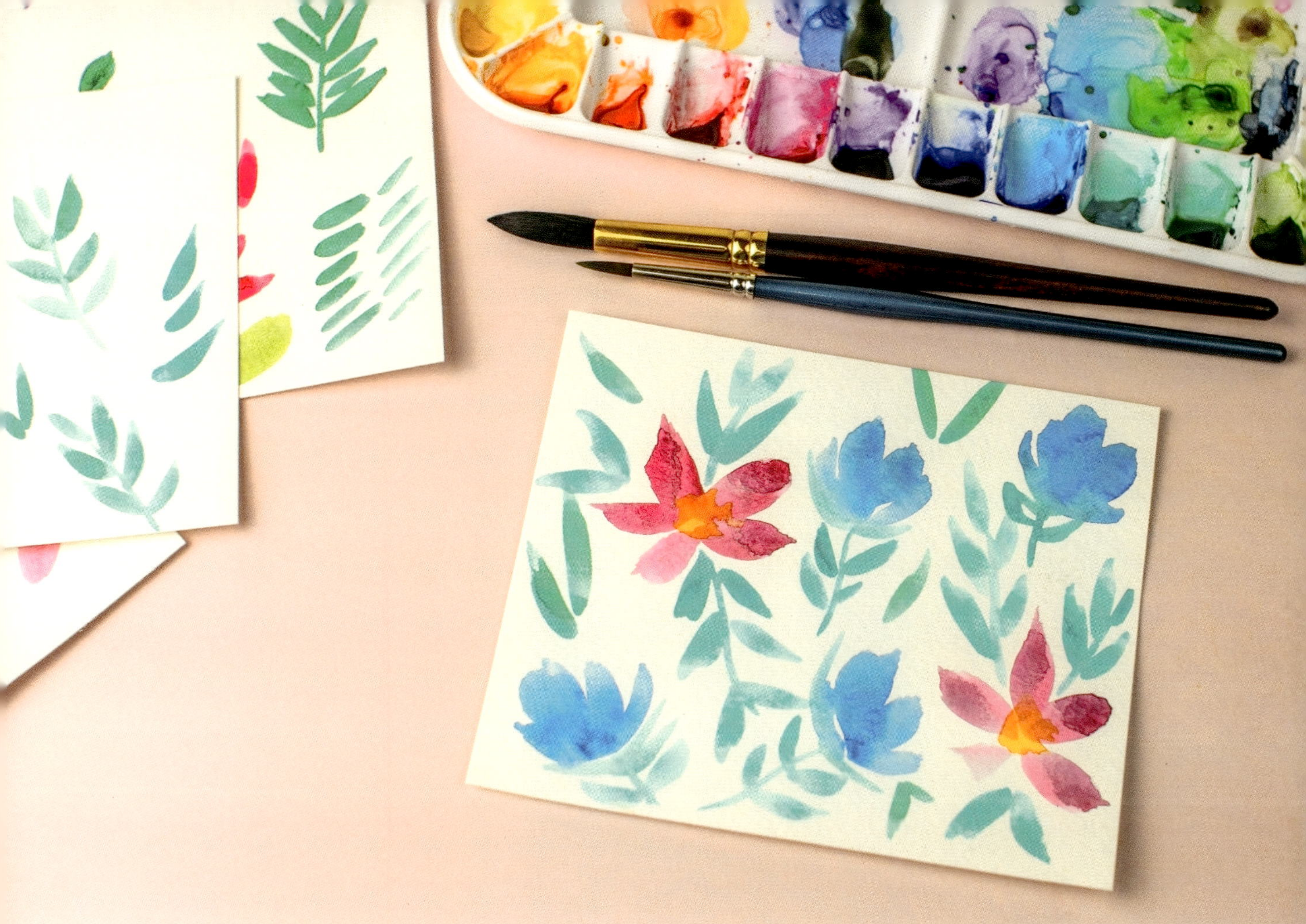

prompt One-stroke flowers and leaves

Now that you have experimented with some expressive brushstrokes, test those skills with some florals. Flowers and leaves are the perfect way to put your expressive painting skills to use, because anything goes.

You will need a couple of different sizes of brushes for this prompt—a larger round brush for big flower petals and a smaller round brush for leaves. But feel free to experiment with all different sizes and types of brushes. Each brush makes its own unique stroke. I like to have a scrap piece of paper with me so I can practice each stroke first.

When working on the flowers, start from the center of the bloom and whisk your brush out. Try to use a single brushstroke for each petal. For the foliage, I like to paint the stem with a quick swoosh first, then use a single stroke for each leaf along the stem. Try to utilize the whole brush, from the very tip to the full belly and back to the tip again, to achieve that pointy leaf shape.

Green swooshes turn into leaves, and a pink flick of the brush makes a flower petal. That is why I love florals: almost anything works to create a beautiful, fast-growing garden!

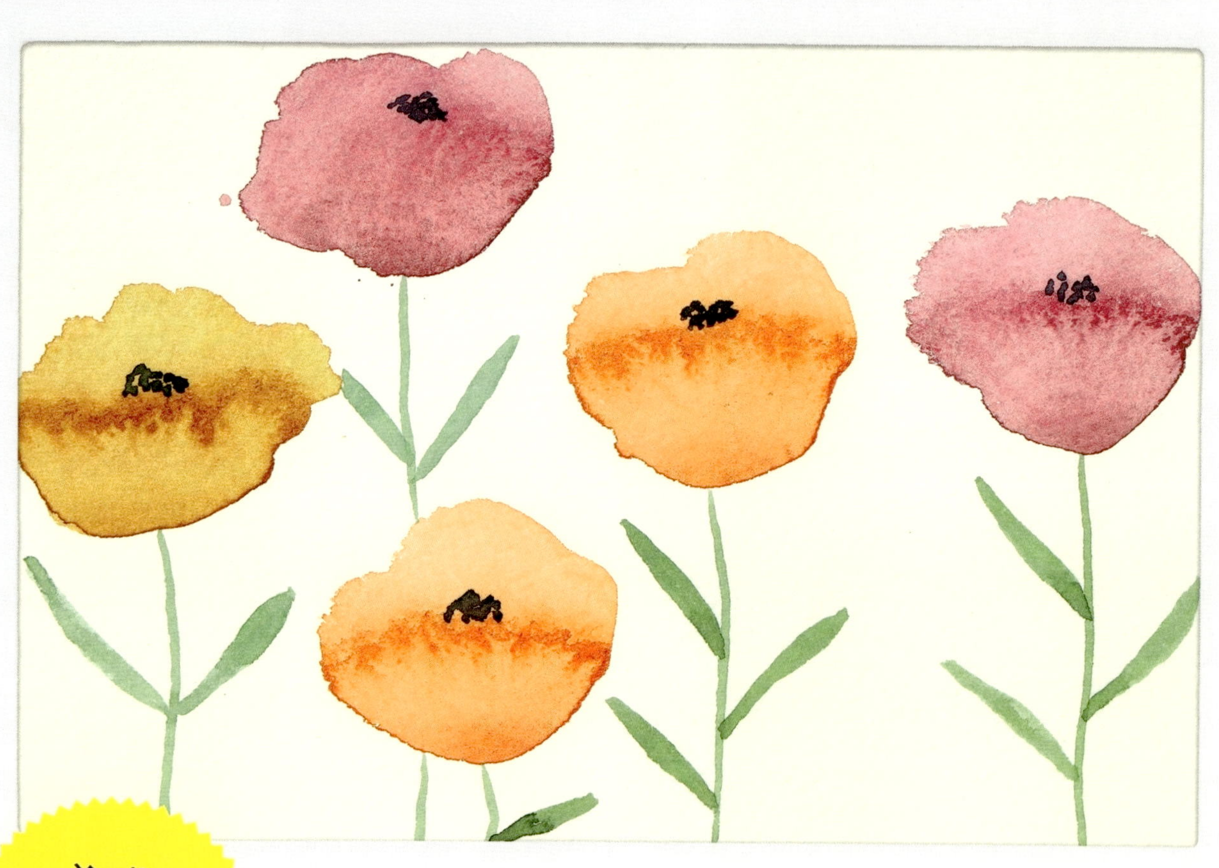

Your finished piece

Each of these flowers will turn out unique, while capturing the magic of watercolor paint.

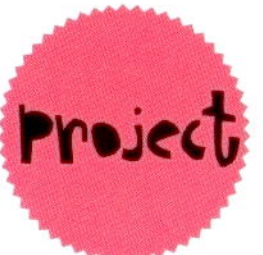

Easy gradient flowers

These flowers are so easy to paint and always turn out beautifully. This is a great example of letting the paint do all the work for you. The flowers won't look like much when they are wet, but wait until the paint dries and you will see the magic! I like to use a big, fluffy round brush for this because it can hold a lot of paint and makes some interesting petal shapes.

YOU WILL NEED

- Watercolor paper
- Watercolor paint
- Large round brush
- Small round brush

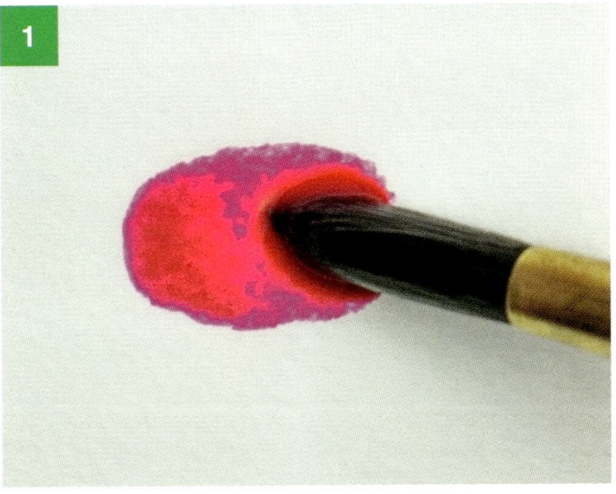

Begin by loading up your large round brush with lots of color and painting a pigmented oval shape on the page. This is the base of your flower.

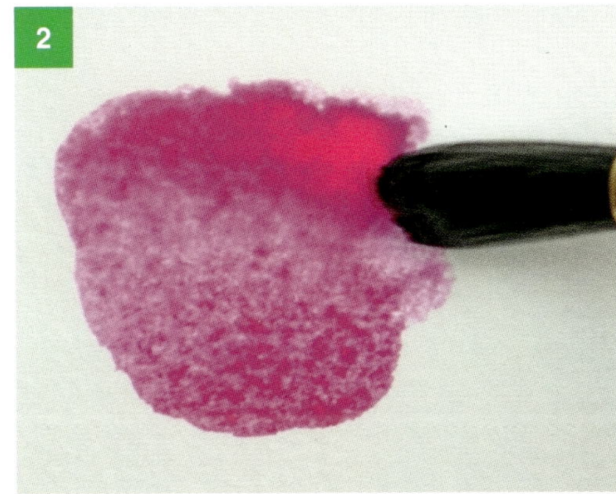

Next, clean your brush thoroughly and dry it. Go back in and drag the pigment up to create petals.

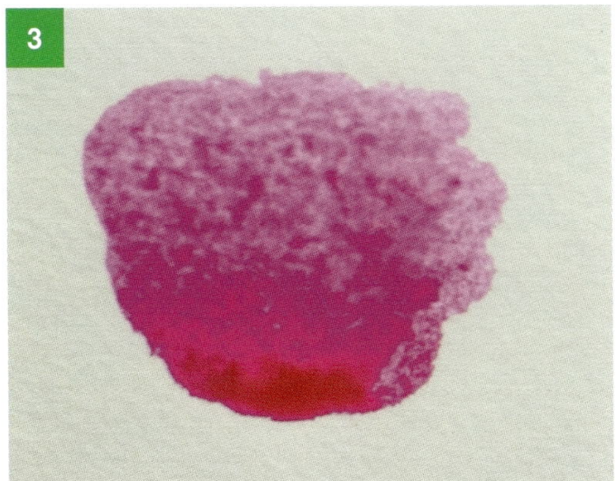

Prop your paper up on something to dry so all the pigment gathers at the bottom of the flower.

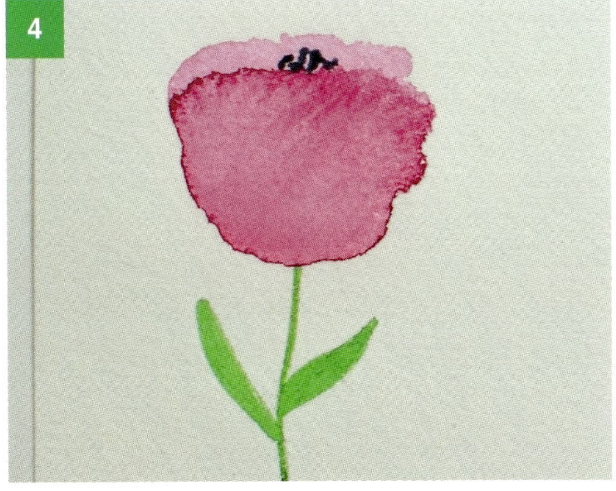

Once the flower is dry, you can add a stem, some leaves, and other details with a smaller brush.

Prompt Create your packing list

Whether it is a real vacation or the trip of your dreams, painting your packing list is a fun exercise. I just love painting everyday objects like the kind of things you pack for a weekend away, because when I see them all laid out on the page they tell a story.

For this prompt, it doesn't matter if you have a trip planned or not. If you don't, it can be just as fun to think up a dream vacation and figure out all the things you would pack in your bag. This exercise is all about taking everyday objects, such as a pair of sunglasses or a towel, and arranging them on the page so they tell the viewer a story.

I started by getting all my objects down on paper with some basic shapes first. Don't worry too much about detail at this stage, and make sure to include everything from what you will wear to what you will read. Maybe you even plan to take along a set of watercolor paints!

After I had the basic shapes complete and dried off, I went back in and added some detail and depth. This is where you can personalize each item and create interest. As a finishing touch, I used a black waterproof pen to outline each object. This is optional—you might like the overall look better without the outline. Now you are ready to take off!

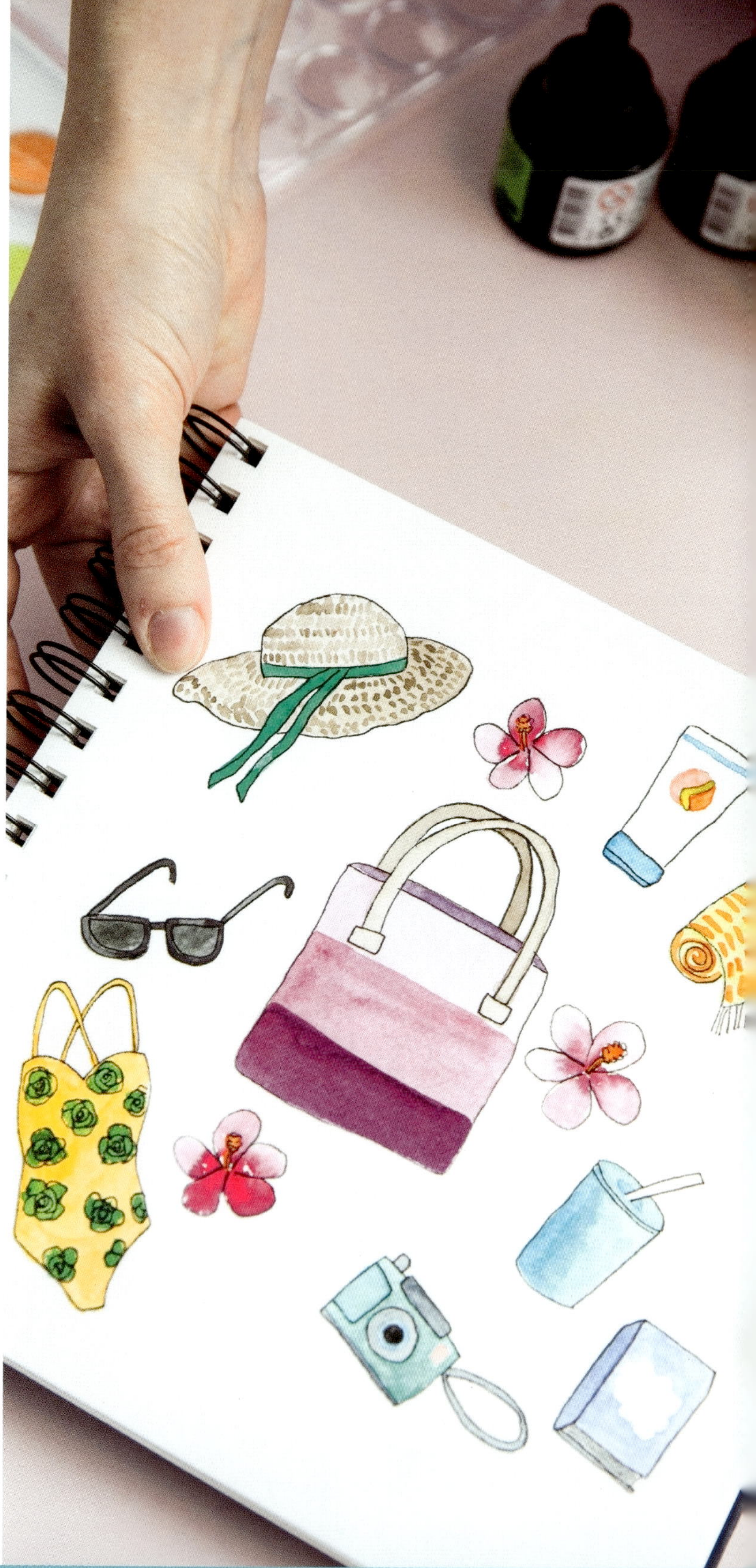

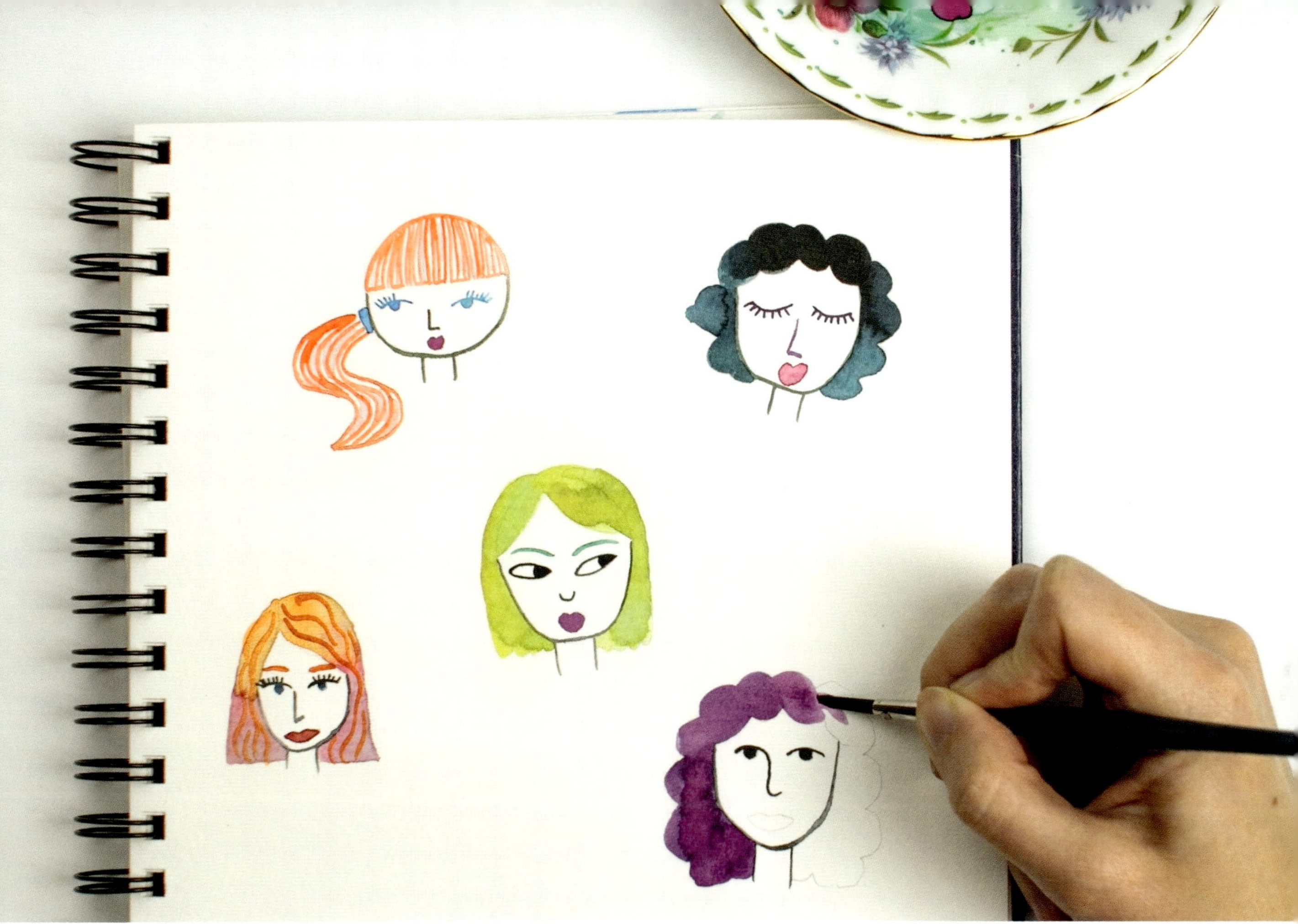

Play Practice painting faces

Committing yourself to a whole portrait can be intimidating. So why not start with a few practice faces? In this exercise, we will practice putting facial features and hair together to create a variety of different heads.

Believe it or not, painting faces can be enjoyable. The problem comes when you try to jump into a full portrait too early. Make one mistake and you feel like you have ruined the whole painting. My solution to this is to fill the page with a variety of practice faces. You will get a chance to experiment with different facial features, styles, placement, and hair. And, in the end, you will have a great reference of faces to look back on and draw from.

I like to start with a light pencil sketch to get the basic shape of each face and the hair. There are so many ways to paint each feature, so be sure to experiment. You can look online or to your favorite artists for ideas, but make sure to only take one or two aspects as inspiration—you don't want to copy someone else's style entirely.

The best part about painting so many faces on one page is that if you make a mistake with one, just move on to the next. With each face you will improve and be more confident. Once you hone your own style, you can challenge yourself with a whole portrait.

prompt 3, 2, 1!

This prompt is designed to get you thinking fast and using your artist's intuition. You will be creating three paintings using only two colors in each. And the kicker? You will need to complete each painting in one minute.

Grab three small sheets of watercolor paper and choose your two colors. I picked blue and pink because it is my favorite color combination. Remember that this exercise doesn't allow for drying time, so pick two colors that will look nice even if those accidental bleeds happen.

Don't do too much planning for this exercise. Before I began, I knew I wanted to make three coordinating patterns and that's about it. If you plan excessively, it will defeat the purpose of the time limit. Instead, practice making decisions on the go and listening to your intuition.

Now set a timer and get started! When the timer goes off, drop your brush right away. If you finish before the minute is up, try to go back in and add a bit more detail. This is a great exercise for when you have very little time or just a few paints available.

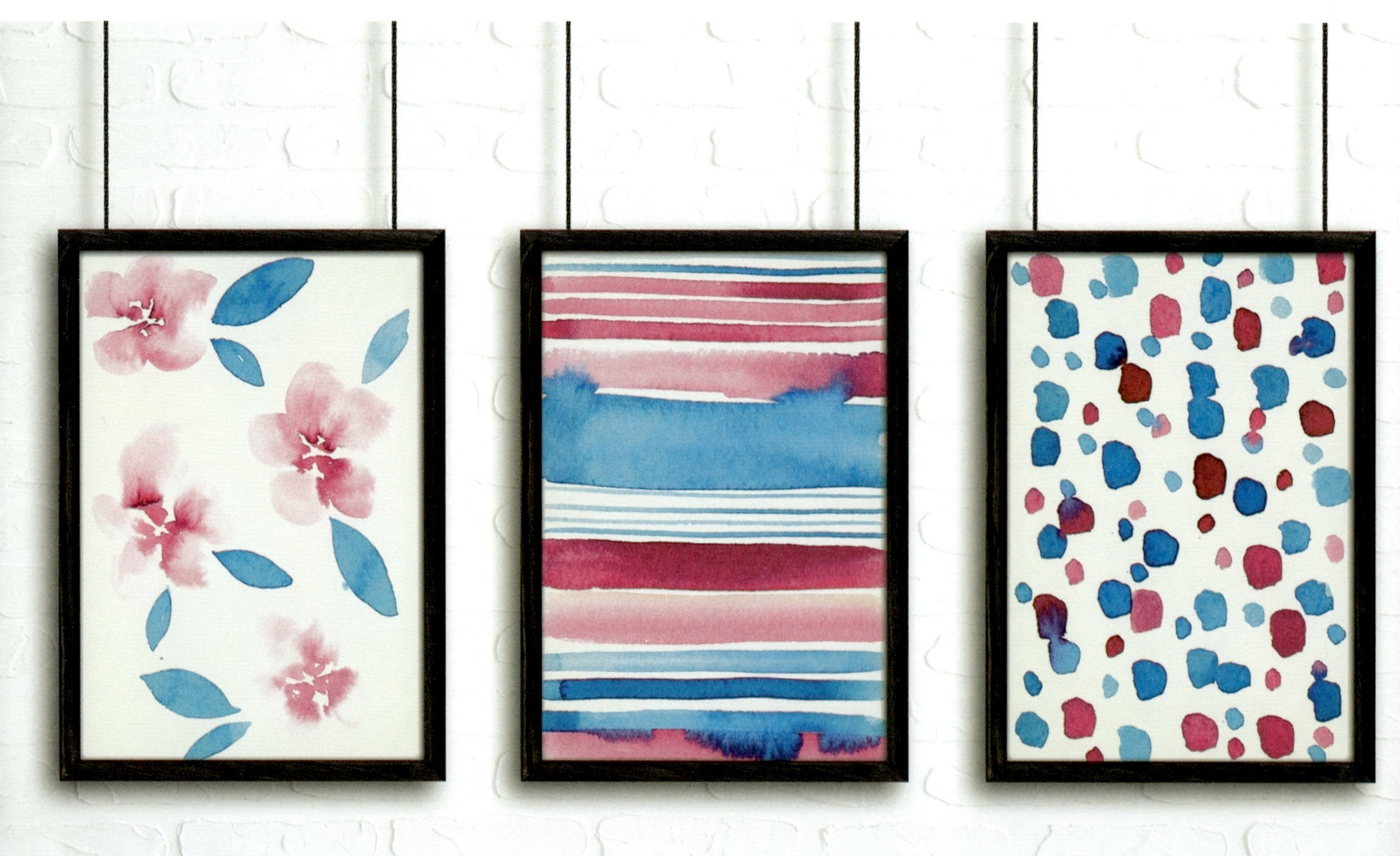

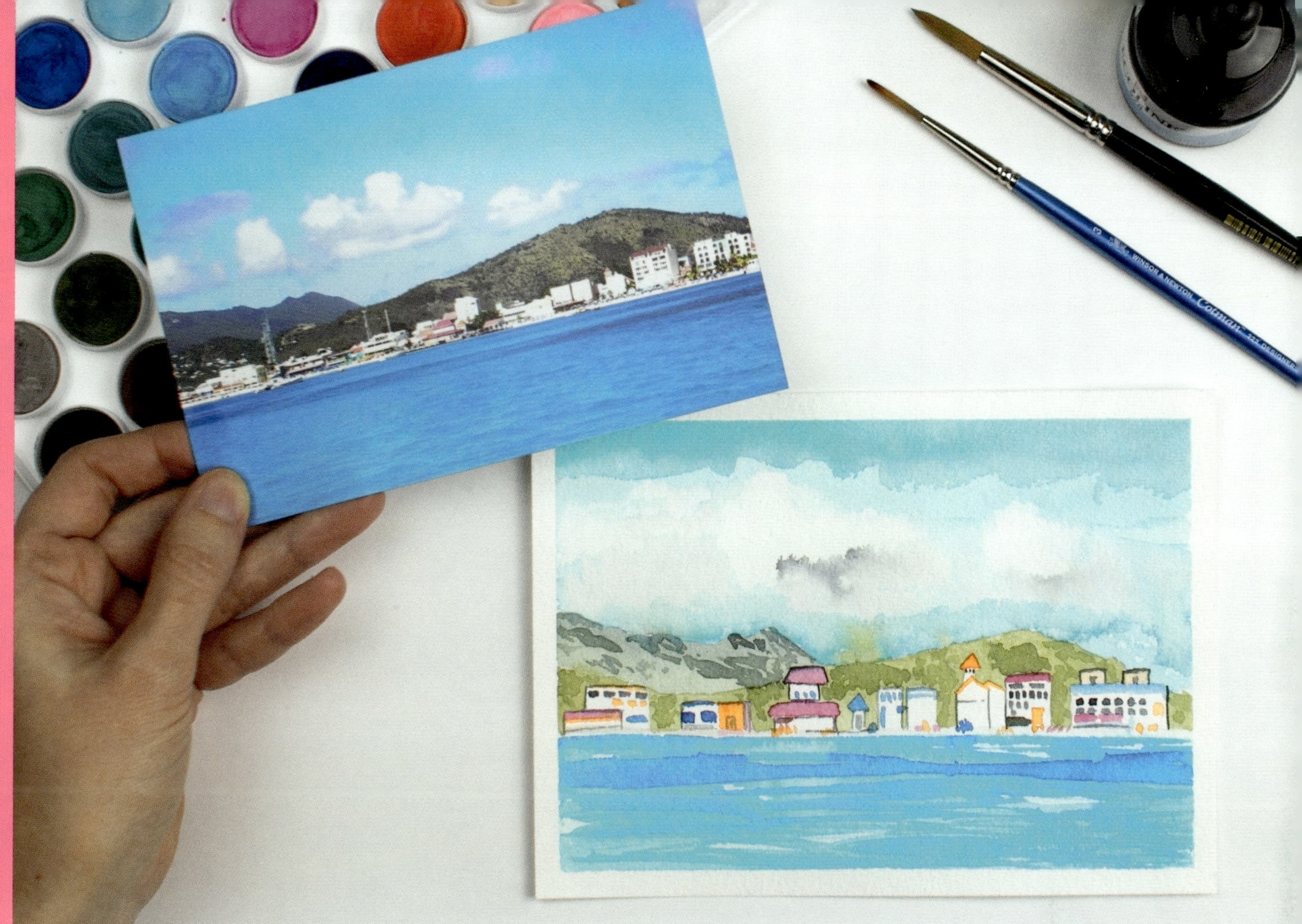

prompt Recreate a favorite photo

Photographs make excellent references. The subject sits still, the light never changes, and the scenery is already cropped for you. This painting can be made even more special by choosing a photo that represents a treasured memory for you.

For this prompt, start by choosing a photo to paint. This can be from your own collection or something you find on the Internet. If you are new to painting, try to choose a simple landscape or nature photo. A photograph with a busy scene or lots of people in it will be more of a challenge to paint.

Make sure to cut your watercolor paper to a similar size to your reference photo. This will help a lot when determining the placement of the objects in the frame. Use a pencil to lightly sketch the large landmarks and objects. In my reference photo, the water takes up about one-third of the photo and the mountains take up another third. Doing quick measurements like this helps to get the proportions right.

As always, remember that you don't need to paint everything exactly as you see it. In my photo, I liked the buildings along the shore, with those pops of color. So I chose to paint them a little bigger to make them the focus of the painting. Now I have a lovely memento from my vacation to hang on the wall.

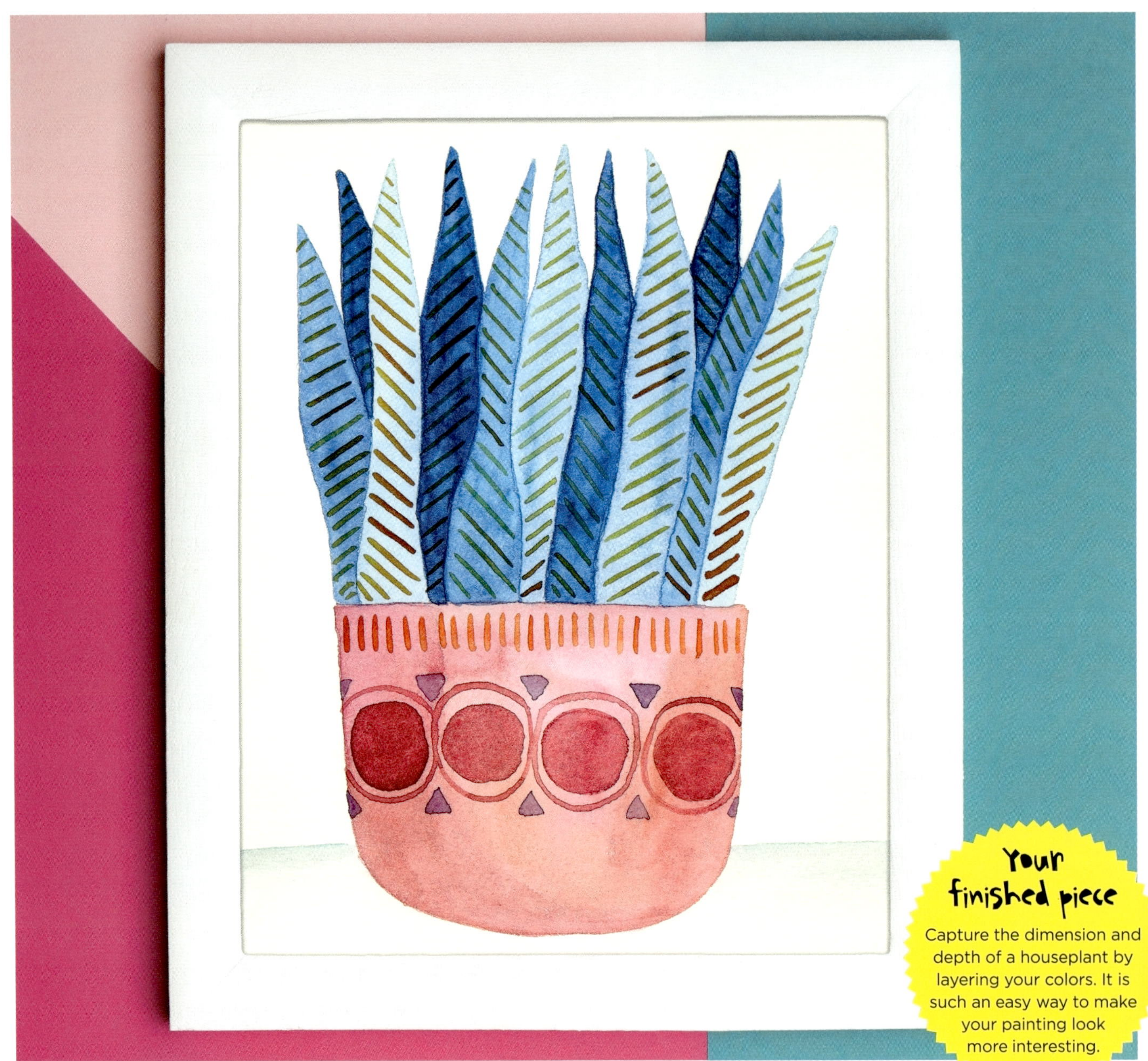

Project Dimensional potted plant

To paint this potted plant, we will be layering color. The darker leaves will look farther back and the lighter ones will appear closer to the front. This layering technique can be used to create depth in any painting. It takes patience to wait for each layer to dry, but the results are well worth it.

YOU WILL NEED

- Watercolor paper
- Watercolor paint
- Pencil
- Medium round brush
- Small liner brush

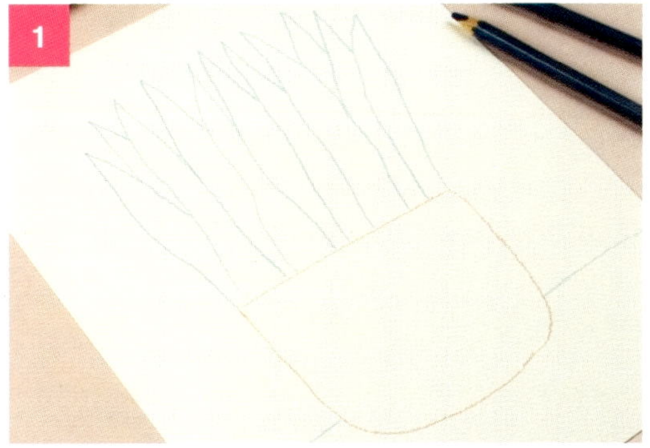

Using a watercolor or graphite pencil, draw a light outline of your potted plant and a line for the surface it is sitting on.

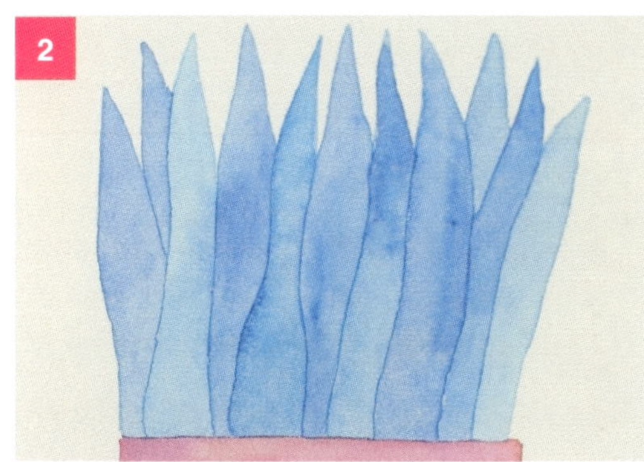

Using your medium round brush, paint a layer of color on the leaves and pot. For now, focus on covering the white; we will get to the dimension later.

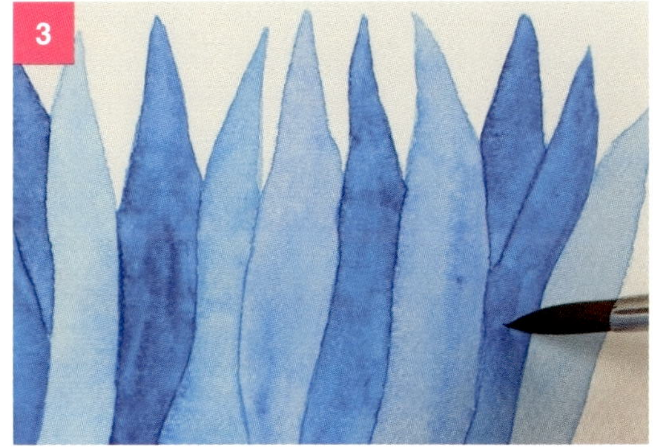

Once the first layer is dry, add a second layer of color to some of the leaves that would be at the back of the plant, in shadow. You can also add a shadow on one side of the pot.

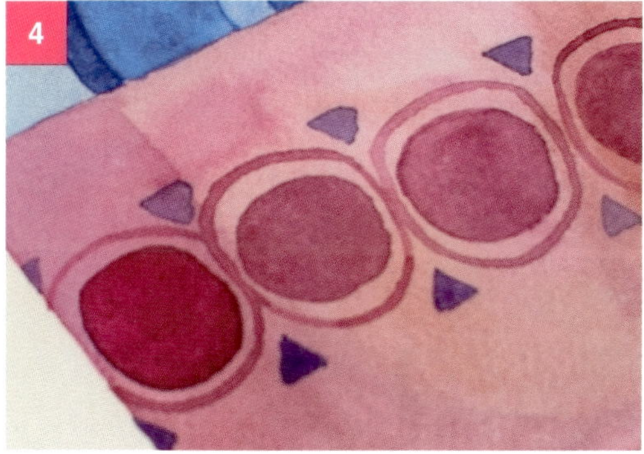

While you are waiting for the leaves to dry, you can add some decoration to the pot. Then go back and add more layers of color to further darken the leaves at the back.

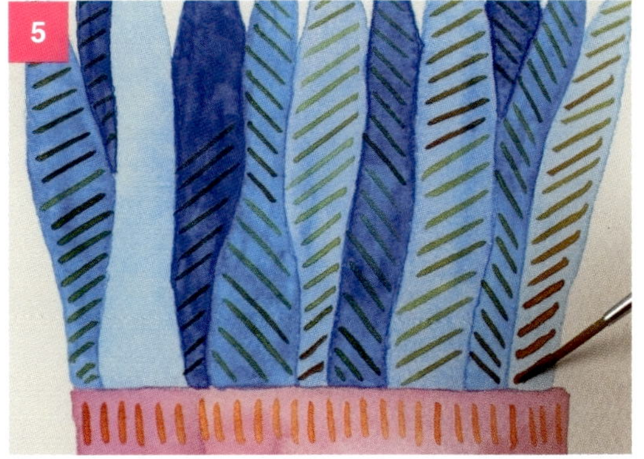

As a final step, add some fine lines to the leaves using a small liner brush. You may want to grab a scrap piece of paper to test out colors and patterns.

prompt Paint a month

You might be asking how exactly you paint a month. In this prompt, I want you to pick your favorite month of the year and represent it with a painting. Paint all the things that remind you of that time, recreate a memory, or paint a seasonal outdoor scene.

This is a good old-fashioned sketchbook prompt, designed to make you think about the visual aspects of a certain time of year. Bring out this exercise any time you don't know what to paint. Every time I do this, it turns out completely differently and always sparks a new idea.

I chose to paint things from October, my favorite month—I adore Halloween, the changing leaves outside, pulling out my cozy sweaters, and it is my birthday month! There is a ton of inspiration and memories for me to draw on.

Start by making a list of all the things that come to mind when you think of your month or by sketching out a scene. Work in layers by painting the basic shape of the items first and then add some details when the first layer of paint is dry. As a final touch, I like to add some decorative aspects such as leaves or flowers.

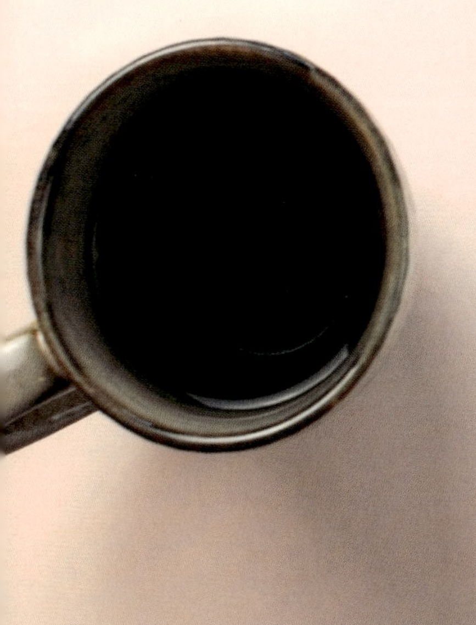

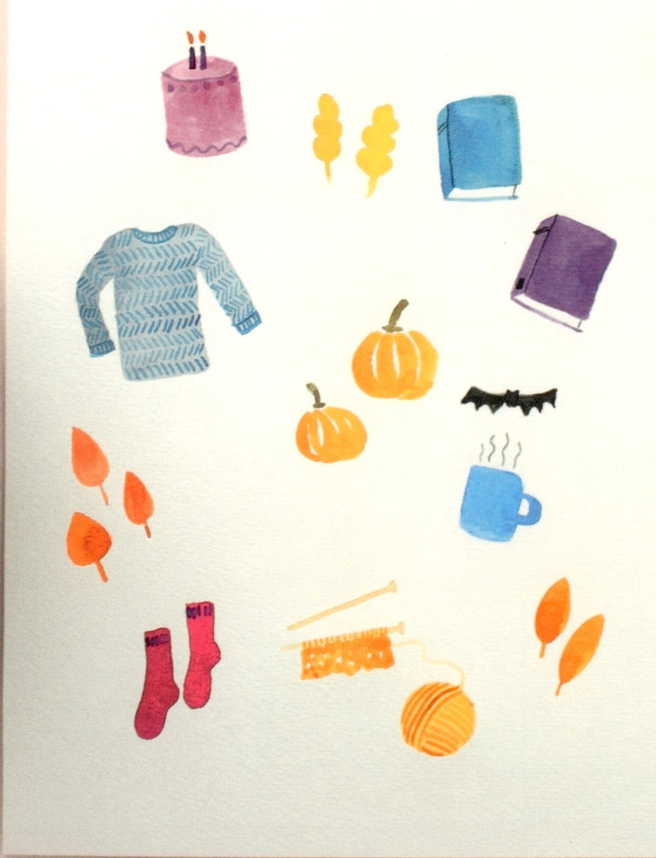

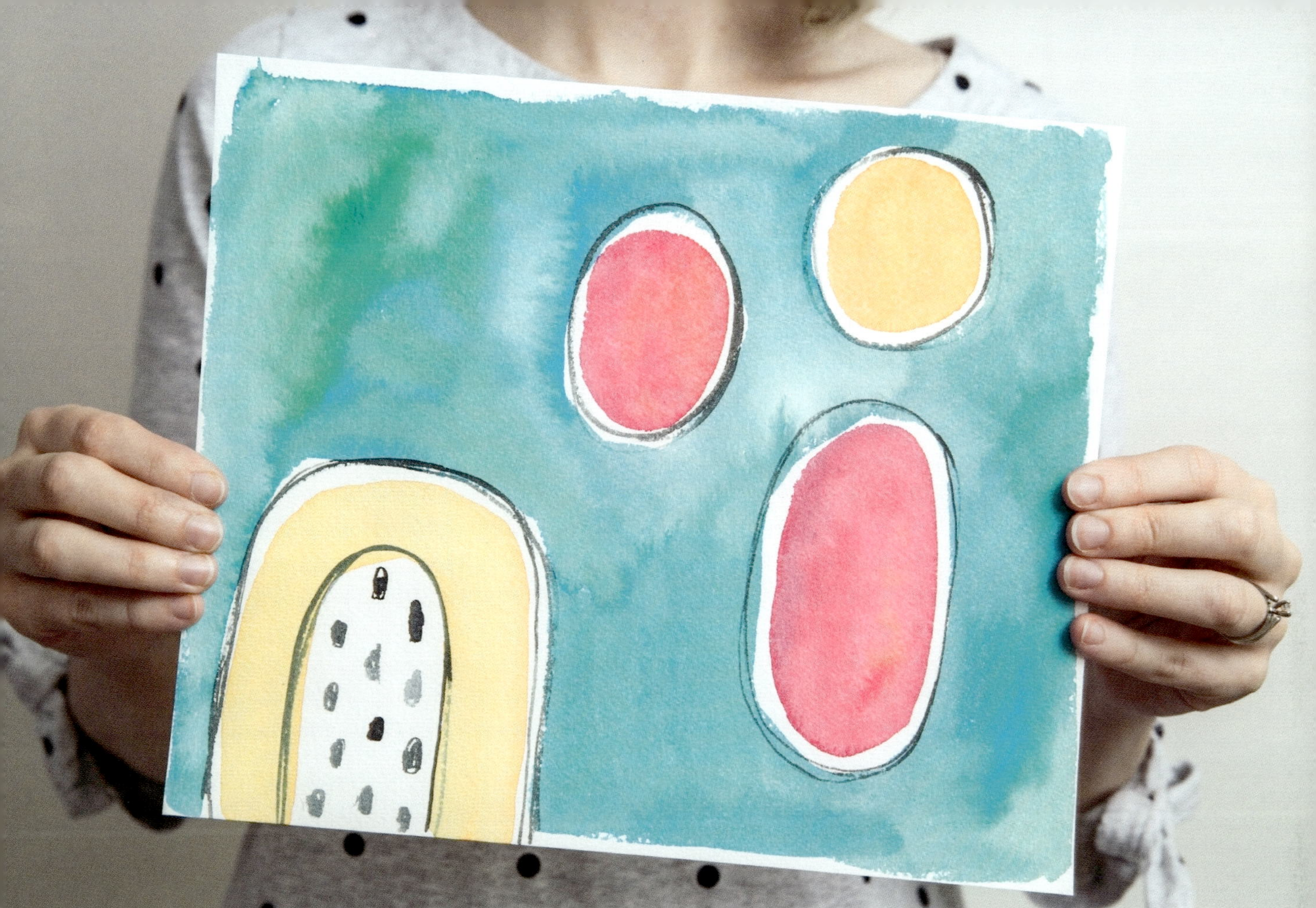

prompt Keep it simple

I believe that art is for everyone. Making beautiful things is fun, relaxing, satisfying, and gives you an amazing feeling of accomplishment—especially when you hang your own art in your home or give it as a gift. But the most frequent complaint I hear is: "I don't have time!"

Making time for art can sometimes feel like a luxury that you don't have. My advice is to keep it simple. Creating art on a regular basis is about developing a habit. Art will not become a part of your daily life if it feels overwhelming or scary.

Try scheduling some art time into your day whenever you can. This could mean painting while dinner cooks or getting up a half hour early. Doing a little bit at a time will soon add up. It is also easy to get caught up in "inspiration hunting." Spending hours scrolling through other people's art won't leave you with much time for your own creative pursuits. Focus on your own art and try not to spend too much time looking at your neighbor's work.

The golden rule is to keep your art supplies accessible. Set up a small art station in your home, with paper and paint all ready to go. Keep it clean and tidy so you can jump right in when an idea hits. Even if you only have room for the primary colors and one paintbrush, that is all you need to create a piece of art.

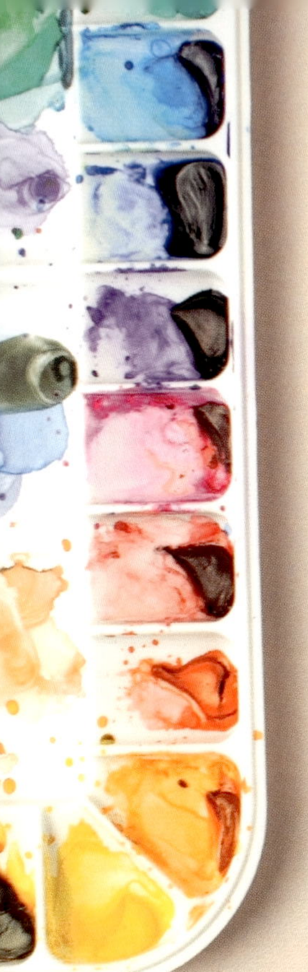

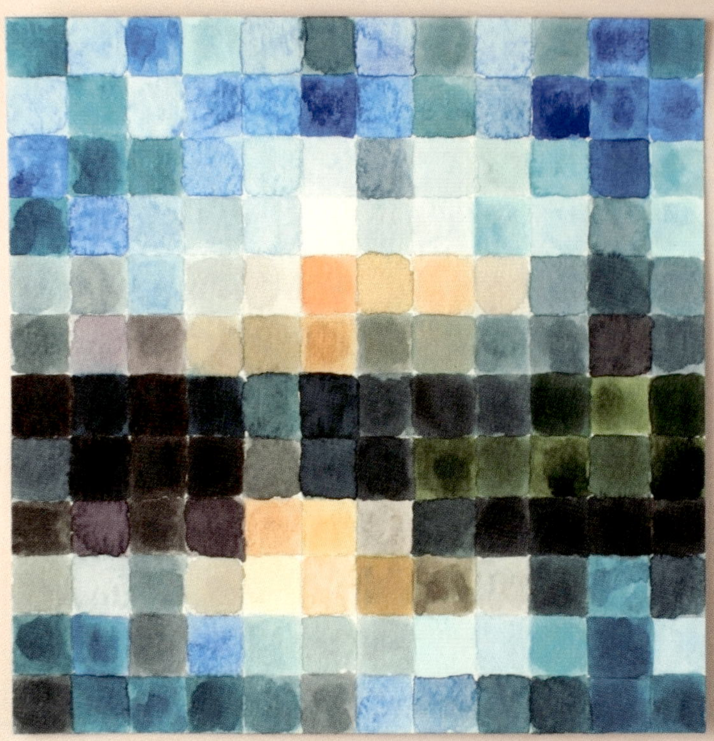

Your finished piece

Your pixel-art landscape painting is complete. Stand way back and squint. Can you see it?

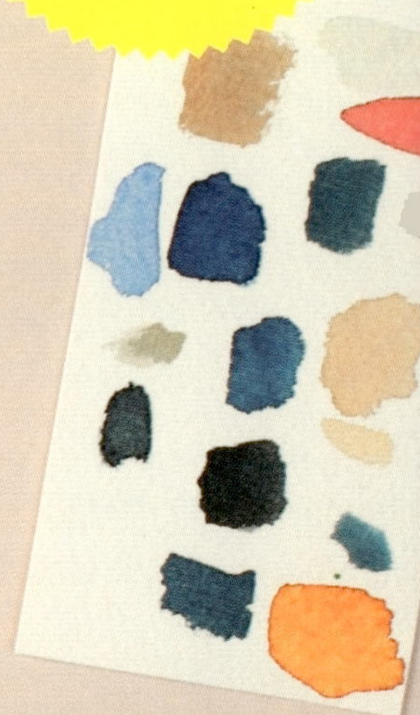

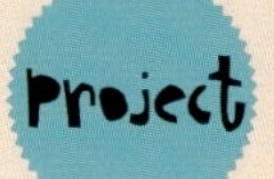

Pixel-perfect landscape

Let's put a twist on the traditional landscape painting. For this project, you will be recreating a landscape photo in a pixel-art style. Have you ever done a paint-by-number? It is a little like that. You will certainly be putting your color-mixing skills to use here. Don't worry; it's not about being perfect–it will look amazing even if your colors are slightly off.

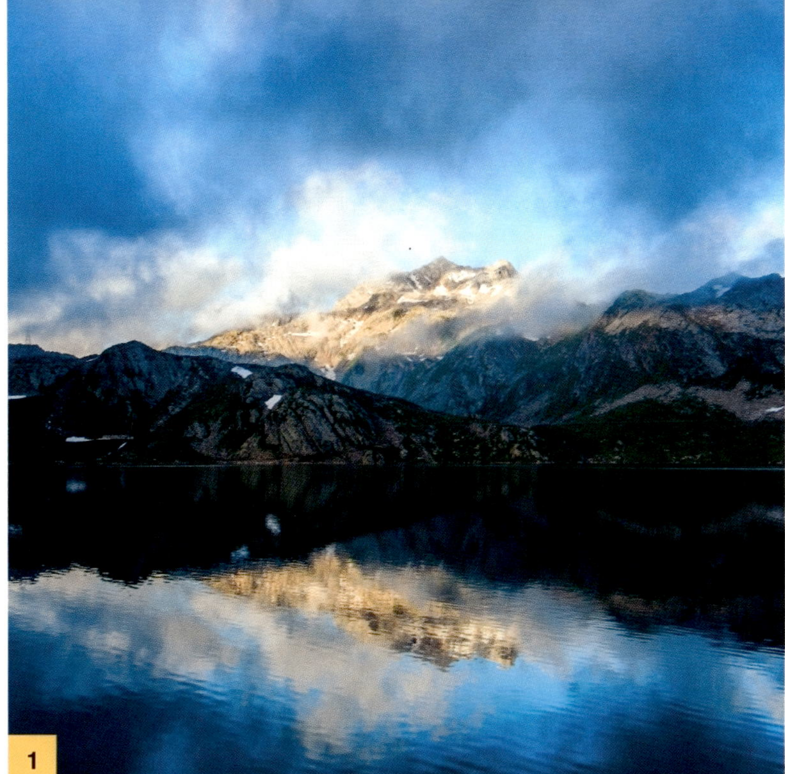

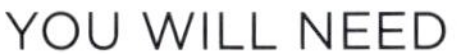

YOU WILL NEED

- Watercolor paper
- Watercolor paint
- Reference photo
- Scissors
- Pencil
- Ruler
- Small round brush

Find a reference photo that has a nice variety of colors. Landscapes that are too monotone will look a little boring when pixelated.

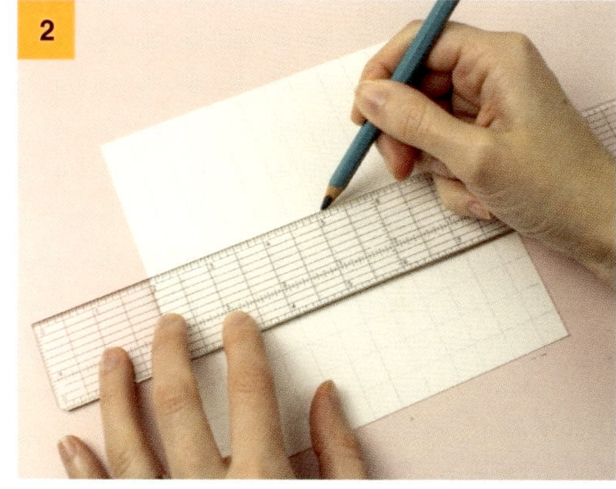

Cut your paper to the same ratio as your reference photo to make them easier to compare. Now draw a grid on your paper. Remember: Smaller squares mean more work to fill them in!

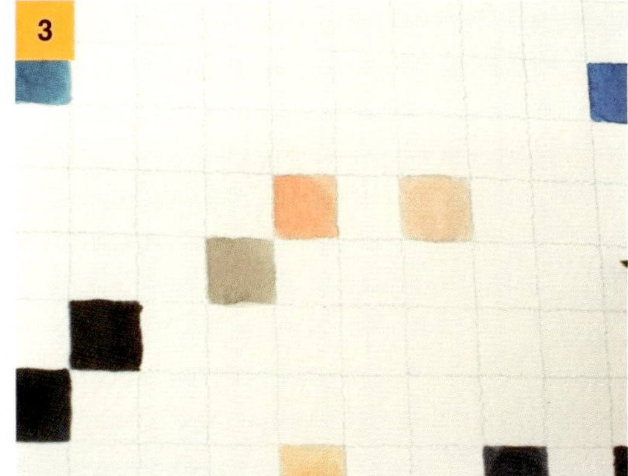

Start filling in the colors. It can help to start with the brightest or darkest colors, or just work from top to bottom. It is not about being perfect, but rather capturing the dominant tones of each section.

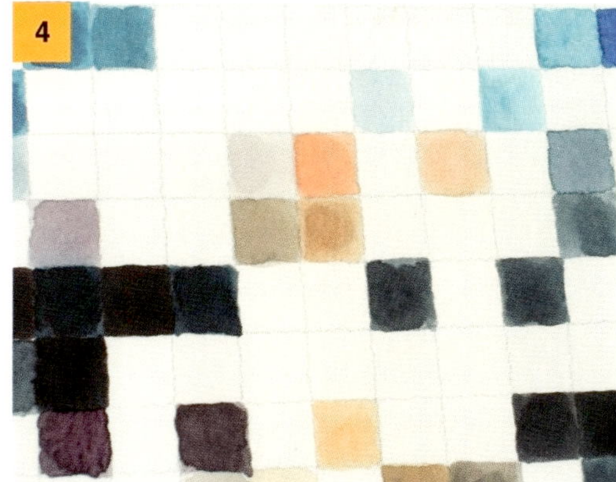

Continue filling in the grid. You might need to work in a checkerboard pattern to prevent the squares from bleeding into one another.

Project Moving paint

You don't always need a paintbrush to create a watercolor painting. In this project, we will be using an old credit card to push paint around the page–you could also try this technique with a plastic squeegee or spatula. You will end up with a completely unpredictable look and a very unique painting.

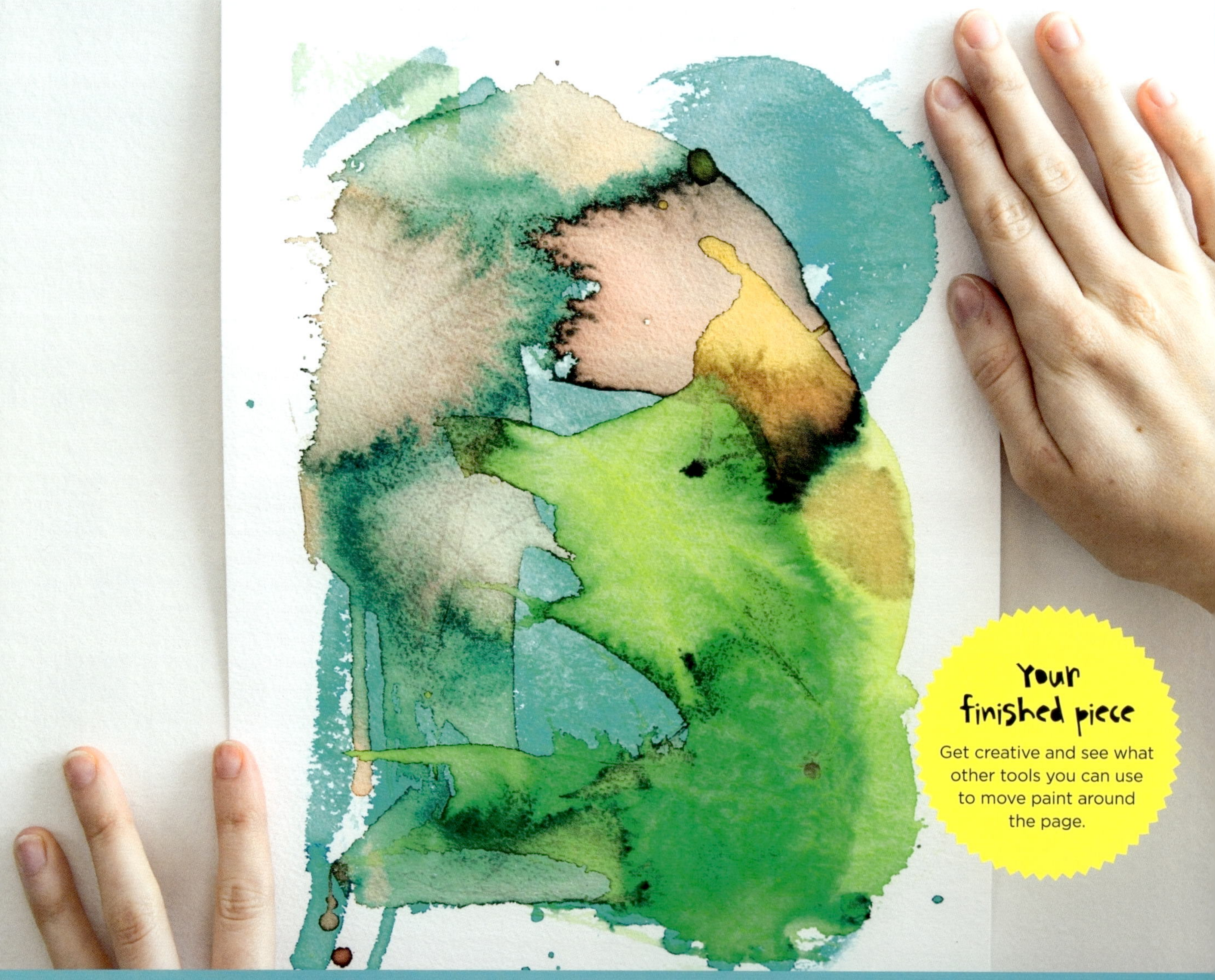

Your finished piece

Get creative and see what other tools you can use to move paint around the page.

YOU WILL NEED

- Thick watercolor paper
- Watercolor paint in at least 3 colors
- Sticky tape
- Small cup
- Old plastic card

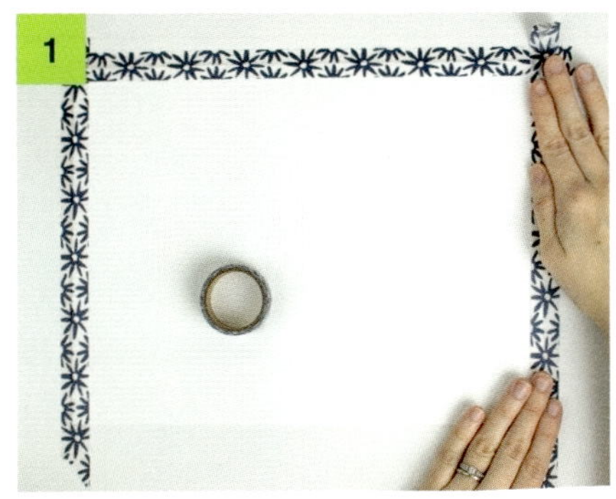

You will need to use a thick piece of watercolor paper for this because it has to be able to take a lot of water. Tape the paper to your work surface to prevent it from curling.

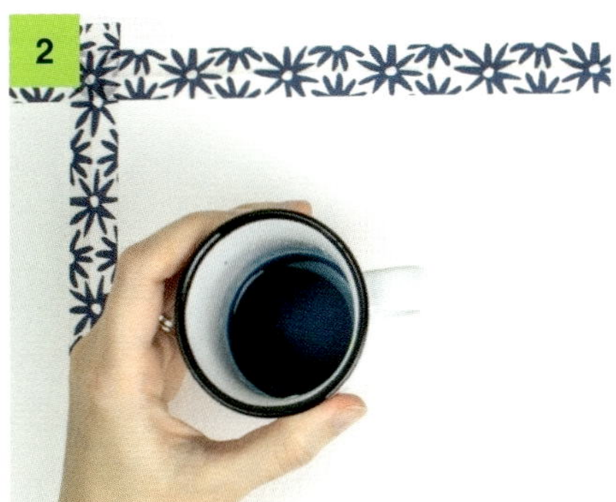

Mix up some paint and a bit of water. I used a few drops of liquid watercolor for this, but any type should work.

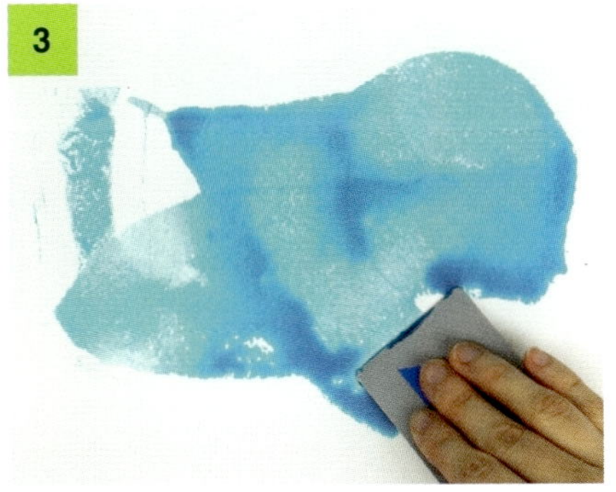

Pour the paint mixture onto the paper and start to push it around with your card. You can take your time here as the paint will stay wet for a long time.

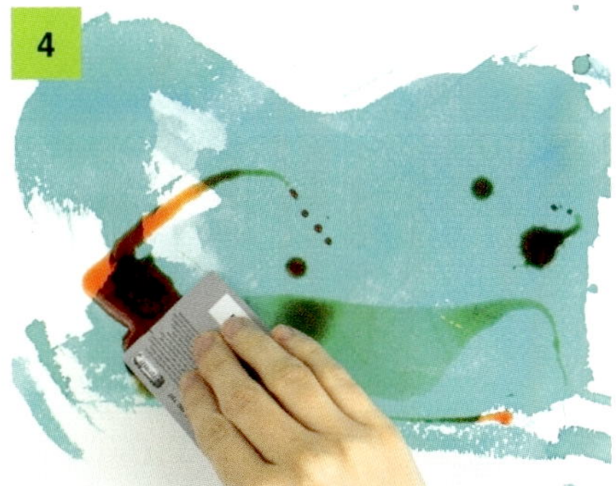

Let the paint dry overnight, then apply a second layer of color. Try not to overwork the second layer as it could lift off the first.

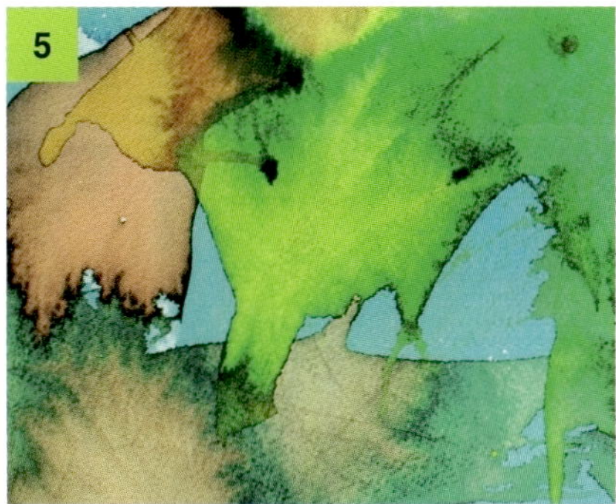

Add a third layer if desired, taking care to let everything dry completely first. You can keep going, adding more layers, but I think it looks nice with three colors.

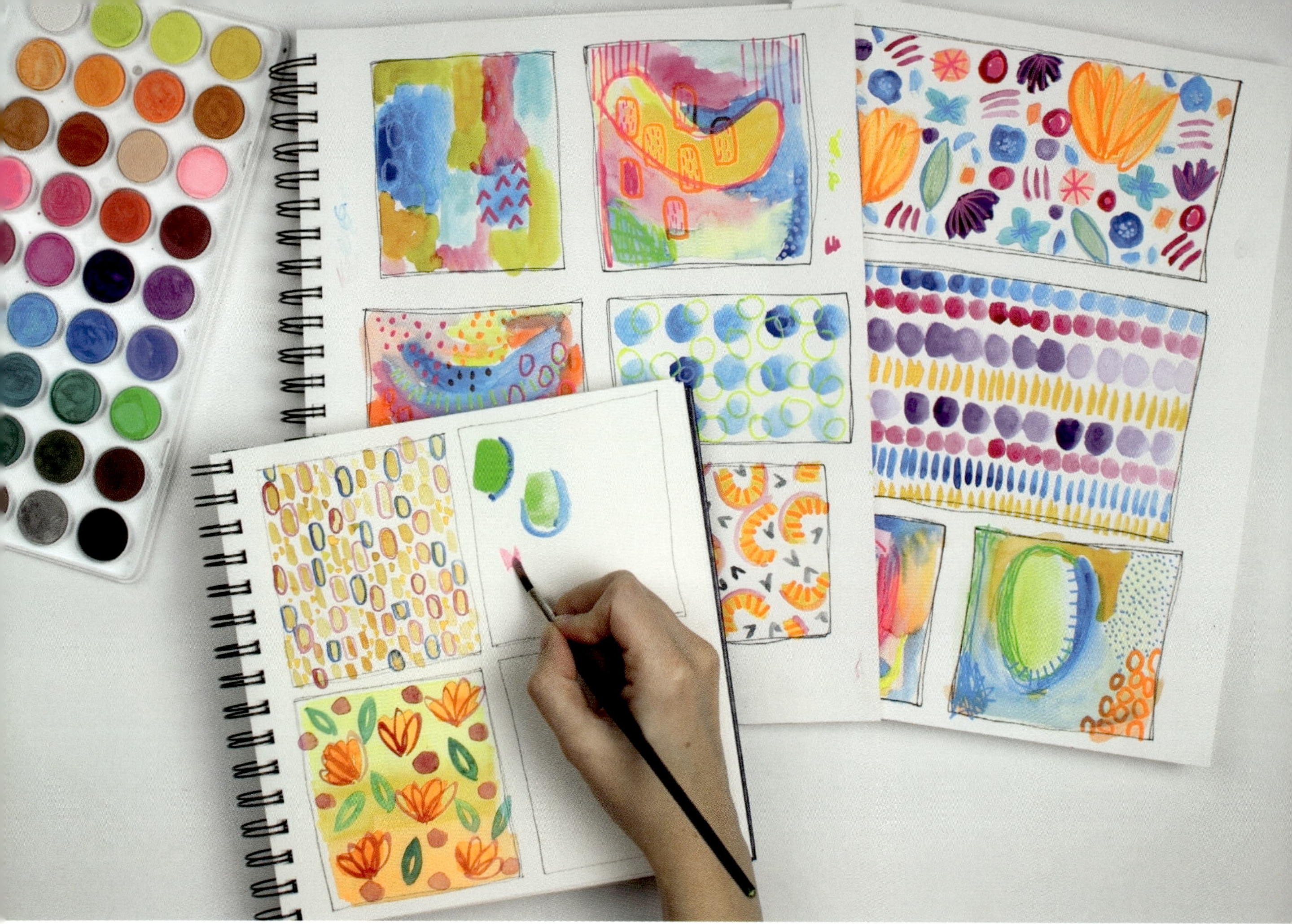

Play Thumbnail it

Thumbnails are invaluable to my painting process. There is nothing worse than spending hours on a painting and using your "good paper," only to end up not liking the painting. That is why I always practice first with a few no-pressure mini-paintings. It helps me work out ideas, color combos, and composition.

When I am planning a painting, I always pull out my sketchbook first for a practice run. You can use a cheap mixed-media sketchbook so you don't feel like you are wasting good paper. Draw a few squares of various sizes on the page with a waterproof pen and start sketching with your paint. This is your chance to roughly lay things out and to see what works. Work quickly and choose your colors intuitively.

This is not just an exercise I do when I am planning a new painting—I often pull out my sketchbook just for fun. These mini-paintings are a speedy way to experiment and work through a bunch of ideas. Sometimes I just sit down in front of the TV and fill these little squares with pattern. When I am low on ideas, I can flip through my thumbnails for inspiration and turn one of them into a bigger piece.

Prompt Layered plaid pattern

Patterns are always so fun to paint. Try your hand at some classic plaid looks with this prompt. They look nice on their own, but you can also incorporate this technique into your other paintings.

Start by grabbing some brushes in a few different sizes. This will help you get a variety of line weights for your plaid pattern. I worked on a few smaller pieces of paper at once for this prompt so I could still do some painting while I was waiting for the other patterns to dry. Working with the larger brushes first, start by painting a large grid on the page. Choose colors that catch your eye.

When the first layer is dry, pick up a medium-size brush and paint another grid in a different color. Continue filling in the plaid pattern with new colors and different line weights until you are happy with the outcome. For the most part, I let each layer dry before adding a new color but I also love to let some colors bleed together.

There are so many color combinations to try and you can change the look by switching up brush sizes. Try painting a delicate plaid using only fine liner brushes. Or try a big, fat buffalo plaid with a large flat brush.

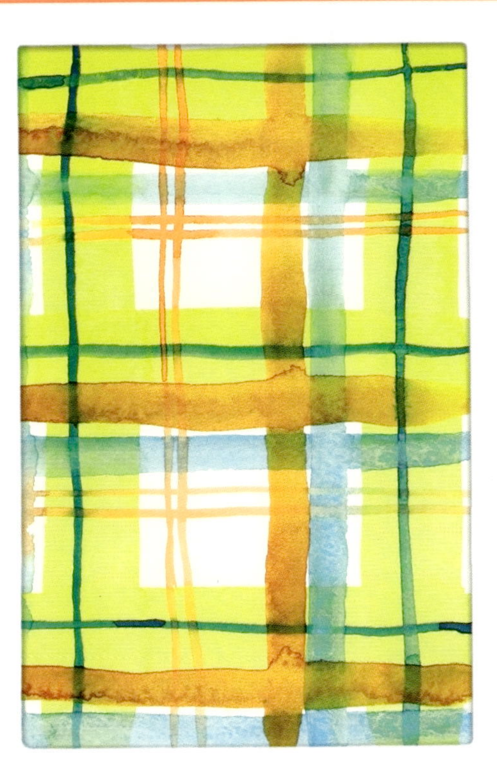

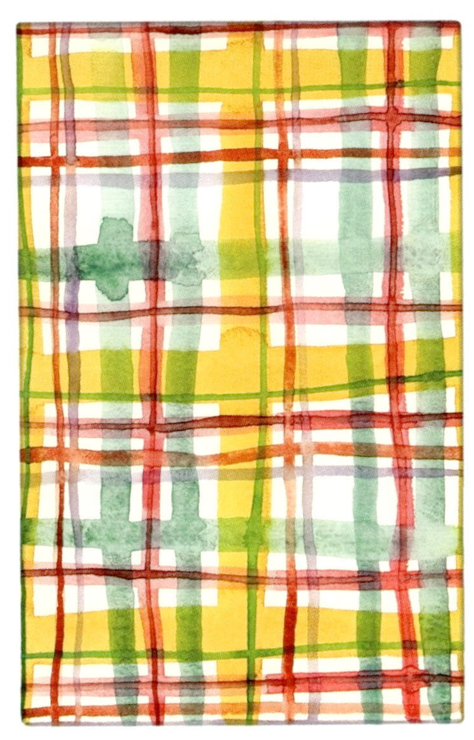

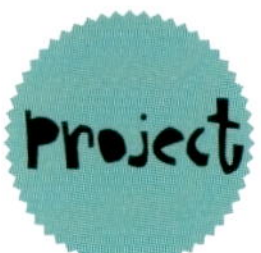

Create a repeating pattern

You can easily create a repeating pattern using computer software, but I think it is beneficial to understand how those repeats work. The best way to do that is to make one yourself. In this project, you will be taking a simple design and creating a pattern block you can repeat endlessly.

YOU WILL NEED

- Watercolor paper
- Watercolor paint
- Scissors
- Clear tape

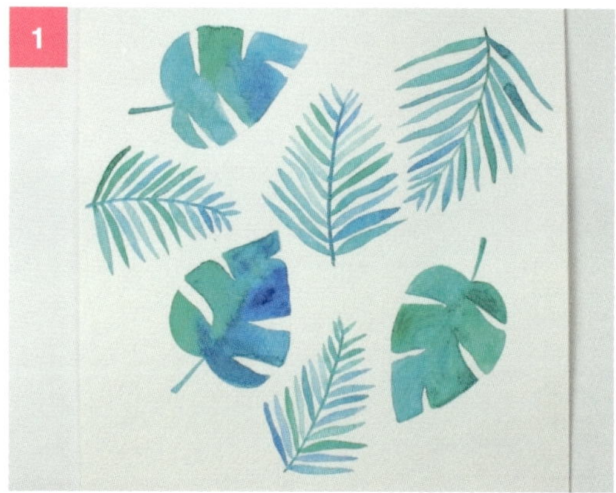

Using any size paper you like, paint a design in the center of the page. Make sure you don't let any of the elements touch the edge of the paper.

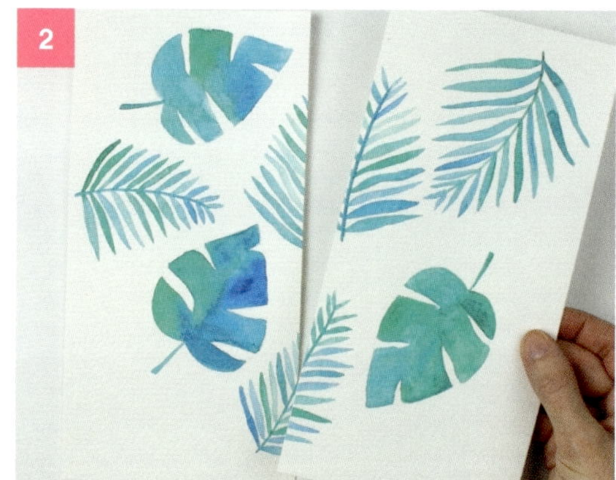

When you are happy with the design, let it dry completely. Then cut the paper in half vertically.

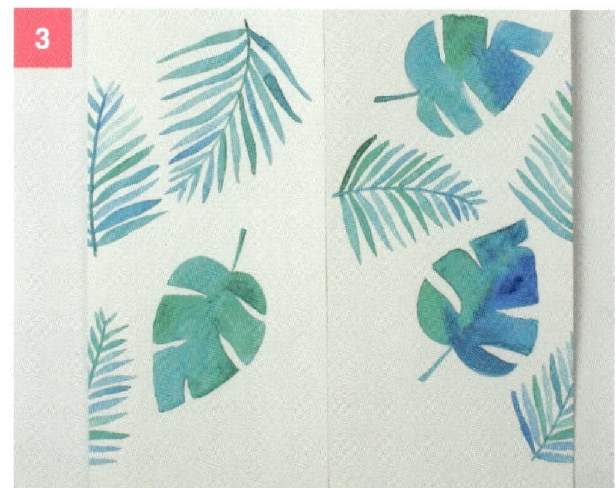

Move the right half to the left side and tape the two pieces together, placing the tape on the back of the paper so you can still paint over the lines.

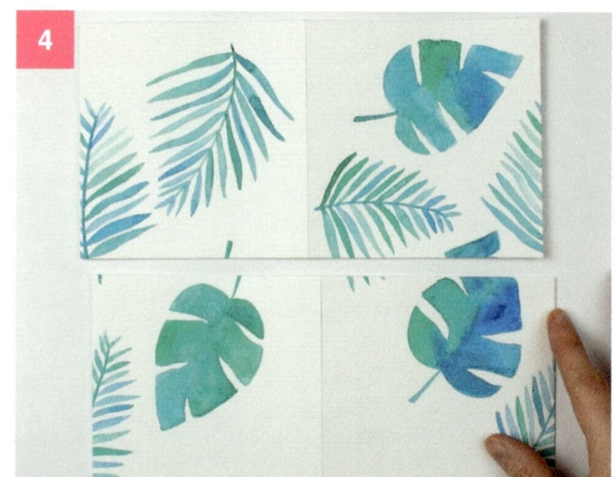

Now cut the paper in half horizontally.

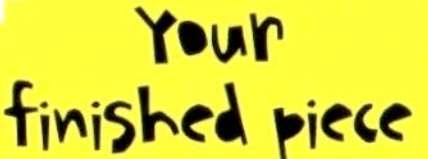

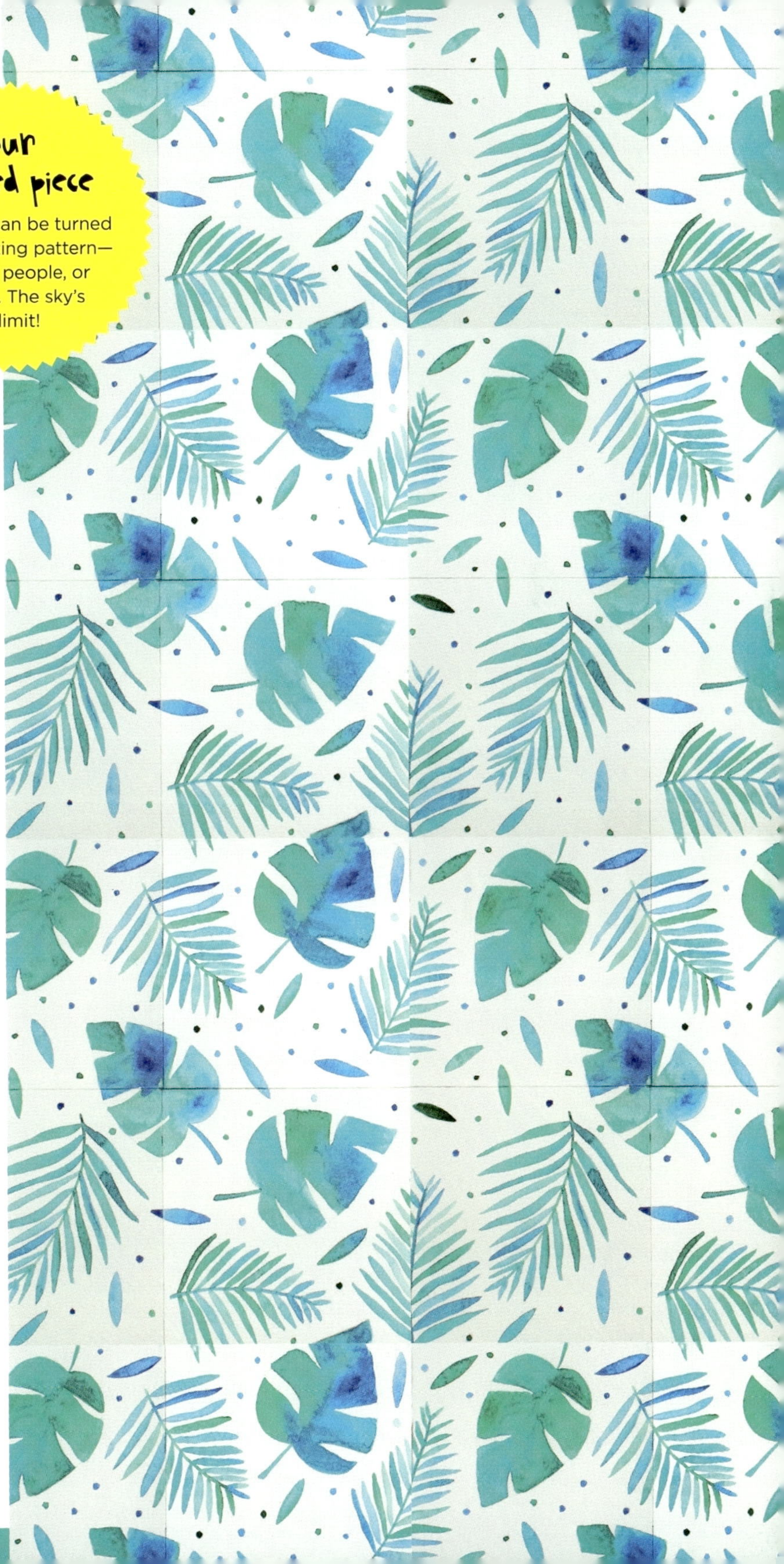

Everything can be turned into a repeating pattern—abstracts, people, or buildings. The sky's the limit!

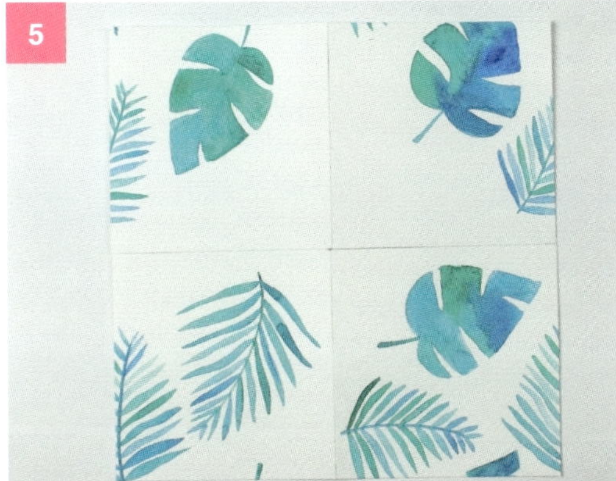

Switch the two pieces around, taping them together on the reverse. Your design is in the four corners and you can start filling in the rest of the white space.

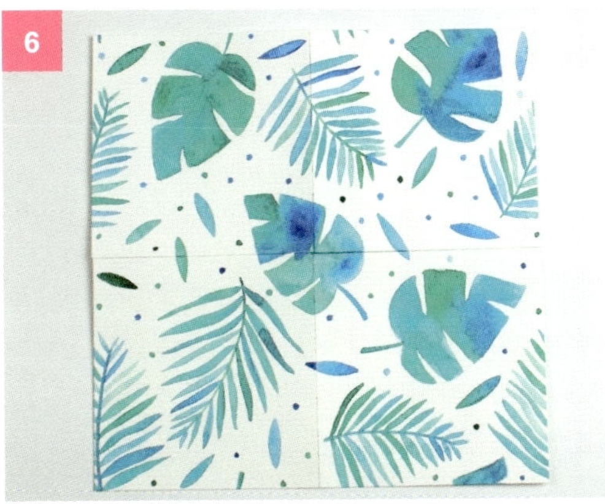

Scan your pattern or make photocopies to create a repeat by hand.

Best friends

One of the great things about watercolor is that it is the perfect companion to so many other mediums. Using ink, colored pencils, markers, or even collage is a great way to add some interest and dimension to your piece. Watercolor will still be the star of the show, but you will soon find that adding in some different art supplies will help you unlock your creativity and have fun with it. There is no need to buy a ton of new supplies; just use what you have—watercolor can be combined with almost anything! We will also use common items found around the house as unexpected art supplies.

Play Watercolor markers

Once you fall in love with watercolor paints, you will want to explore all the other forms of watercolor out there. One of my absolute favorites is watercolor markers. These markers pack a ton of pigment and can be used in so many ways.

One of my favorite ways to use watercolor markers is to quickly fill in a large space with color. You can use multiple different colors and then blend them together with a brush dipped in clean water. The colors blend and move on the paper just like watercolor paints. You don't have to worry about getting color into every nook and cranny because the pigment can be moved around and spread across the page with water later.

Another fun way to utilize the markers is to create a small, on-the-go palette. Grab a scrap of watercolor paper and put down some circles of color. The color can be reactivated later and used just like a tiny travel watercolor set. You can also use watercolor markers to add some semi-transparent details to your paintings. The marker form gives you a little more control over the pigment for small details.

Tip

Watercolor markers can be expensive, so if they are not within your budget, why not try some washable kids' markers? Any water-soluble marker will work.

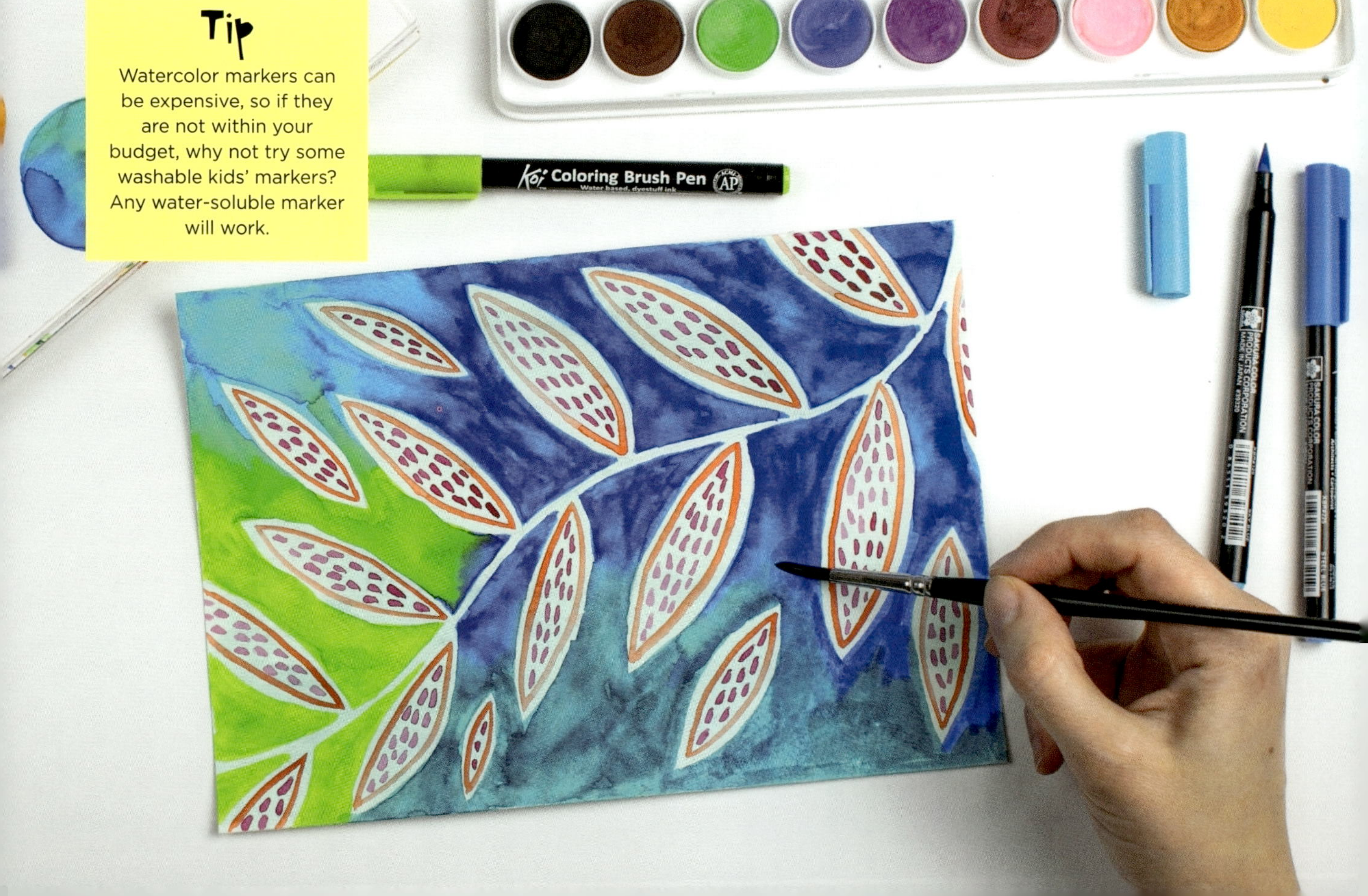

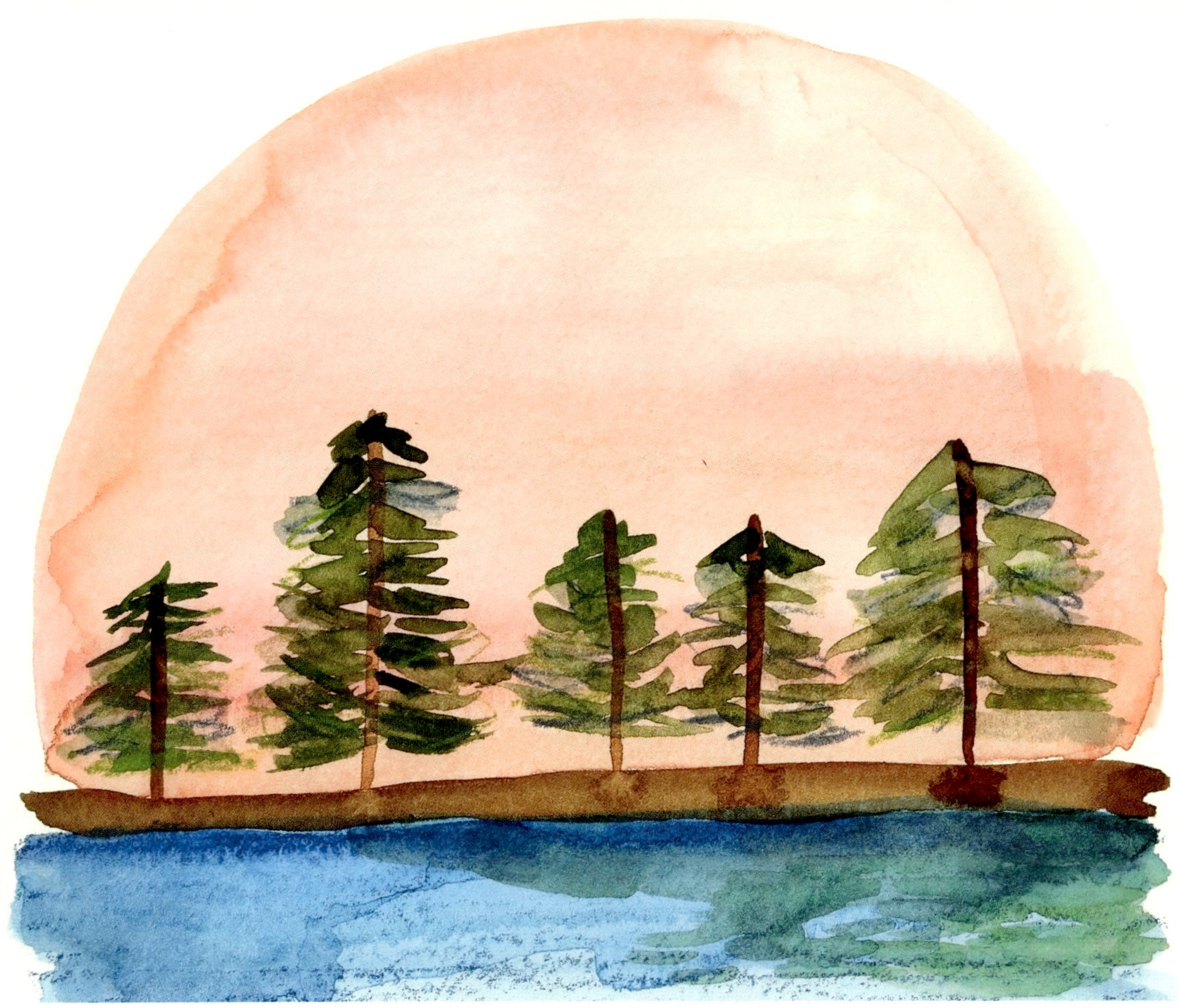

Play Watercolor pencils

Watercolor pencils are another fun addition to your art-supply stash. They are portable, inexpensive, and used just like regular colored pencils. But when you add water, that is when the magic happens!

The simplest way to try out watercolor pencils for the first time is to draw something and add water. Draw anything you like and fill it in with colored pencils. Once your drawing is complete, take a clean brush dipped in some water and start bringing the scene to life. You will notice the colors are much more pigmented when they are wet, so don't worry if your pencil drawing looks a little faded at first. Be sure to use a light touch with the pencils and water to avoid overworking the paper. Once everything is dry you can add a second layer, but not much more than that.

You can create an entire piece of art with watercolor pencils, but they are also wonderful for adding some final detail to a painting. As with markers, you get the control and precision of a pen but the look of watercolor paint. You can use the pencil dry for fine details or dip the tip of the pencil in water for an interesting effect.

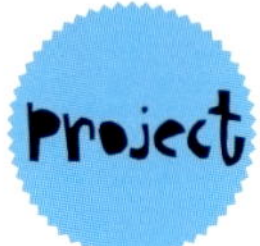

Rainbow abstract background

You are going to be soaking this page with water, so make sure you are using a watercolor pad that is gummed on both sides, or securely tape your paper to a hard surface. Grab your markers and spray bottle full of water, and let's get started!

YOU WILL NEED

- Watercolor pad or paper
- Watercolor markers
- Stick tape (optional)
- Spray bottle
- Paper towel

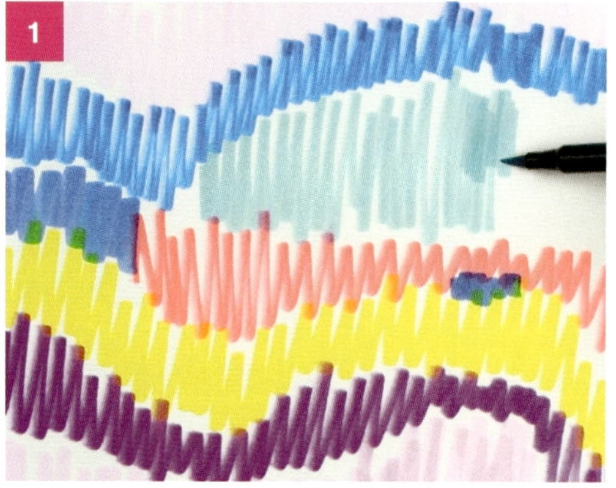

Choose as many colors as you like and start filling the page using water-soluble markers. Don't worry about getting a solid covering, because when youadd the water, the pigments will all bleed together.

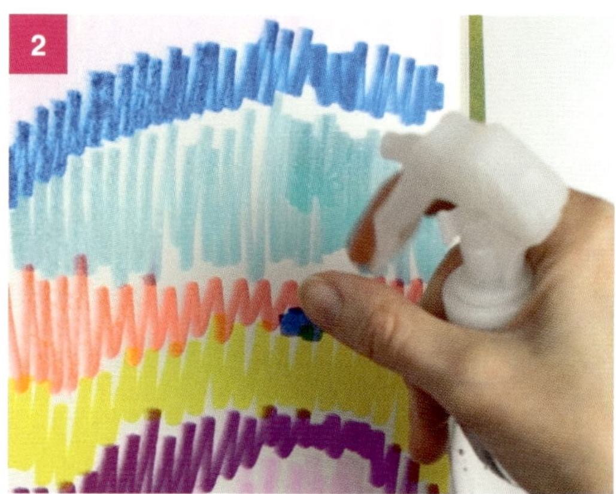

Grab your spray bottle and start spraying the paper with water. Go for a light misting at first to see how your markers perform.

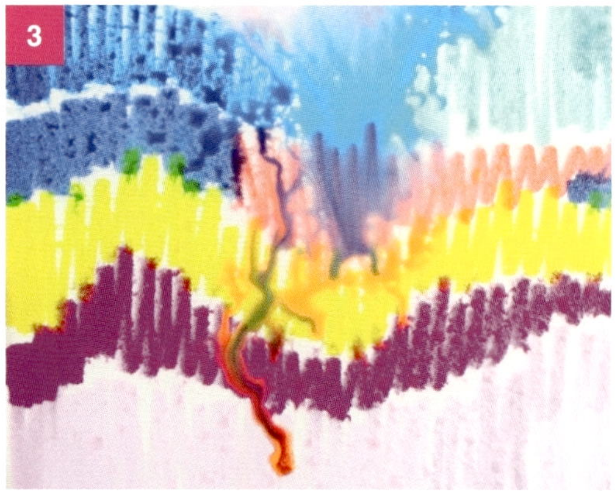

Keep adding water where you want to see more movement. You can even pick up the paper and tilt it to help things along.

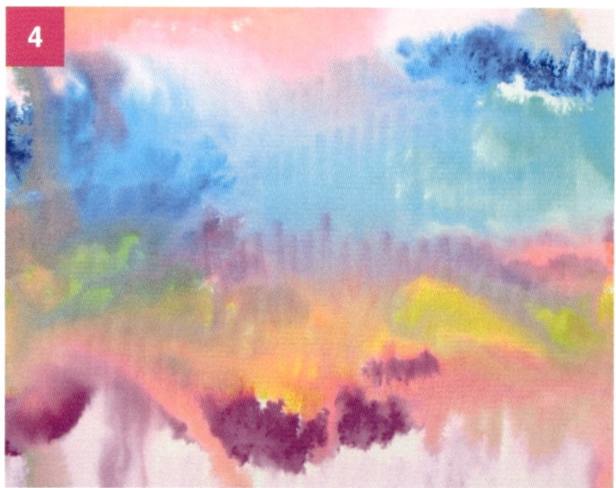

Clean up any big pools of water with a paper towel and leave your painting for at least 24 hours to dry. It will look different when you see it the next day.

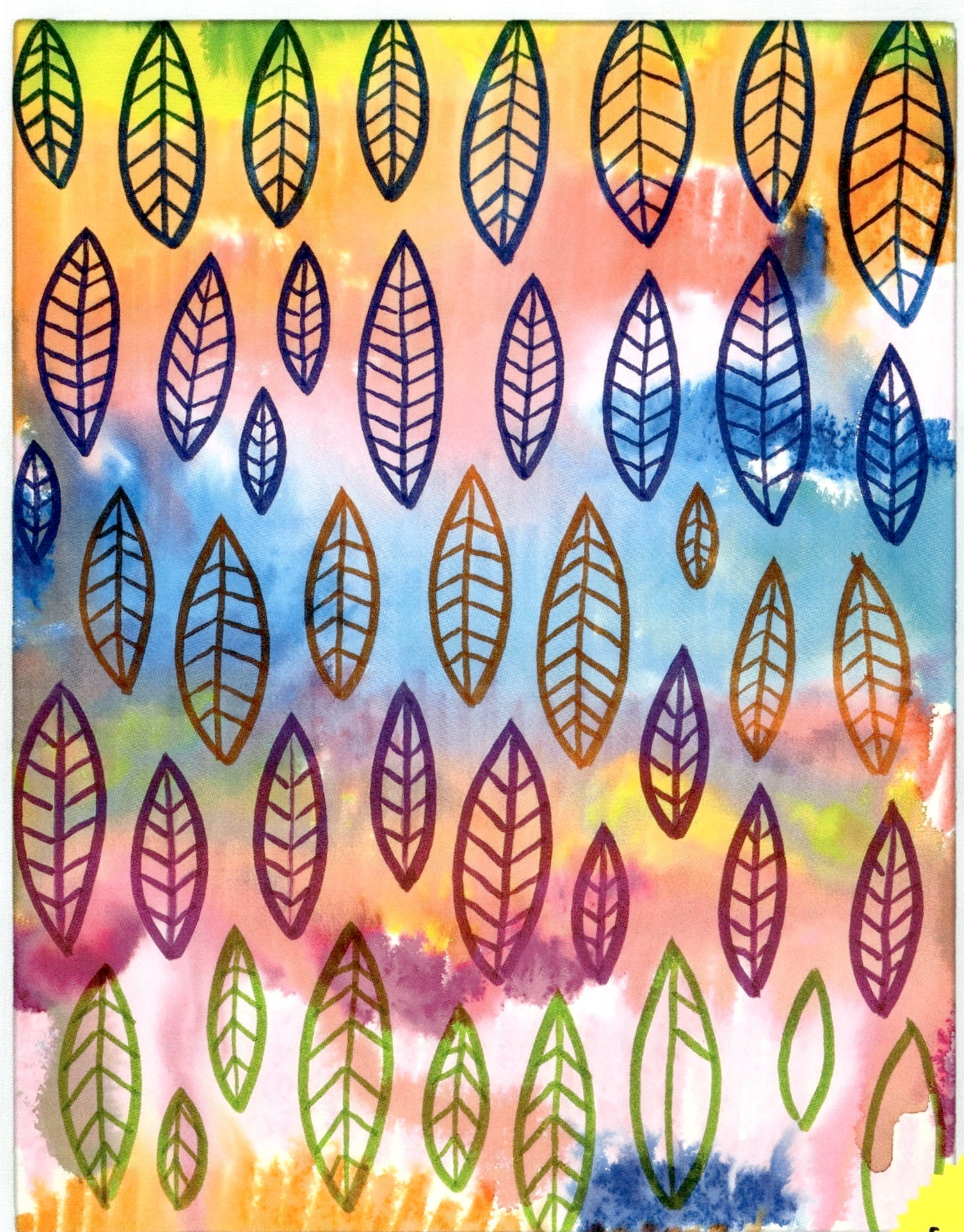

Your finished piece

Use your rainbow background for art journaling, collages, or a starting point for a colorful painting.

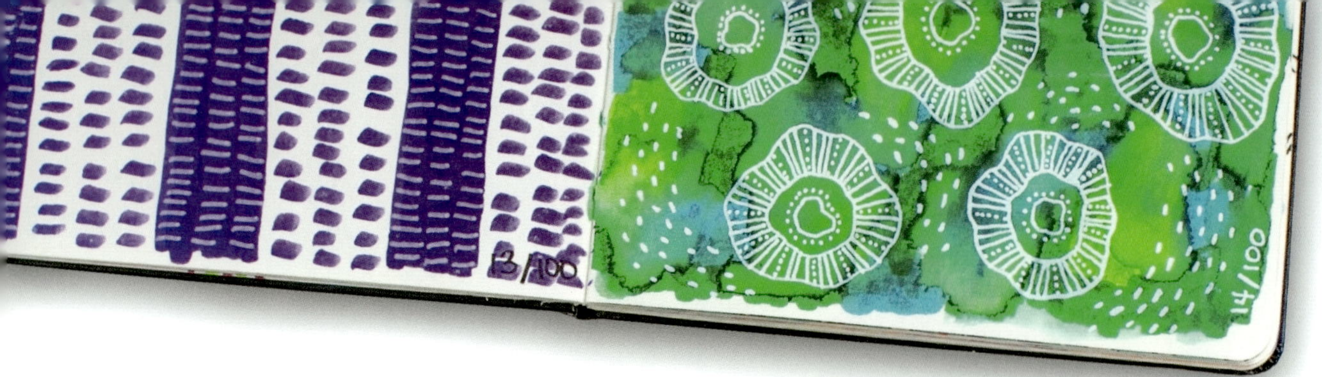

Play White gel pen detail

Almost every painting can benefit from some white highlights and detail. It is easy to get carried away with gel pens—you will be finding every excuse to break out your white ink.

As you know by now, once you put down paint on the page, there aren't many ways to take it away again. Watercolor works beautifully in layers, but only from light to dark, and when the layers are still fairly transparent. So, having some white ink in your arsenal can be invaluable. Adding some opaque white details to a watercolor piece can make the colors pop, and gives depth to an otherwise flat design. There are many different white pens on the market, ranging from gel ink to acrylic and even oil paint. I love to experiment with them all. Just when you think a painting is done, you can add some white highlights or details and totally transform it. You can even use white pen to cover up or fix a mistake. It is a perfect companion to any watercolor set, and once you get your hands on one, you won't be able to stop. To keep your white pens in top condition, wipe the tips after using them and store them tip-down in a jar.

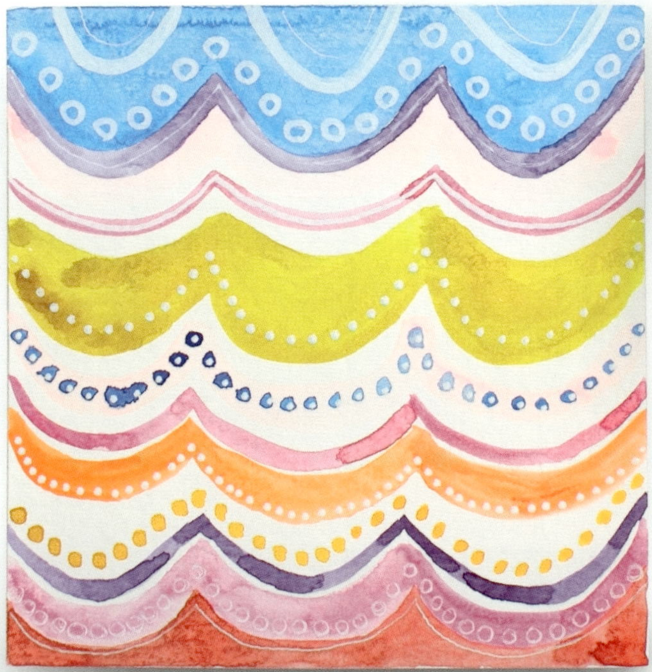

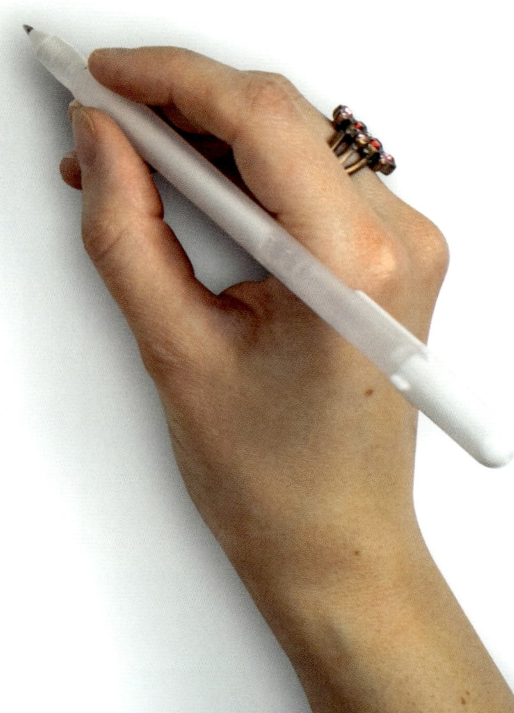

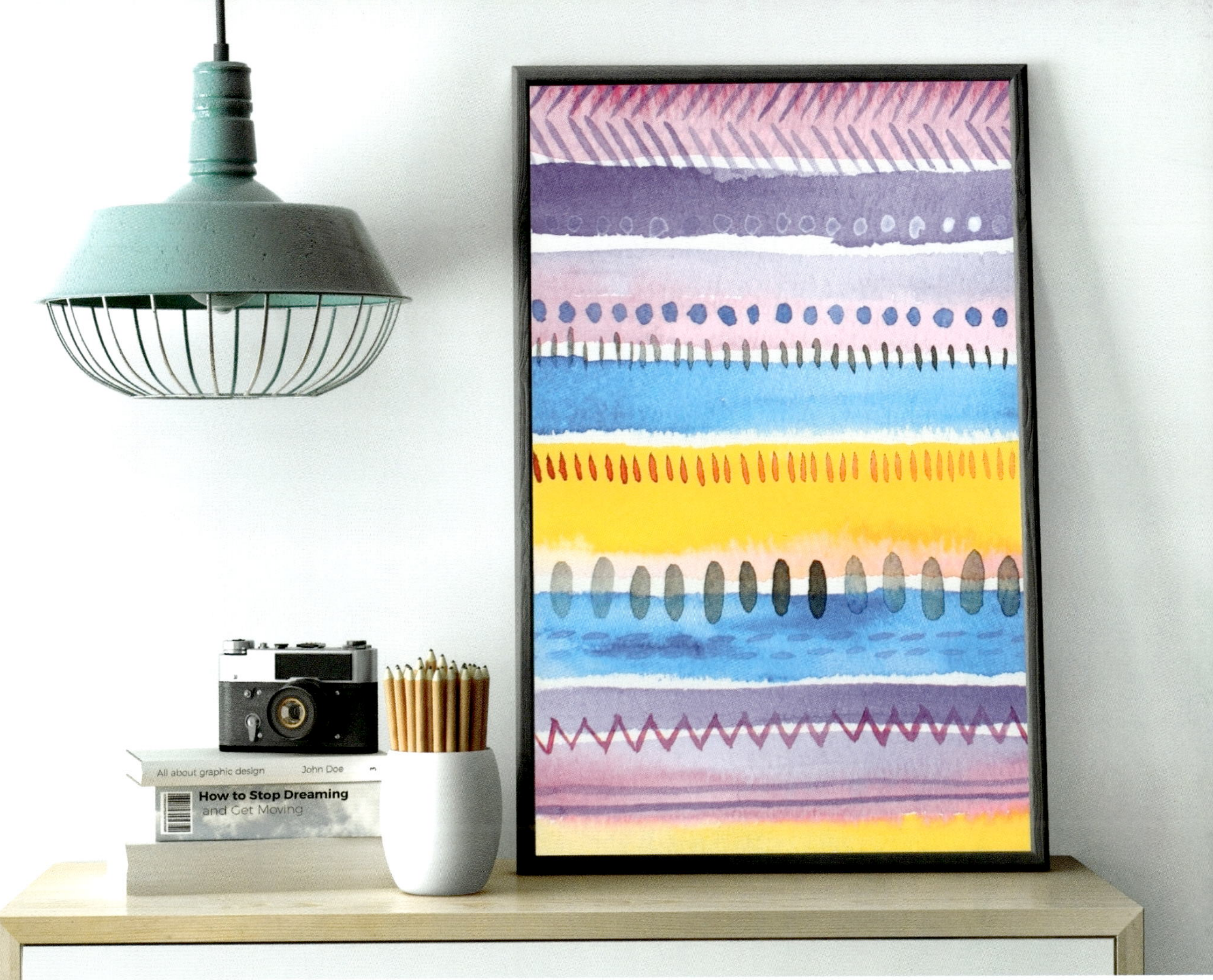

prompt Not-so-simple stripes

Let's take some of your new art supplies out for a test drive by adding detail and depth to this simple stripe design. You will be able to try out new color combinations and see how your gel pen and markers work with your existing supplies.

One of my favorite ways to paint is to start with a simple pattern or design and transform it into something "not-so-simple." It is satisfying to see a plain stripe pattern turned into something more.

Start with four or five different colors and begin painting stripes on the page. Use a couple of different brushes to vary the lines. Some stripes may be separated with a little white space and some may blend together. Get all your stripes down first and let dry. After your stripes are dry, begin adding detail with more paint, watercolor markers, and a white gel pen. Go as crazy as you like! Keep adding zigzags, dots, and dashes until you are happy with the look. Now that you have a feel for how your new supplies work with your current palette, you can start including them more in your paintings.

Project Swirly watercolor galaxy

When watercolor paint is allowed to move freely on the page, it makes the most beautiful swirls and blooms. It always reminds me of a faraway galaxy! For this project, we will use some space-inspired colors and let the paint work for us to create a watercolor universe complete with stars.

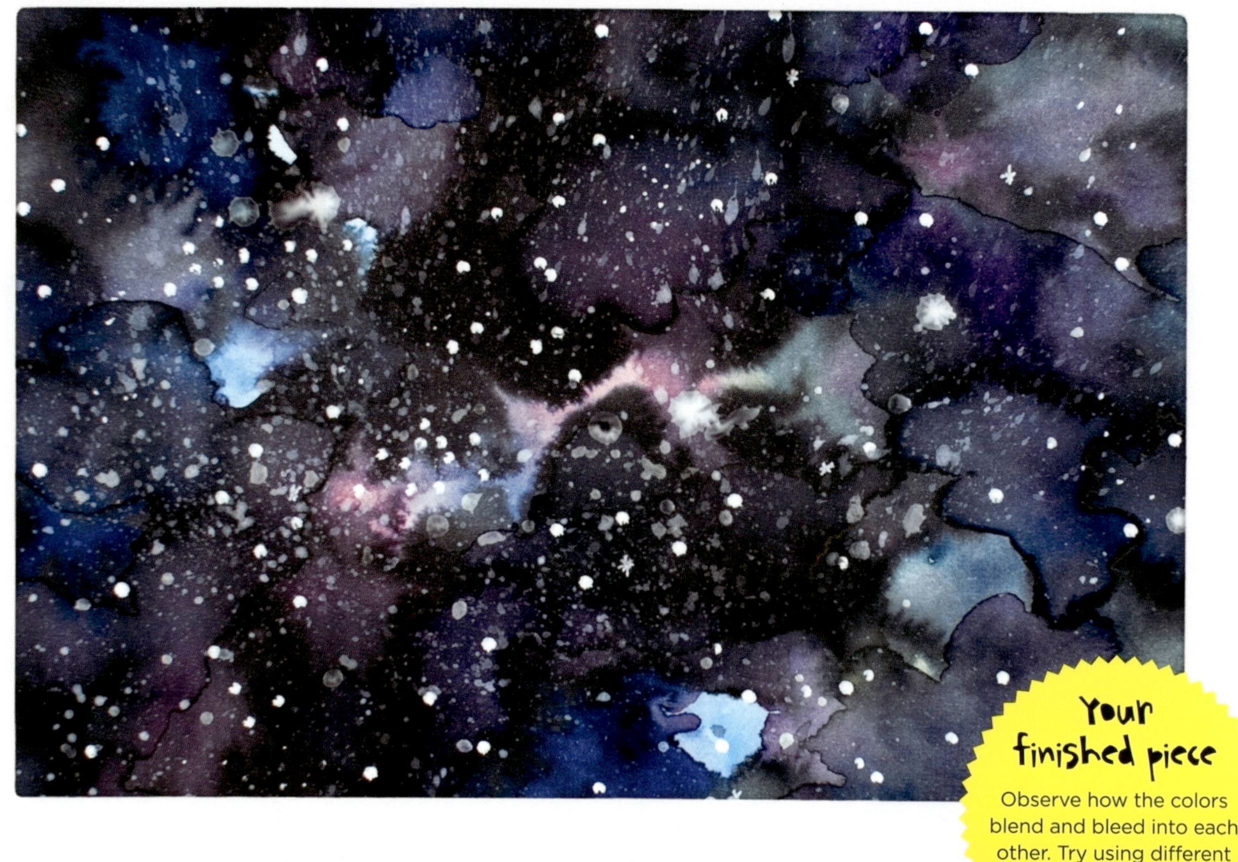

Your finished piece

Observe how the colors blend and bleed into each other. Try using different colors as the base layer and see what happens.

YOU WILL NEED

- Watercolor pad or paper
- Watercolor paint in black, blue, pink, and purple
- Sticky tape (optional)
- Large round brush
- Medium round brush
- White acrylic paint or gel pen

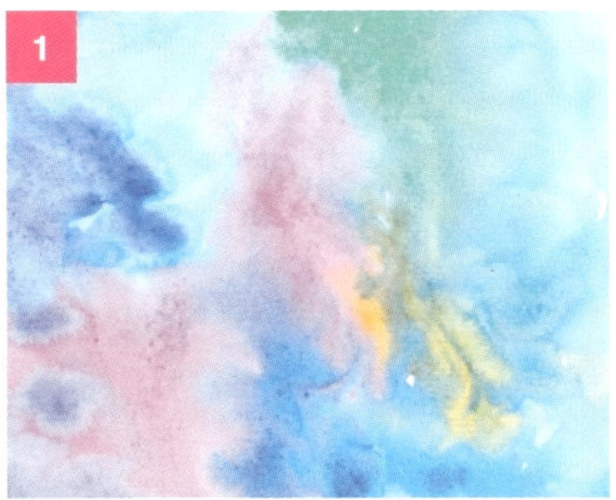

Using a large round brush, start with a base layer of color. I like to use blue, pink, and purple, but feel free to add whatever colors you want for your galaxy.

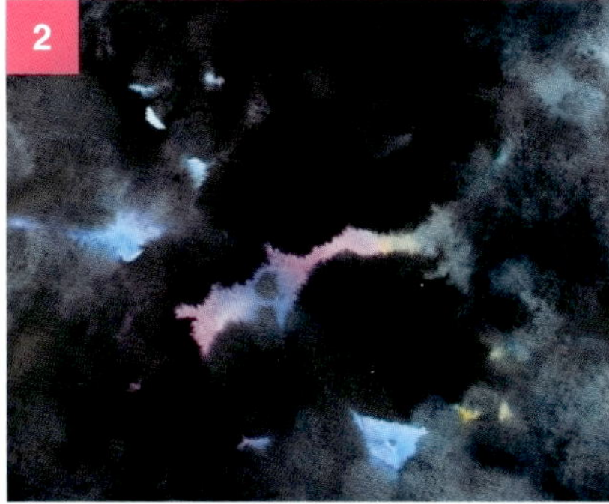

Working quickly while the first layer is still wet, add a layer of black paint. Don't cover up every bit of color—let some lighter areas peek through.

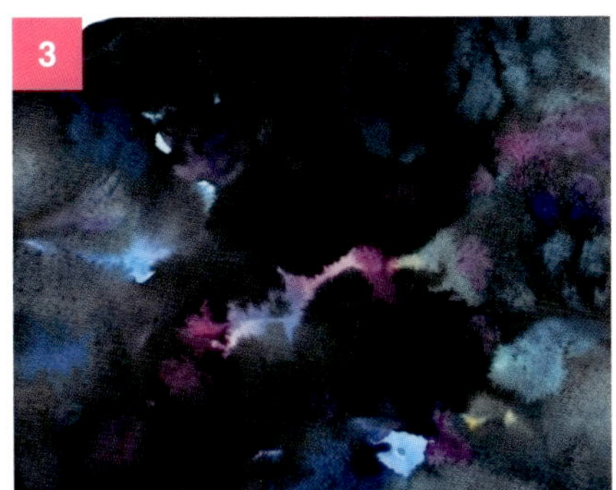

Again, while the whole page is still wet, with a medium round brush add some blobs of color on top of the black. The color will slowly spread as the paint dries.

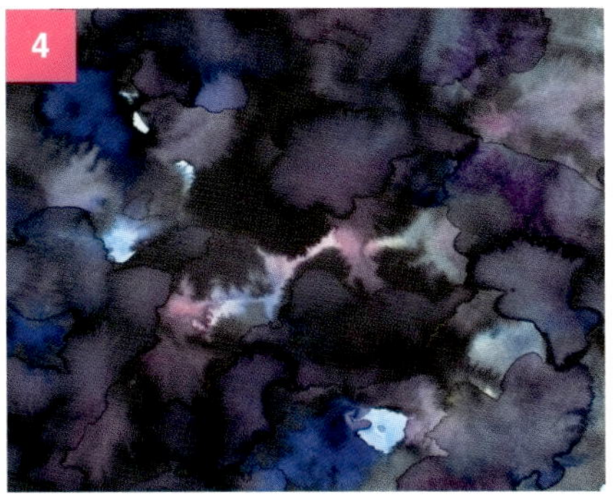

Wait for everything to dry and then go back in with a bit more black and/or color where you think it is needed.

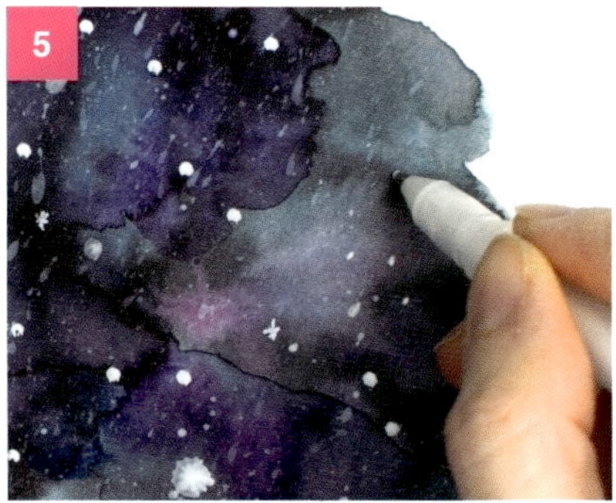

Now add some stars. Using an old frayed brush, spatter white acrylic paint over your galaxy. You can add even more stars with a white gel pen.

Play Resist techniques

With watercolor paint, there are a few different ways to create a resist—the technique of applying something to the paper that will "resist" the paint and leave it clean underneath. You can use these techniques to create interesting patterns, textures, or highlights in your work. It is best to experiment with these techniques first so you know how they behave.

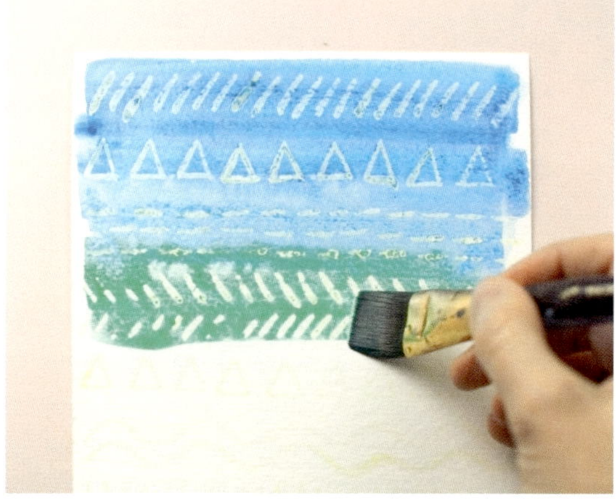

Masking fluid

The best way to preserve the white of the paper is to use masking fluid, which is a latex-based fluid that resists paint. Using a paintbrush (one you don't mind wrecking), it is applied like paint. Once everything is dry, remove the masking fluid with your fingers or an eraser.

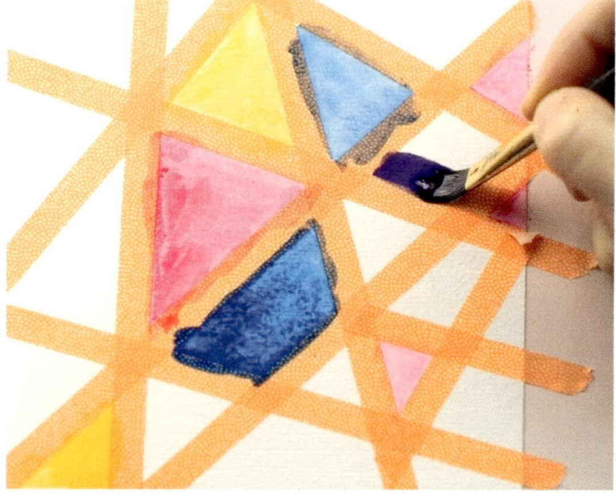

Tape

You can use tape to create a nice clean edge on your paintings, but did you know you can incorporate it into your art as well? Use a semi-sticky tape such as painter's tape or washi tape to block off large areas of your page or create a fun design.

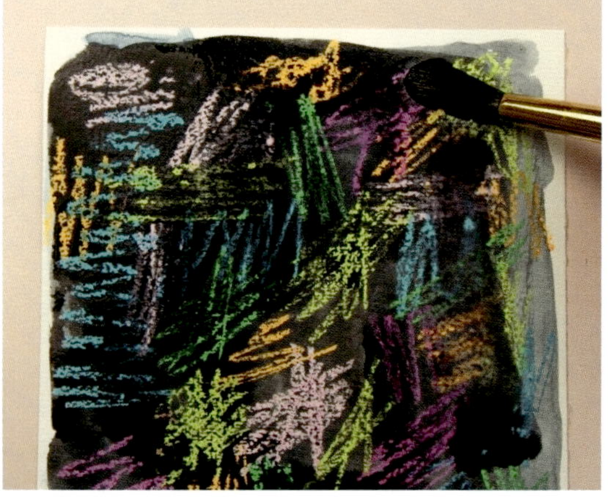

Wax crayon Using wax crayon is a bit different to tape or masking fluid because you can't remove it afterward. The results can be very interesting, so grab some different colors of crayons—including white—and experiment away!

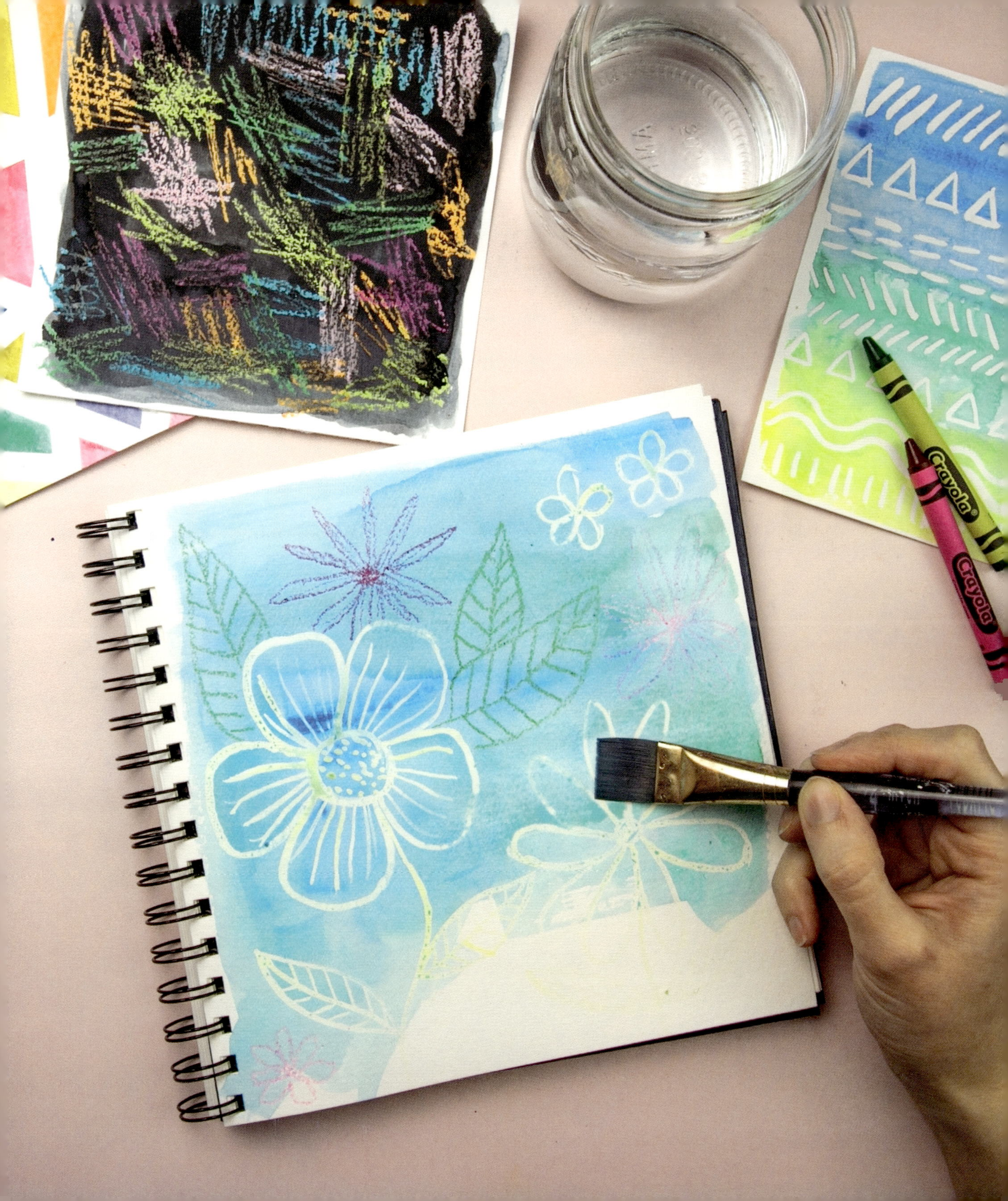
Crayola
Crayola

Play Rubbing alcohol effect

Rubbing alcohol dropped into wet watercolor paint will repel the pigment, leaving big blooms of lighter color. This can be used to create cool textures and shapes that look like they came from a lava lamp.

Remember that old bottle of rubbing alcohol laying around in your first-aid kit? Time to dig it out and put it to use—yes, you can even find art supplies in your medicine cabinet! A reaction happens when you drop alcohol onto wet watercolor paint. The alcohol pushes the pigment away and leaves you with little blobs of lighter paint when it is all dry.

Experiment with different ways to apply the alcohol. Try a dropper, a paintbrush, splatter it, or even use a spray bottle. Each tool will create a different effect. You can add alcohol to the paper first and paint on top of it for an interesting resist effect. Just be sure not to apply the alcohol directly to your paint palette because it can break down the binders in your paint.

Just like watercolors themselves, this effect can be hard to predict, but that just makes it more intriguing to play with.

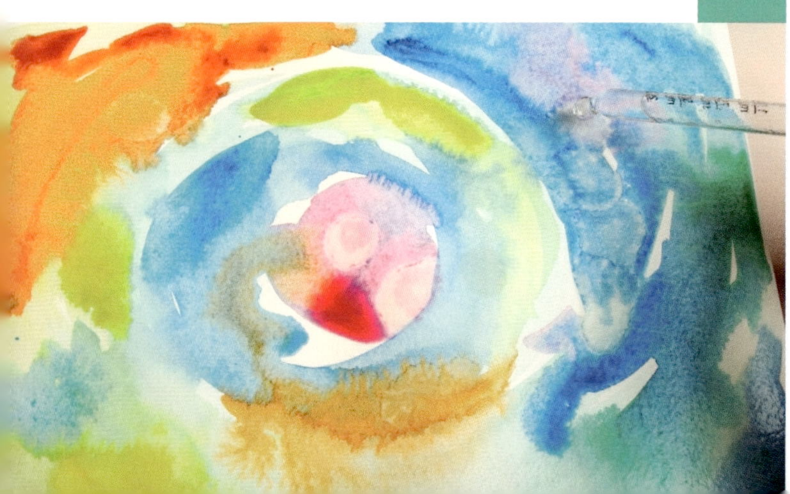

Prompt Go big and bold

Ready to make a big impact? Get an extra-large sheet of watercolor paper, grab your paints, and create a big, bold painting. This eye-catching piece of artwork is so easy to make and will look amazing in any room of your house.

There is something magical that happens when you take an ultra-simple design like a stripe or dot and blow it up huge. It suddenly looks so striking, when it might look a tad boring on a small sheet of paper. It means that big paintings are one of my favorite things to create.

It can take some bravery to attack a huge sheet of watercolor paper with a brush, but if you keep things simple you will quickly find out how fun it is. I love stripes, dots, squares, triangles, and dashes because they are all so easy to paint. For a modern look, keep your color palette to a minimum or even stick with a single color.

If you work with your paper taped to the wall, be prepared with a drop cloth for some drips and mess. If you want to keep clean lines, lay your paper down on a table instead. You might want to grab a few sheets of paper, because this project can be addictive!

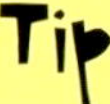

Mix up your paints in small cups ahead of time so they are easier to use with a large brush.

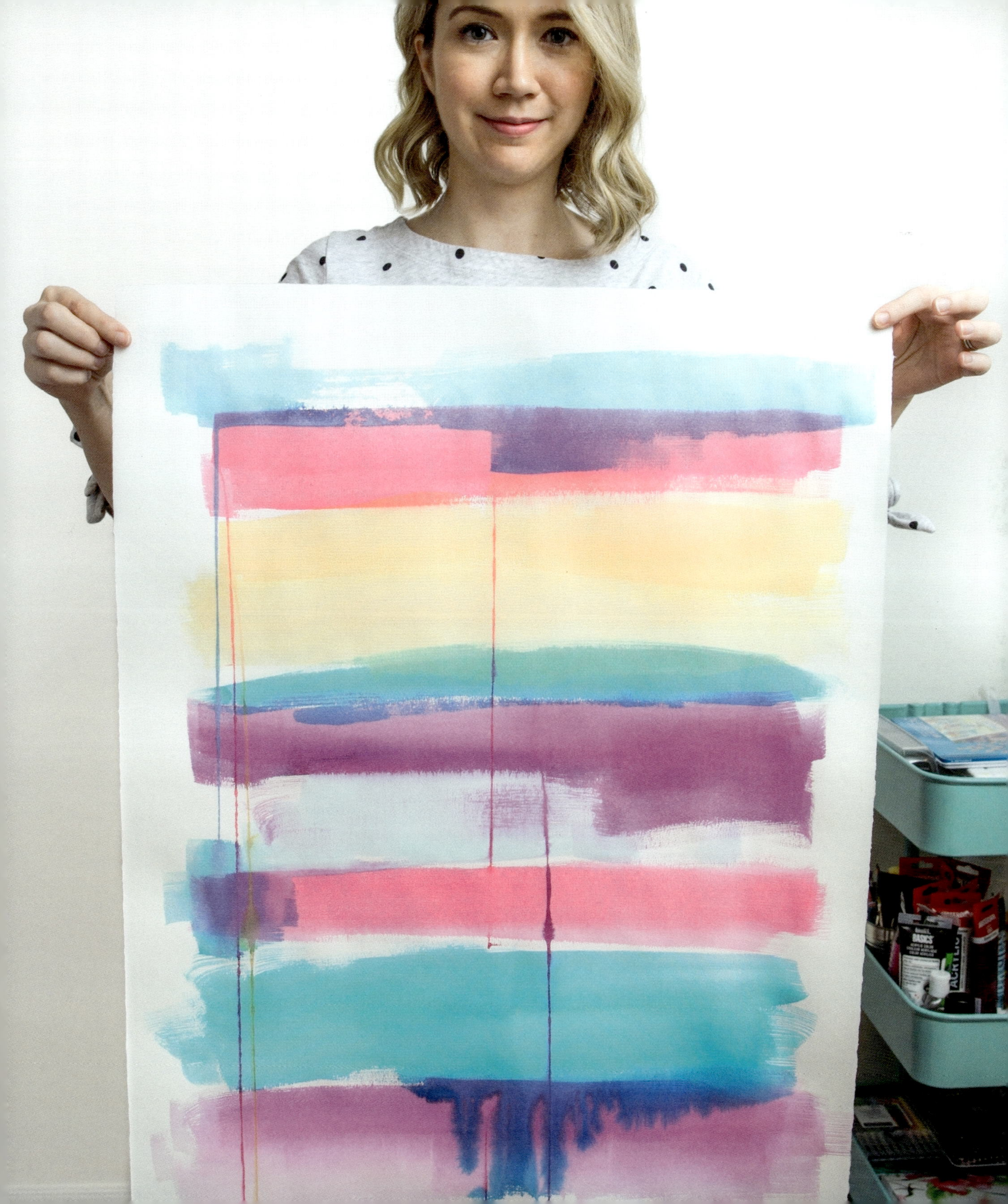
BASICS

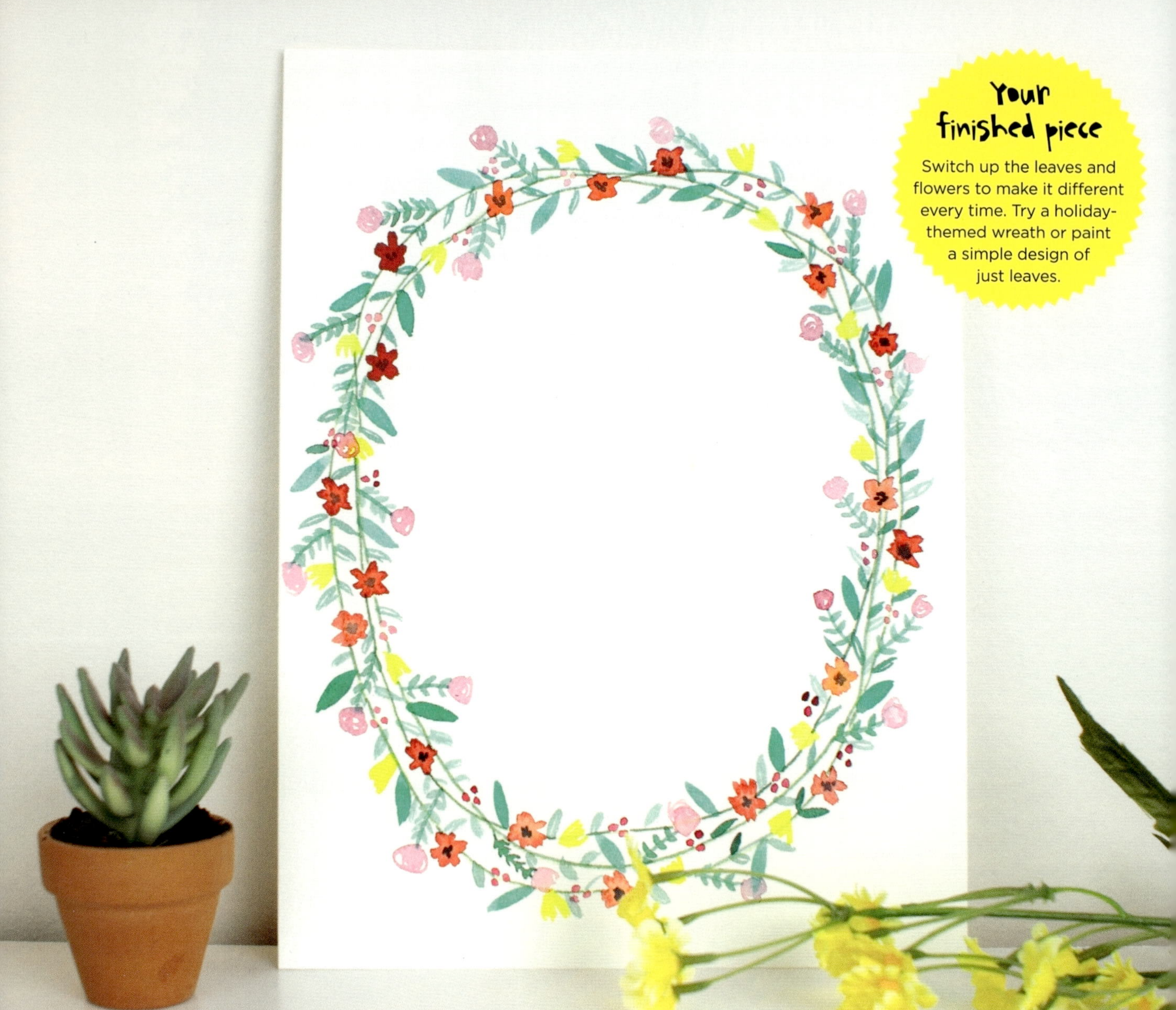

Project Start small and grow a wreath

A frame for calligraphy or a quote, a starting point for a beautiful card or invitation, or just some fun drawing practice in your sketchbook, painting these little wreaths is a lot of fun and easier than you might think. And it can easily be changed up for a different look every time.

YOU WILL NEED

- Watercolor paper
- Watercolor paint
- Pencil
- Small round brush
- Fine liner brush

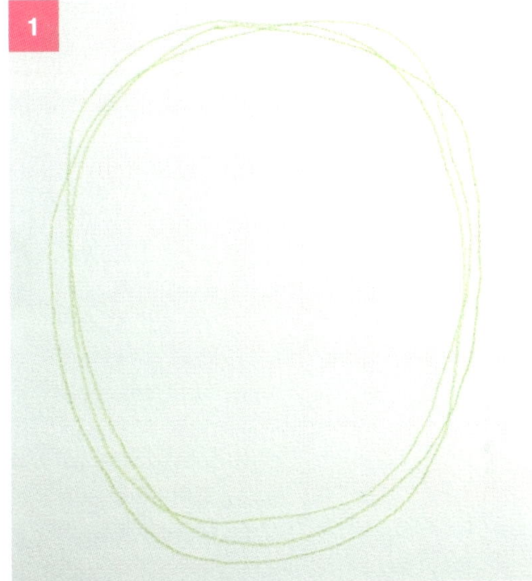

Start by drawing a spiral on your paper using a graphite or watercolor pencil. It definitely does not have to be perfect; just go around in a circle three or four times.

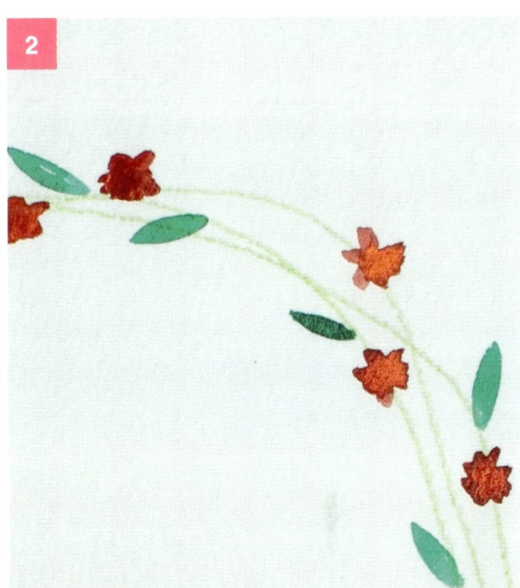

Now start adding some flowers and leaves. I like to start with my largest motifs first with a small round brush, so I can fill up some space.

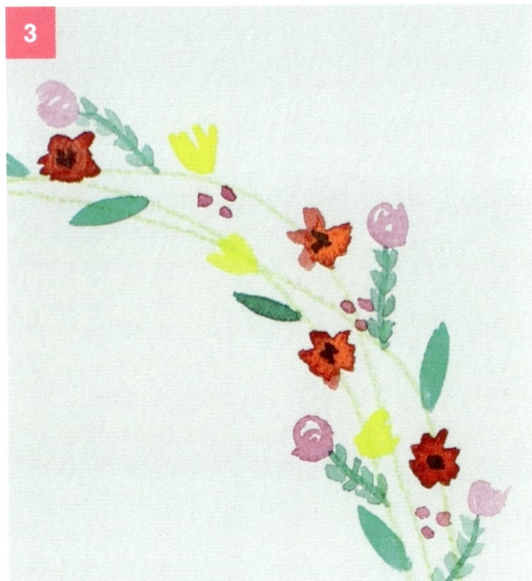

Continue by adding smaller flowers, buds, and greenery. I like it when all the leaves are pointing in the same direction, so I rotate the paper as a go.

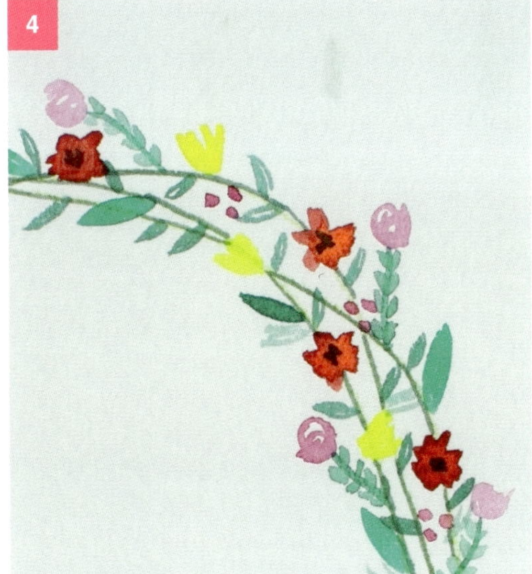

Finish by filling in any empty spaces with more leaves and flowers. As a final step, I traced over my original pencil line with a fine liner brush and some green paint.

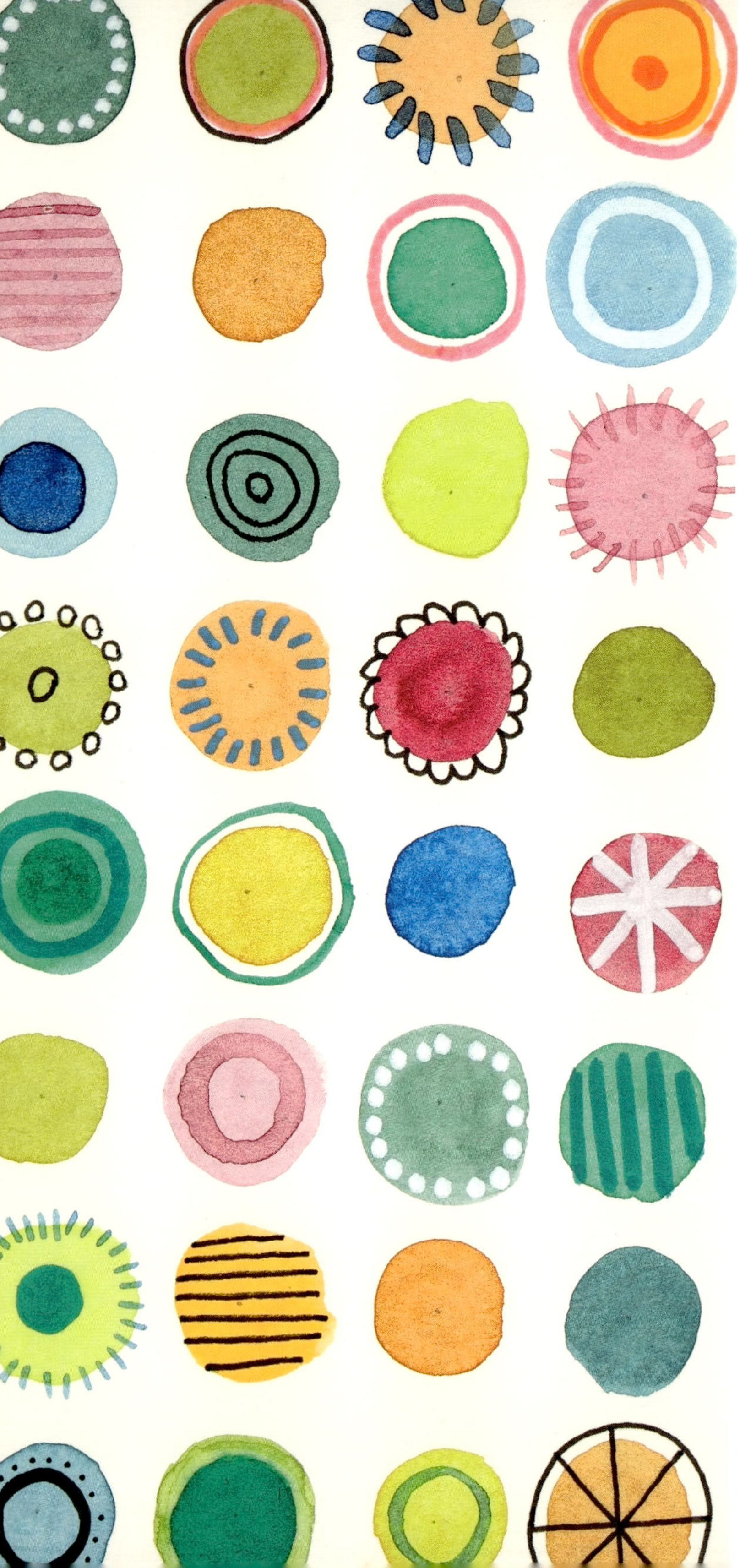

Prompt

Not-so-simple circles

Remember what we did a few pages back with a stripe design (see page 83)? Now let's try it out with a polka dot! Circles are something that anyone can paint, but it's what you do with them next that will make the pattern uniquely yours.

Every time I do this little exercise I get a completely different result. Depending on the colors you choose, the supplies you use, and even your mood, you will get a brand new pattern. For this dot pattern, I measured out an equal distance between each circle, but it also looks amazing if you scatter the circles randomly.

I chose a wide range of colors, from a few neutral shades to bright pops of pink. I find it is nice to have some variety when adding the details so I can see how each color combo works together. After I painted a basic polka-dot pattern, I grabbed some watercolor markers, gel pens, a black waterproof pen, and some more paint. This is the part where you get to customize the page.

This kind of exercise might seem simple, but it teaches you a lot about color combinations and balance in the process. After completing a meditative pattern like this, I almost always jump into a new painting feeling full of ideas.

Play Watercolor salt texture

Yes, that's right! Regular table salt sprinkled on wet paint can create a wonderful texture. This technique can be used to create an icy look for a snowy painting, a starry sky, or a sandy beach. There are so many ways to incorporate salt into your work!

Salt can be an interesting addition to your watercolor painting supplies. It is unpredictable and can create a wide range of textures. Spend some time experimenting with different sizes of salt grains and pigments. The look will vary even between colors.

When salt is sprinkled on wet paint, the crystals start to soak up the pigment. Using the salt sparingly will create more of a starry-sky look, while using a heavier hand will give a sandy texture. Be sure to start sprinkling when your paint is still quite wet. Then you will need to wait until everything is completely dry before scraping the salt off the page with your fingers. It can take longer to dry than usual, so patience is key, because you can ruin the texture if you remove the salt too early! Use your imagination and see where you can incorporate this cool texture in your next painting.

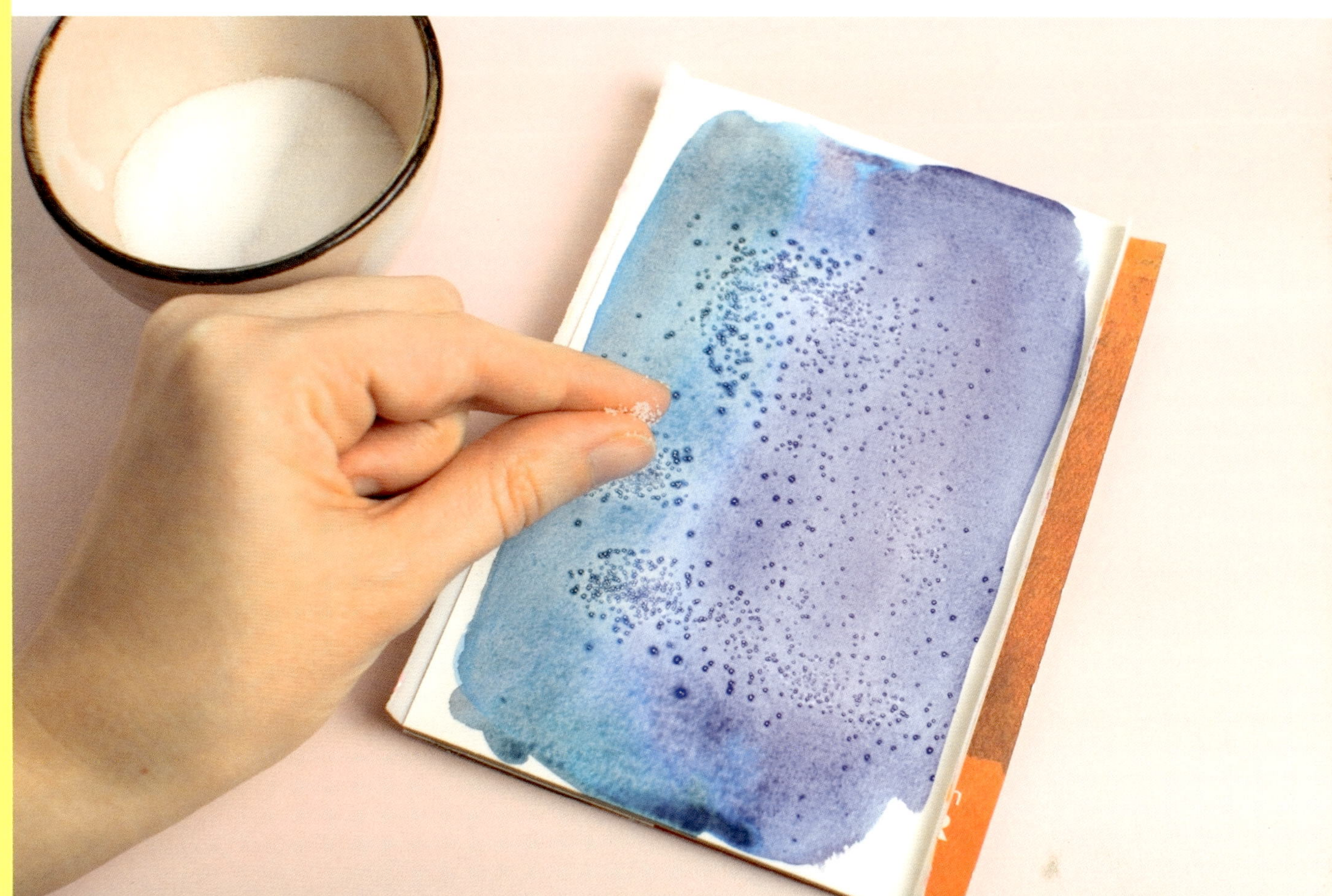

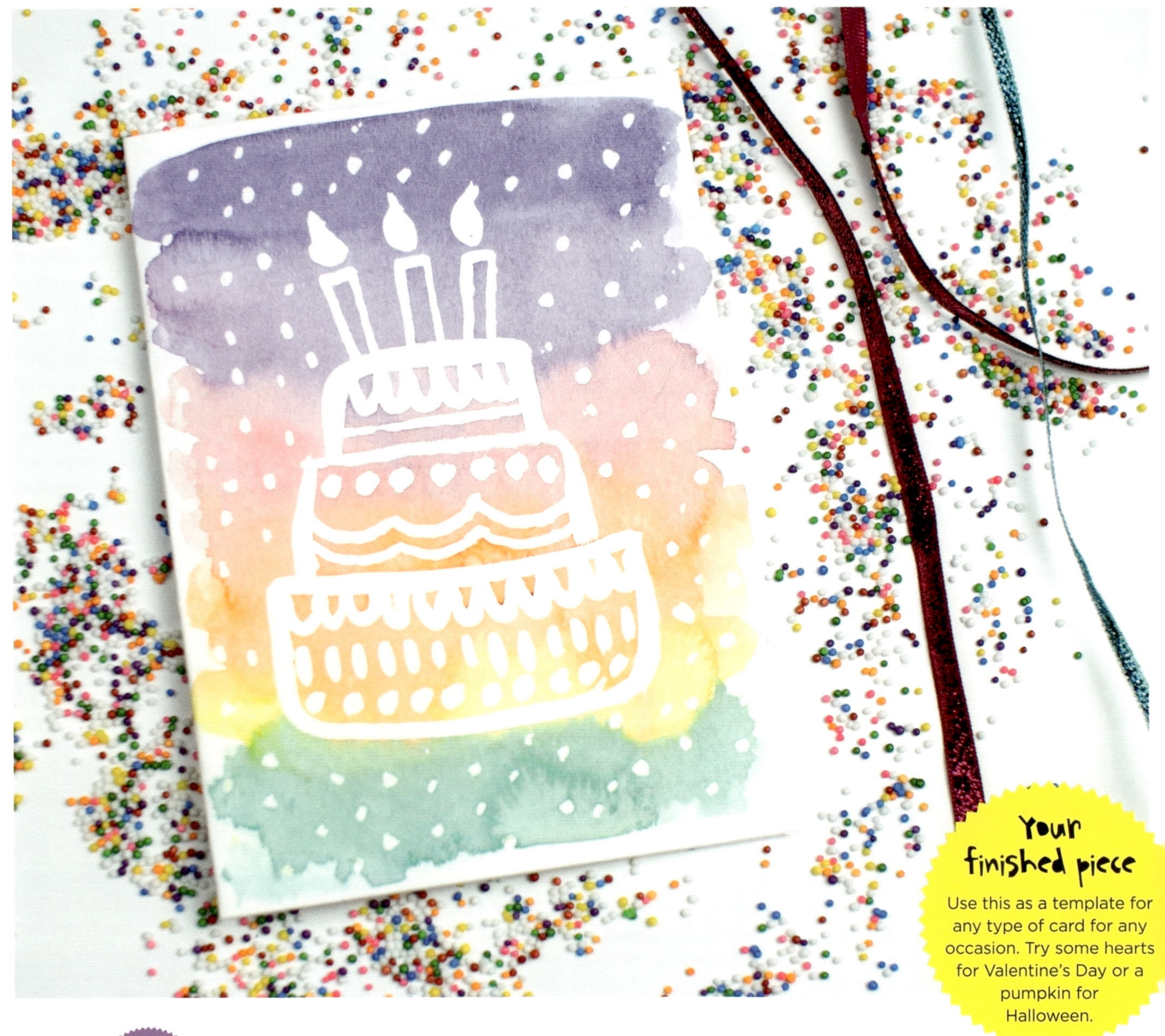

Your finished piece

Use this as a template for any type of card for any occasion. Try some hearts for Valentine's Day or a pumpkin for Halloween.

Project

Resist birthday card

Making cards for people was how I became interested in art. It is like a tiny canvas where anything goes, and the best part is giving it to someone special. For this project, I took a sheet of watercolor paper and folded it in half to make a card. Be sure to use an old paintbrush for this because masking fluid doesn't clean off easily.

YOU WILL NEED

- Watercolor paper
- Watercolor paint
- Small round brush
- Masking fluid
- Flat brush
- Eraser (optional)

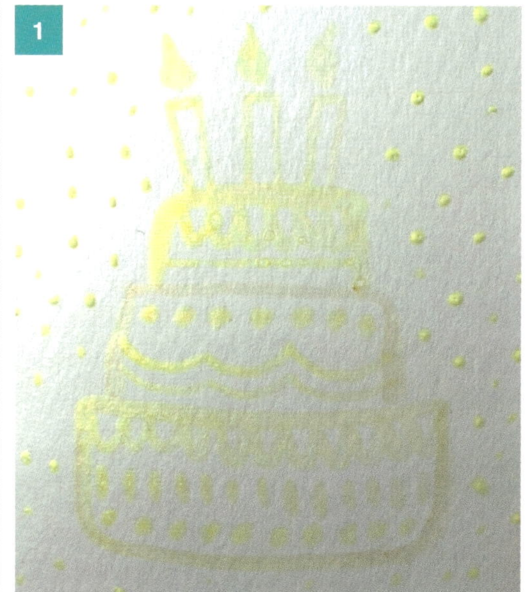

Begin by painting your design on the card with a small round brush and masking fluid (I like to use the kind that is tinted yellow so it is easier to see).

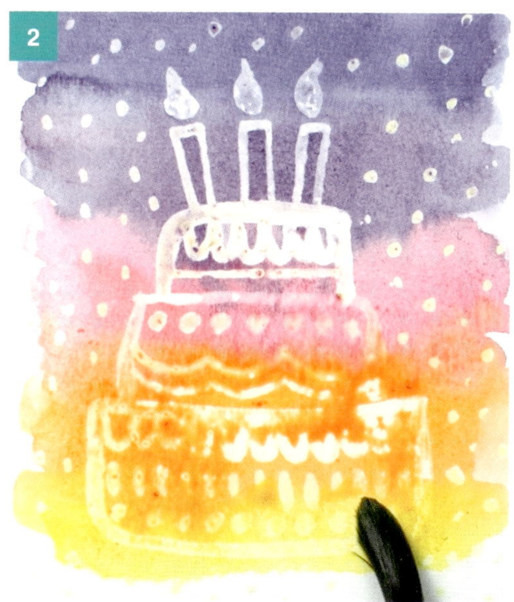

Once the masking fluid is dry, paint over the whole design using a flat brush. I chose rainbow colors, but pick any colors you like.

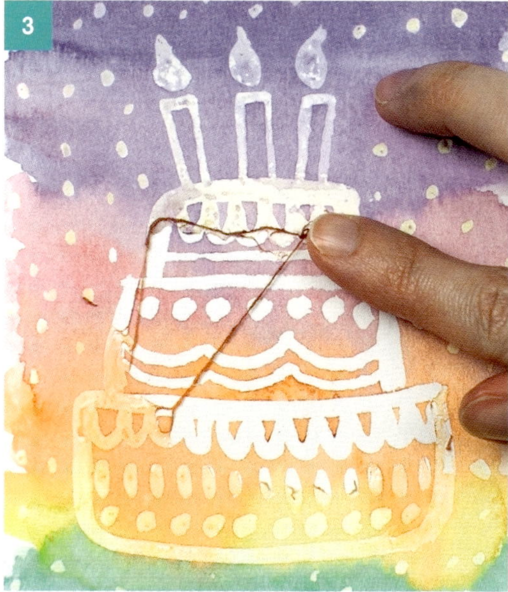

When the paint is dry, peel off the masking fluid using your fingers or an eraser.

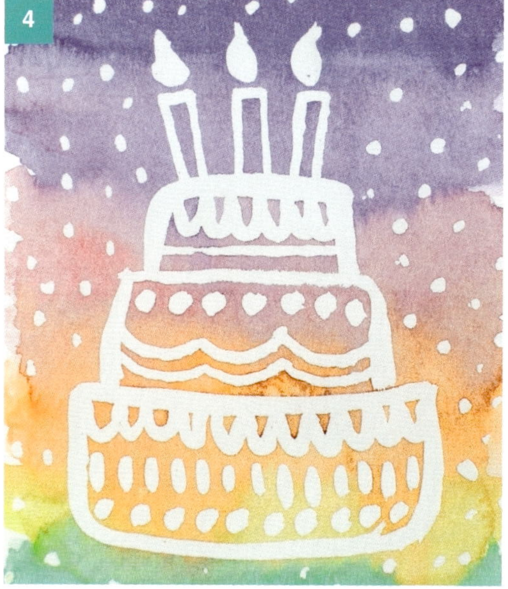

You can add a bit more detail to your card or leave it as it is. It's such a fun effect!

Tree texture using watercolor pencils

YOU WILL NEED

- Watercolor paper
- Watercolor paint
- Medium round brush
- Watercolor pencils

I love the scratchy, rough texture of colored pencils, and as watercolor pencils are water-soluble, you can get some very interesting effects that would not be possible with paint alone. This little tree pattern looks more complicated than it is, but it is all in the details. Some unexpected color choices help, too!

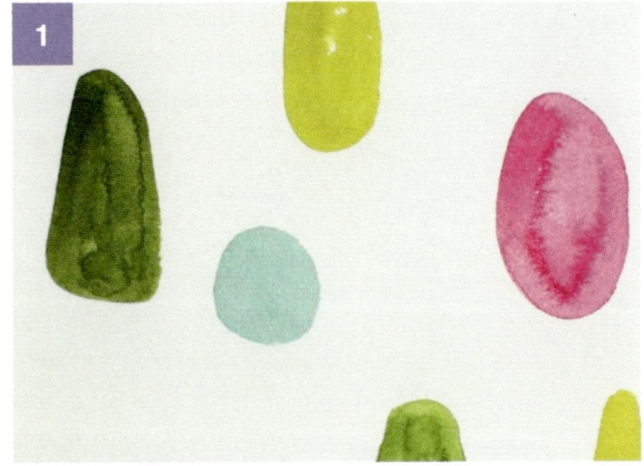

Start by painting some tree tops in a variety of different shapes. Don't be afraid to use colors other than green.

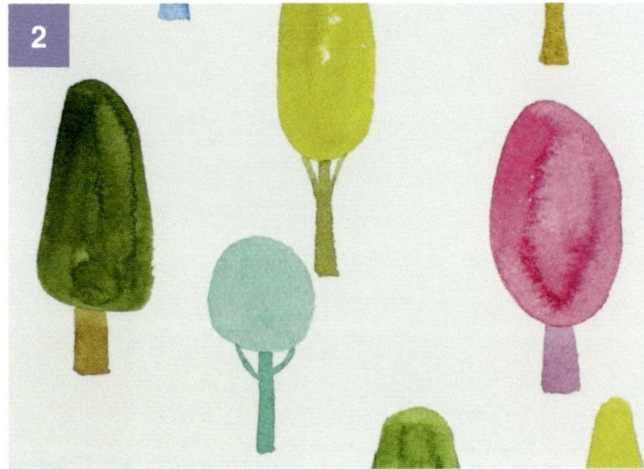

Add your tree trunks in varying sizes and styles. Again, don't be afraid to think outside the box when it comes to color.

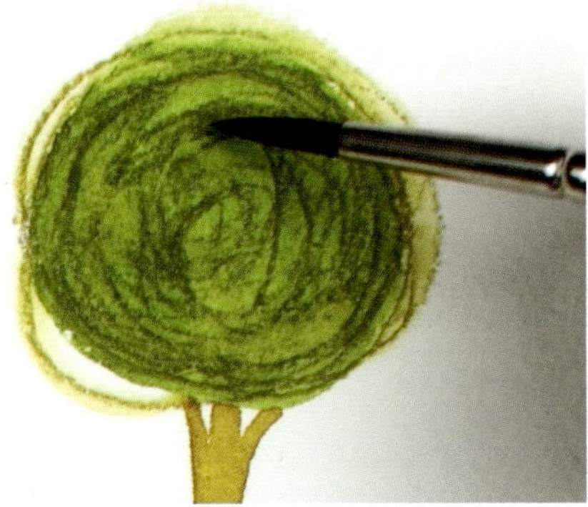

Using watercolor pencils, add some pattern and texture on top. For some of the trees, I did a little blending with a clean, wet paintbrush. The result (right) is a cute little forest with unique trees.

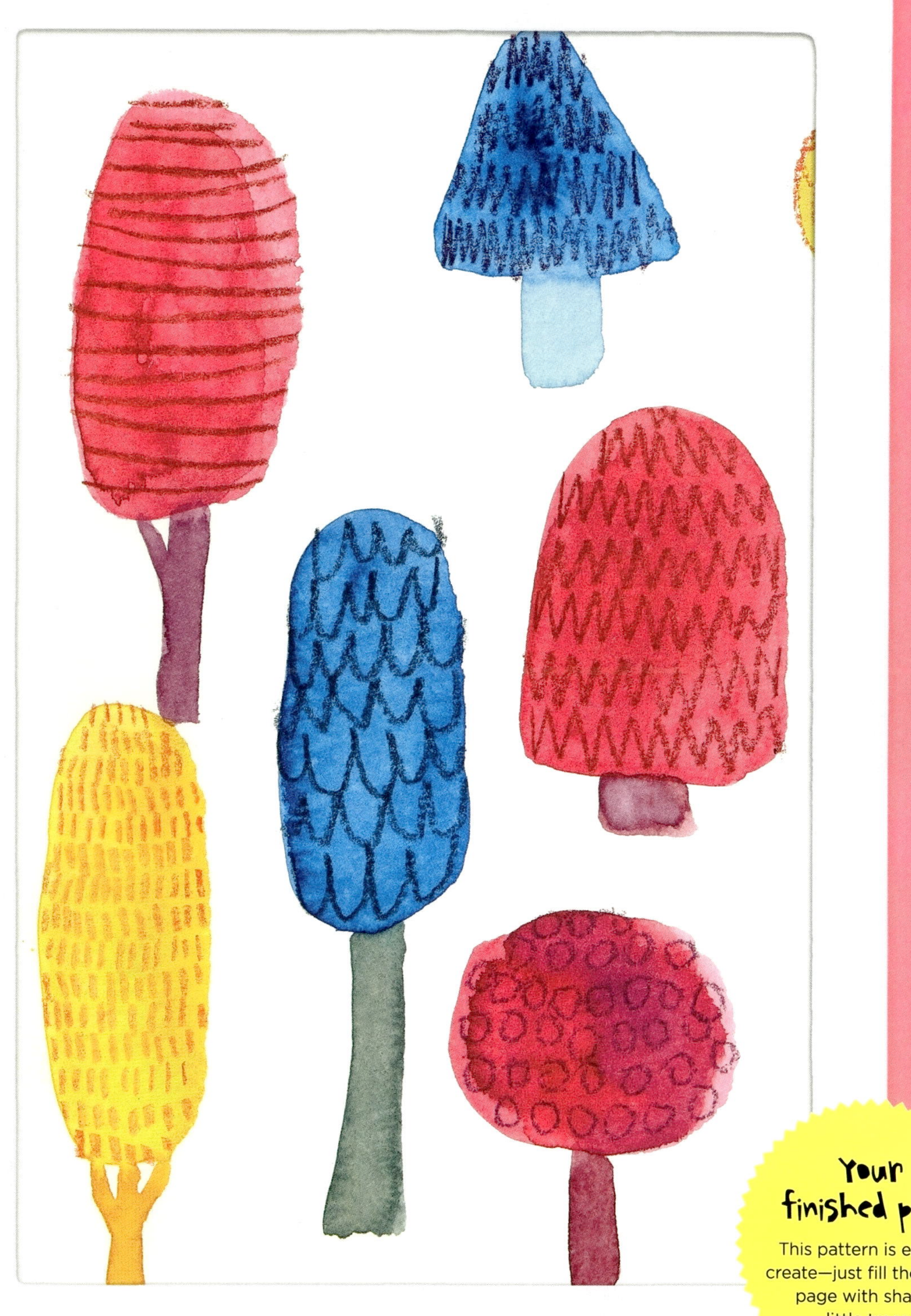

Your finished piece

This pattern is easy to create—just fill the whole page with shaped little trees.

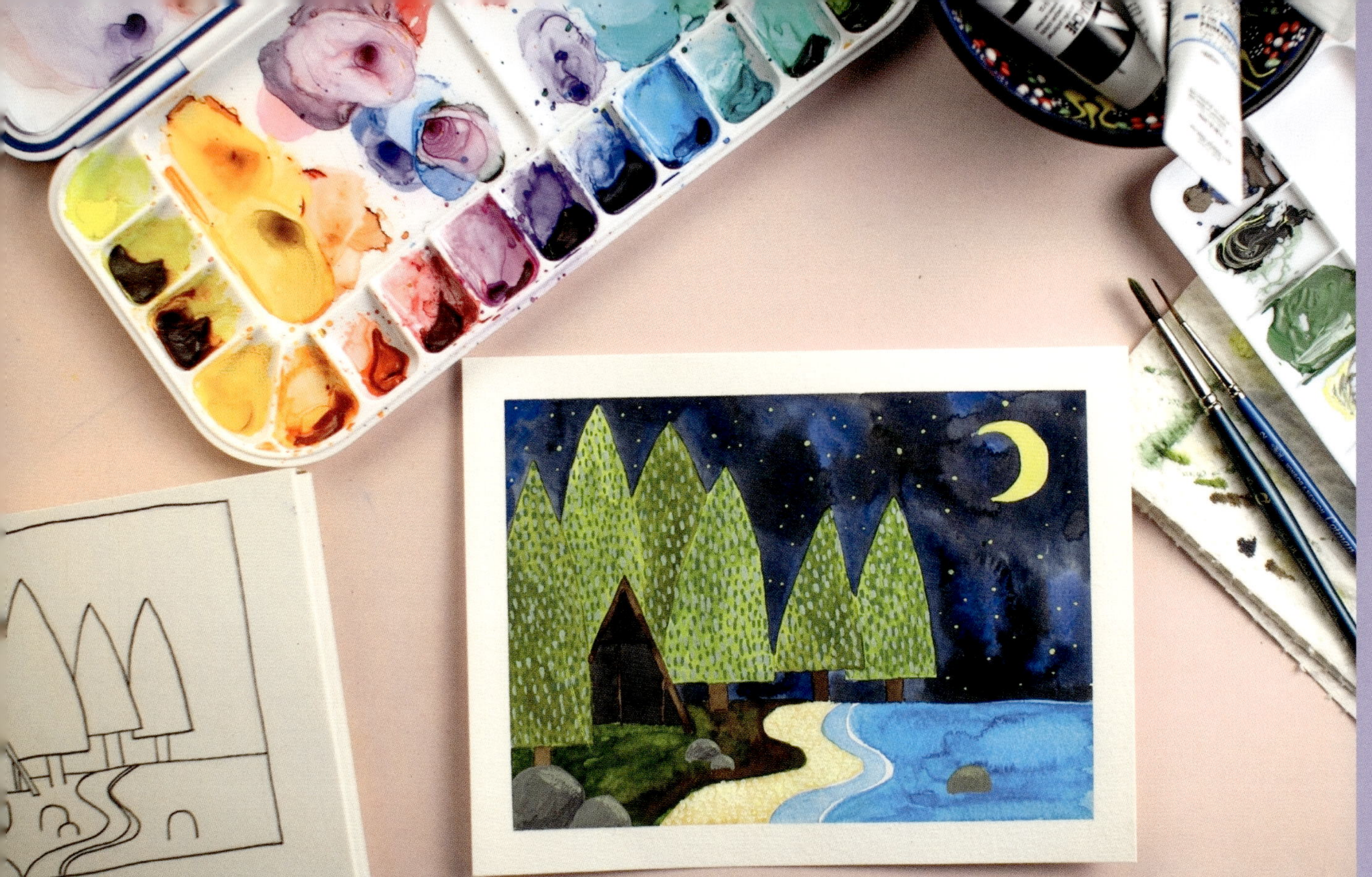

Play Watercolor plus gouache

Watercolor and gouache are a match made in heaven. Now that you are familiar with how to paint using watercolor, adding gouache into the mix is going to feel very natural. While the two mediums are similar, the differences they have can complement each other.

There are two main differences between watercolor and gouache. The first is that gouache is more opaque. If you are using high-quality paint, you can usually achieve a completely opaque layer with only one coat. However, it doesn't have the same sheerness that watercolor has. The other difference is that gouache doesn't flow and blend like watercolor.

So what makes them work so well together? They are both activated with water and can be pulled across the paper in much the same way. Like watercolor, a little gouache goes a long way. These paints are highly pigmented, come in small tubes like watercolor, and will last a long time.

I love to use gouache when I need more opaqueness. An example is painting the stars and moon onto a dark night sky. It also works beautifully for adding some special detail, where watercolor would be too translucent. If you want to get started with gouache, begin by purchasing only the three primary colors, white, and black, and mixing the colors you need. Even a small tube of white can be useful for adding highlights and detail.

prompt Mixed-media florals

It is time to put everything together in a happy mixed-media floral painting. Watercolor plays nicely with so many different mediums, so grab whatever you have at hand. Watercolor pencils, markers, pen, gouache… Let's see how it all works together.

Watercolor paint makes a great base for a mixed-media painting because everything can be layered on top so easily. You can get the beautiful translucency of watercolor and then build more depth and interest using other mediums.

It can be challenging to switch between mediums, especially if you are not as familiar with this approach, but that's all part of the fun! You will end up with surprising results when you mix and match different art supplies. And it will give you a good excuse to take home something new from the art store—not that I ever need an excuse to spend money there.

For this painting, I started with a watercolor base. Then I added some gouache to the main flower to make it pop. I added some leaves and stems using watercolor pencil to get that scratchy texture. I also blended some watercolor markers for other flowers and leaves. For a final step, I added some white detail with a gel pen. Florals are very forgiving, so enjoy challenging yourself.

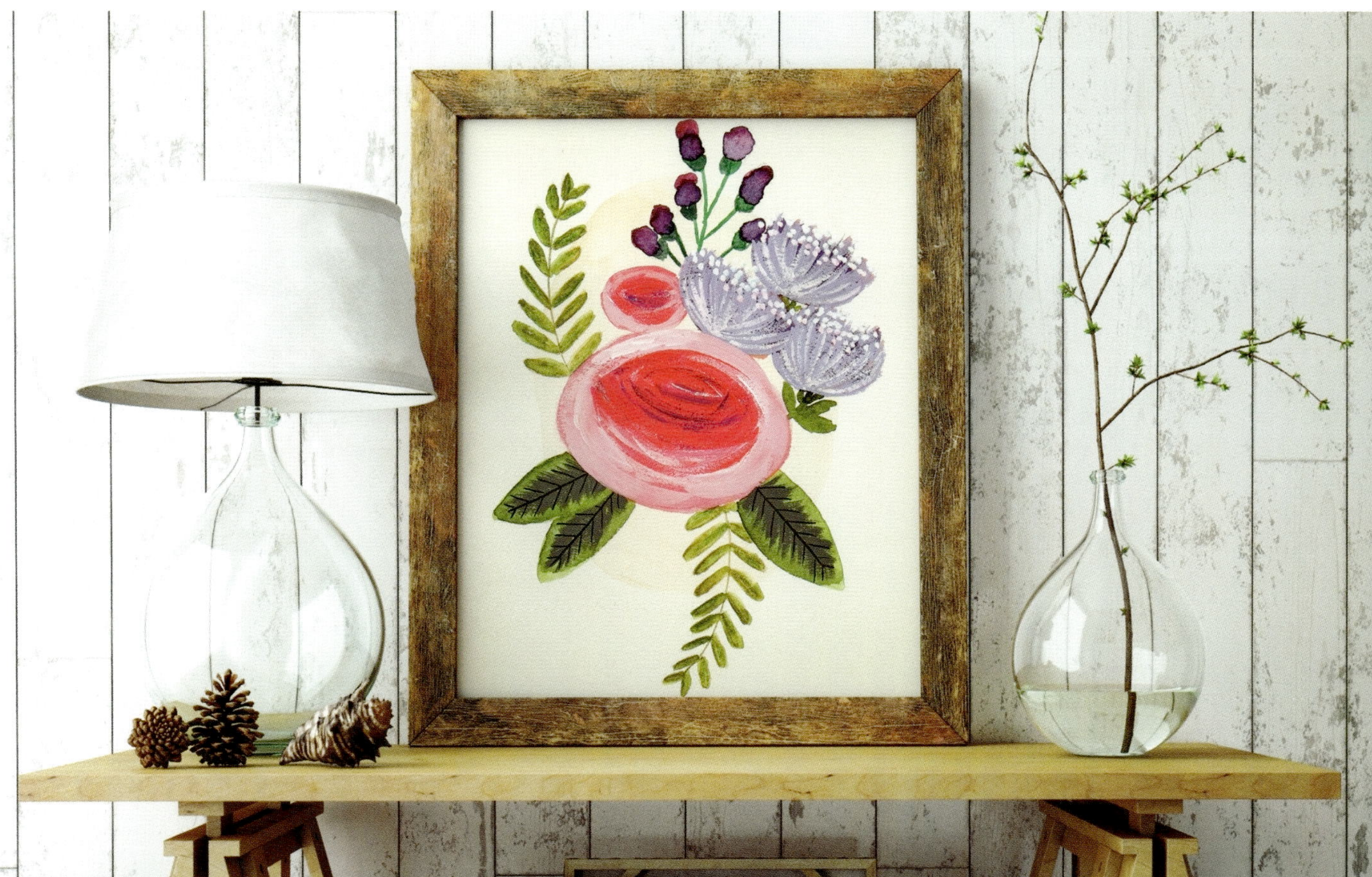

Tea time with pen accents

YOU WILL NEED

- Watercolor paper
- Watercolor paint
- Medium round brush
- Black waterproof pen
- White gel pen

My black waterproof pen and white gel pen almost never leave my side. They are both wonderful additions to any painting and can be so much fun when creating a crazy pattern like this tea-time spread.

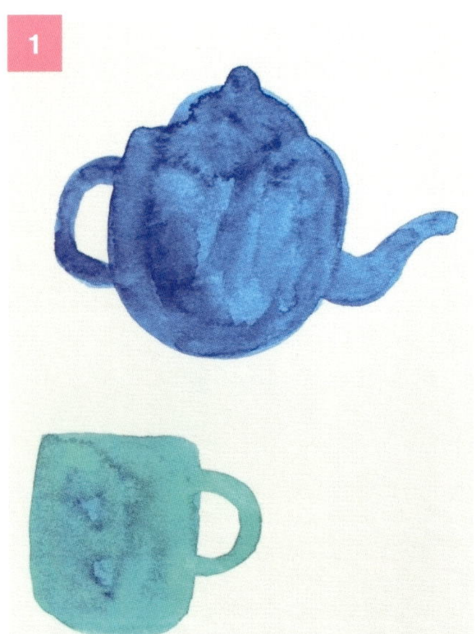

Start by painting some simple cups, mugs, and teapots on the page with a medium round brush. I went with a few shades of blue and teal to keep it cohesive. Let dry.

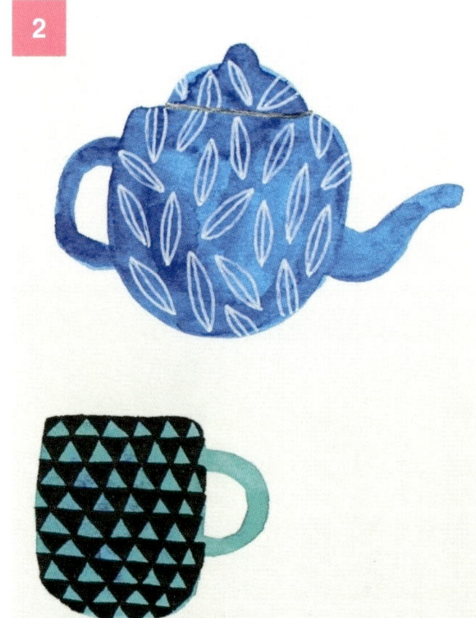

Grab your black and white pens, and start creating some fun designs on your cups and teapots. Each motif can be totally different, or you can create a matching set.

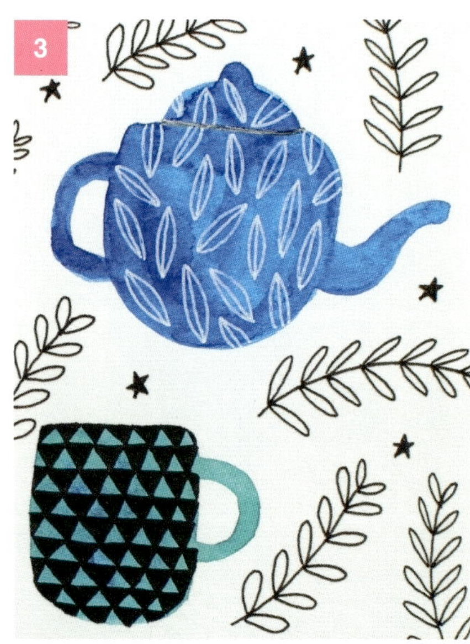

To make the picture more interesting, add some pattern to the background of the page.

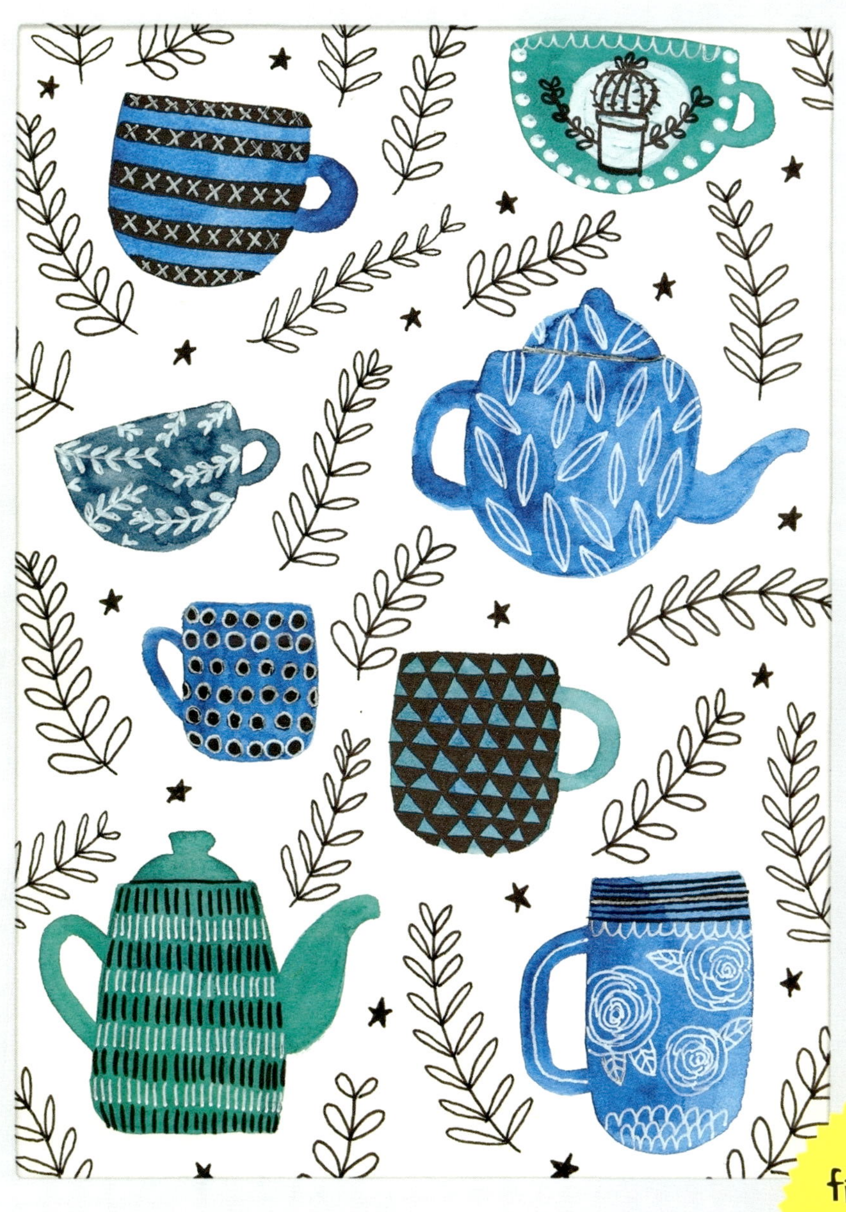

Your finished piece

Switch up this painting with any motif you like. Start with simple silhouettes and then go crazy adding pattern.

Prompt New life for an old painting

No matter how long you have been painting, you will still end up with pieces that you are not that fond of. Afterall, not every painting can be your favorite. How can you give these discarded paintings a new life? Collage is the answer!

When I am working on an abstract piece, I tend to work quickly and try to pick colors intuitively, which results in a few happy accidents and surprises, but also means that at the end of a painting session, I have a lot of discarded ideas.

I might like the colors in one, the shapes in another, and the small details in a different painting, but none of them is quite right. It is a shame to throw these away, so, recently I started saving them for collage work. I keep a little stack of imperfect paintings and whenever I am in a collage kind of mood, I grab one and start snipping.

These scraps can make a base for a new painting. You can cut out what you don't like and keep the good stuff. If you have been working through this book, then chances are you have a few mistake paintings lying around already. Too pretty to throw away, but not pretty enough to display. So, grab a pair of scissors and some glue, and breathe new life into that painting!

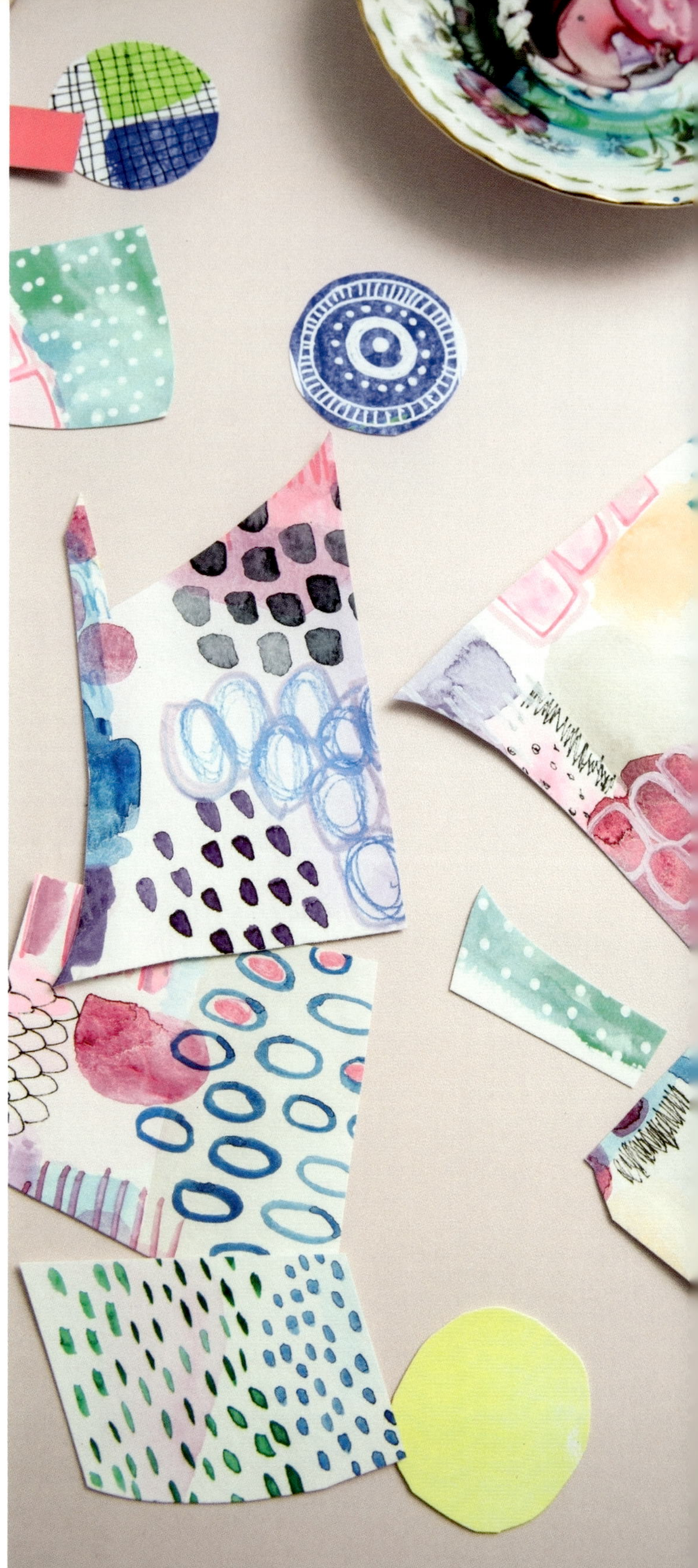

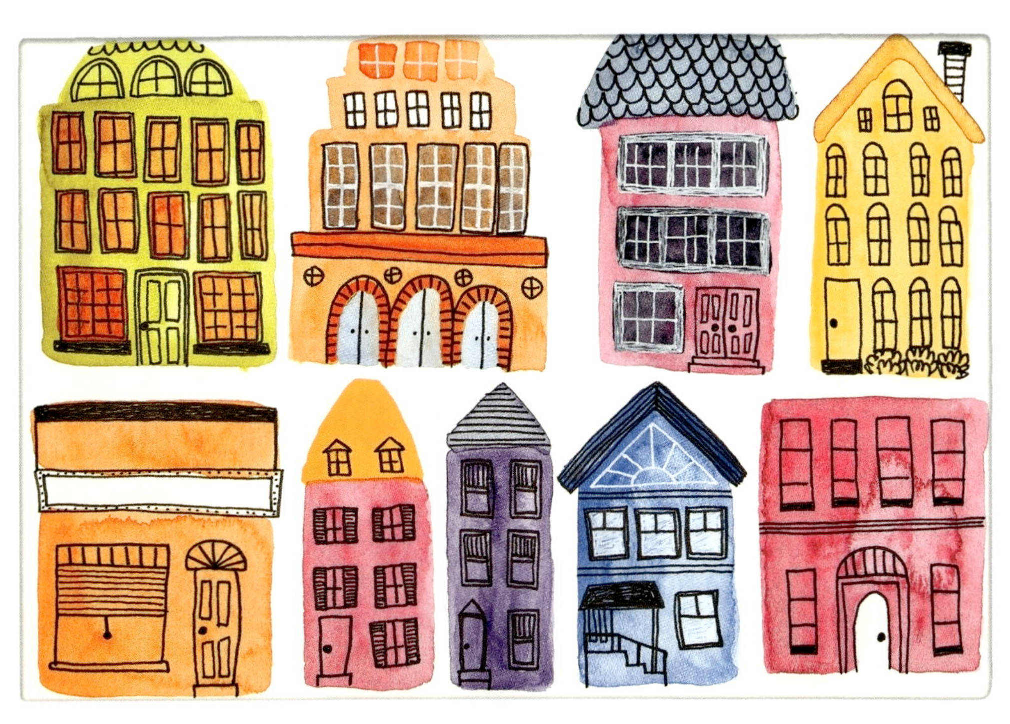

prompt Paint a tiny town

Turn some rectangles and triangles into a sweet, candy-colored town using the magic of a black waterproof pen and a white gel pen. It's all in the details with this prompt!

This is the best kind of painting to create while on vacation or when you are taking a little time for yourself in a coffee shop. Just find a nice patio or window to sit by and quietly observe the neighborhood around you. This can be a deliberate and relaxing piece to create. You can even slowly add a new building to the page each time you come across something interesting.

Start with a base layer of some general building shapes. Try to find a variety of sizes and styles, and leave some white areas for doors and windows.

Once the first layer is dry you can add some detail in other colors. Now for the fun part! This is the step that takes the most time and will require some observation. Grab a black waterproof pen and a white gel pen, and start adding details to the buildings. That means windows, doors, signs, steps, and anything else that catches your eye. I don't like to recreate the buildings exactly as they are, but instead pick out some of my favorite details, and even mix and match some architectural aspects.

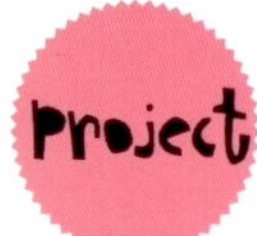

Doodles in a floral explosion

There is something so wonderful about seeing a whole page of intricate and colorful doodles working together. This project is very forgiving, so keep things loose and abstract—you will always end up with something interesting.

YOU WILL NEED

- Watercolor paper
- Watercolor paint
- Medium round brush
- Black waterproof pen

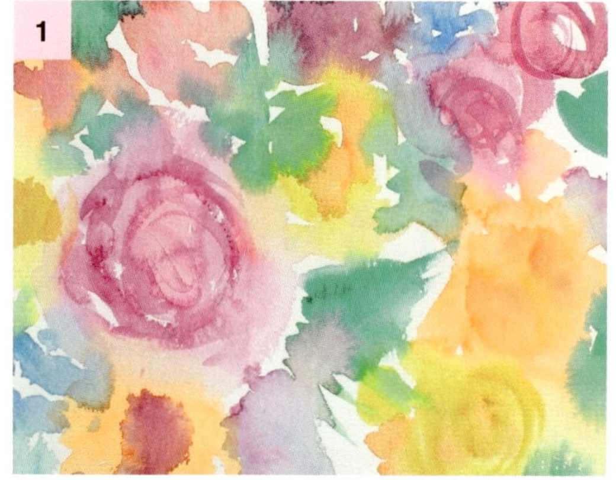

Start by painting some loose flower shapes on the page. You are not trying to paint a flower, just the basic structure of one. Then add a few hints of green for some leafy areas. Again, they don't need to resemble actual leaves.

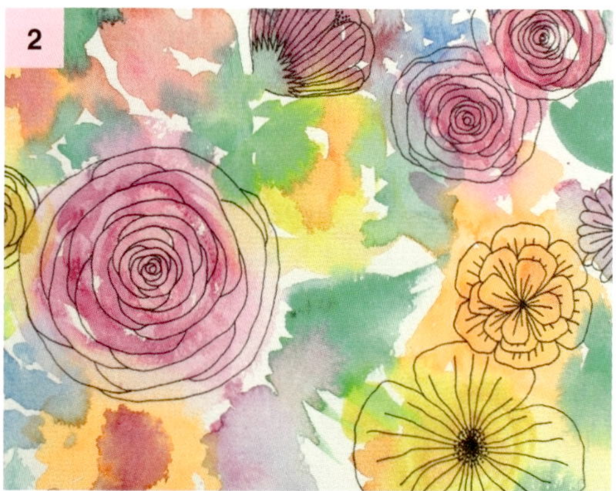

Once everything is dry, start doodling some flowers with the black pen. Begin in the center of the flower and build the petals out from there. I like to start with some of the big, obvious ones that jump out at me first.

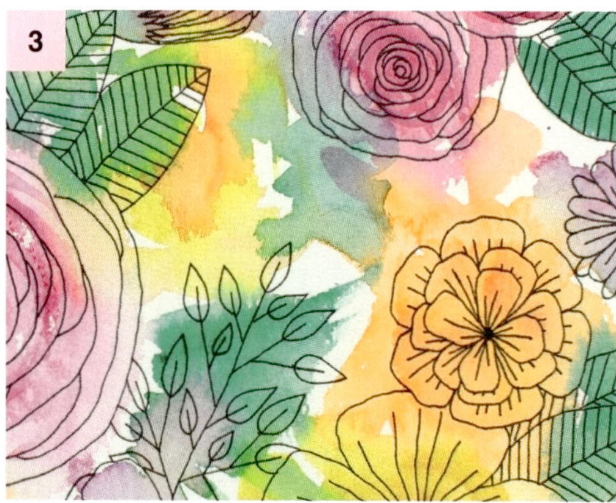

Then use some of the green areas to add a few leaves to complement your flowers. Draw a variety of greenery going in all directions.

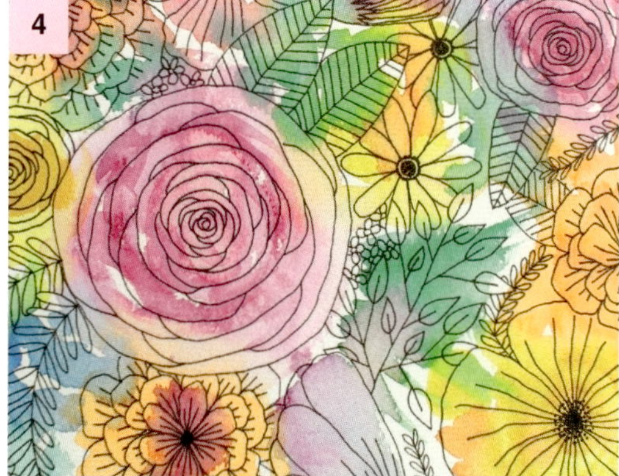

Continue filling the page with doodles until you are happy with how it looks. You can even color some areas black for a little contrast. I like to add clusters of tiny flowers to fill the space.

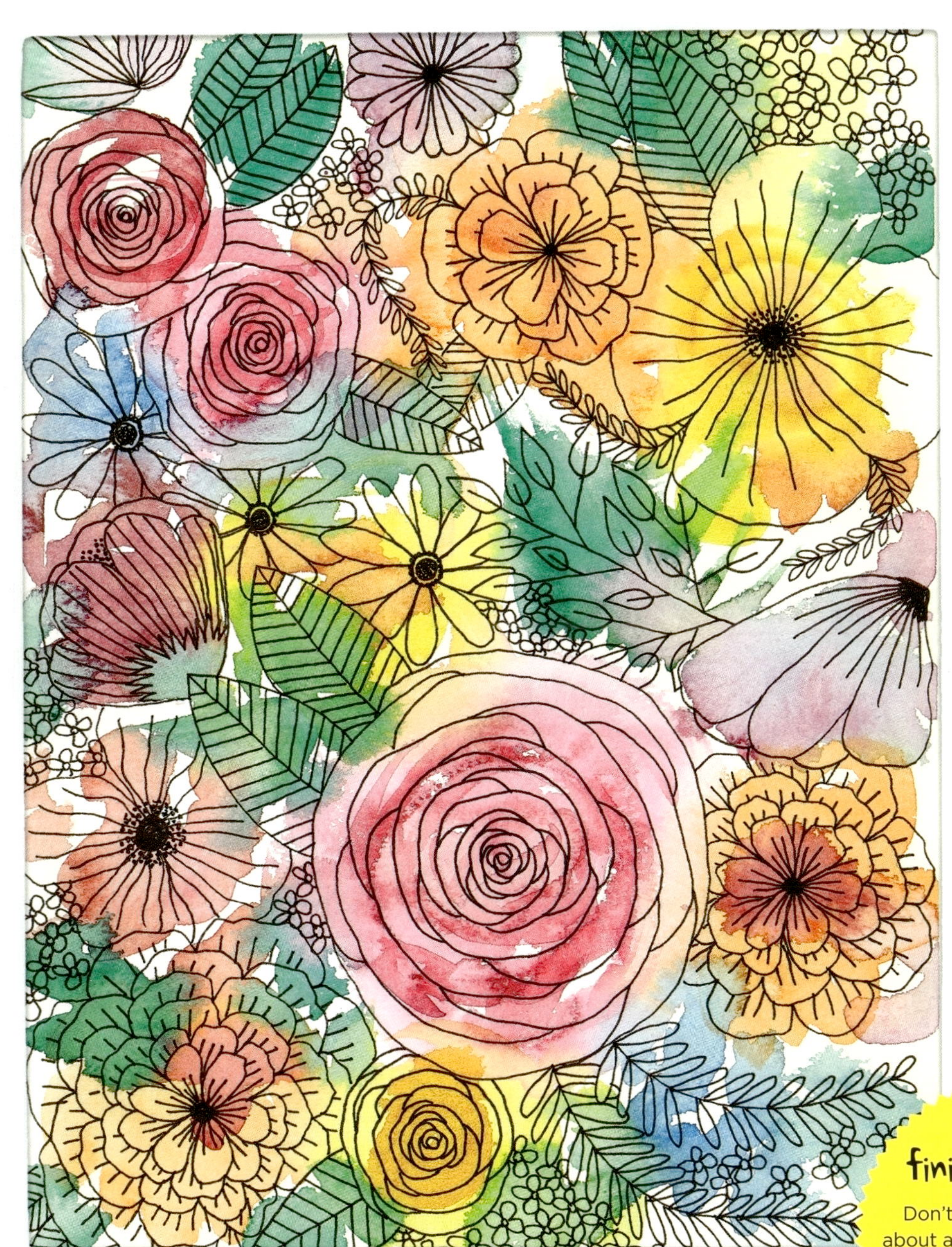

Your finished piece

Don't worry too much about a color palette here. Pick the colors that speak to you and it will all come together when you add the doodles.

Paint a frosty winter scene

This painting of a cozy little cabin uses a couple of different techniques to give it a wintery feel. The cool color palette makes you think of ice; the salt gives the sky a frosty look; and the white gel pen creates big fat snowflakes.

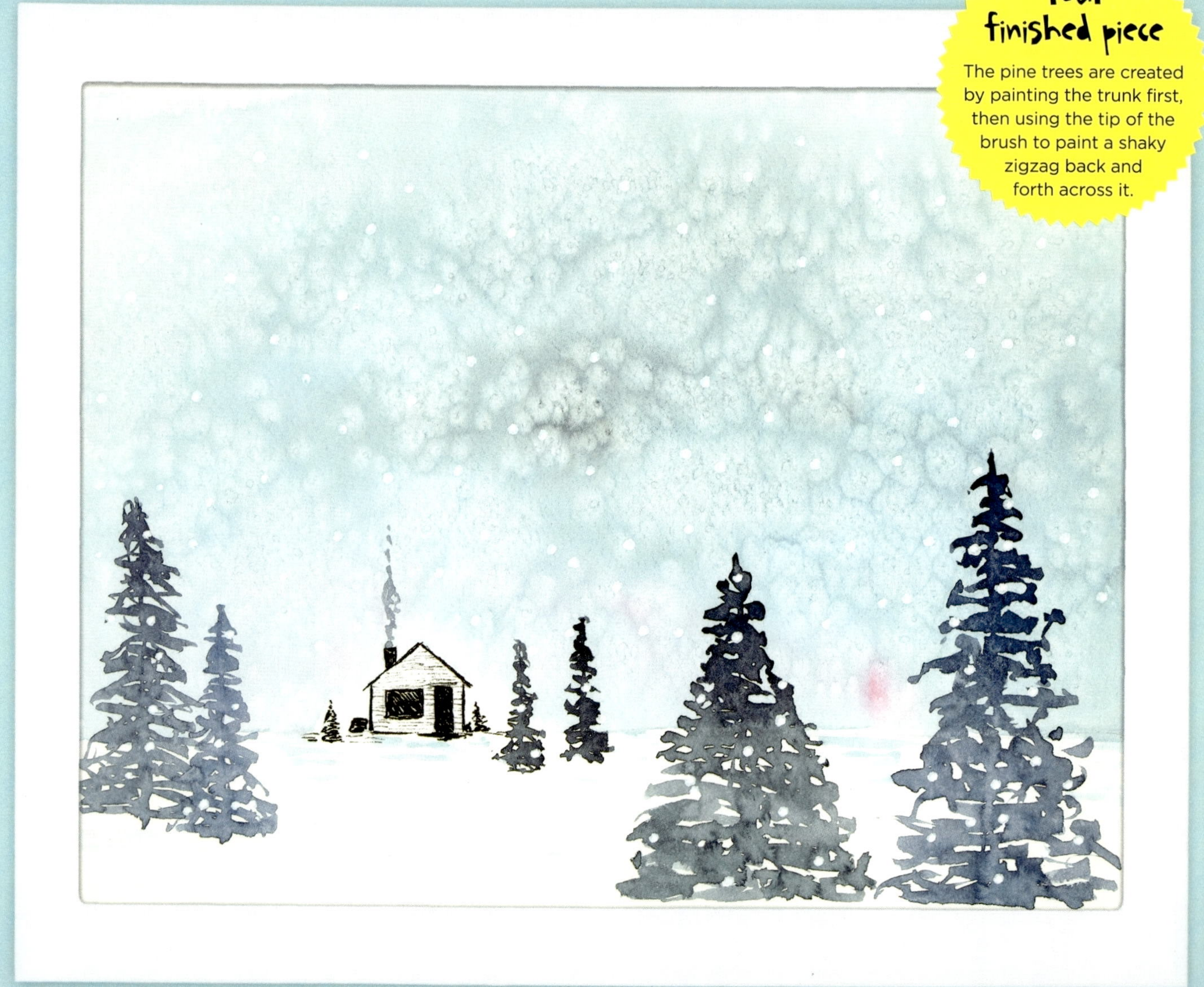

Your finished piece

The pine trees are created by painting the trunk first, then using the tip of the brush to paint a shaky zigzag back and forth across it.

YOU WILL NEED

- Watercolor paper
- Watercolor paint
- Pencil
- Black waterproof pen
- Small round brush
- Salt
- White gel pen

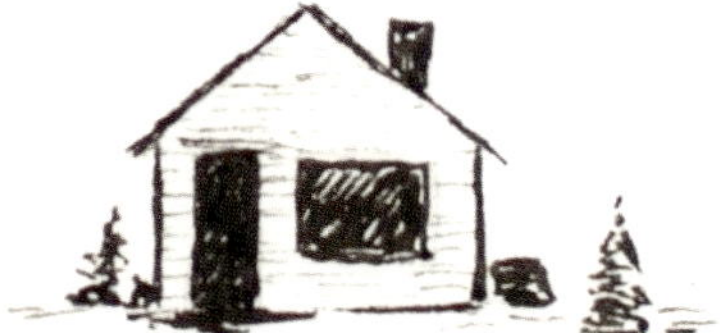

Begin by sketching out a horizon line about a quarter of the way up the page. Then draw a little cabin using a waterproof black pen.

Wet the sky area of the page with clean water, then fill it in using a mix of gray and blue, taking care to paint around the cabin. While the sky is wet, sprinkle on a little salt.

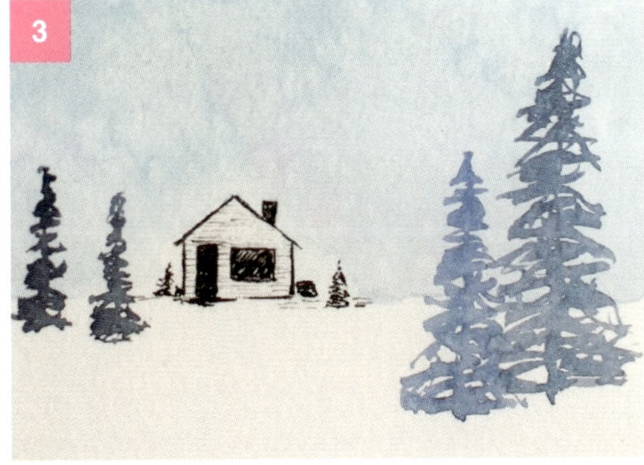

When the page is completely dry, remove the salt. Then paint some trees. Vary the size and placement to make them look closer and farther away.

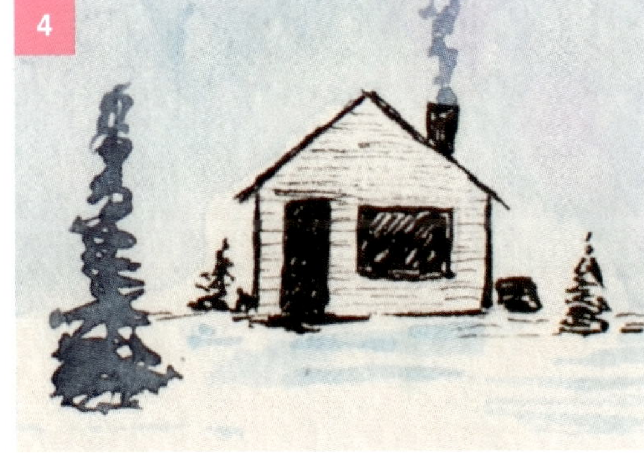

Using a very watered-down blue, paint some blue highlights on the snow. You can also add some smoke coming from the cabin's chimney.

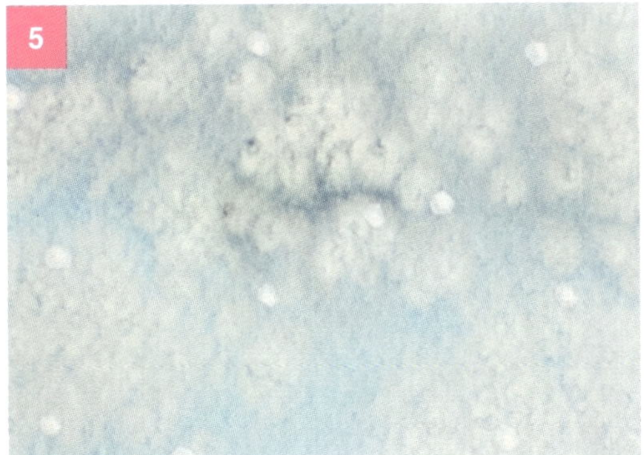

When everything is dry, add some snowflakes using a white gel pen. You could even add a scattering of snow on top of the trees.

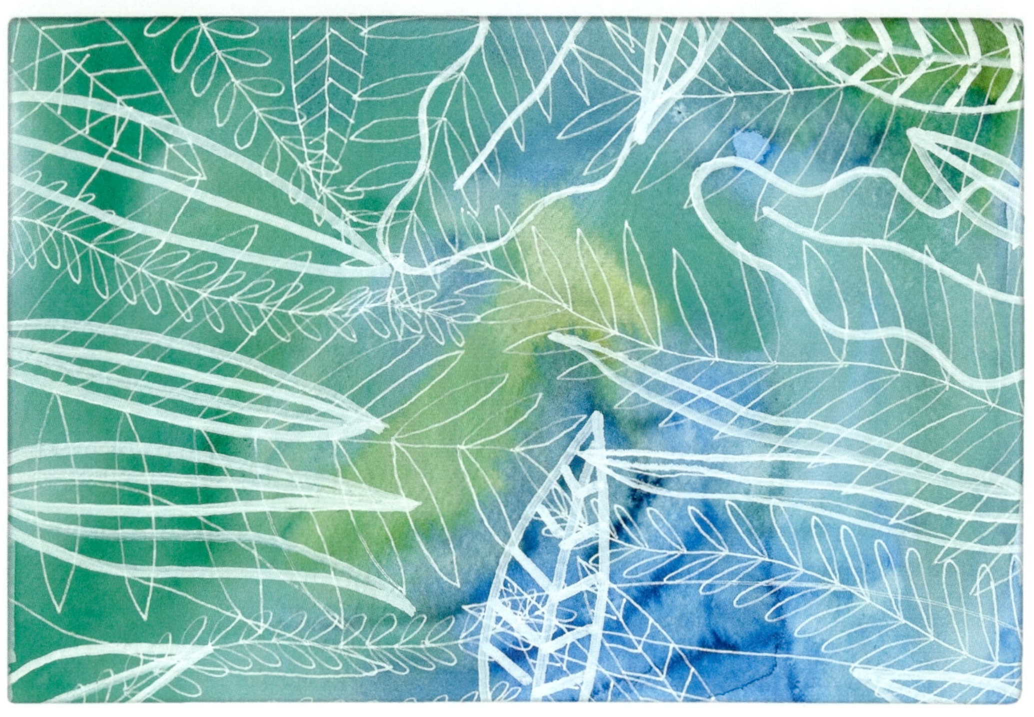

prompt Gel pen leafy tangle

If you have a long train ride ahead of you or just need some quiet time, this is the perfect painting for you. After you lay down a base of your favorite colors, simply draw and draw until you fill the whole page.

This is one of those exercises that is so simple and enjoyable you won't even notice you are sneaking in some great drawing practice. I love to create this kind of art while relaxing after a long day. Once you get into it, the leafy drawings are quite meditative. It also allows you to practice drawing new leaves and foliage.

Start by laying down some of your favorite colors. I like to use a watercolor pad that is gummed on both sides, so the page doesn't curl. Let the colors blend however they want to, to create those beautiful blooms. Now get a white gel pen or paint marker and start drawing your leaf shapes coming in from all angles. Draw a variety of shapes and sizes, and be sure to experiment with new types. I love the look of having them all layered on top of one another—a true tangle of leaves and plants. This painting would also look attractive with a light-colored base and black pen instead of white.

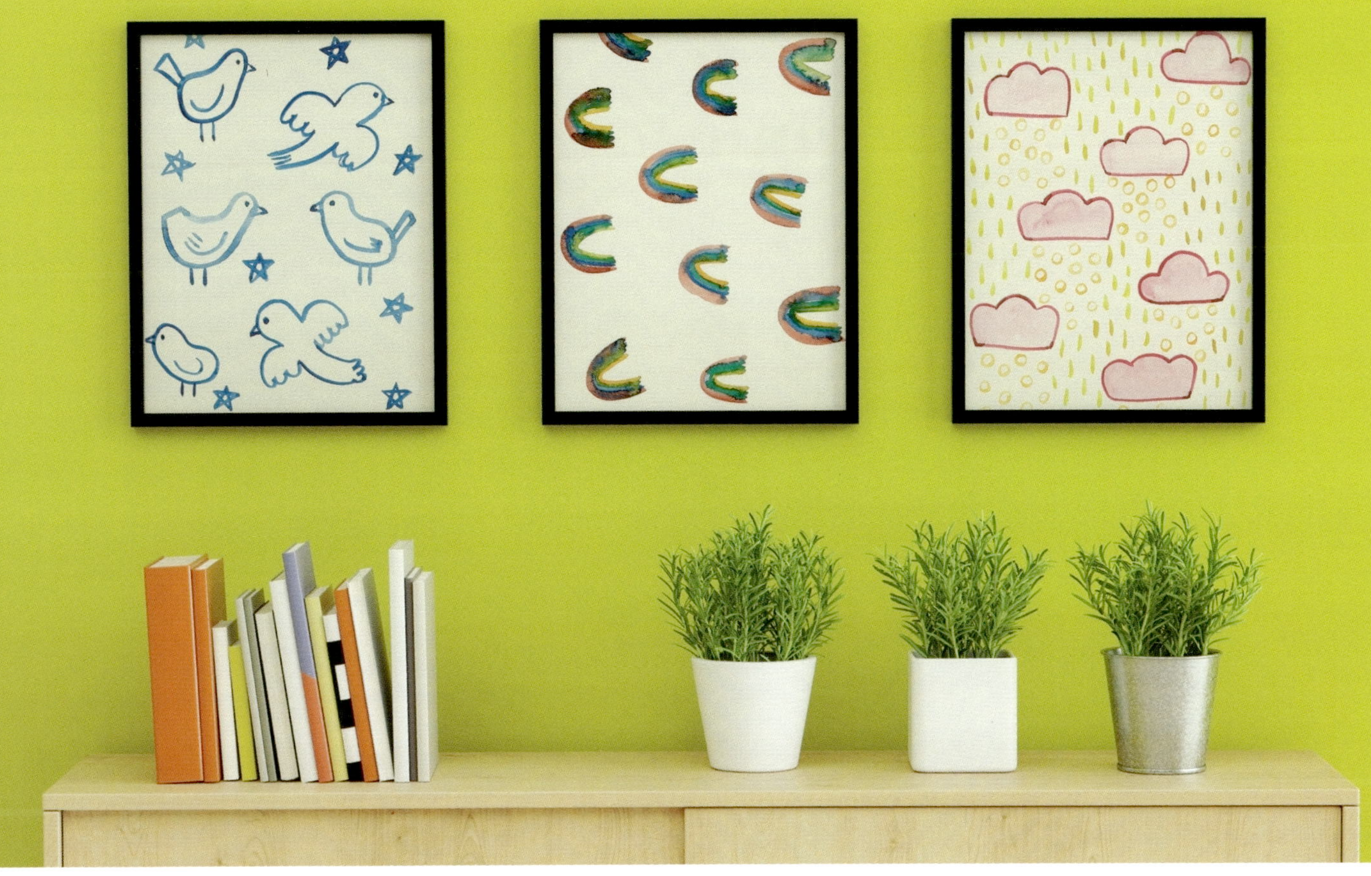

prompt Find the essence

What is the essence of a rain cloud? How simplified can your painting be before the subject becomes completely unrecognizable? In this prompt, we will be throwing the rulebook away and painting like a kid again.

There is a lot you can learn from watching a child paint or draw. Their style is completely their own and they create with such confidence. There is a cliché that says abstract art can be done by a child, but anyone who has tried to paint or draw in a more primitive style knows that it can be difficult to let go of their insecurities and capture the essence of a subject.

As a fun exercise, grab a couple of large sheets of watercolor paper (it is so much more fun to work big) and paint like there are no rules. You don't need to show anyone these paintings; they will be for your eyes only. Choose a recognizable subject, such as a bird or tree. You want something with a couple of distinct features that you can play with and distort. Break your subject down into those distinct features. For a bird, it would be the body, beak, and wings. Experiment with how simple you can make the subject before it becomes unrecognizable. When you forget about the rules, you might find yourself feeling more creative than ever.

Project Show your love

What do you love the most? Whether it is gardening, cats, hiking, or music, this painting is the perfect way to showcase all of your favorite things. From far away it will look like a heart, but up close you will be able to see all of your favorite details.

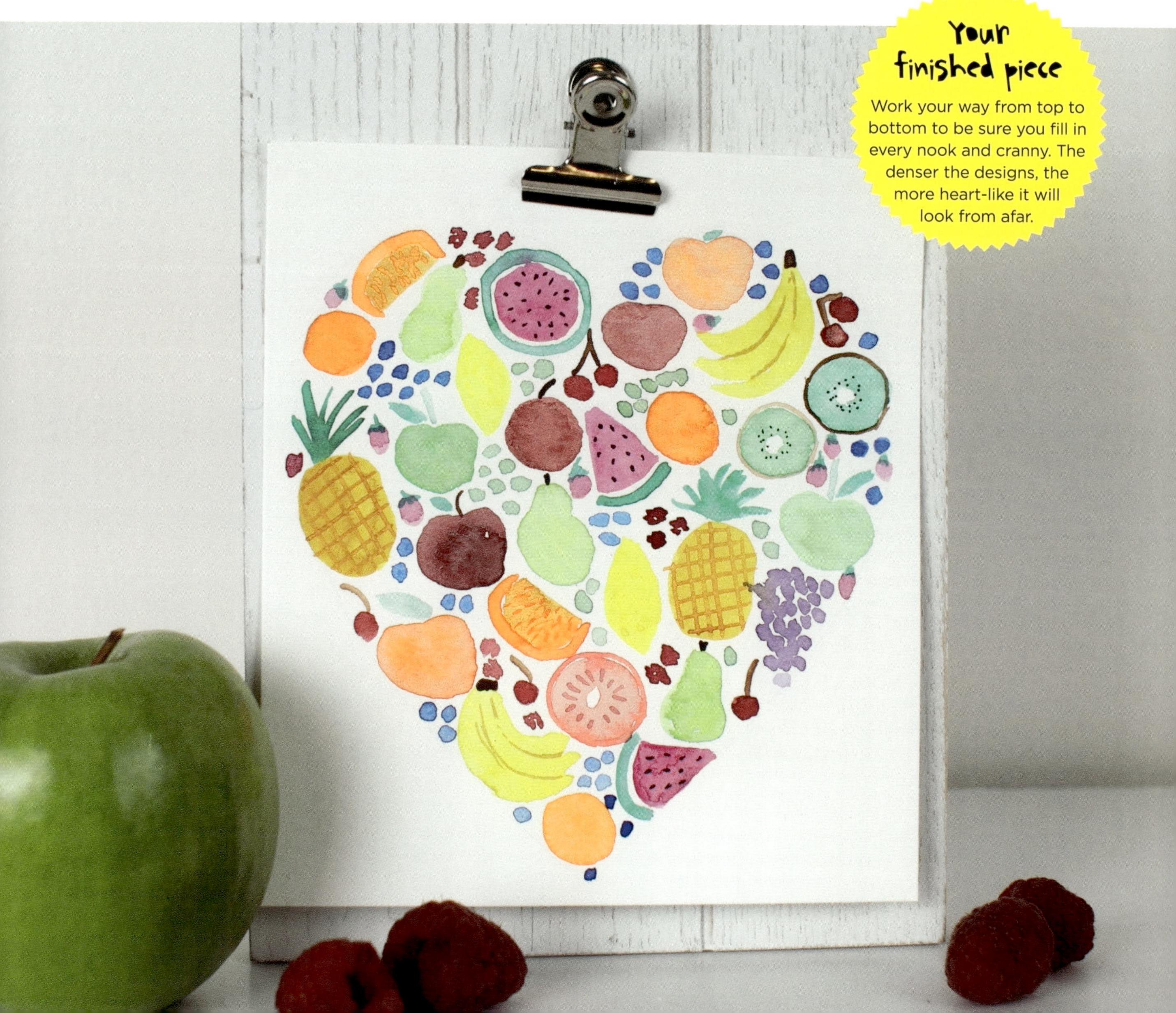

Your finished piece

Work your way from top to bottom to be sure you fill in every nook and cranny. The denser the designs, the more heart-like it will look from afar.

YOU WILL NEED

- Watercolor paper
- Watercolor paint
- Pencil
- Small round brush
- Small liner brush
- Black waterproof pen
- Eraser

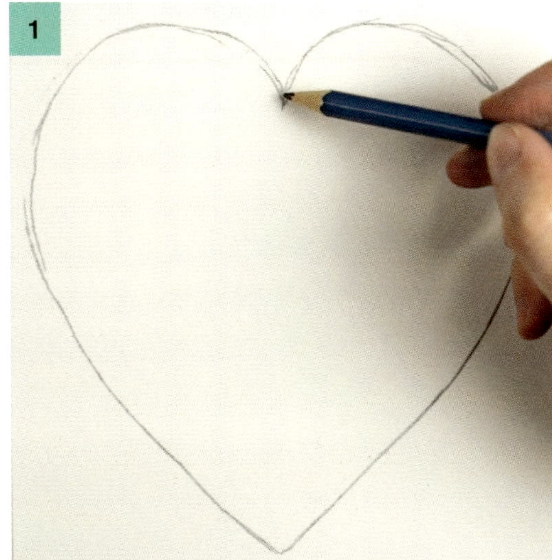

Start by lightly sketching a heart using a pencil. You will be erasing this later, so you don't want the line to be too dark.

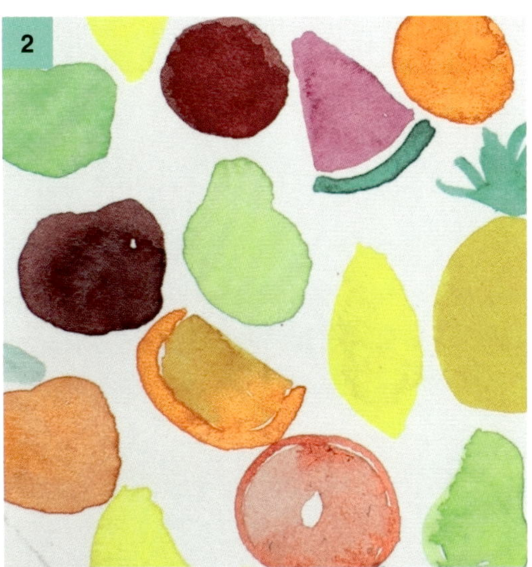

Using a small round brush, start filling in the heart shape with some of your larger illustrations. Don't worry about grouping them close together.

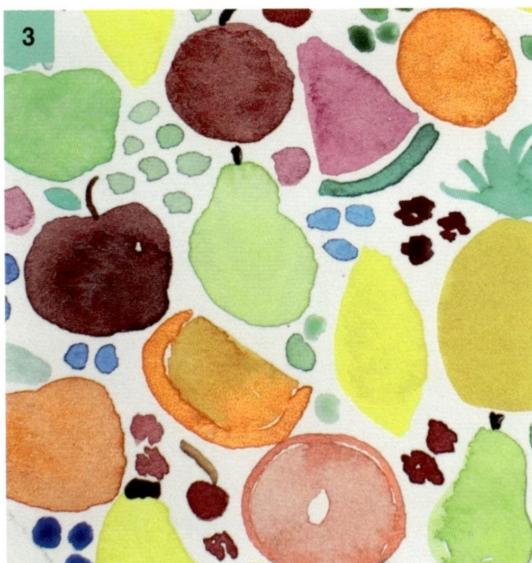

Now fill in all those gaps with smaller illustrations or even just some random shapes. Be sure to get right up close to the pencil line.

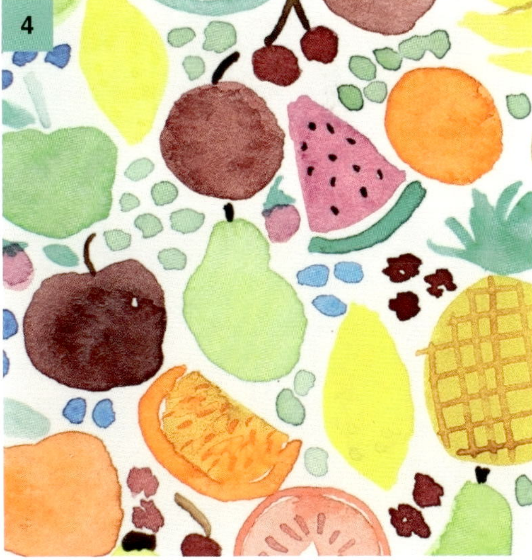

Add detail to your piece with a small liner brush and some black pen accents where it makes sense. Don't forget to erase the pencil line.

4

Pulling it all together

Are you over the fear of the blank page yet? Well, to tell you the truth, that never really goes away! However, these next exercises will help you fill an entire sketchbook and develop your creative confidence even further. We all have our strengths and weaknesses as artists, and I want to show you how to play to your strengths and start developing your own style. My hope is that you will finish this book filled to the brim with creative ideas and energy to keep painting. We will even be creating pieces for displaying in your own home and for gift-giving, so you can share your talents with the world.

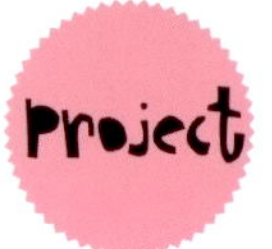

Create a colorful jungle

Imagine you are in a sensuous, multicolored jungle. Look up at the treetops and see the different kinds of leaves and branches overlapping to create a canopy, with spots of sunlight peeking through. This painting recreates that canopy while showing off the beautiful way that watercolor can layer.

YOU WILL NEED

- Watercolor paper or pad
- Watercolor paint
- Sticky tape (optional)
- Large round brush
- Small round brush

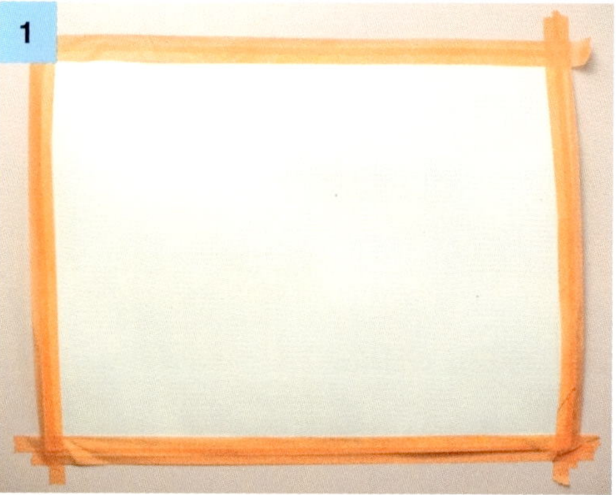

Start by taping the paper to your work surface, or use a watercolor pad that is gummed on the sides, to prevent the paper from curling.

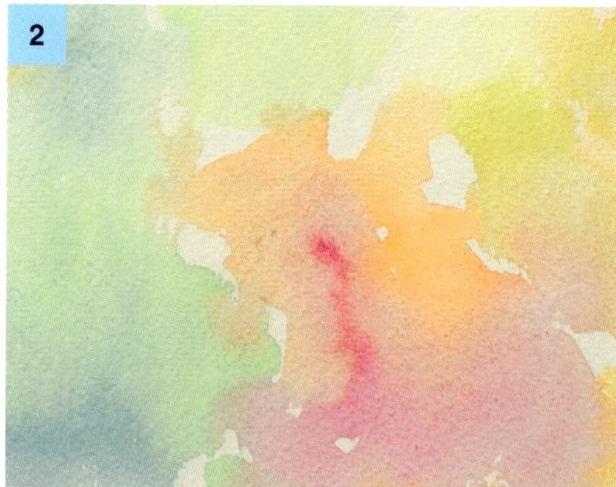

Next, create a base layer of bright colors using a large round brush. Work loosely and let everything blend. Keep some parts of the page white.

Once the first layer is dry, remove the tape if using and paint some large leaves all around the outside of the page with a small round brush. Use paint that has been watered down a bit so it is easier to layer.

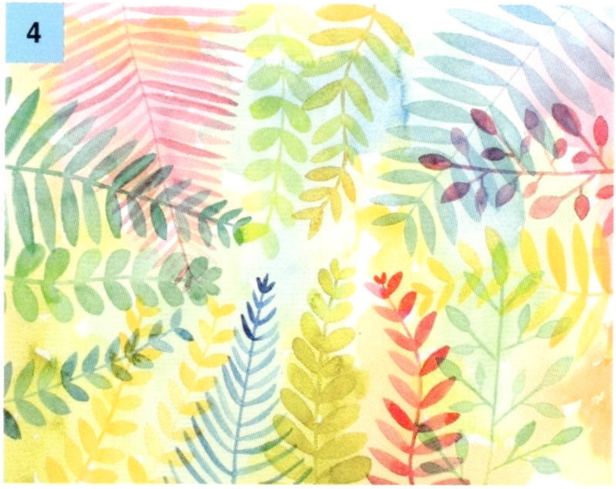

Continue painting leaves and branches so they all begin to overlap. Keep working until you are happy with your jungle.

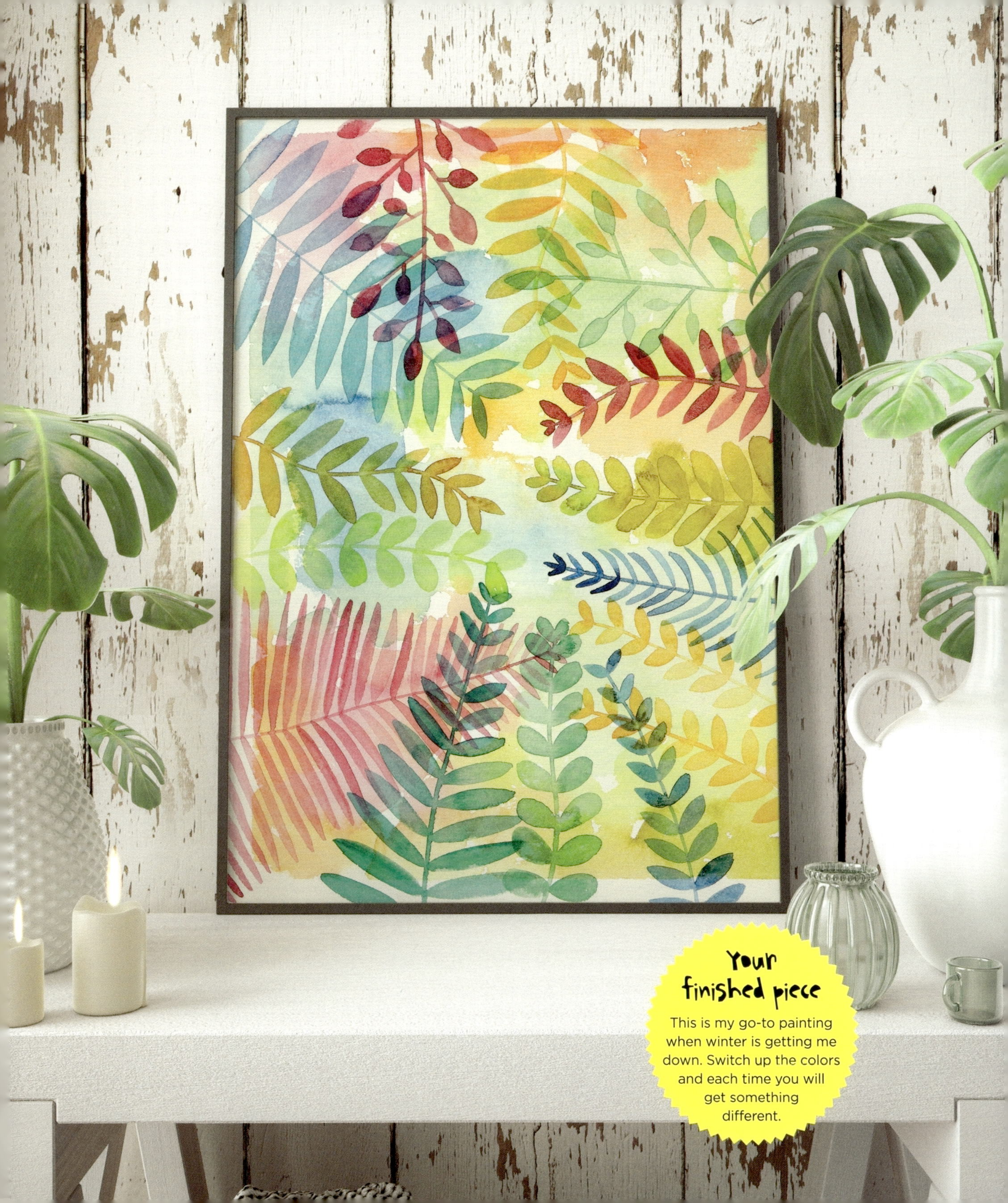

Your finished piece

This is my go-to painting when winter is getting me down. Switch up the colors and each time you will get something different.

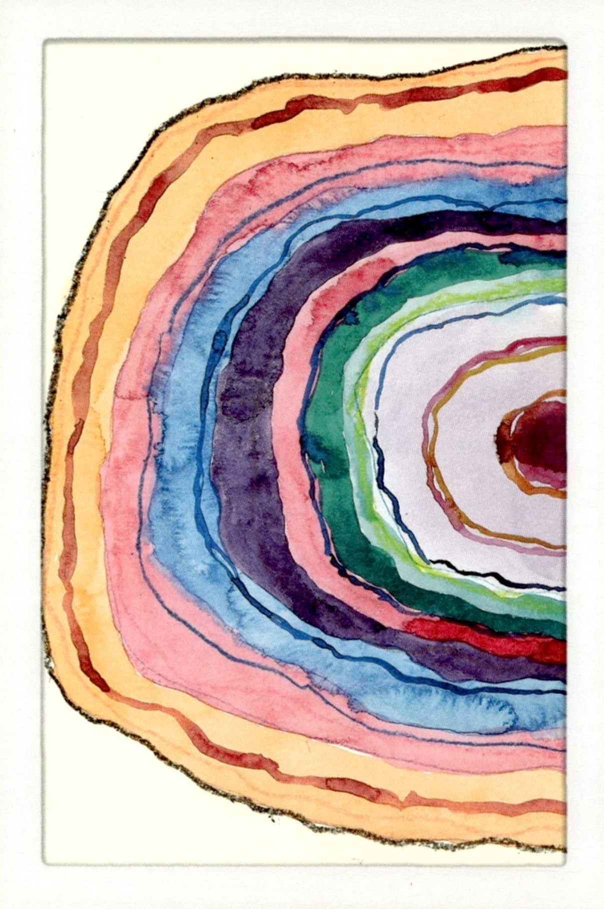

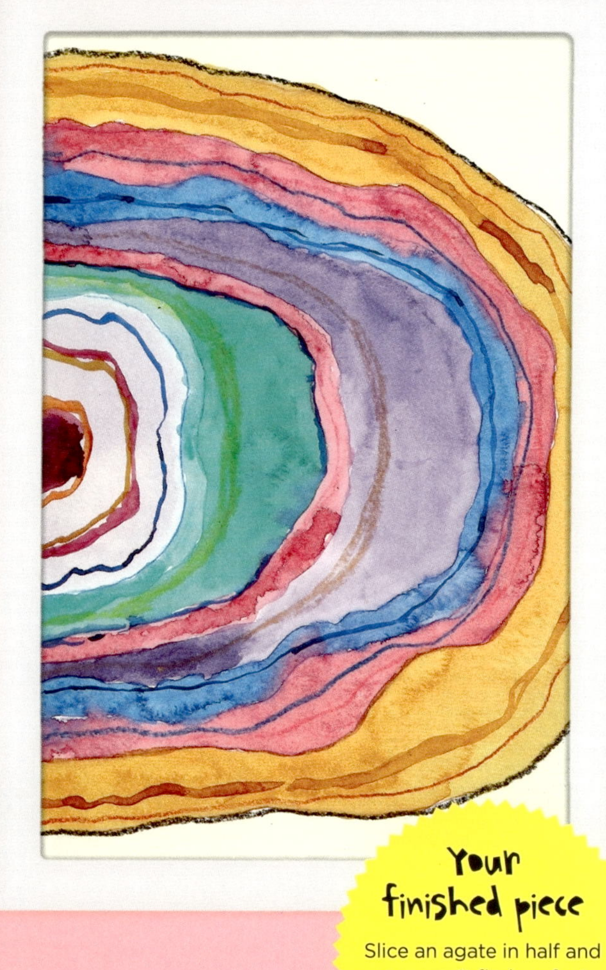

Your finished piece

Slice an agate in half and you won't find perfect circles. Hold the brush loosely to copy those wavy, natural lines.

Project Compose an agate diptych

Why not just paint some circles and then cut the sheet in half? Well, that would be the easy way. I like to think of these paintings as sisters, not twins. When you paint each half separately, you can make slightly different color choices and create two unique pieces of art that complement each other.

YOU WILL NEED

- Watercolor paper
- Watercolor paint
- Sticky tape
- Pencil
- Large round brush
- Small round brush
- Wax crayons

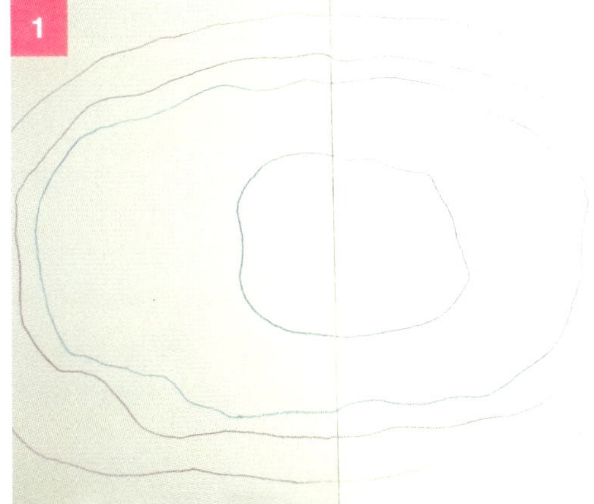

1

Start by taping two sheets of watercolor paper together. Draw some wobbly circles that span both sheets of paper using a pencil.

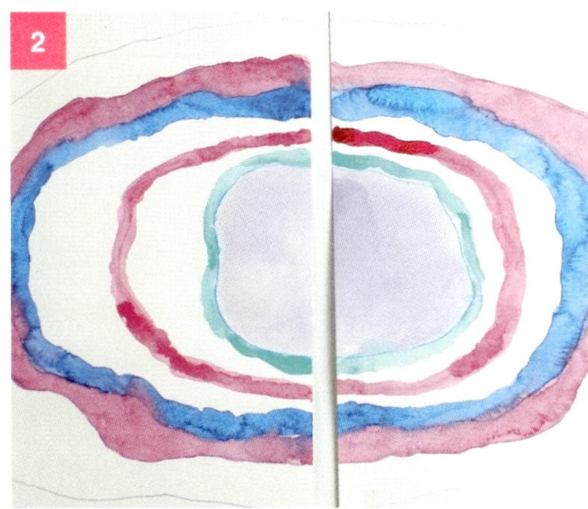

2

Remove the tape and fill in some of the larger areas with paint using the large round brush. Let some sections bleed together.

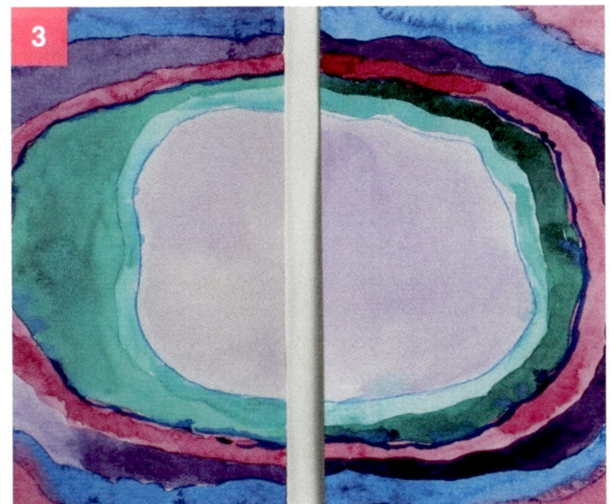

3

Once the first layer is dry, fill in the rest of the white space. Choose slightly different colors for each half, so each painting is unique.

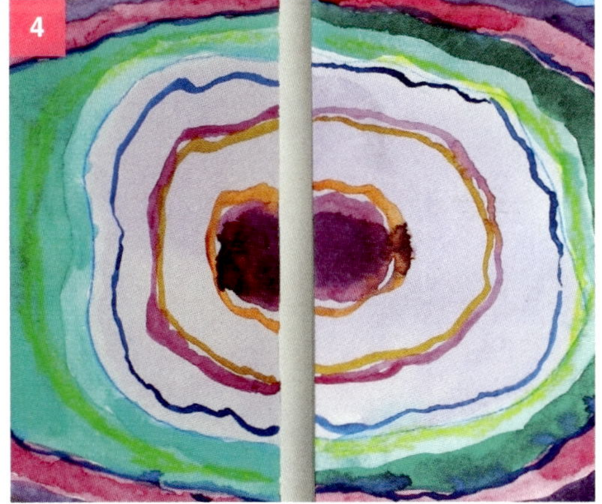

4

Now use the small round brush to add some small, wiggly lines for detail. You want the picture to resemble something found in nature, so avoid smooth lines. Add some wax-crayon lines for a rough texture.

Project Custom alphabet

Start with a reference alphabet that you will use as your guide. I typed the whole alphabet using a font I liked, then printed it out so I could trace it onto my watercolor paper. Once you have that base, you can do anything you like, so use your imagination!

YOU WILL NEED

- Watercolor paper
- Watercolor paint
- Watercolor paint
- Reference alphabet
- Pencil
- Eraser
- Small round brush
- Fine liner brush, gouache, or pens

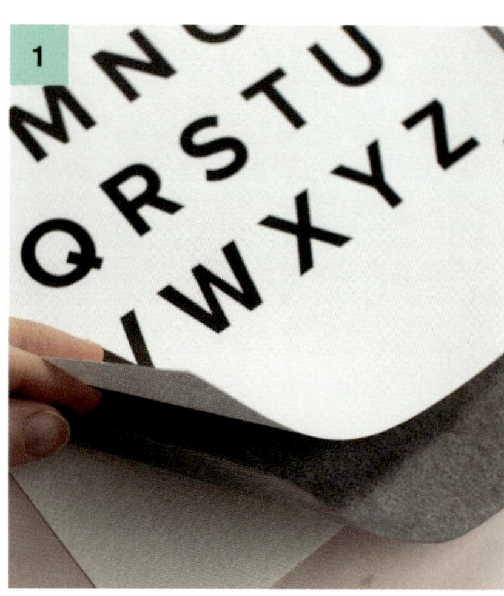

Sandwich a sheet of carbon paper in between your watercolor paper and alphabet, and trace the letters. Keep a light touch and erase any lines you don't want.

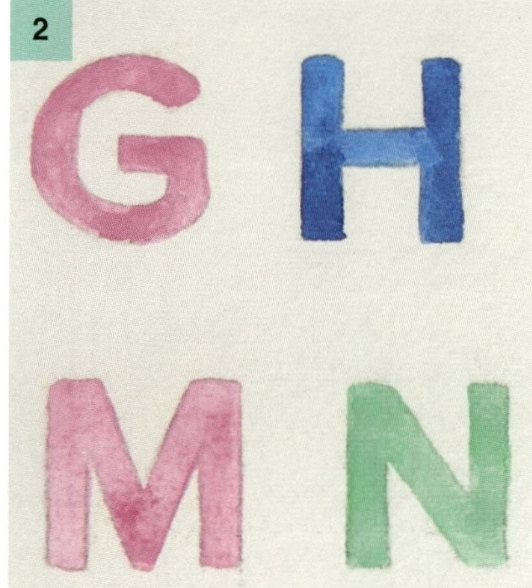

Fill in the letters with paint using a small round brush. You can keep every letter the same color or come up with a color palette. Play with the shape of the letters to make them your own or just fill them in.

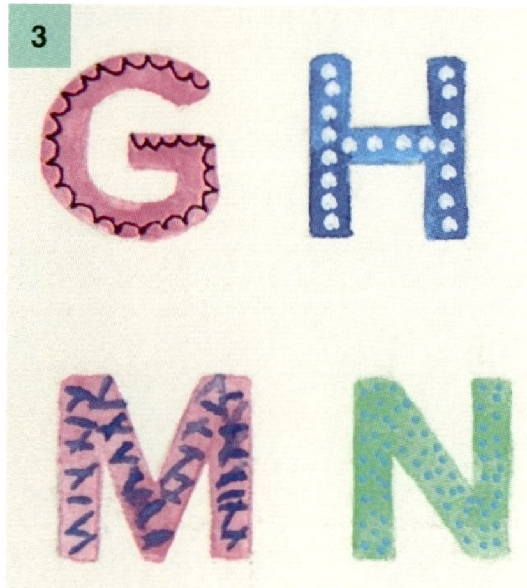

Once your first layer is dry, add detail to your alphabet with a liner brush, gouache, or pens. Make each letter unique or keep a uniform look.

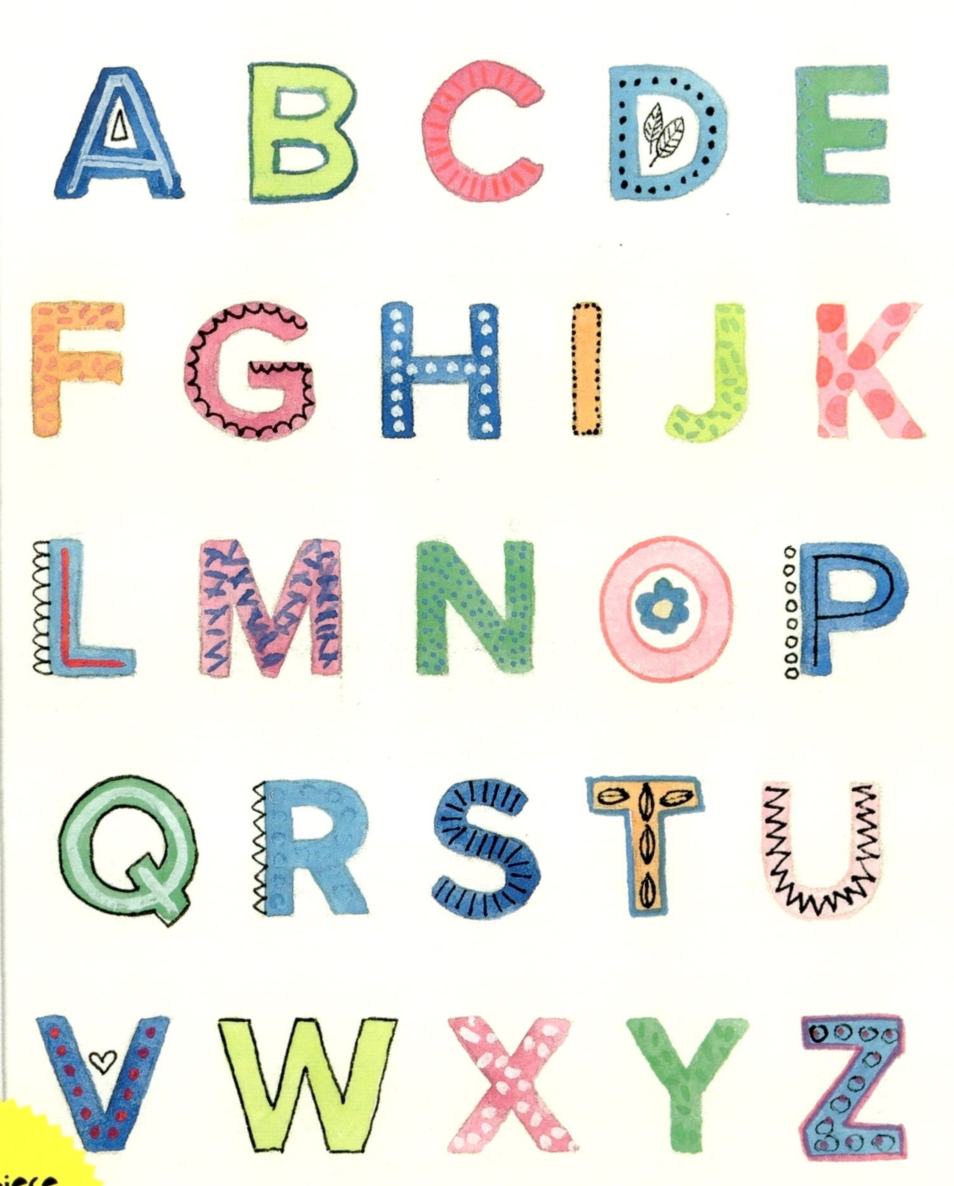

Your finished piece

Customize the alphabet to suit anyone's interest. Use food for someone who loves to cook, or plants for the gardener in your life.

Project Paint a mandala

Mandalas are abstract designs in a circular form. They can be very complex and precisely measured or much less structured, like this one. But they all have one thing in common: they all start with a dot in the center of the page; each new element is built upon that dot and grows from there.

YOU WILL NEED

- Watercolor paper
- Watercolor paint
- Pencil

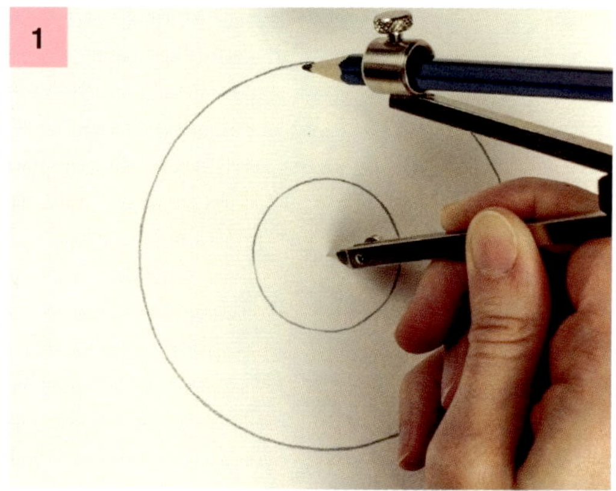

1 Draw some light circles on the page that you can use as a guide. Use a compass or just trace around some circular objects.

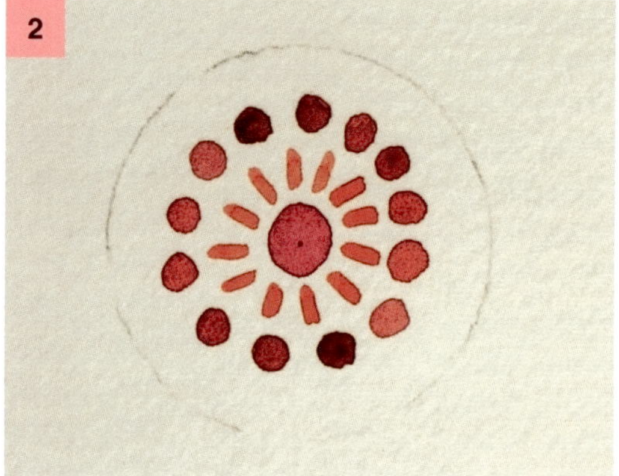

2 Every mandala starts with a dot. Place yours in the very center of your circle so you can build on it later. Make some simple marks around your dot. They can be dashes, dots, scallops—anything you want.

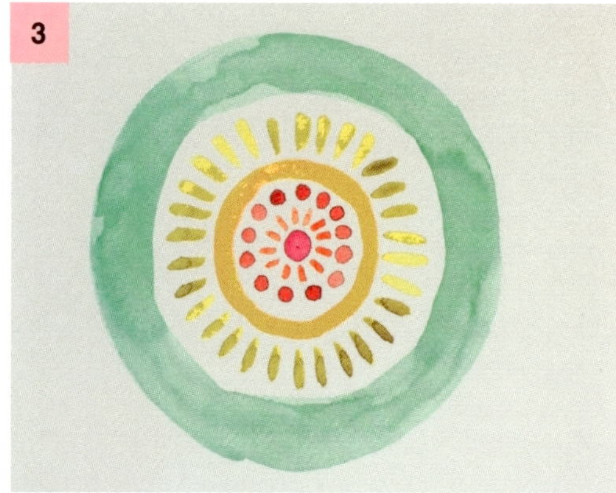

3 Continue to build your marks. I like to fill some areas with color so I can add more detail later.

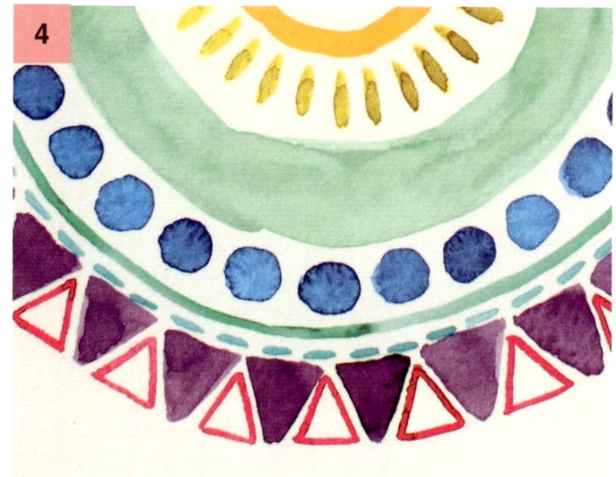

4 Keep building your mandala one mark at a time until you reach the outer edge. Once the page is dry, add a few more details before deciding if your painting is finished.

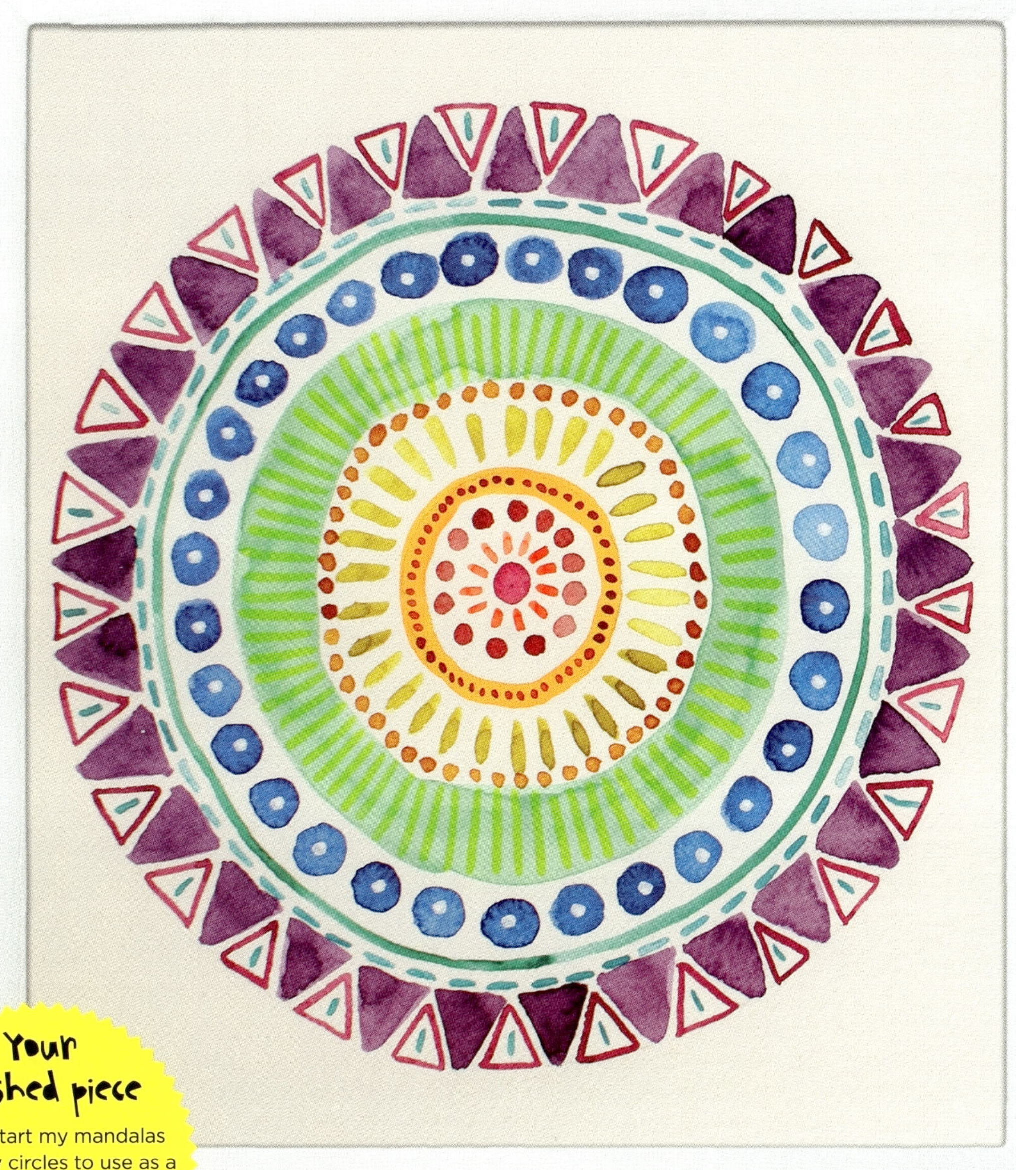

Your finished piece

I like to start my mandalas with a few circles to use as a guide. It helps to keep me on track. You can add more guides if you like or just wing it.

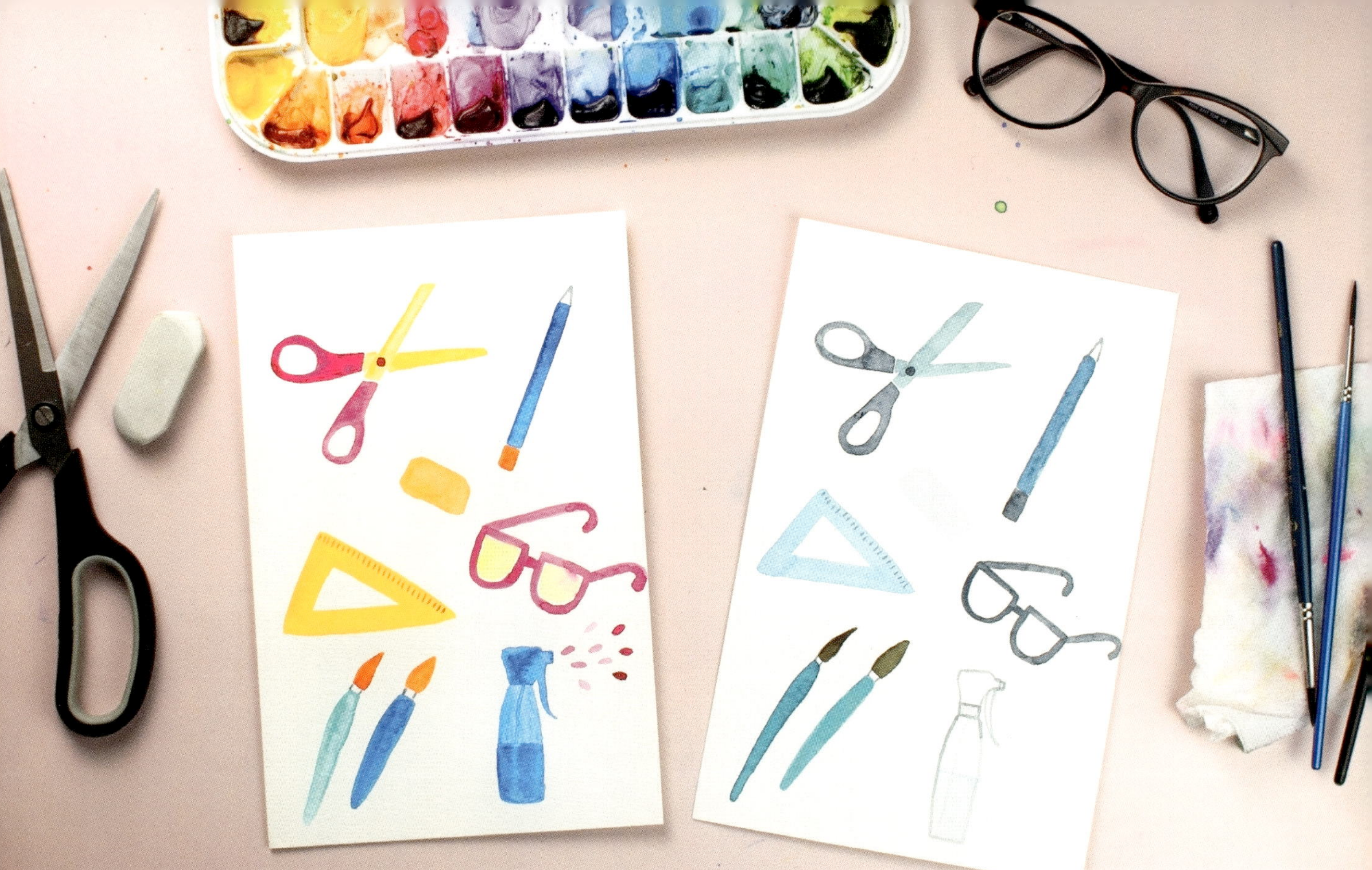

prompt Unexpected color choices

A surprising color choice can turn just about any painting into something special. A green tree is nice, but a pink tree is especially eye-catching. Everyone knows apples are red and green, but how about painting a blue apple? Choosing unusual colors for your piece can open up multiple possibilities.

Painting what I see around me is how I get most of my ideas, but painting exactly what you see in real life can get a little boring! Or at least, I think so. Sometimes when I am painting something that is a little ordinary, I pick unusual colors to give it more interest.

Color can dramatically change a piece of art, so why not give this exercise a go? Grab two sheets of watercolor paper and your paint palette. On the first page, paint some items that are on your desk or around you. Just regular, everyday objects. When choosing colors, try to pick ones that are true to what you see. Now get your second sheet of paper and paint the same objects, but this time choose unexpected colors. Don't worry if they don't look realistic; that is the point! Keep in mind the color theory you learned earlier in the book and choose colors that sing when placed next to each other.

So which painting do you like best? I am sure they both have good qualities, but chances are your eyes are drawn to the one with the unusual colors.

Play Keep an experimental sketchbook

Keeping a sketchbook is an important practice for any artist. You can show it to other people, but I like to keep mine private. It gives me a place to experiment without worrying about the outcome.

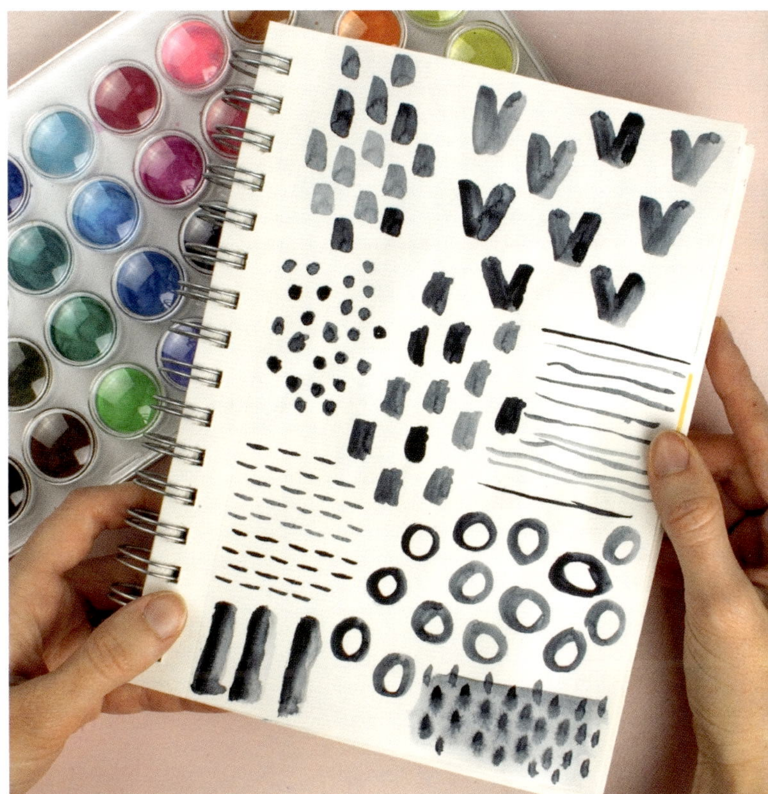

High-quality watercolor paper and paint can be expensive. This leads to every sheet of paper and every drop of paint becoming precious. And, if you are always worried about ruining a new sheet of paper, you will never paint anything!

That is why I always have a messy experimental sketchbook on the go. It is usually a mid-range, mixed-media sketchbook that isn't specifically for watercolor paint, which makes it much cheaper than watercolor paper. In addition, I love to use an inexpensive craft store (or even dollar store) paint palette. You obviously won't get the same results as with thick, expensive paper and high-quality tube paints, but what you do get is the freedom to try new things and make mistakes. You can fill a page with random marks or practice painting the same flower a hundred times. This cheap little sketchbook will prove to be well beyond its material worth.

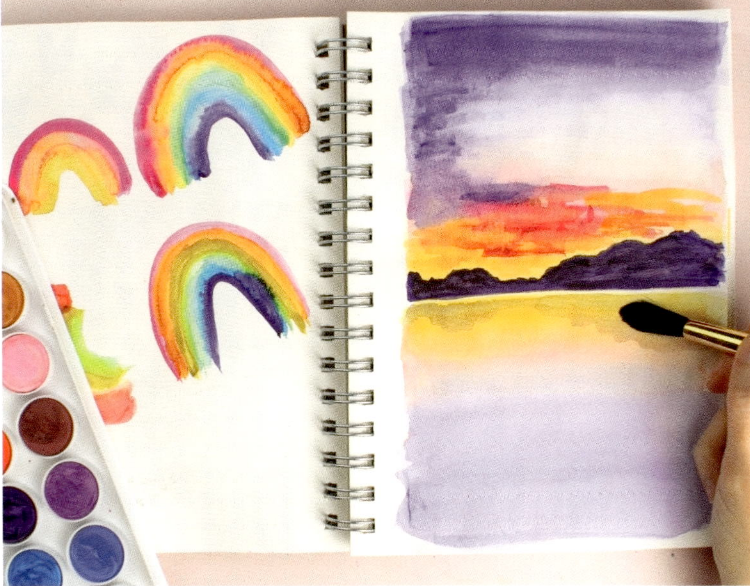

Personalized letter painting

Personalized monogram paintings can make wonderful gifts. Frame one and give it as a wedding gift, Mother's Day present, or a gift for a new baby. Switch up the color scheme and the flowers to personalize it further.

YOU WILL NEED

- Watercolor paper
- Watercolor paint
- Letter stencil (optional)
- Pencil
- Small round brush

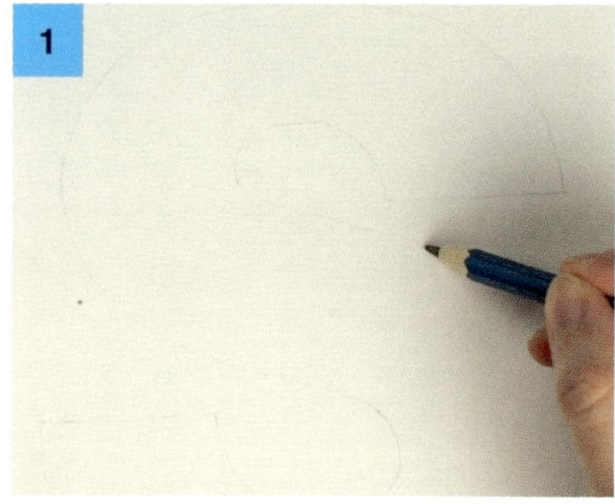

Start by sketching out a letter in pencil. Use a stencil or draw it freehand. Make sure the letter is fat enough to fit lots of flowers inside.

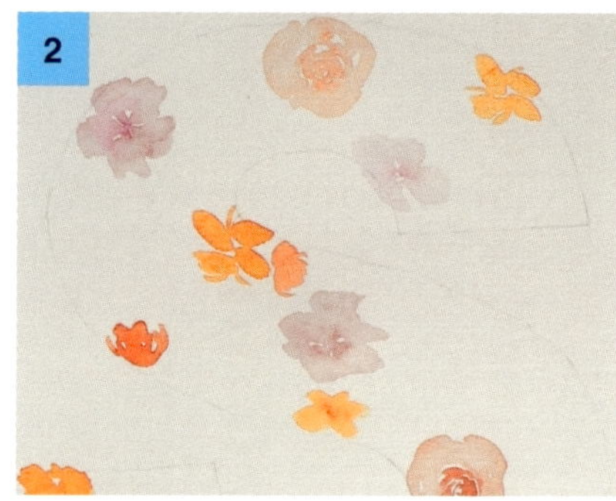

I like to start with the big flowers first so I can ensure they are evenly spaced. Using your small round brush, paint some flowers in two or three different colors.

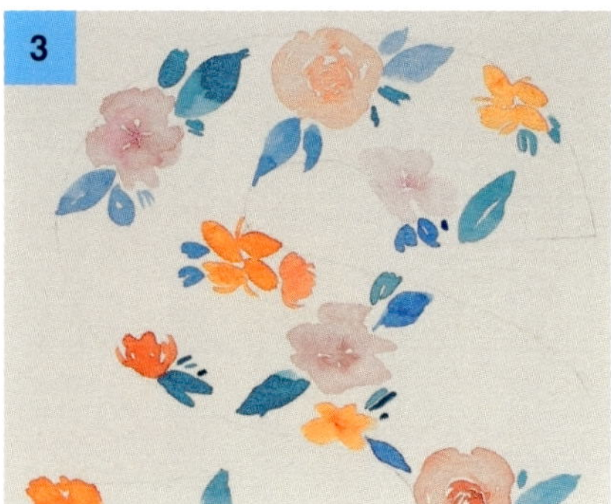

Add some large leaves to go with those statement flowers.

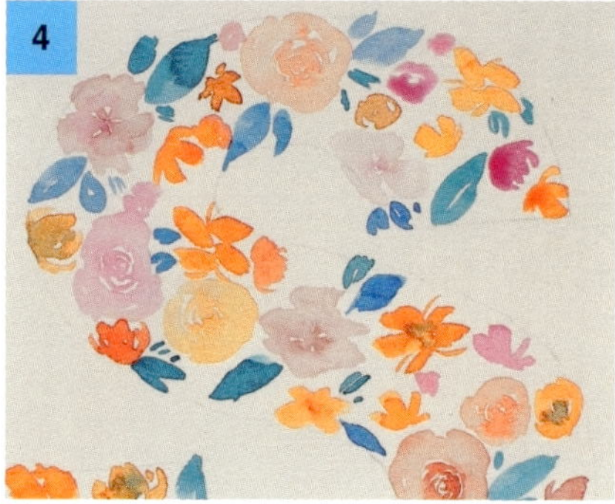

Next, add smaller flowers and smaller leaves to fill in some of the gaps. You can switch to a smaller brush or keep working with the small round brush.

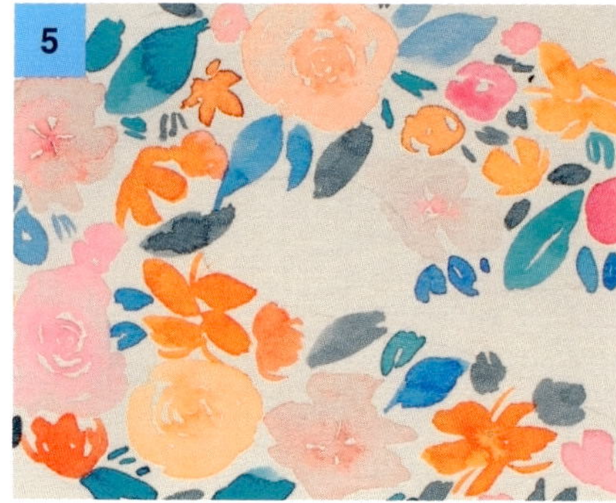

Fill any leftover white spaces with tiny flowers or small dashes to indicate a leaf. Don't be afraid to go over the pencil guide.

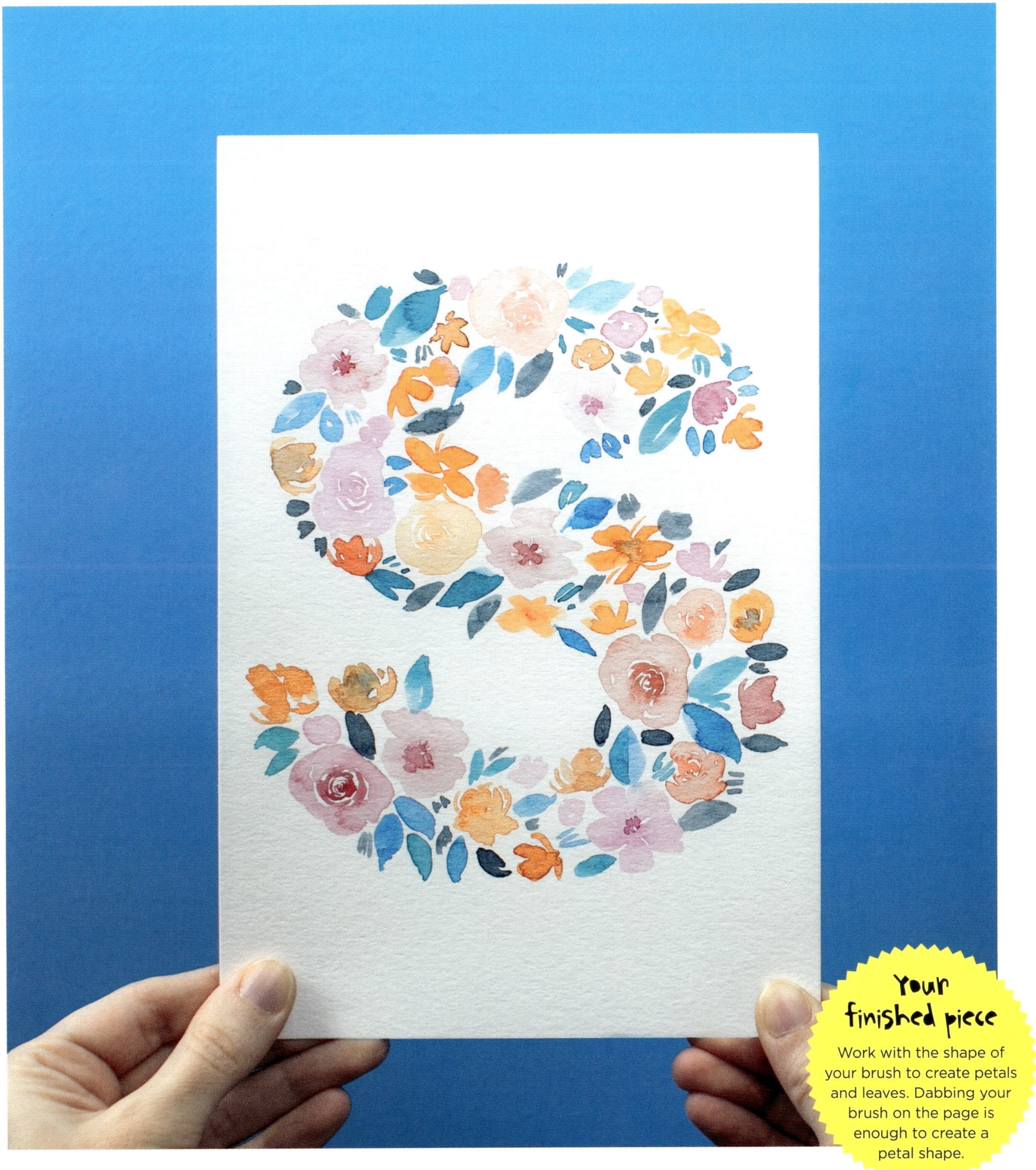

Your finished piece

Work with the shape of your brush to create petals and leaves. Dabbing your brush on the page is enough to create a petal shape.

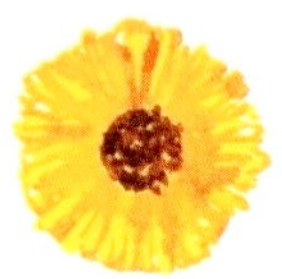
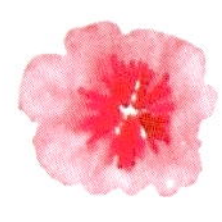
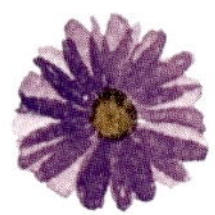
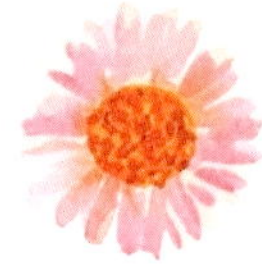
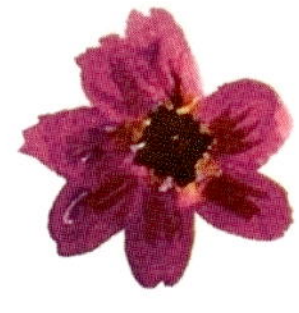
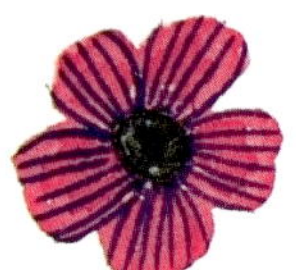

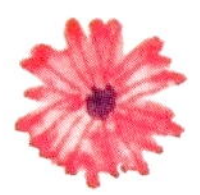

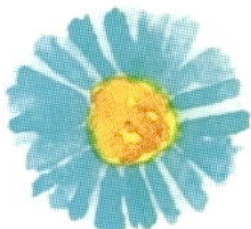
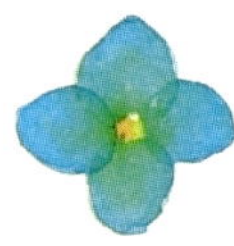
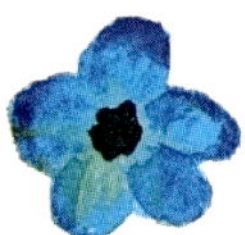
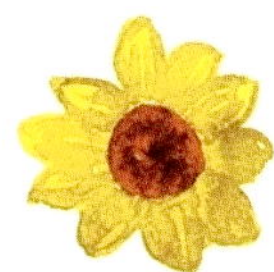

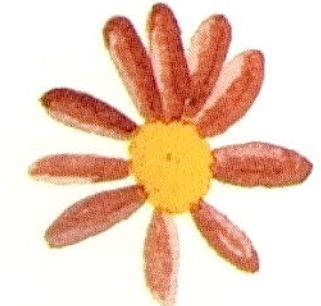

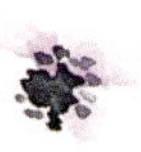
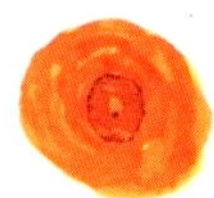

Your finished piece

The key to this painting is to keep a lot of white space around every flower so each one of them can stand alone.

Project Pressed-flower painting

This painting was inspired by delicate little pressed flowers I once found in a book. They were so tiny I had to look closely to see all the details. I love how the tiny flowers in this painting are spaced so far apart that they each have a chance to shine on their own, but all together they make a lovely pattern.

YOU WILL NEED

- Watercolor paper
- Watercolor paint
- Pencil
- Ruler
- Small round brush
- Small liner brush

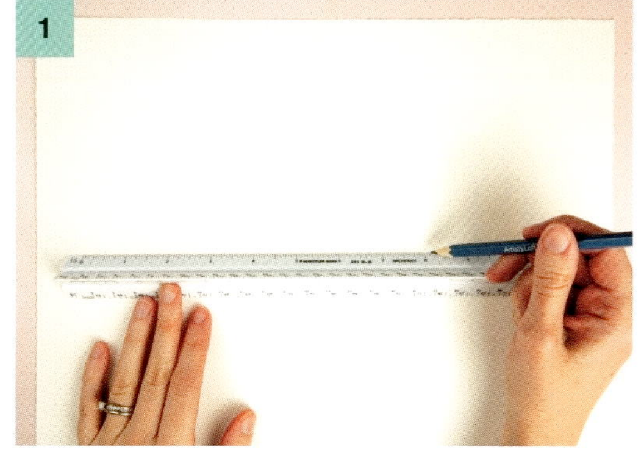

Make some small dots with a pencil equal distances apart from each other on the page. It might take a little math to get the number of dots right.

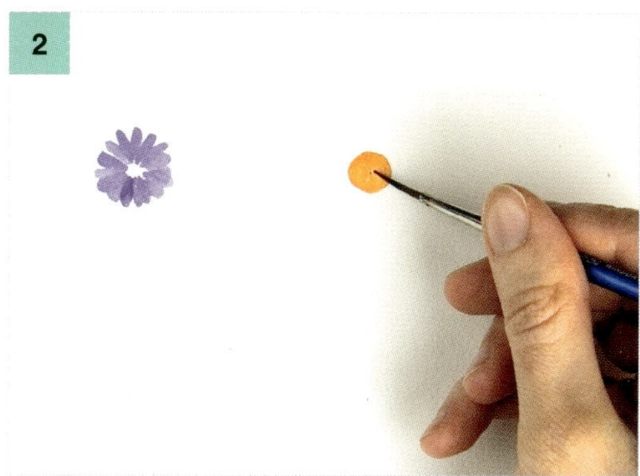

Once you have a dot grid on the page, start painting little flowers on each dot. If you are not sure how to begin, paint a small circle and grow the petals around it later.

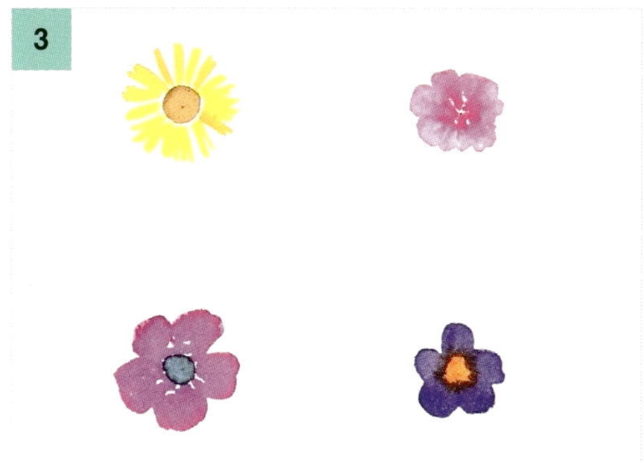

Continue filling the page with simple flower shapes. We will be adding some detail and depth in the next step, so don't worry if the painting looks flat.

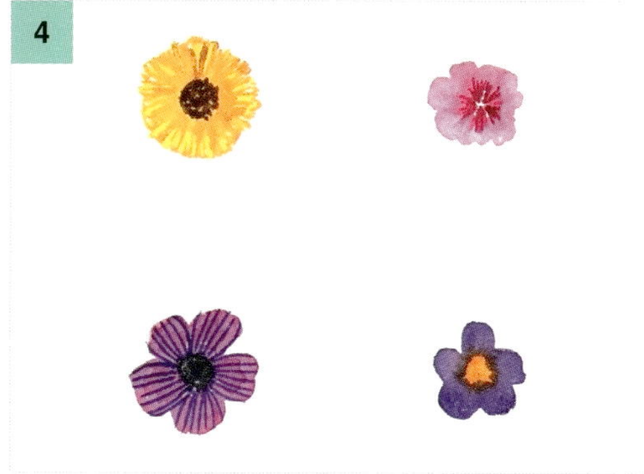

Revisit each flower individually and see where you can add some extra detail using the small liner brush. Sometimes you can add some shading to the petals or texture to the center of the flower.

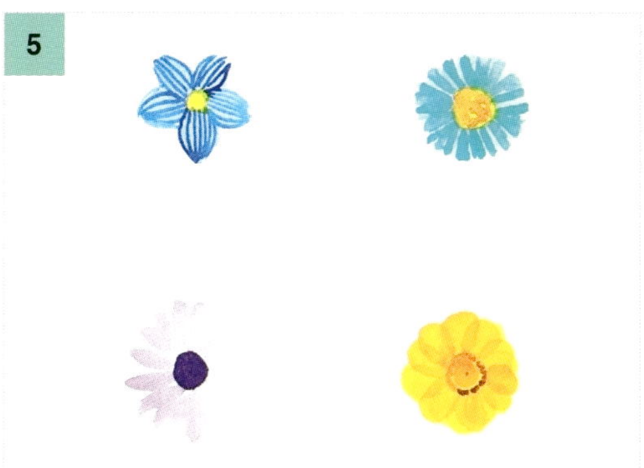

When you think you've finished, revisit each flower to see where you can add more depth.

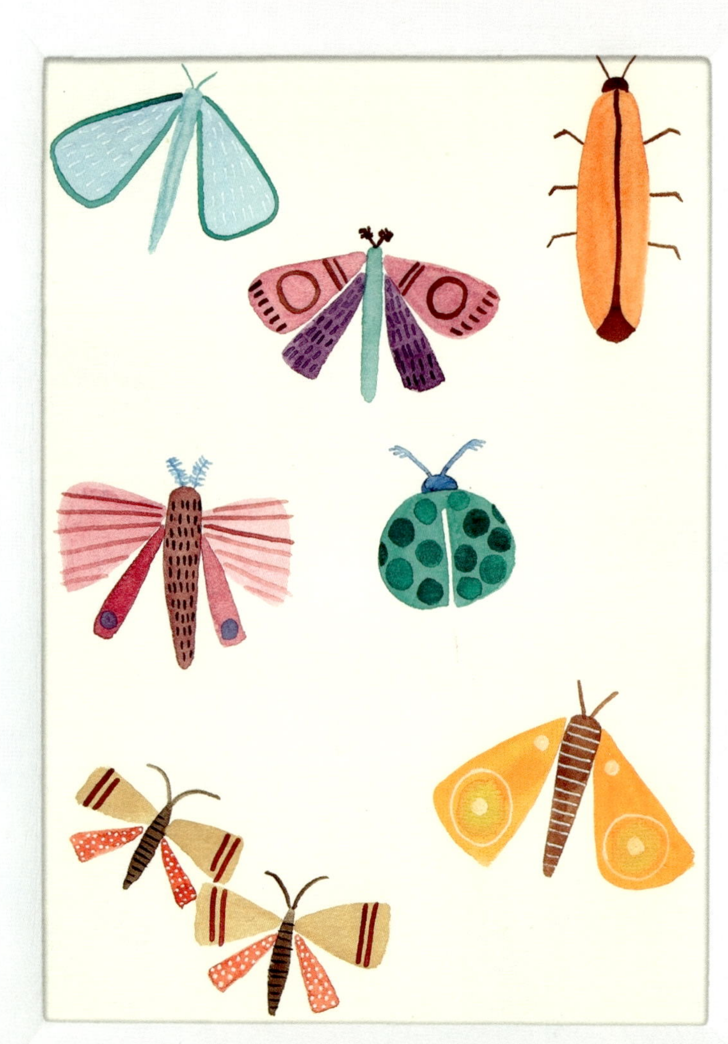

prompt

Beautiful bugs

Bugs creep me out, but anything can be made beautiful with bright watercolor paint! So even though I will never get near a bug in real life if I can help it, I love painting them. Bugs come in all shapes, sizes, and colors, so take your pick and let your creativity flow.

The reason bugs such as butterflies and moths are so fun to paint is that they are really forgiving. For this prompt, you only need to paint a cylinder for a bug body with some wings attached.

Then, paint some fun stripes, dashes, circles, or anything else you can think of to decorate your bugs. Don't be afraid to use some unusual colors. And bugs always seem to travel in groups (shudder), so make sure to paint a whole gathering of bug friends. With their pretty, polka-dot wings and striped bodies, I think I might actually like these little creepy crawlies!

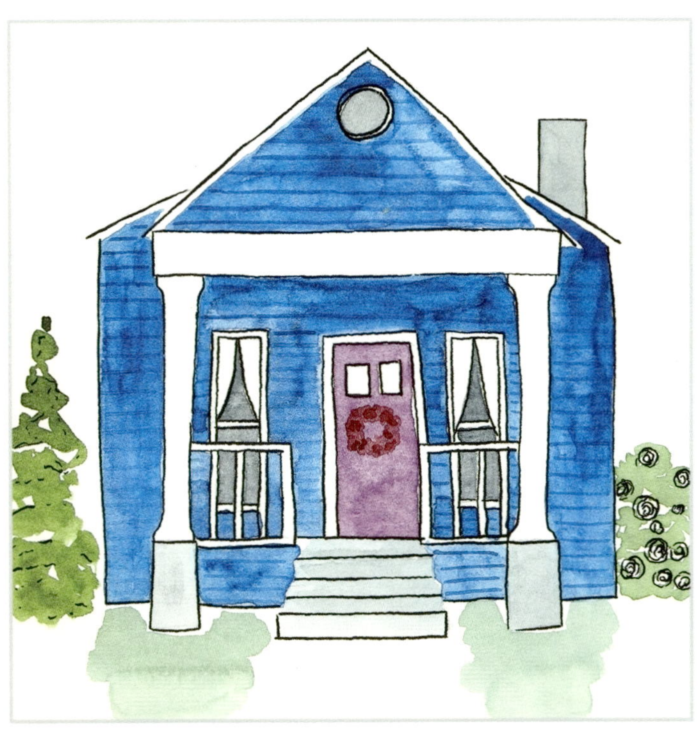

prompt Paint your dream house

Painting houses can be so soothing—it almost feels like you are building something. You can use a reference photo for this prompt or your imagination, and create your dream house from scratch.

I used to be intimidated by painting houses or buildings because I was overly concerned with perfecting every corner and detail. I soon realized that a wonky house is cuter than a straight one, and the secret to painting an interesting building is to pick out a few details you like and not to worry too much about the rest. If you focus on a couple of distinguishing features and put away your ruler, your painting will be full of personality.

For this type of painting, I like to start with a rough pencil drawing in my sketchbook. Once I get a feel for the house, I will lightly sketch it out with pencil on a sheet of watercolor paper. This way I know where everything will be placed ahead of time and I can plan my colors. Filling it all in with paint is the fun part. Have you always dreamed of a bright purple door? Choose any colors you like to bring your dream house to life.

The final step is to outline everything with a black pen and add some special details such as a wreath on the door or a rosebush in the side yard. Lose yourself in this painting!

Watercolor gems

Give your watercolor gems a natural look by using several different colors and shades. If your gem is yellow, try adding the colors from either side of the color wheel, such as green and orange. Texture and color variance will create depth, and painting each facet a different shade will make those gems pop off the page.

YOU WILL NEED

- Watercolor paper
- Watercolor paint
- Pencil
- Small round brush
- White gel pen

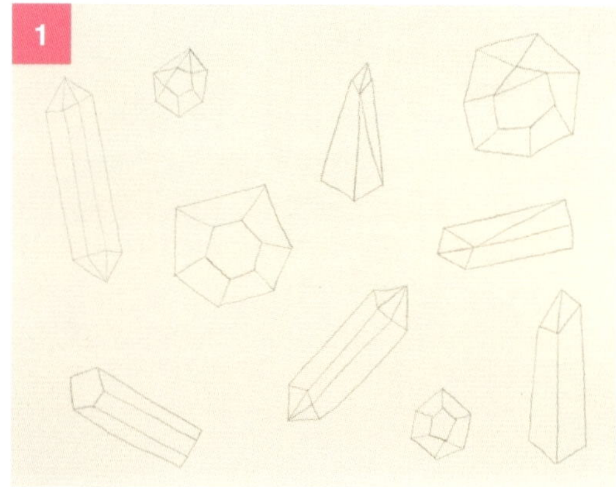

Start by drawing a variety of gems in pencil. If you are unsure what to draw, start with a multi-sided shape, then divide it into some triangles.

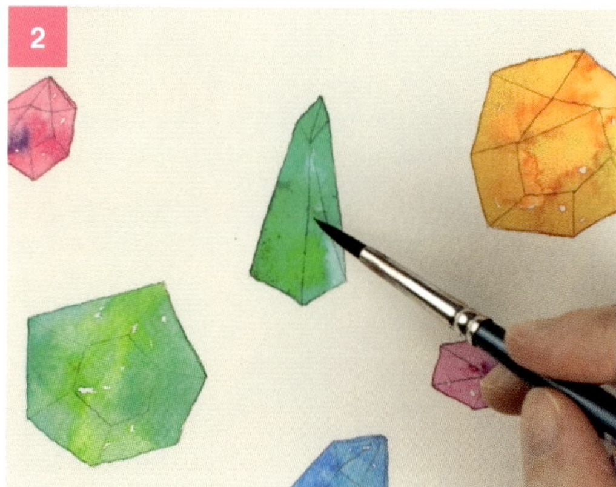

Next, paint a first layer of color, filling in the whole shape. Vary the shades, let it all blend together, and leave some white specks for a realistic look.

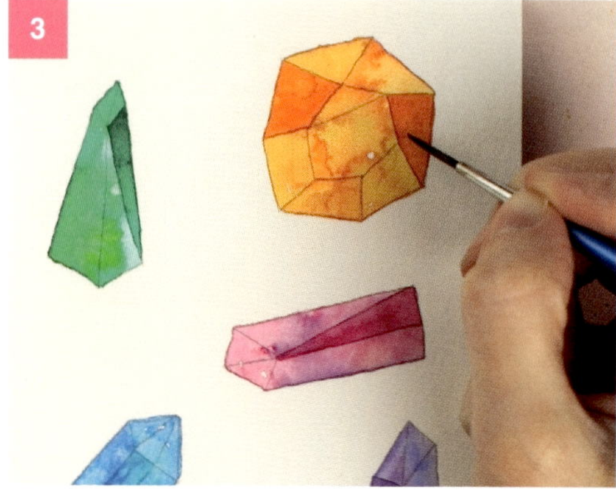

Once the first layer is dry, paint some of the facets of your gems in varying shades to create depth. Let them dry and do this a few times over if you want.

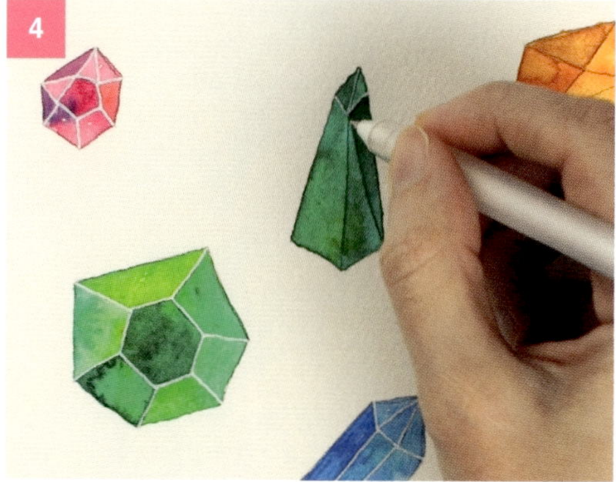

Now retrace the original pencil line with a white gel pen. Those are some lovely gems!

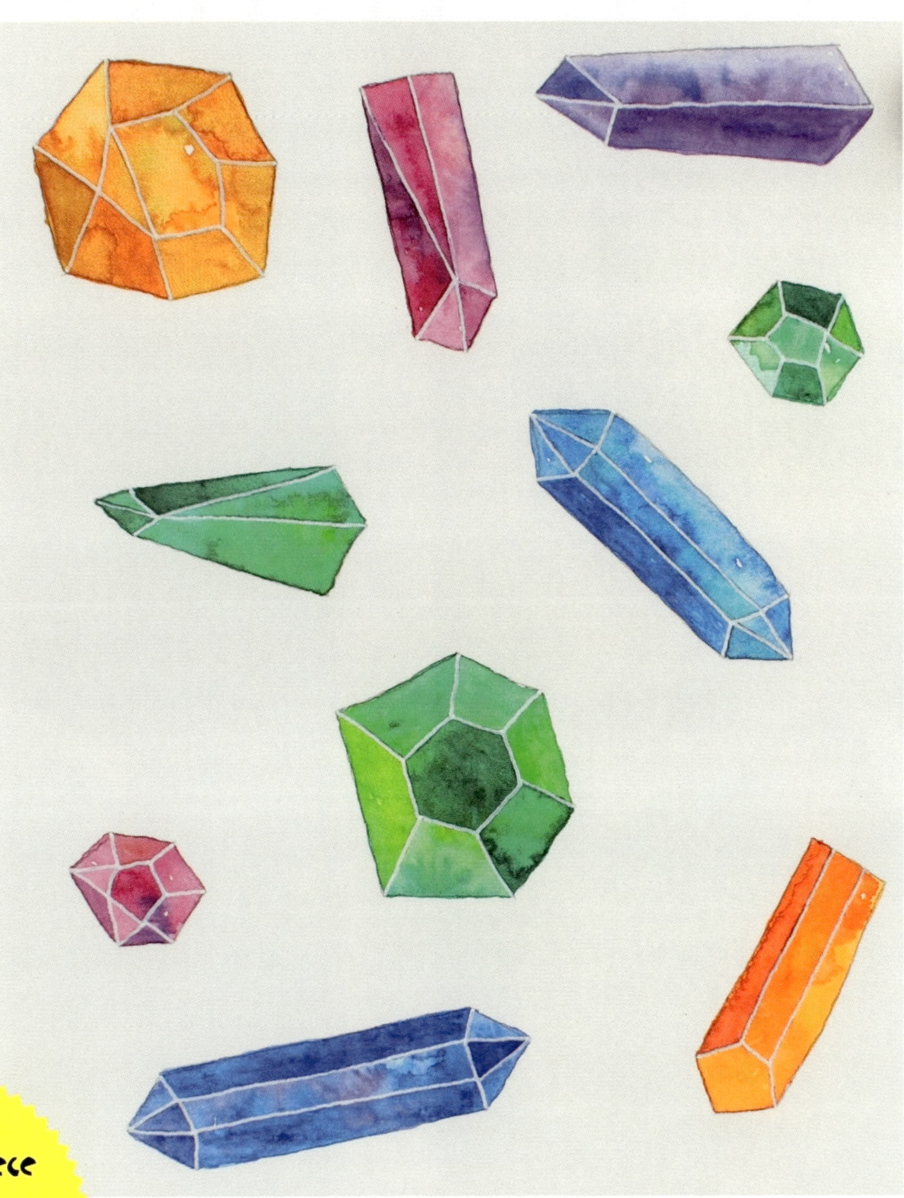

Your finished piece

Try painting a thin outline of your gem in masking fluid. Paint your gems as usual, then peel off the masking fluid after the paint is dry.

prompt Mini-landscape paintings

I adore landscape paintings, but this is a type of art that I struggle with. I am always looking for ways I can try my hand at landscapes while simplifying the process. The answer to my landscape woes is going miniature.

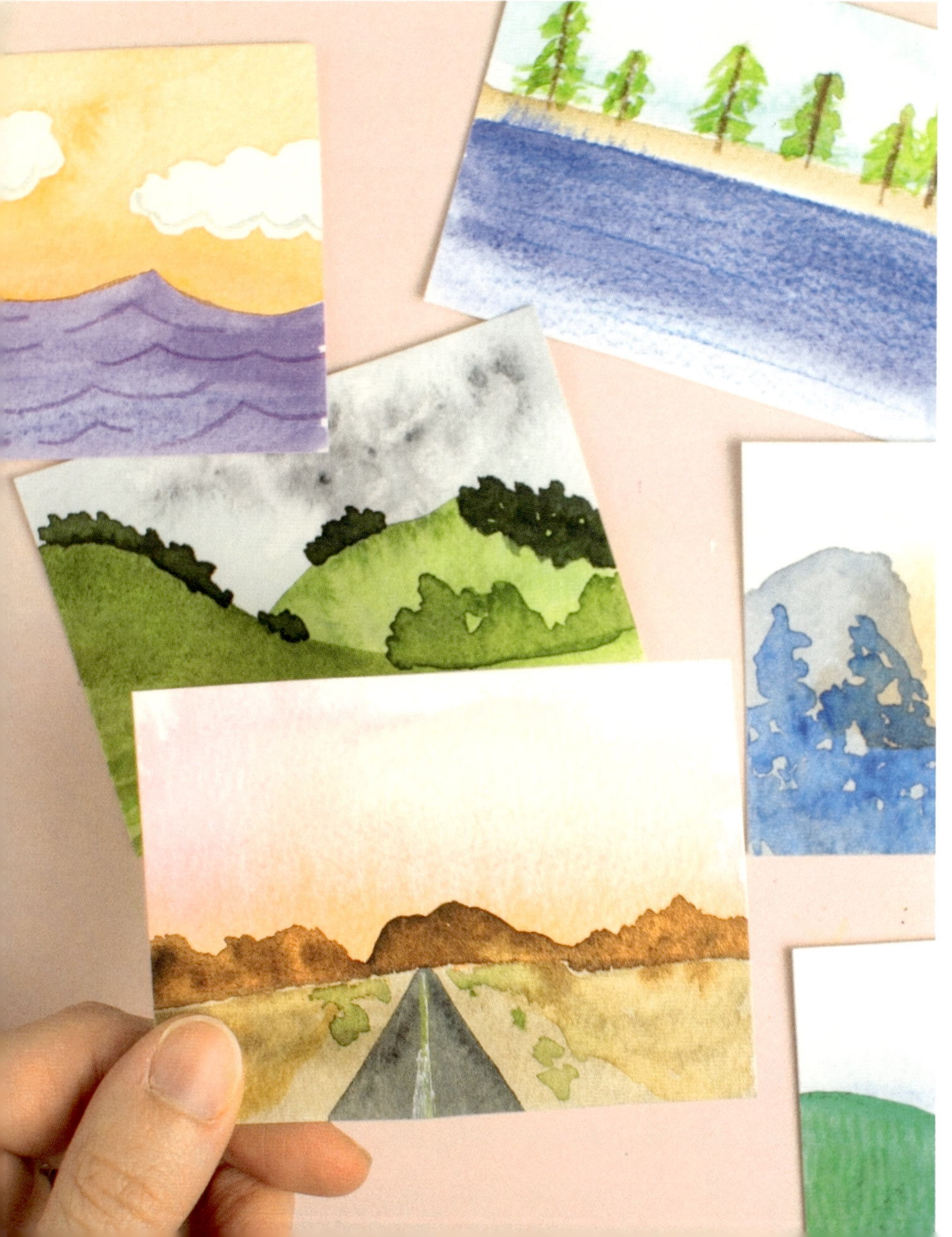

Adorable, tiny, unmistakably landscape paintings. How does that happen? There seems to be so little to each of the paintings, yet they all read as landscapes. Our brains are good at recognizing patterns, so when we see a horizon line and some sky, we automatically know what it is. You can, of course, add as much tiny detail as you want to these paintings and even switch up the colors.

I started by drawing some rectangles on a sheet of watercolor paper. I painted each landscape, let everything dry, and then cut out each painting. If you paint them all on a larger sheet of paper, they won't wrinkle as much, and the paint will end up going right to the edge. Most of these are worked in several layers—I painted a few at the same time so I could have something to do while the first ones were drying. It is possible to try out a whole range of landscapes in just a few minutes.

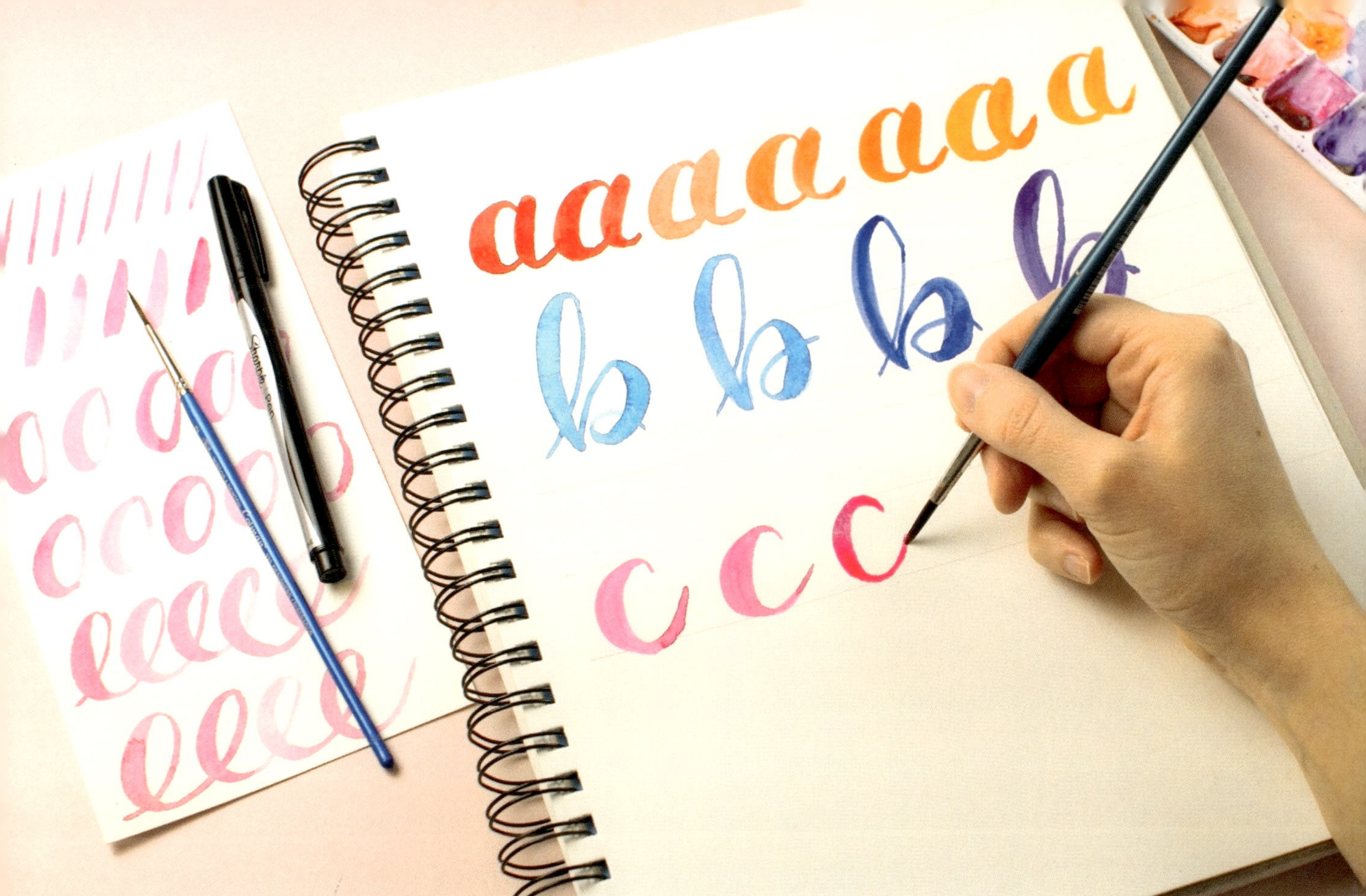

Play Flowy hand-lettering

A paintbrush and watercolor paint are the perfect tools for hand-lettering. The shape of the brush allows you that beautiful, thick-to-thin variation in your letters. Fair warning: it does take practice to master.

Before you even think about lettering some actual words, my advice would be to practice a few general shapes and brushstrokes first. This will help you get a feel for the art form. Each brush will feel a little different, and even the roughness of the paper can make a difference. I like to use a small or medium round brush with a good point.

The general rule is that downstrokes are thick and upstrokes are thin. So when you move your brush down the page, apply pressure for a thick line; when you are painting upward, ease up on the pressure for a thin line. Easy enough, right? It just takes practice.

Start by painting some thin upstrokes and some thick downstrokes. After that, you can move on to circles, C-shapes, and loops.

Once you have mastered the basics, you can move on to some actual letters. I like to draw some guidelines on the page in pencil so I can keep all my letters uniform. Going through the whole alphabet may seem laborious, but it is awesome practice and will also provide a reference for when you letter a whole quote.

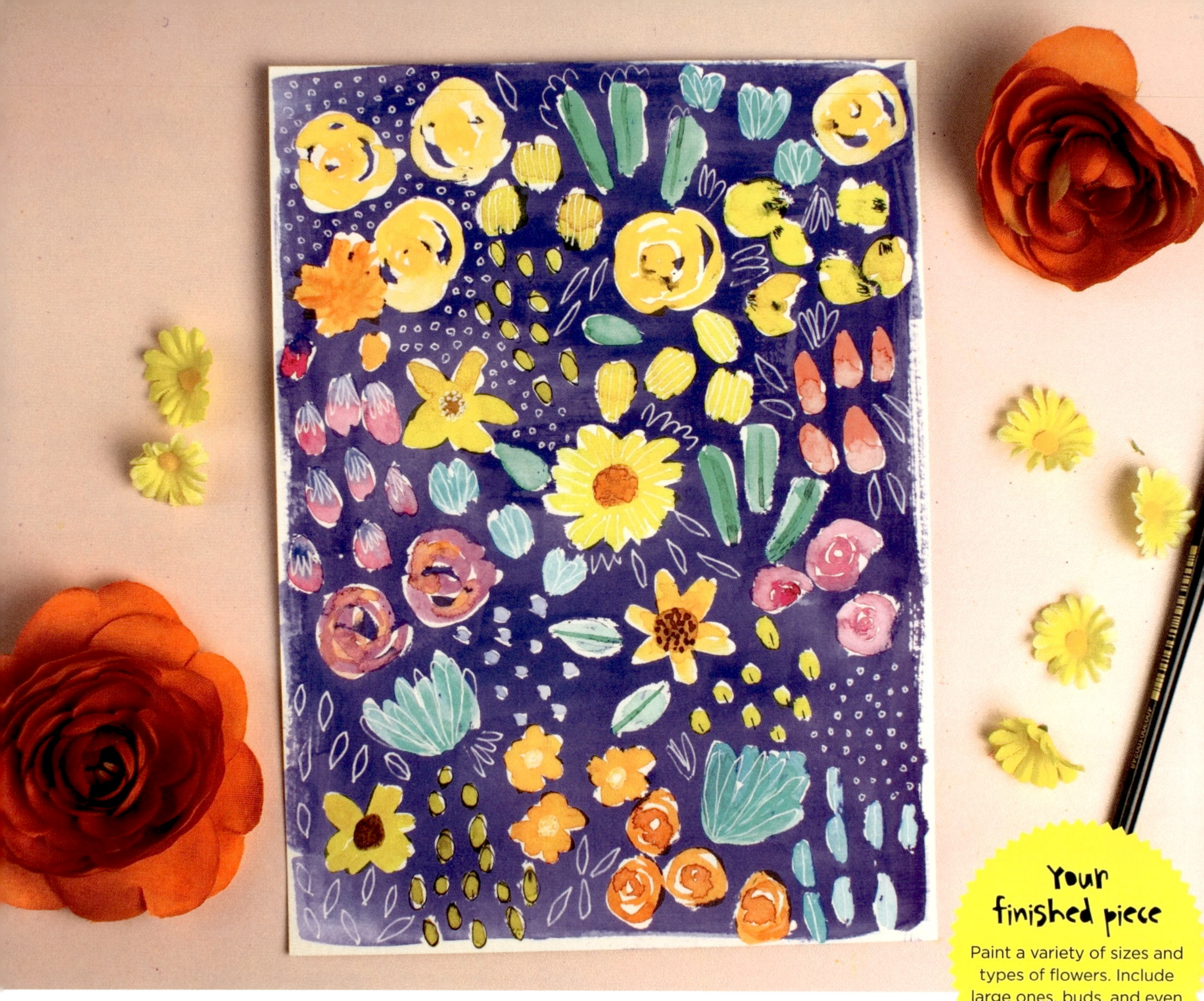

Your finished piece

Paint a variety of sizes and types of flowers. Include large ones, buds, and even some single petals.

Project Moody floral pattern

It is always a challenge to paint something with a dark background using watercolors. It normally involves a lot of careful planning and precise painting. That is why I love this project so much. You get a lot of spontaneity because the masking fluid is difficult to control—the messy look works well here.

YOU WILL NEED

- Watercolor pad or paper
- Watercolor paint
- Sticky tape (optional)
- Small round brush
- Medium flat brush
- Masking fluid
- Eraser (optional)

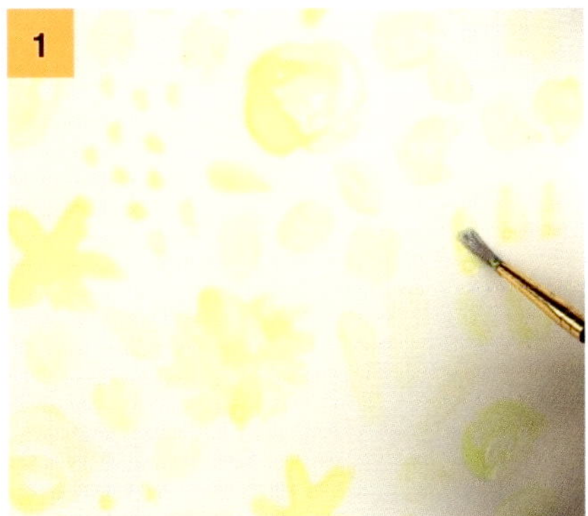

On a watercolor pad, use the small round brush to start painting some flower-like blobs all over the page with masking fluid. They really don't have to resemble flowers that much; embrace the messy look!

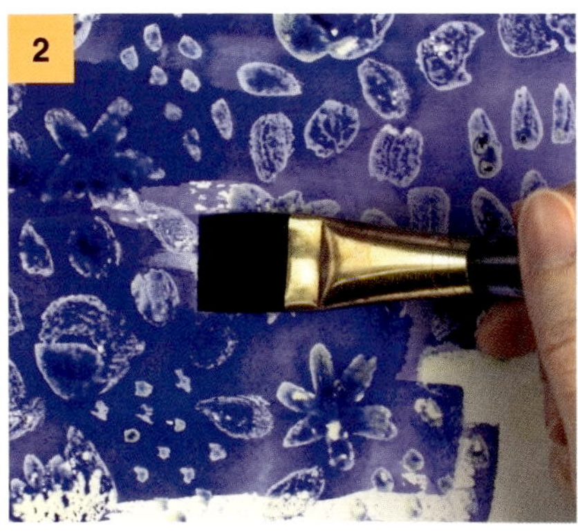

Once the masking fluid is dry, cover the page with a dark color using the medium flat brush. I used dark violet, but dark blue, green, or black would work just as well.

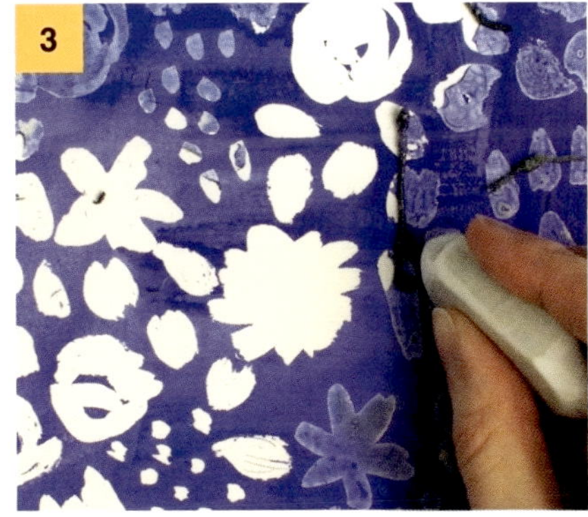

When the paint is completely dry, remove the masking fluid with an eraser or your fingers. Now you can see what you have to work with.

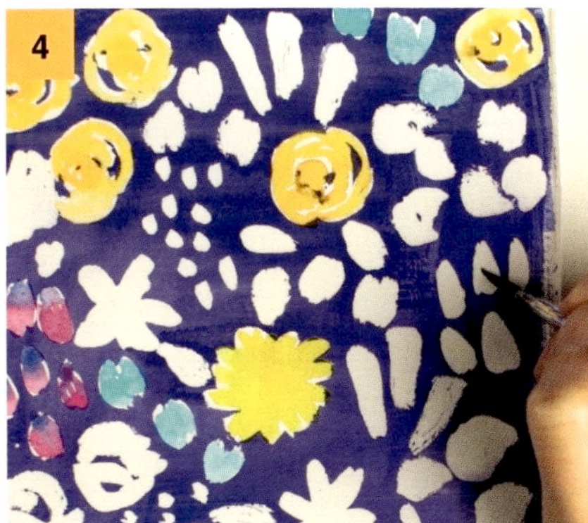

Start by filling in the white spaces with some color. Again, I love the messy look here so don't worry about being perfect: it will still read as floral.

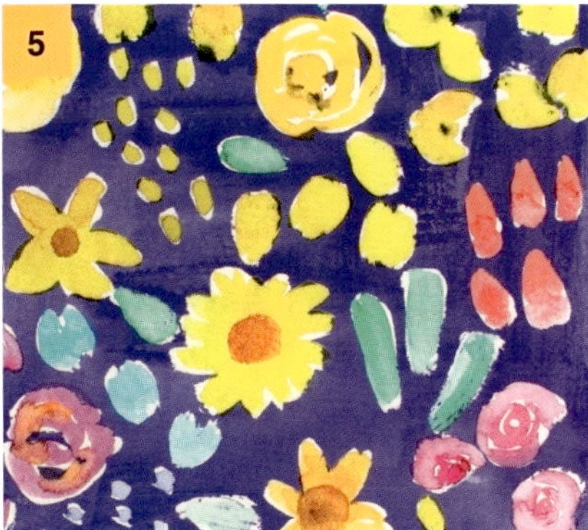

Continue filling in the white space with your flowers. You could even use a white gel or black pen to add a little more detail.

Prompt A record of your day

If you like the idea of keeping a journal but don't relish writing, this exercise could be a suitable alternative for you. You will be keeping a visual record of your entire day by sketching out and painting everything you did.

I have tried so many times to form the habit of keeping a journal, but it never seems to stick. It is much more appealing when I combine it with my love of art. When I look back on those pages, I can literally see the memories on paper. Some of my favorite ones are playing with my son or cooking a special dinner. This prompt is especially relevant while on vacation, because you will have some particularly treasured moments to paint.

You could bring out your sketchbook throughout the day to record each event as it happens, but I like to sit down before bed and sketch it all out then. I start by thinking about a few things that happened during the day which would make good paintings. They definitely don't have to be special things. It can be breakfast time, or an afternoon walk–look back on the everyday moments.

I start with a little pencil sketch to get everything laid out on the page and then I bring out my watercolor paints to add color. After it all dries, I like to outline everything in a black pen, but that is optional. Don't forget to add the date to the back of the paper, or even find a way to incorporate it into your painting.

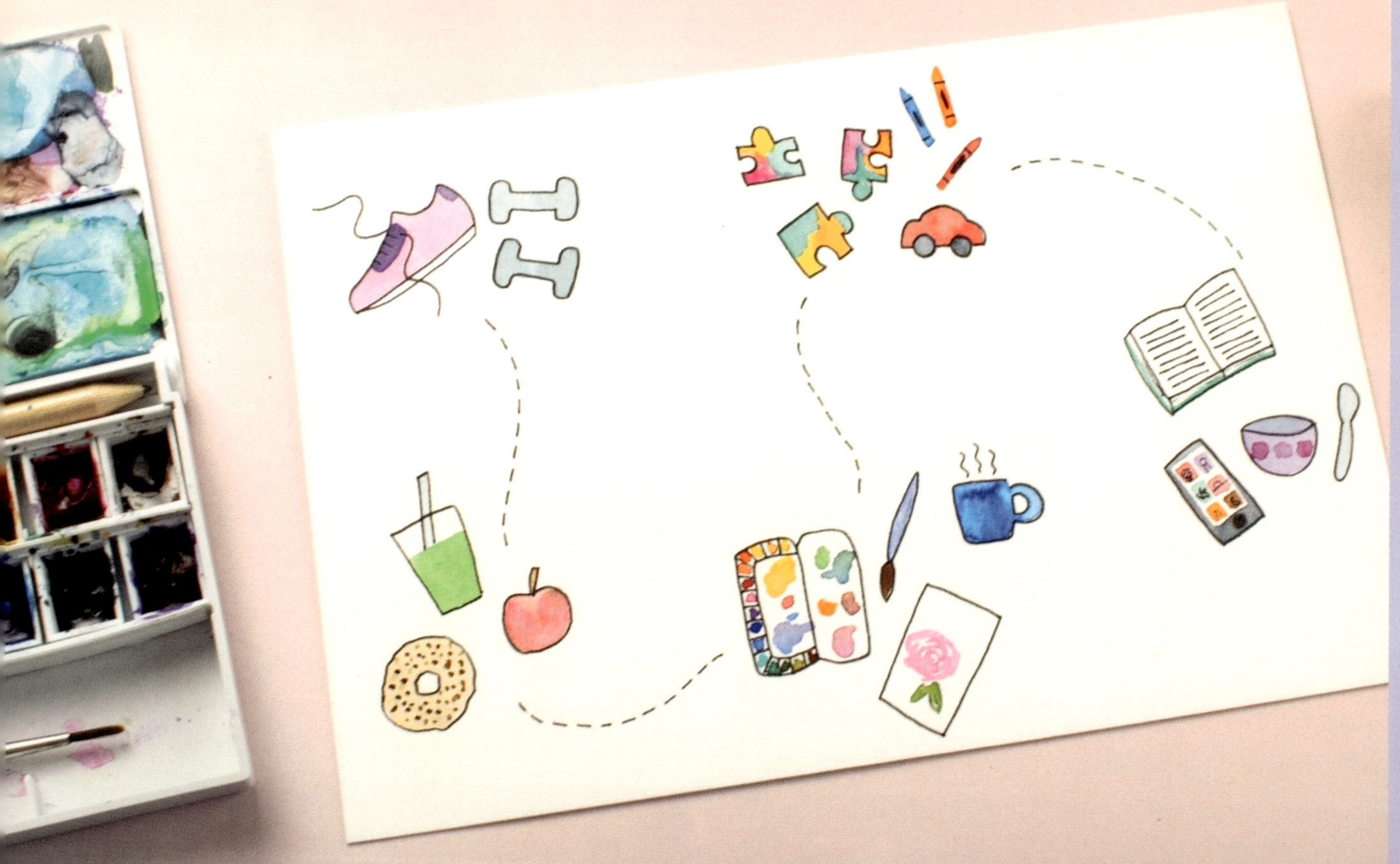

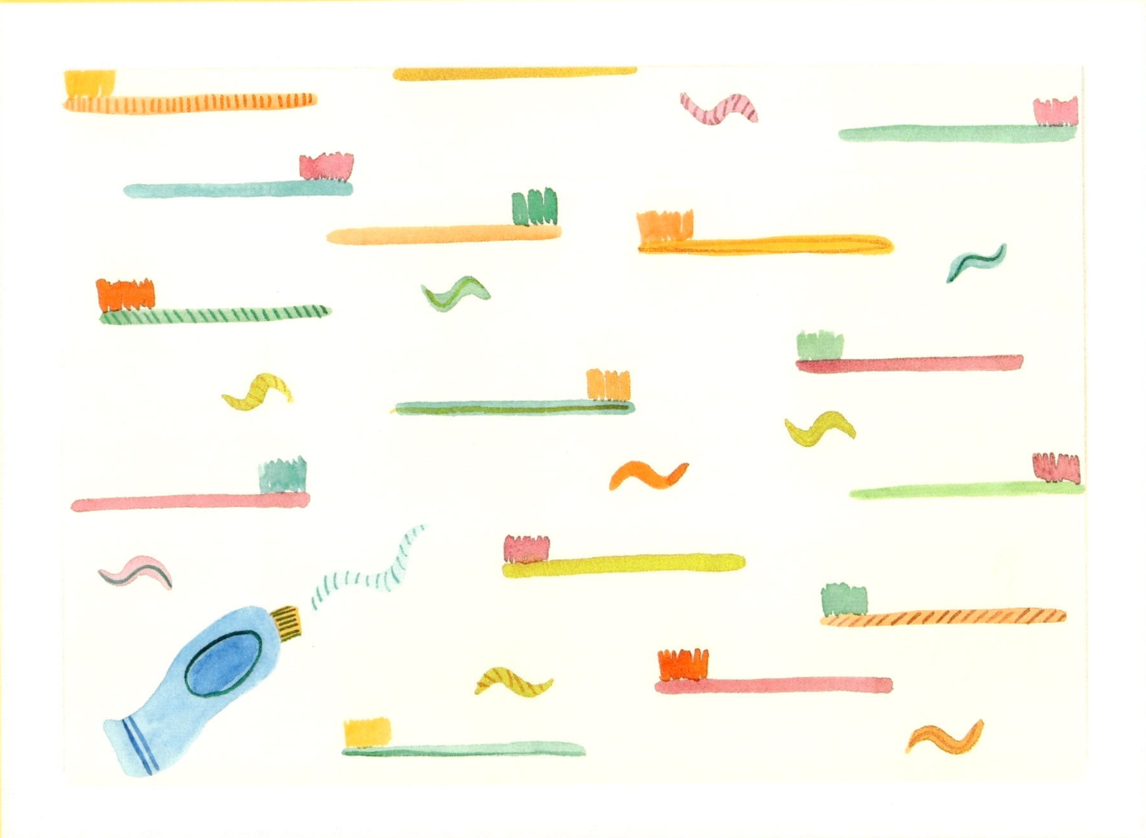

prompt Mundane pattern

Colorful flowers and cute animals are always a joy to paint, but taking something less-than-pretty and painting it in your style can present more of a challenge. In this prompt, you will be using a mundane object as inspiration for a happy pattern.

A common question that all artists get asked is, "Where do you find your inspiration?" And the answer is usually the same: everywhere! Sometimes it is found on a walk through a lovely forest, sometimes on a beach vacation; other times it can be found right at home. You don't need to travel to a beautiful location to find artistic inspiration. Those regular days at home or work can seem like they are lacking in beauty, but if you take a look around, you will be able to find inspiration anywhere.

What you need to do is train your eye to spot interesting shapes or patterns. And if you still can't find anything that catches your eye, choose something normal and mundane and make it fun. I took these toothbrushes, something most of us don't give a second look, and painted them in multiple colors with some pattern. Fill the page with silly toothbrushes and suddenly you have a piece of art inspired by a boring task you do every day.

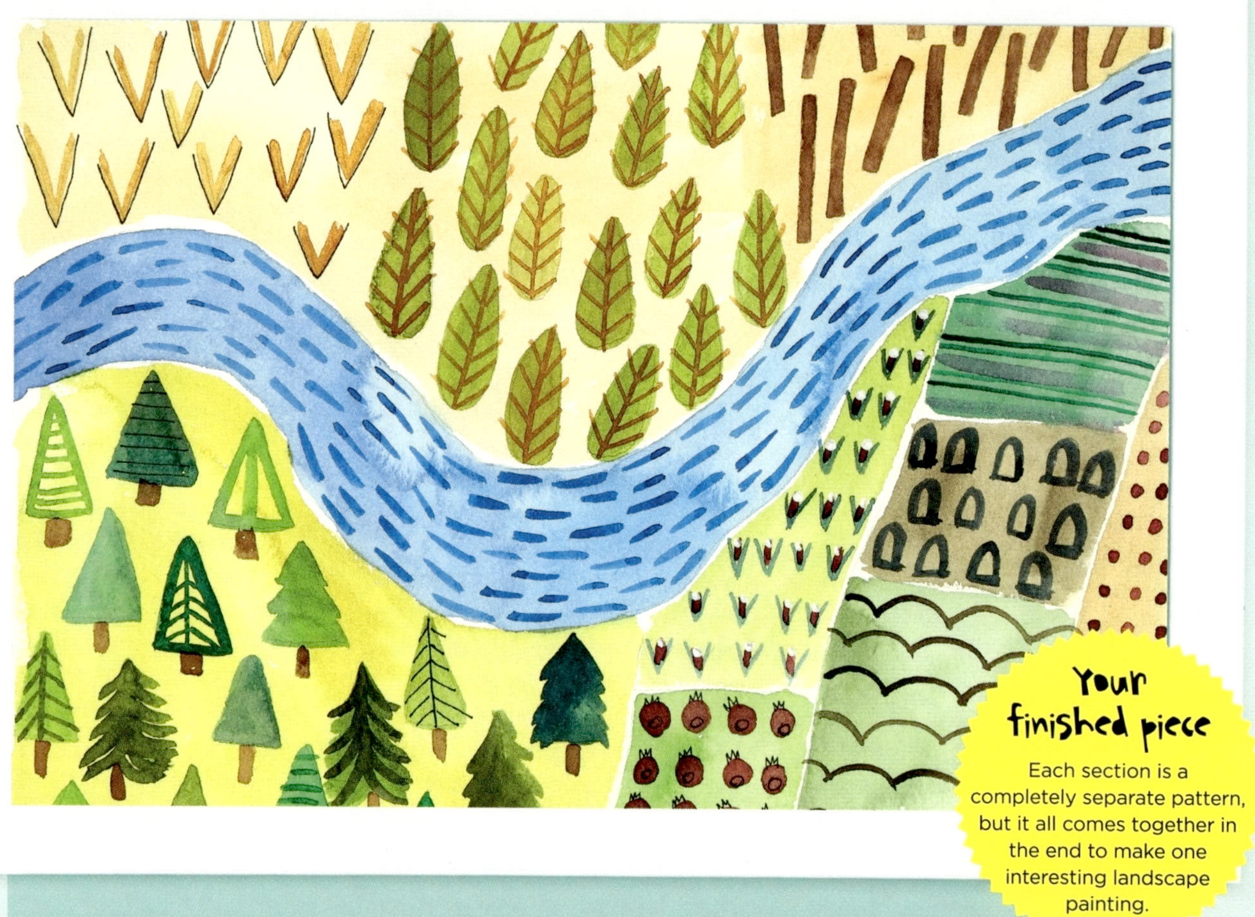

Your finished piece

Each section is a completely separate pattern, but it all comes together in the end to make one interesting landscape painting.

Project

Create a patterned landscape

As I mentioned before, I love landscape paintings but I struggle with them. So I am always looking for ways to simplify this type of painting. I call this a patterned landscape because you fill the page with patterned sections that come together to form an outdoor scene. For example, instead of painting a wooded area, paint a forest pattern. It's a bit of a landscape quilt.

YOU WILL NEED

- Watercolor paper
- Watercolor paint
- Pencil
- Medium round brush

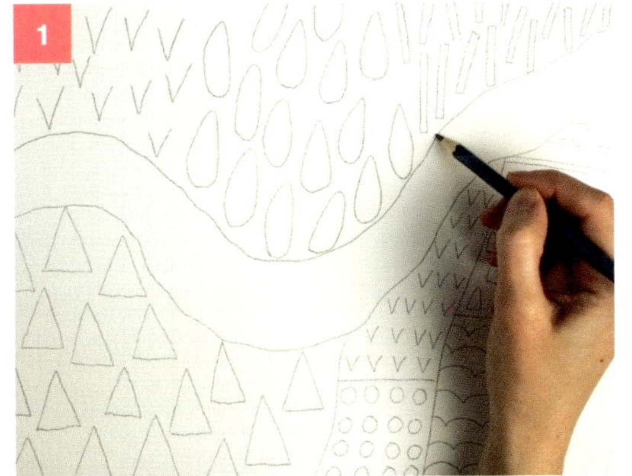

Sketch out a simple landscape scene using a pencil. I drew mine looking from the top down so I could maximize the pattern coverage.

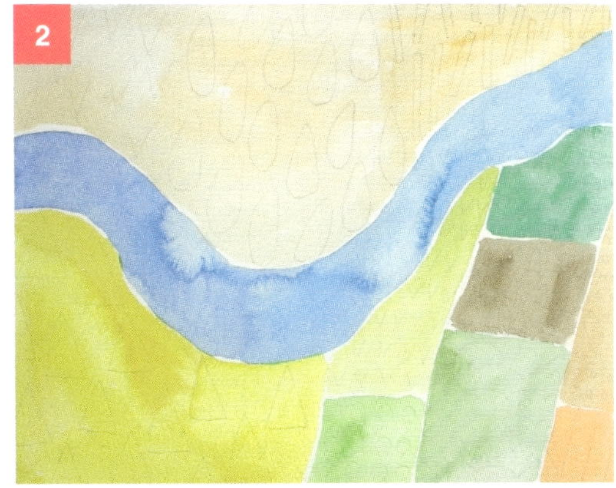

Paint a base color for each section. You can take your time and fill in all the white gaps, but I prefer the messy look. Let dry.

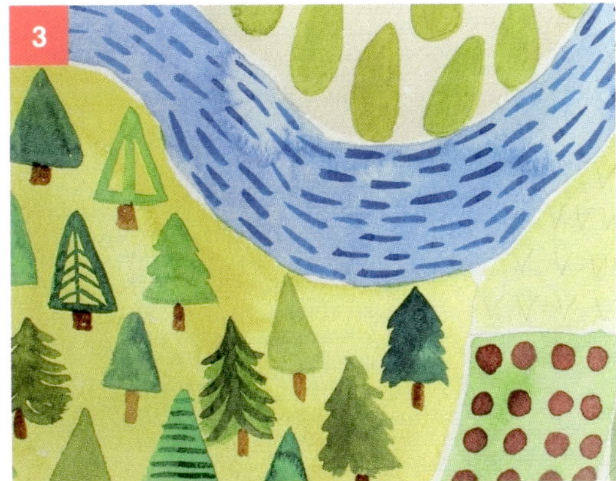

Start filling each section with pattern. I like to make sure there is variety in the sizes of my motifs.

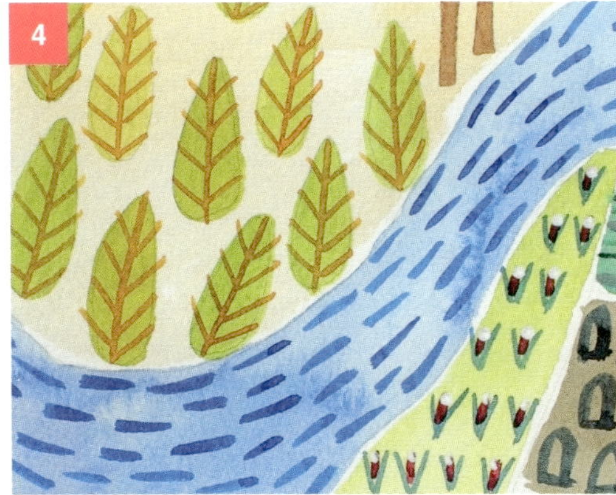

After everything is dry, go back to add some extra detail. You can use more paint or even grab some pens and markers.

Paint a terrarium in a jar

In this project, we will be growing a cute little terrarium in a jar. I love this kind of painting because it is a template I can repeat over and over, and never get the same result. As a bonus, these watercolor terrariums have lasted longer than any plant I have ever owned. I will never tire of painting plants.

YOU WILL NEED

- Watercolor paper
- Watercolor paint
- Pencil
- Small round brush
- Small liner brush

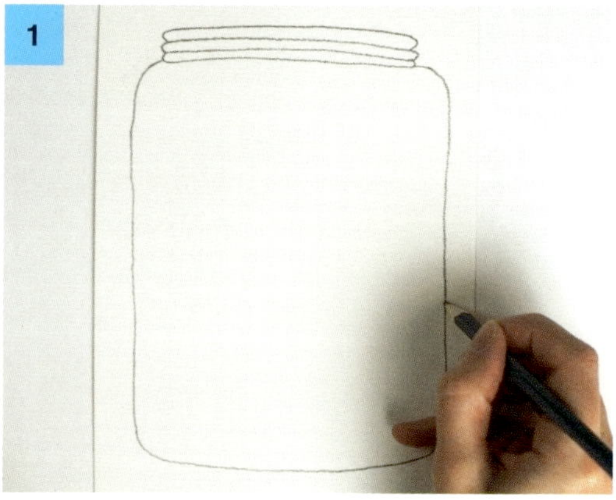

Using a pencil, sketch out a jar shape that fills the page. This is where you will grow your terrarium.

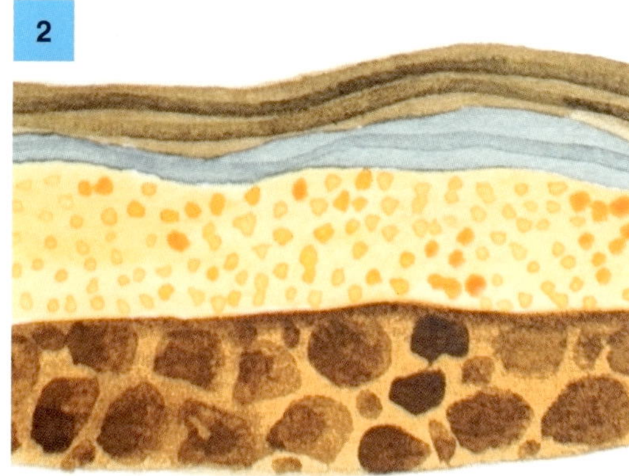

Start by grabbing a small round brush, and paint a few layers of soil and rock in the bottom of the jar.

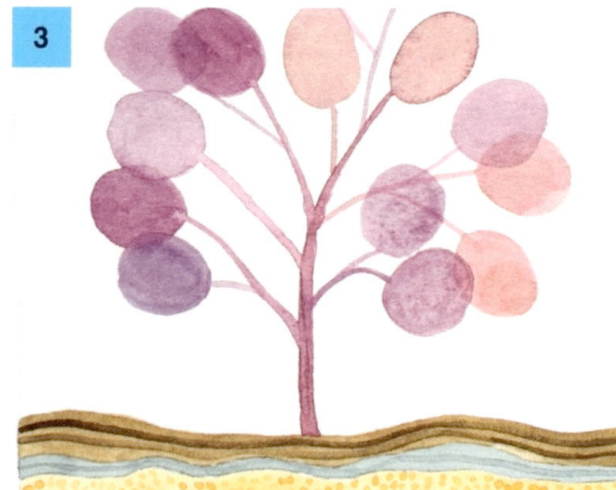

Then add a plant or two. You can keep it simple or completely fill the jar with lush greenery in any color.

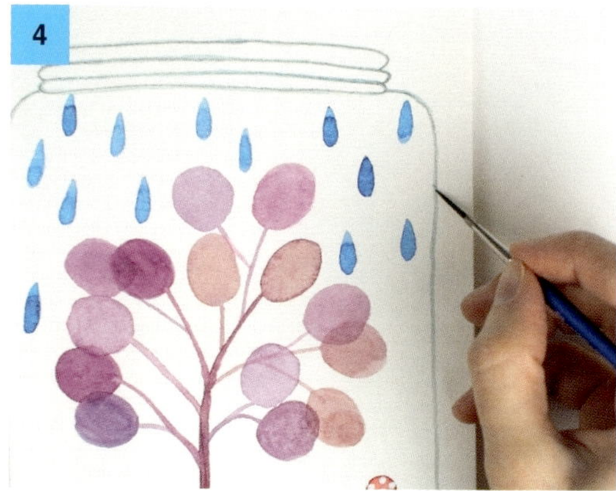

Add your special touch. It could be a weather element, some garden decor, or an animal. Finish by outlining your jar in paint using a liner brush.

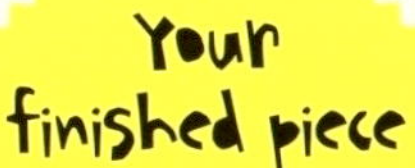

When you paint your terrarium, add a personal touch such as an animal or some kind of weather. It will make the jar unique.

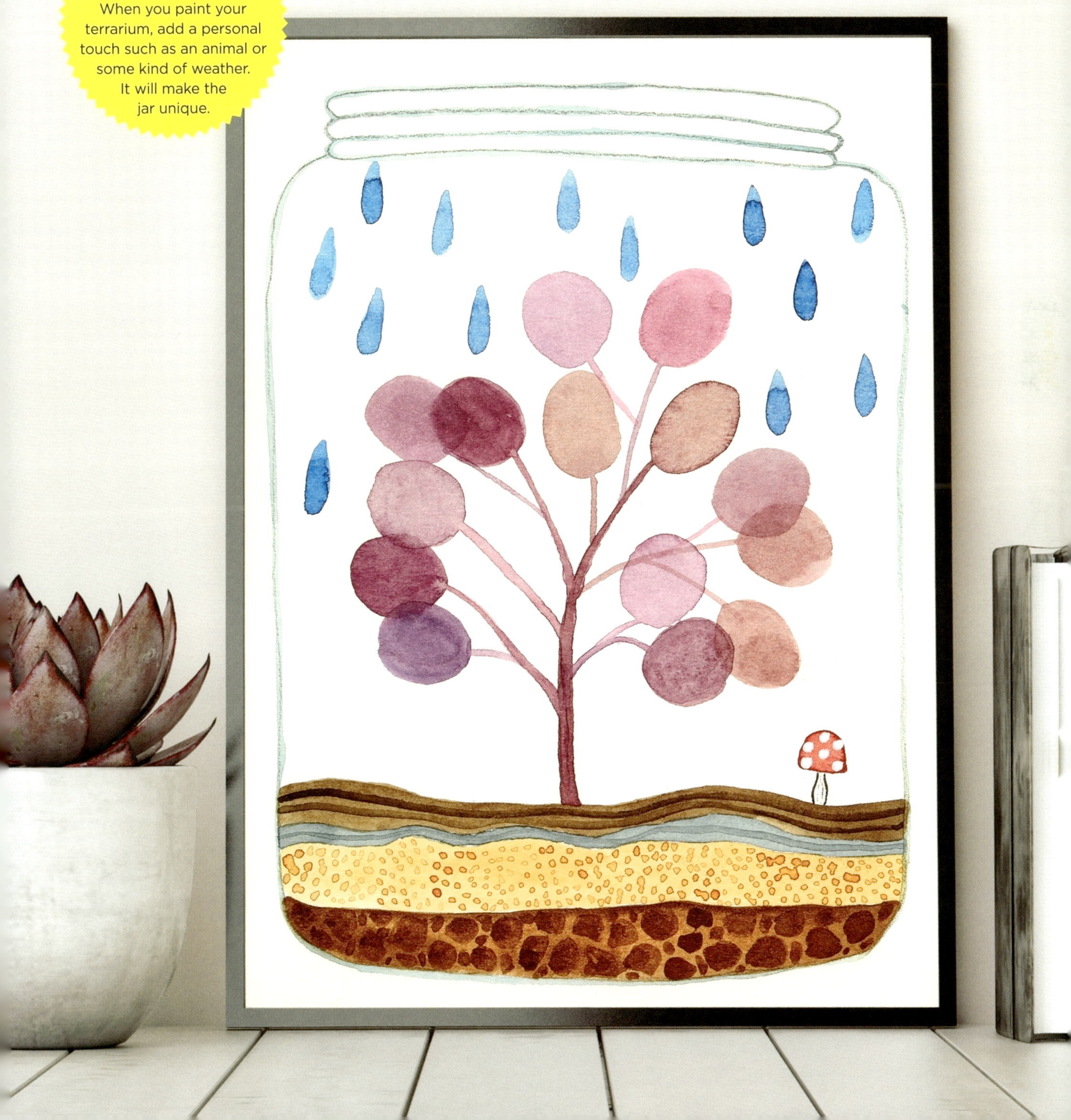

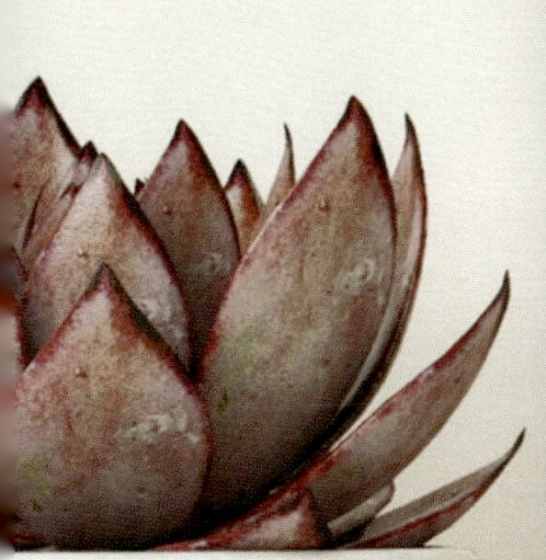

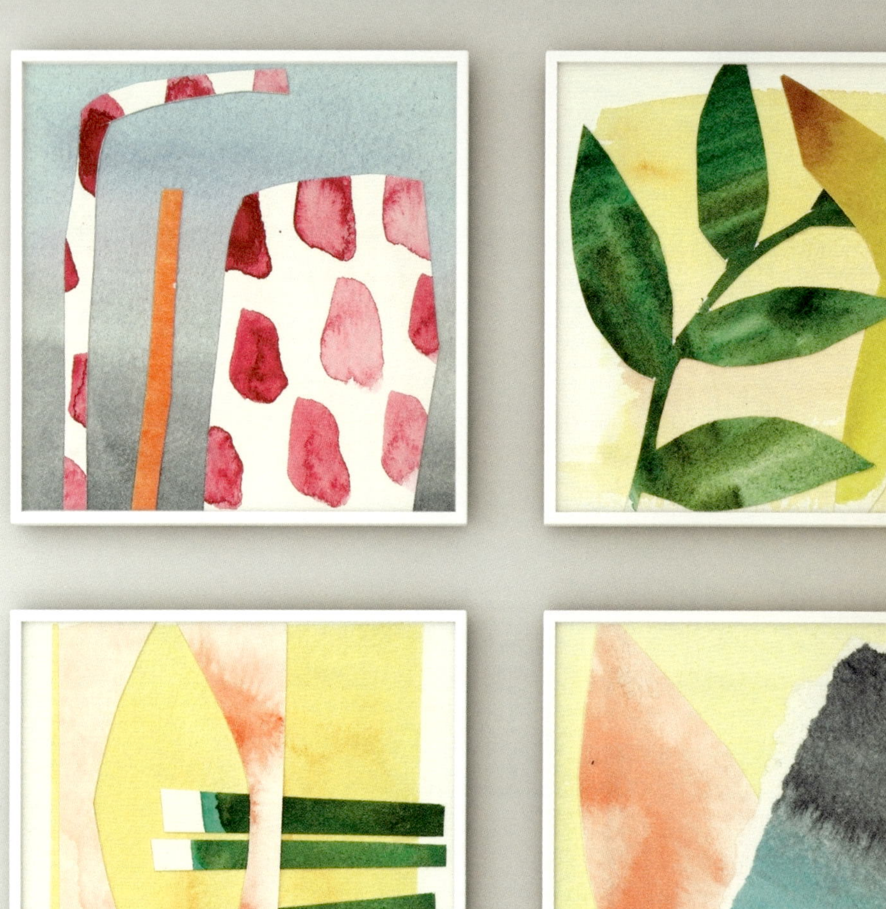

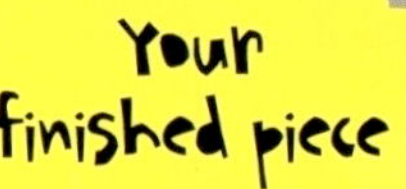

These studies are a fantastic way to test out new color combinations. Rearrange them until you get an interesting look.

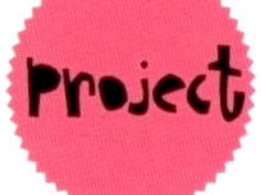

Simple collage studies

I always seem to accumulate a lot of watercolor scraps. It sometimes comes from cleaning my brush on a piece of paper, testing out new color-mixing recipes, or a painting gone wrong. This activity will help you to create something arty from those scraps. They also serve as color and shape studies to reference later in your artwork.

YOU WILL NEED

- Watercolor paper
- Watercolor paint
- Watercolor scraps
- Scissors
- Glue

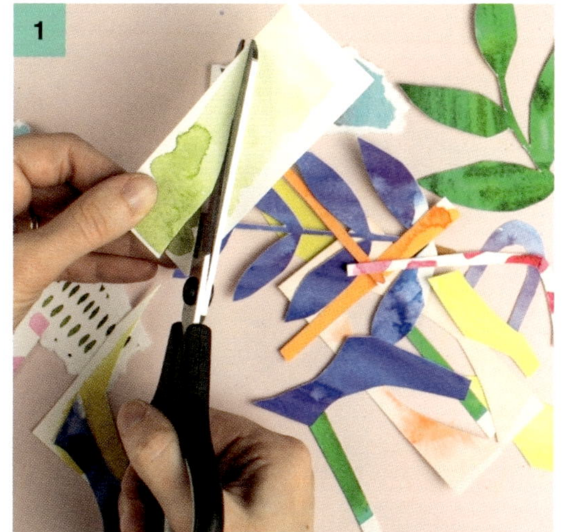

Gather all your watercolor scraps together and start cutting them. Your shapes can be representational or abstract, random cuts.

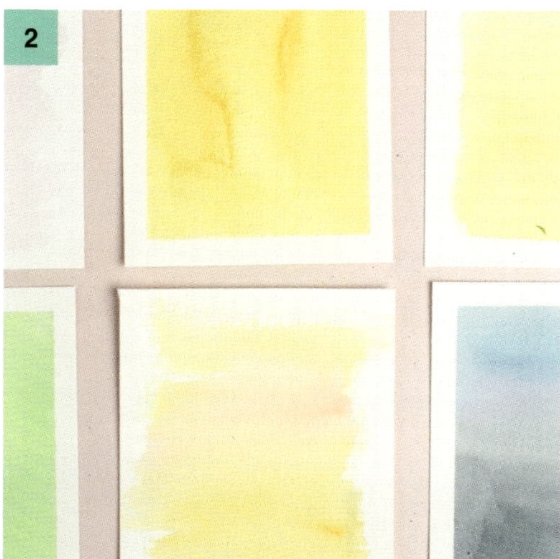

Prepare a base for your collages. I cut a few small pieces of watercolor paper and gave them each a simple background color.

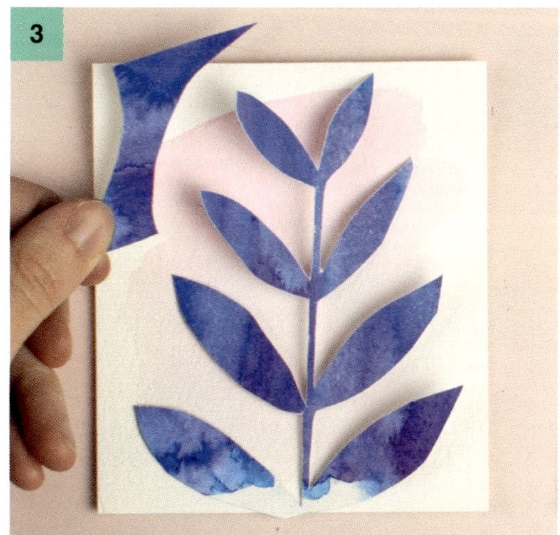

Experiment and rearrange like crazy! I like to keep things simple, with only one or two scrap shapes per piece.

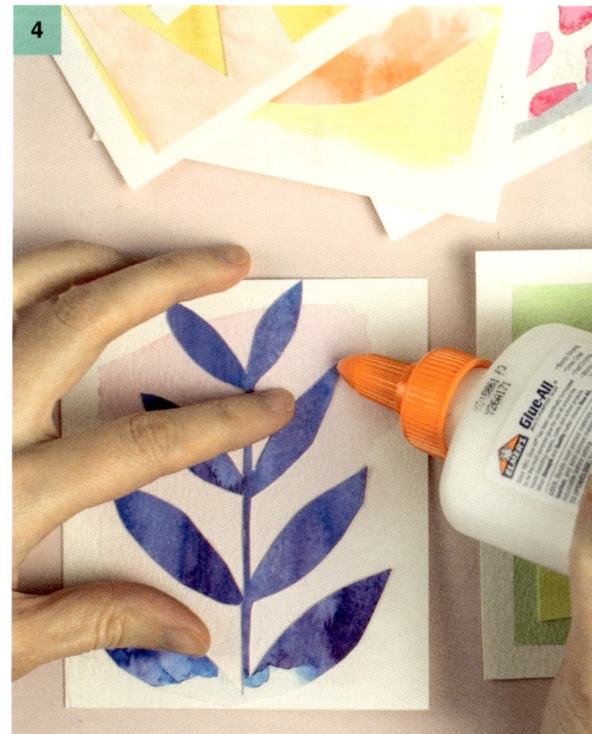

When you are happy with how the shapes look, start glueing it all together. I love how the simple pieces form a collection.

prompt

Custom phone wallpaper

There are so many ways to display your art: framing, making prints, taping onto the wall. But the easiest way to show off your art is by turning it into custom cell phone wallpaper.

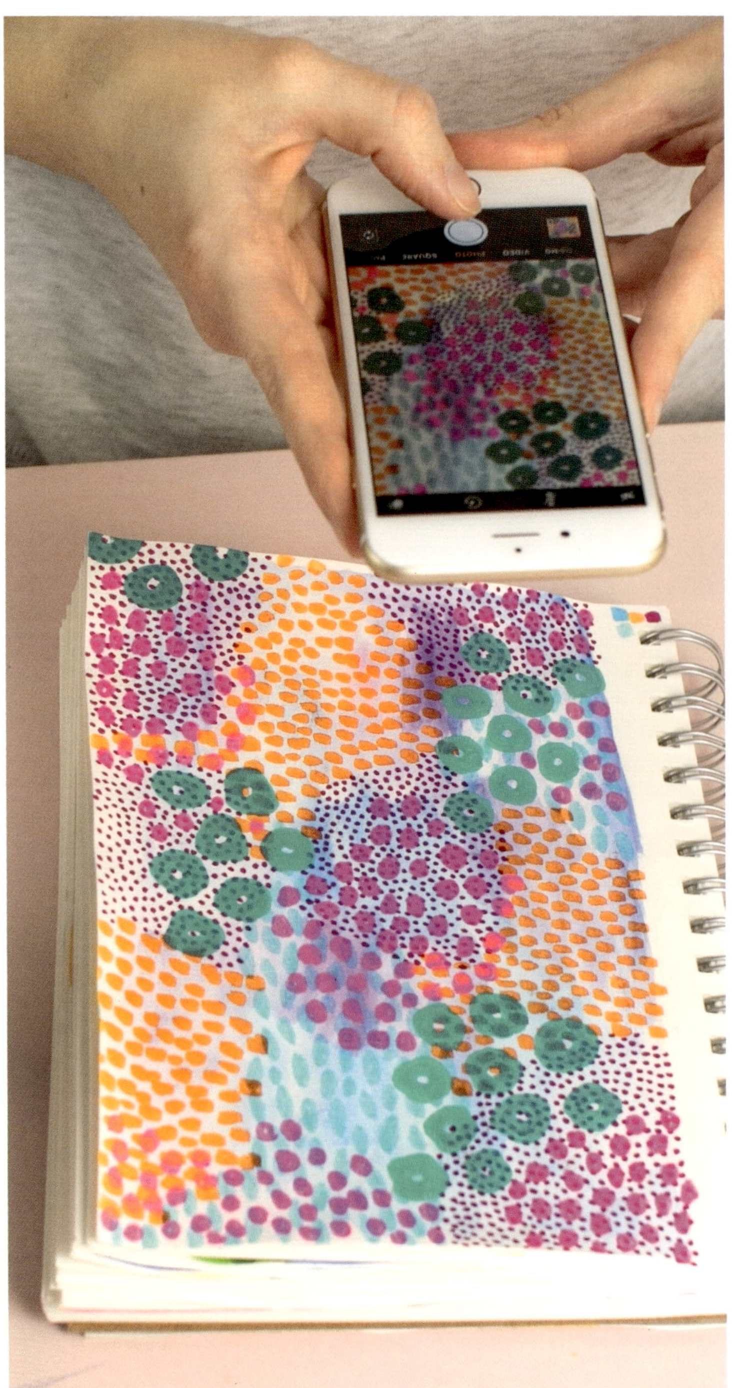

One of my favorite ways to relax is by making abstract or patterned pages in my sketchbook. These pages don't serve a purpose, they are just fun to make and don't require a lot of brain power. Experimentation time is key for me, but sometimes I feel like these pieces of art are piling up without being put to use. So, recently I started taking photos of my favorite pages and using them as my phone wallpaper.

This is easy to do. Start by finding a well-lit area, such as near a large window or even outside, to take your photo. Move your phone in close to the page so the art completely fills the frame. You can edit your photo in a mobile photo-editing app to brighten up the whites and increase the saturation, or just leave it as is. Then set the photo as your wallpaper.

It is lovely to catch a glimpse of my own artwork every time I pick up my phone. I change my background often and even send some of my favorites to friends and family so they can use them too.

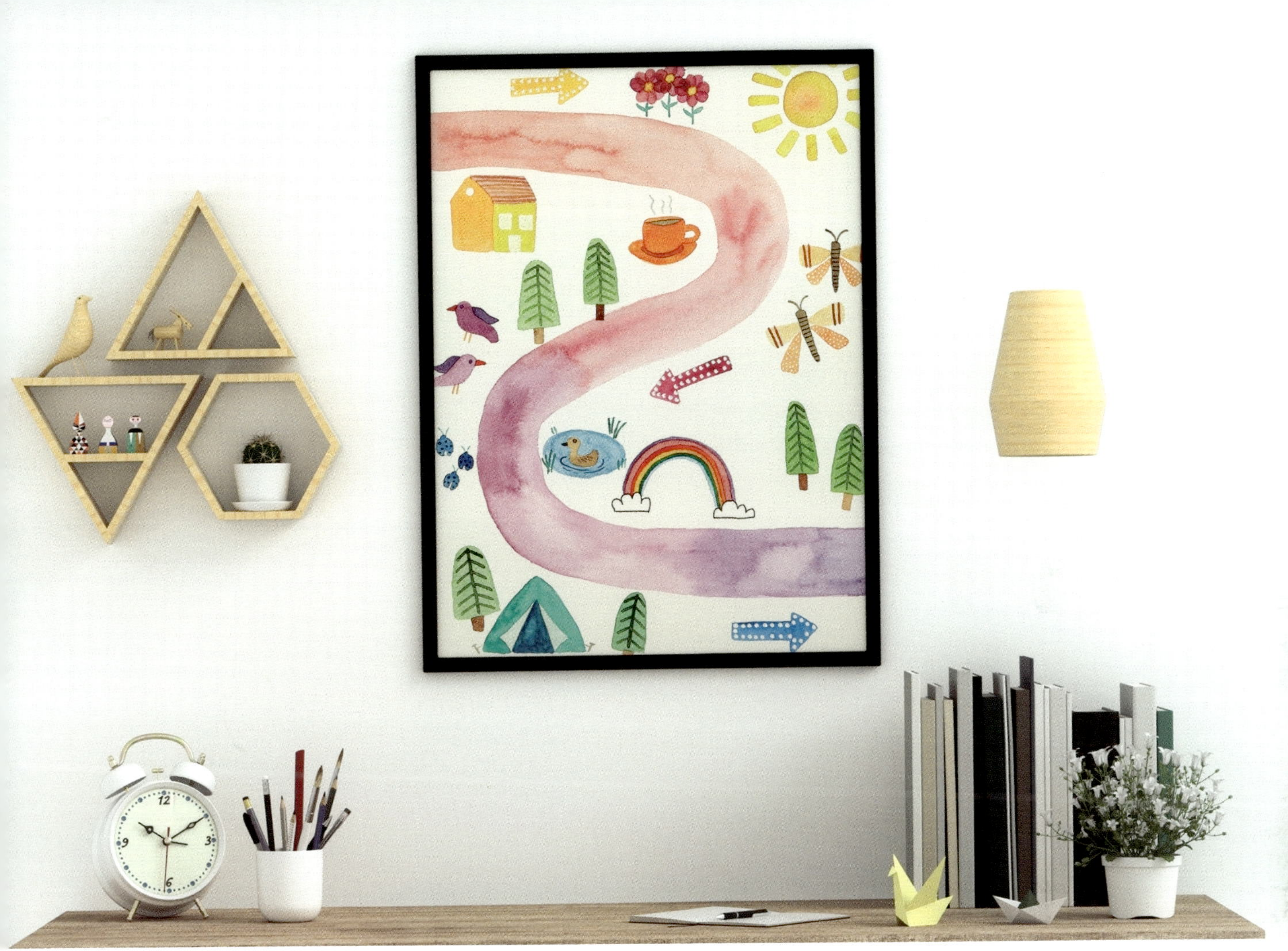

prompt Map it out

In this prompt, you will be painting a map. Where does your map go? Wherever you want! The aim is to make it big, bold, and colorful. So, grab your paints and your favorite brushes, and let's create your own unique map.

Not all maps have to be a depiction of a physical place, and your map certainly doesn't have to be to scale in this painting. Map out anything you want: your creative process, your average day, an imaginary trip, or even your whole life. I love how this painting draws your eye down the path, so you can visit every detail along the way.

Start by painting a path down the middle of your page. It can be curvy, straight, whatever you want, but I think most journeys have a few twists and turns. You can also sketch it out with a pencil first, but I prefer the spontaneity of putting paint directly to paper in this exercise. Now add all the places you want to visit along the way. You can even add signs or notes for people who will be reading your map. Enjoy figuring out how to represent each stop on your journey visually.

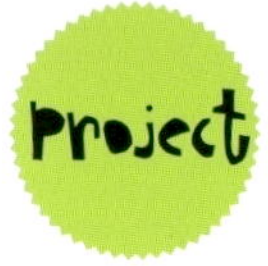

Paint your own stamp collection

By now you probably know that I love any project where I can use up some scrap watercolor paper. Always save your scraps! In this exercise, you will be cutting up paper to create tiny works of art for your stamp collection.

YOU WILL NEED

- Watercolor paper or sketchbook
- Watercolor paint
- Pencil
- Ruler
- Scrap paper
- Brushes of your choice
- Scissors
- Glue

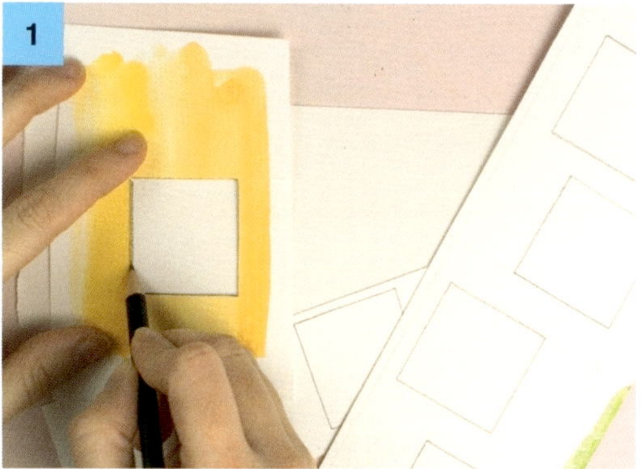

Start by measuring out some squares on your scrap paper, keeping some space in between each one. You could even create a cardboard template.

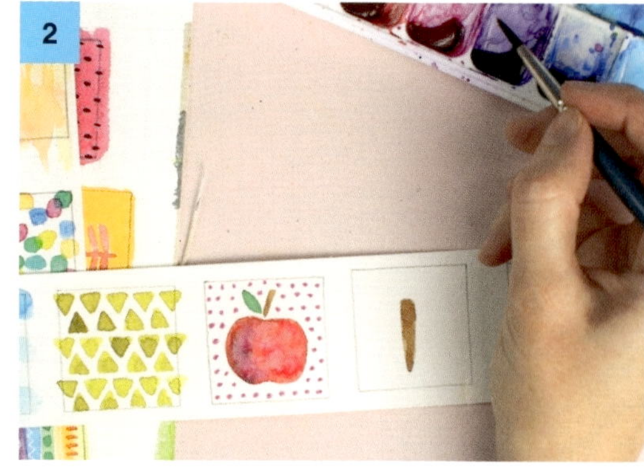

Next, fill in each square with a small painting. You can go abstract or paint patterns, landscapes, or even tiny animals—the choice is yours.

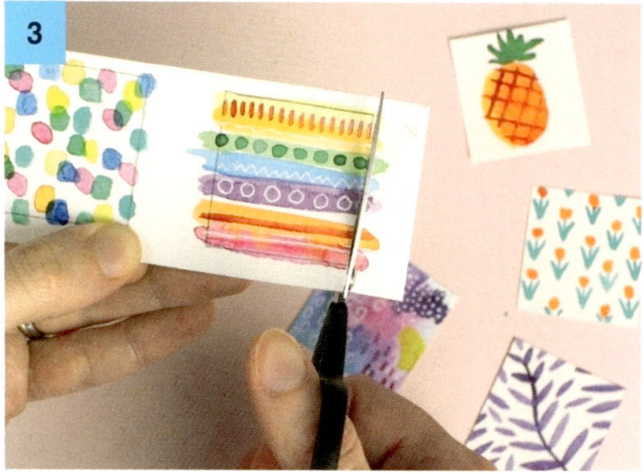

When the paint is completely dry, cut out each stamp.

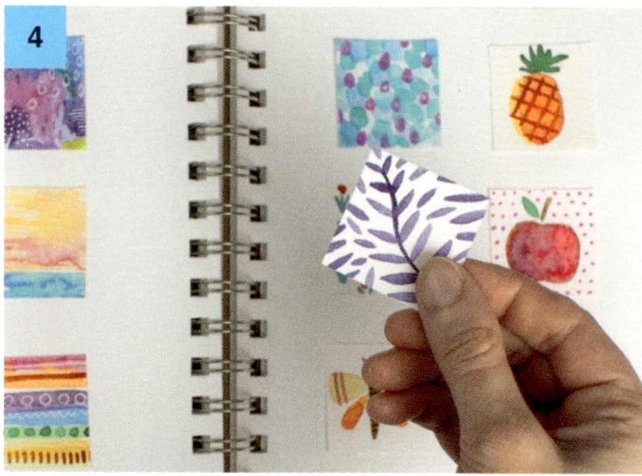

Arrange and rearrange the stamps in your sketchbook. You could also use a sheet of paper if you want to display your work. Once you are happy with the layout, glue down the stamps.

Your finished piece

You don't have to fill the whole page on the first day. Save your scraps and keep adding to your collection whenever inspiration strikes.

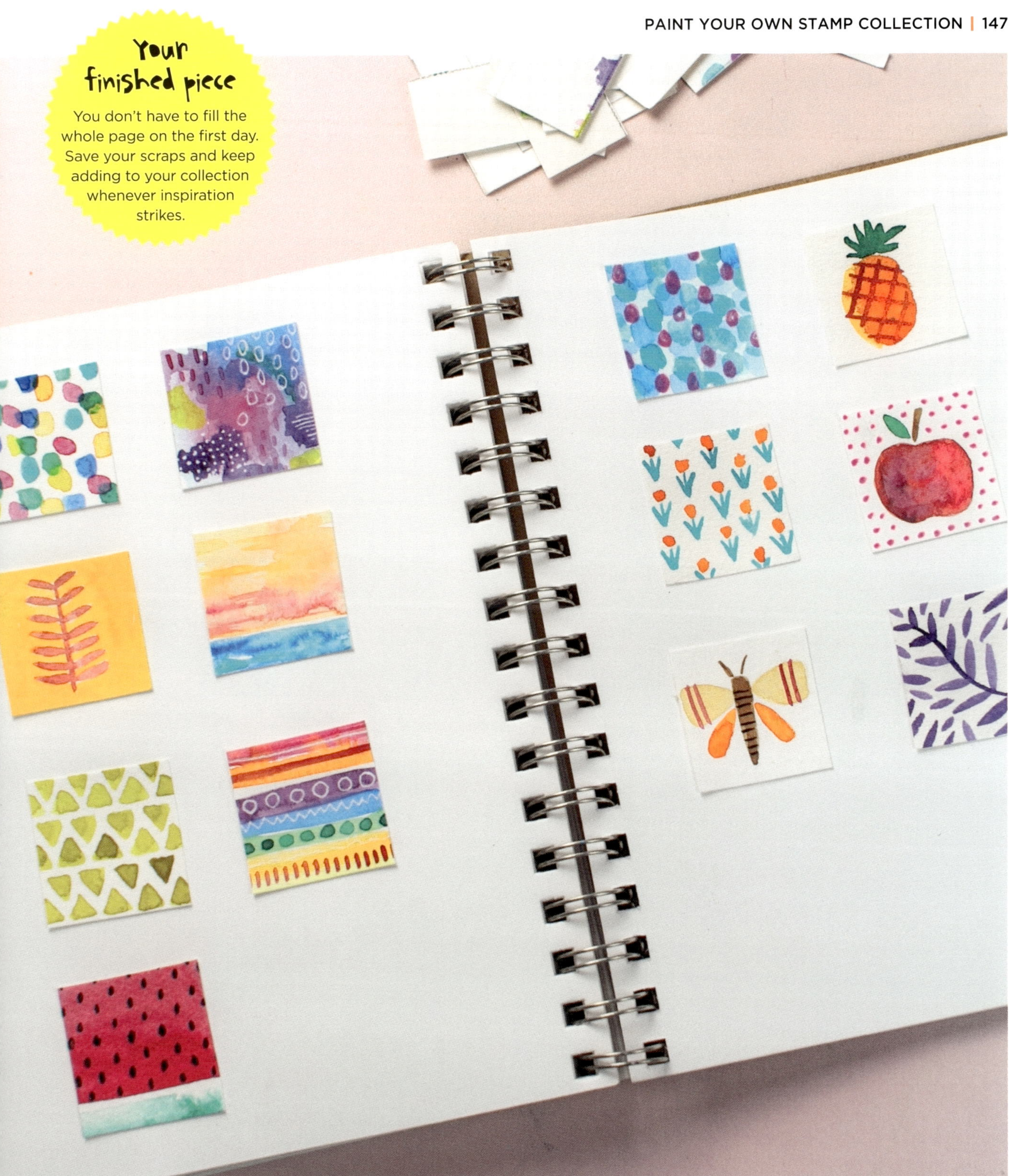

Prompt Make painterly bookmarks

Instead of using a gum wrapper or old receipt, I started painting my own bookmarks, and now I can always find one when I need it. They also make great gifts for the book lovers in your life.

I love when I can turn my paintings into something useful. Hanging art on the wall is obviously great, but there are other functional ways to display your art. Finding ways to put your mark on something practical incorporates more art into your life and makes every day a little prettier.

There are a couple of ways you can create your bookmarks. You can start by measuring out a rectangle on a sheet of paper and drawing a pencil guideline; paint whatever you want and then cut along the pencil lines. You can pre-cut a bunch of bookmarks and work with those. Or you can paint like crazy without giving any thought to the size of the bookmark and then cut a favorite section out of the painting (this technique is an ideal way to involve your kids). Choose your favorite method and start creating.

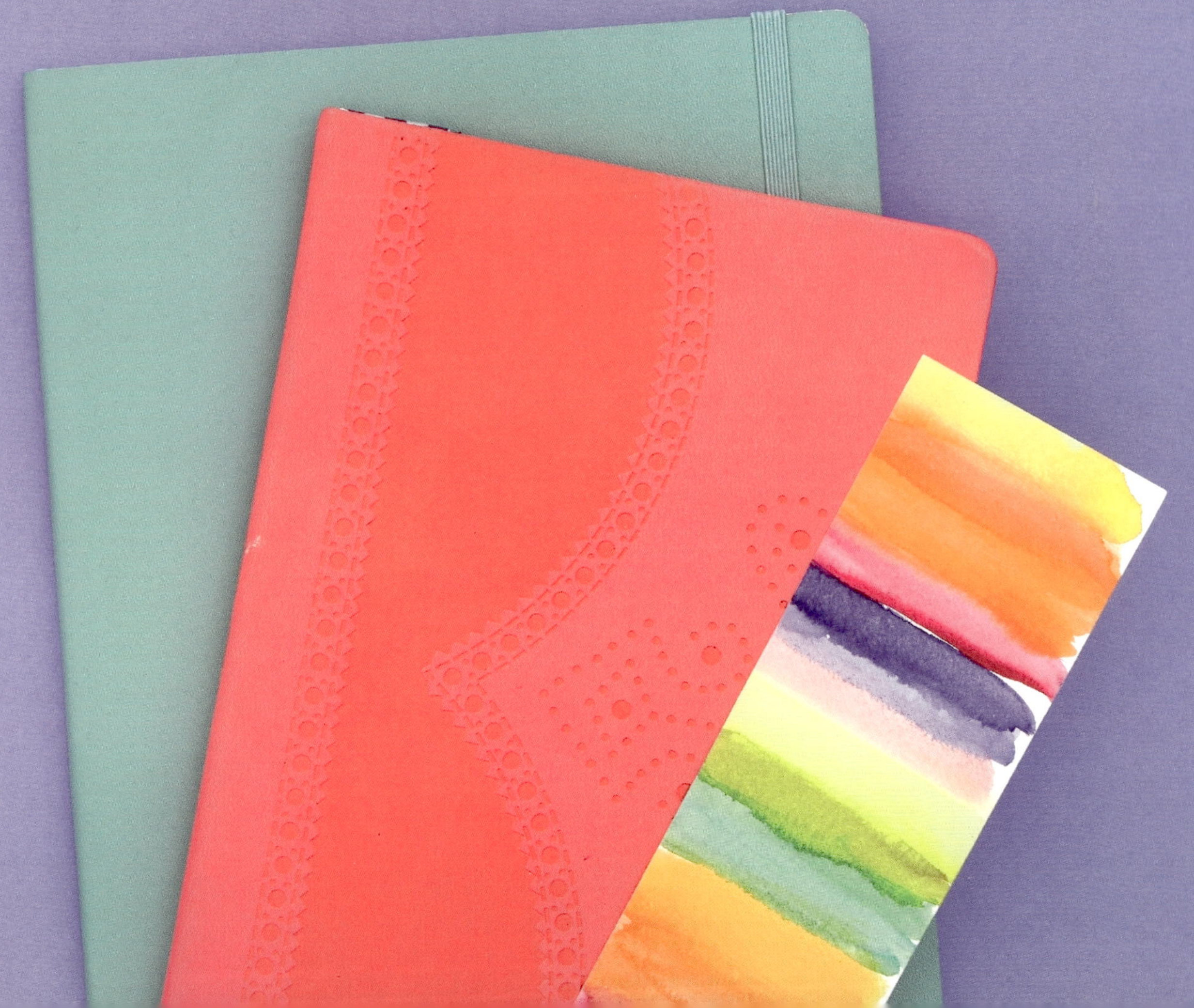

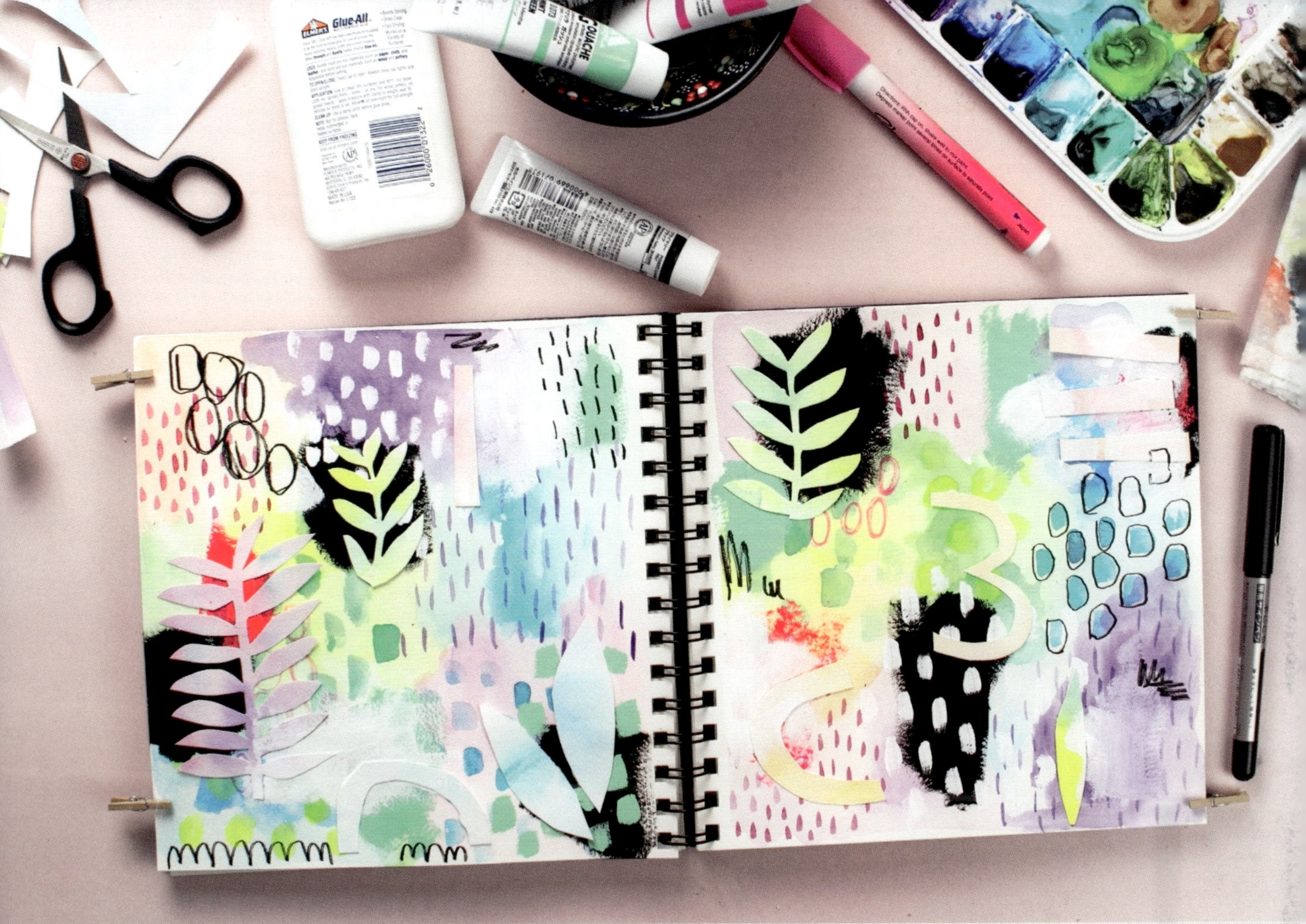

prompt

Put it all together in an art journal

Art journaling is all about using art to record your thoughts, feelings, memories, and emotions. The best part–there are absolutely no rules! Use any art supplies you want, go crazy with color, and combine your favorite techniques.

There is no wrong way to keep an art journal, but I think an art journal is a bit different to a sketchbook. A sketchbook is where I work out ideas and practice techniques that I would like to use on a final piece. My art journal is a book of finished pieces, and they are usually private and personal. Sometimes I combine writing or words with my art; other times I stick with symbols. It all depends on how I am feeling.

I also love using a wide variety of art supplies in my art journal. On this page I used watercolor, gouache, acrylic paint, collage, paint markers, and black pen. I try to start with an emotion or feeling I have been trying to work out and see where it goes. There is no right or wrong way to paint the emotion "happy" or "love," or to record how you have been feeling lately. So grab your favorite supplies, using them and choosing your colors intuitively.

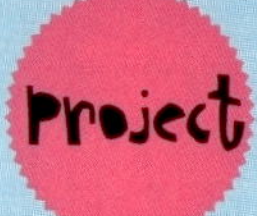

Design your own stationery

Fun with watercolor does not need to stop at the end of your sketchbook. Put those paints to use all over the place! Creating custom stationery is so easy to do, and whoever is on the receiving end of your letter will appreciate the special treat.

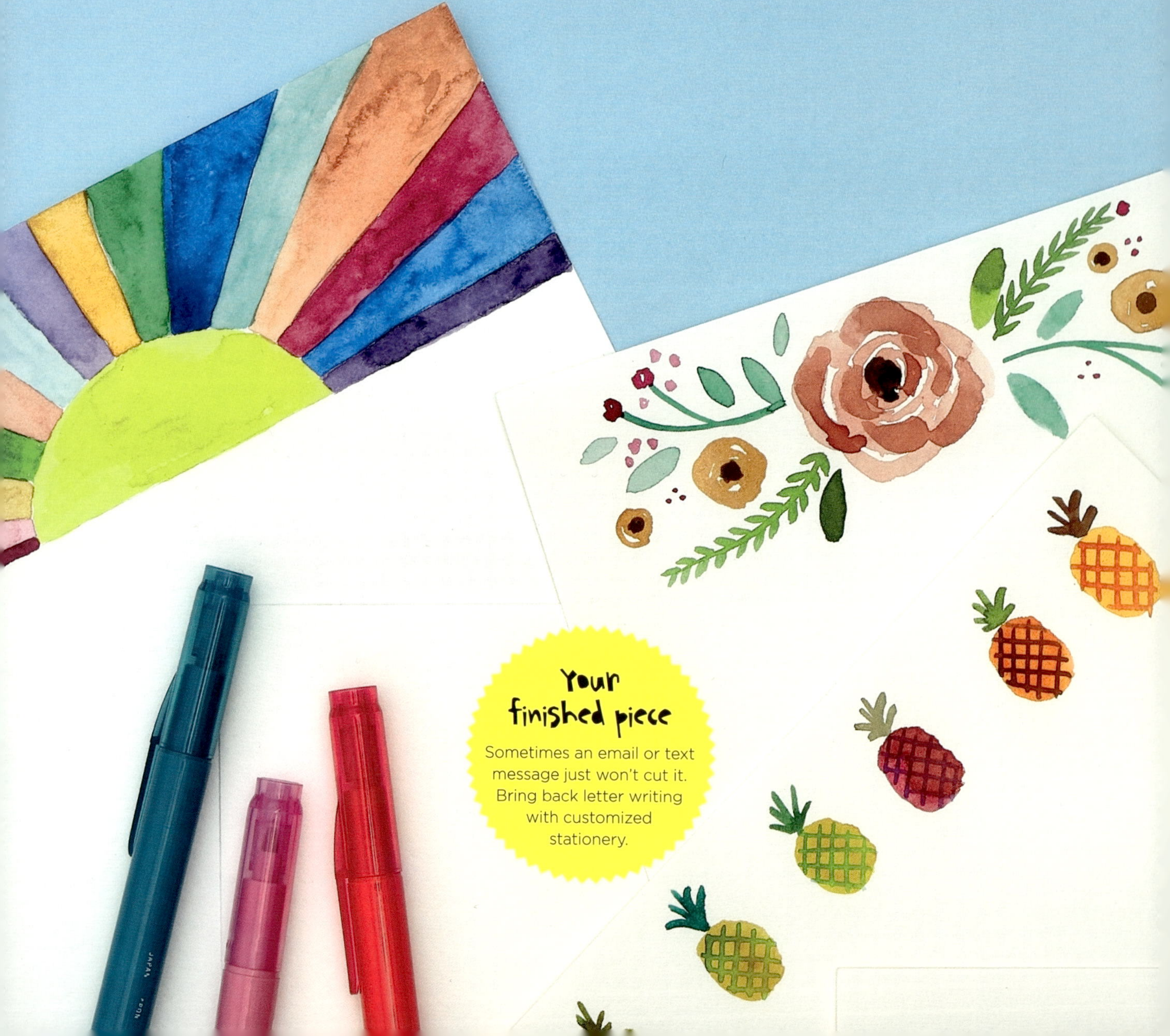

Your finished piece

Sometimes an email or text message just won't cut it. Bring back letter writing with customized stationery.

YOU WILL NEED

- Watercolor paper
- Watercolor paint
- Brush of your choice

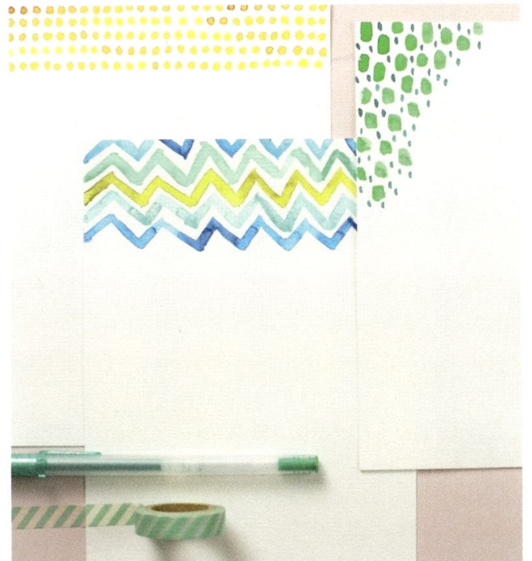

Geometric patterns A straightforward geometric pattern is a perfect choice for decorating stationery. If you need to create a large number of cards quickly, a stripe or zigzag is the way to go.

Simple color Just let the watercolor paint do what it does best: flow, blend, and bleed. A simple swoosh of color will look gorgeous for any occasion.

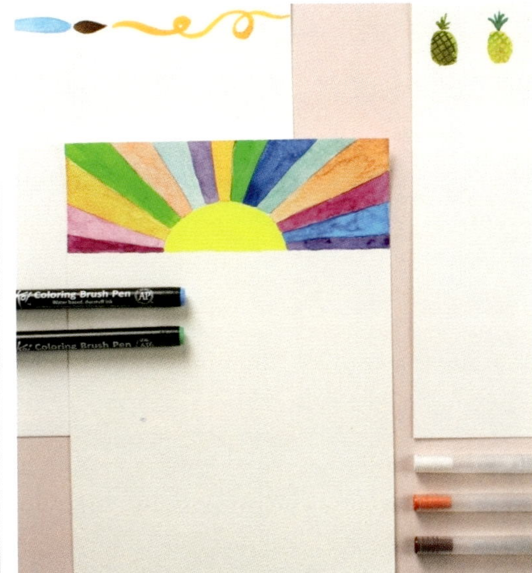

Get symbolic Decorate your stationery with a special symbol that shows off your individuality. Personalized stationery makes a thoughtful gift that is useful, too.

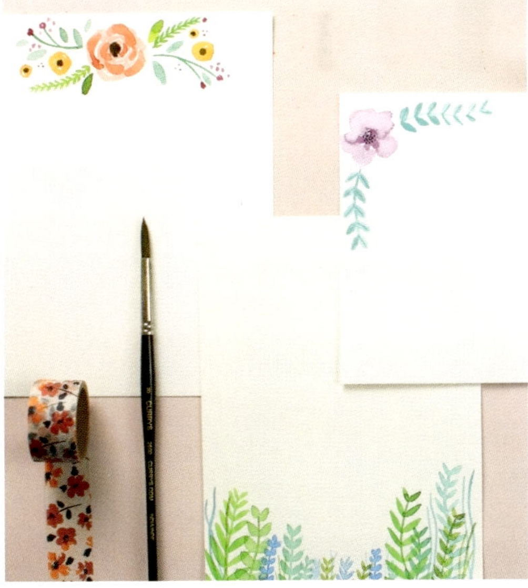

Florals and foliage No matter what the question, flowers are always the answer. You can use a flower burst as a beautiful header, paint foliage creeping in from the edges, or surround your writing with color.

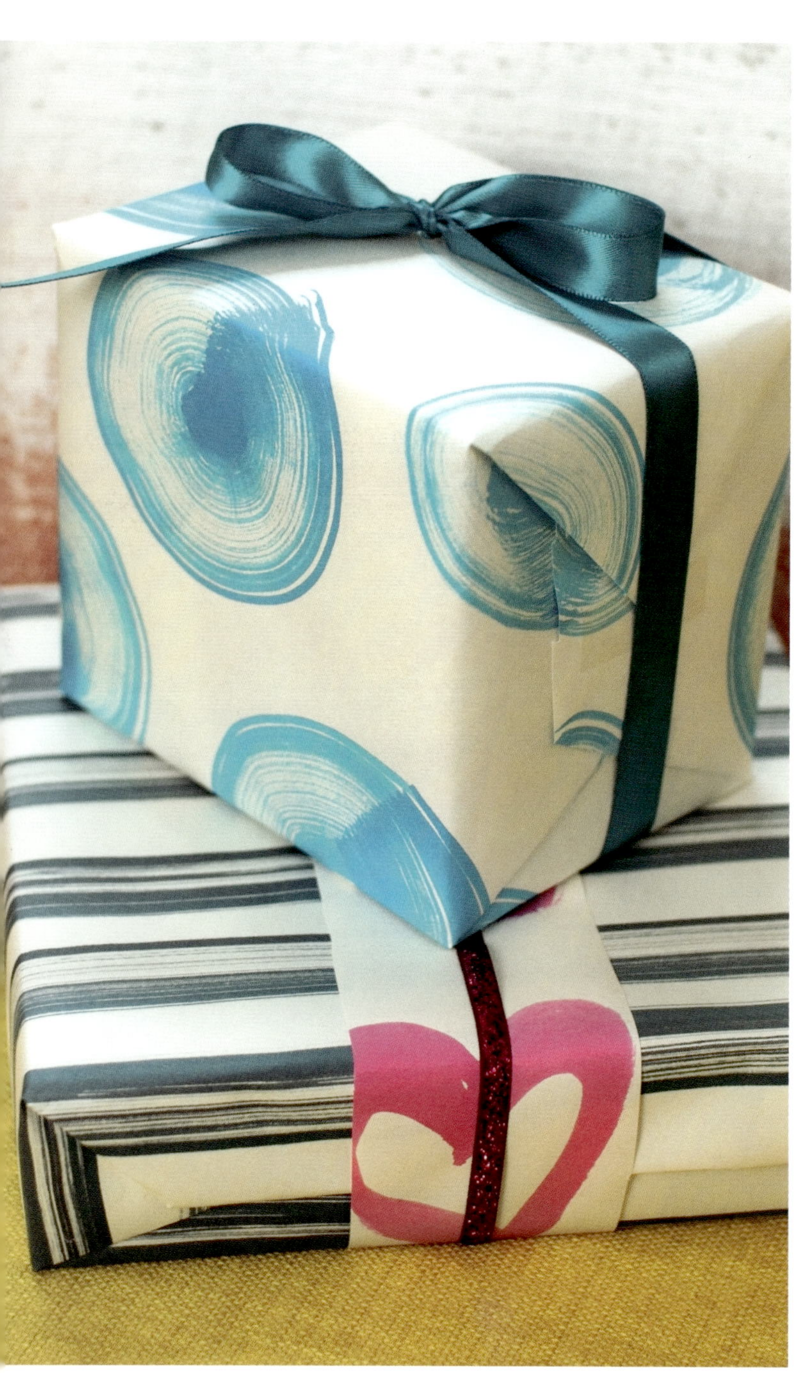

Prompt Create bold gift wrap

For gift-giving, adding a special touch with a personalized card or hand-painted gift wrap is so thoughtful and practically doubles up as the gift itself.

Finding paper that can take watercolor paint but is also thin enough for gift wrap is a little tricky. Too shiny and it won't absorb the paint; too flimsy and it might tear. I used some children's drawing paper that comes on a big roll. It isn't as nice as working with thick watercolor paper—the colors aren't as vivid and blending is a lot harder, but I am still very pleased with the results.

It is a good idea to tape your paper down to a hard surface before starting. Once it is secure, you can experiment. For some interesting texture, try using an old frayed brush. As drawing paper will soak up the paint quickly, you need to work fast. So, for gift wrap, I like to go big and bold. Try designs that you can lay down quickly and don't require any layering. These hand-painted papers will add so much personality to your gifts.

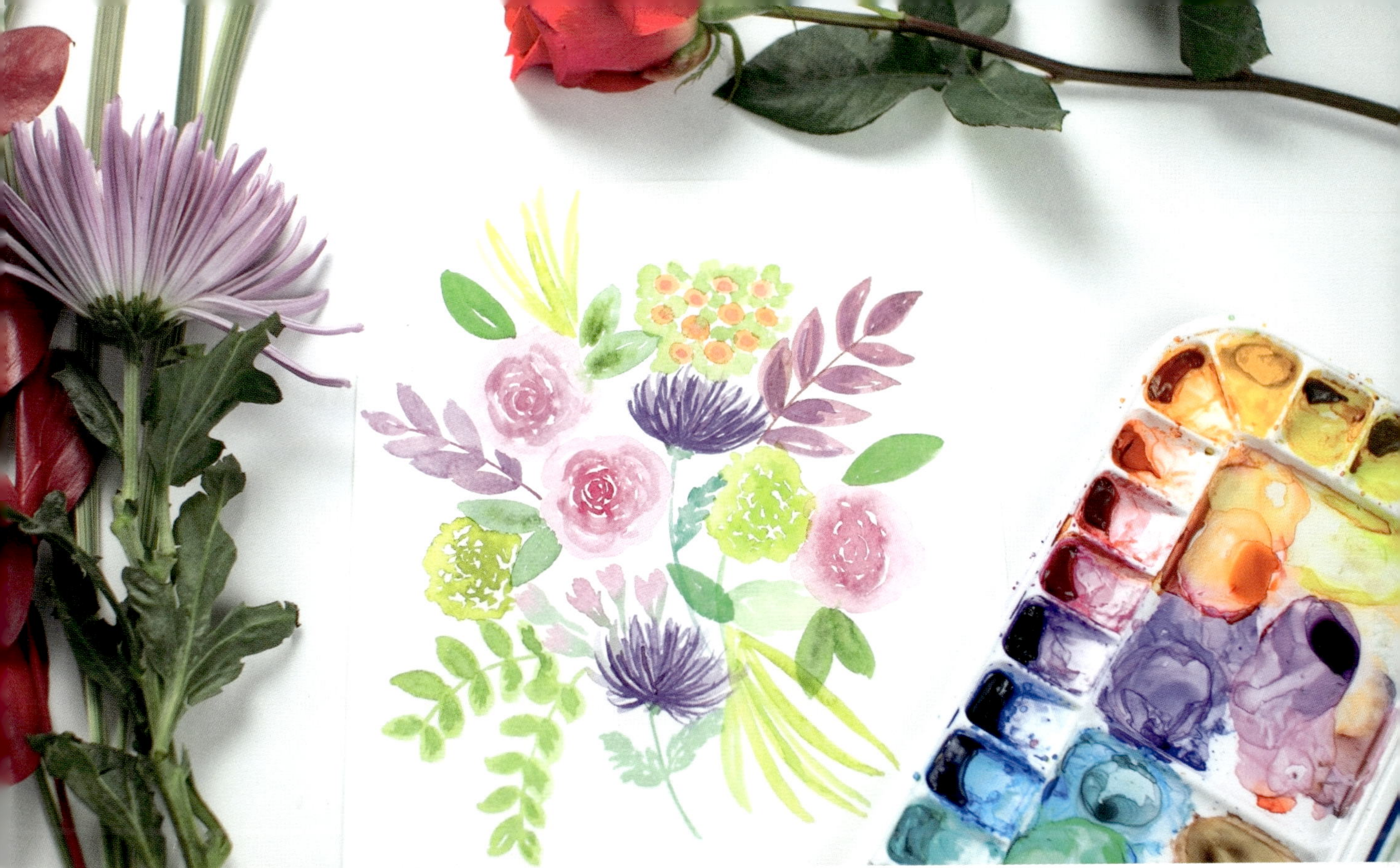

prompt Deconstruct a bouquet of flowers

Painting a bouquet of flowers is a classic still life painting exercise, but sometimes getting all those angles and the composition right can be tricky. Here we will be breaking down a bouquet and painting each flower individually.

It may seem like a small distinction from painting flowers while they sit in a vase, but giving yourself time to focus on each bloom individually can help you slow down and observe. I also like how it turns a traditional still-life into a more abstract piece and allows you to place each flower exactly where you want it in the composition.

Start by pulling out a couple of the largest flowers and work on those first, placing them in the center of the page. Work your way out, grabbing the smaller flowers one at a time. You can group similar flowers together, arrange them in a pattern, or just place them randomly around the page. Don't forget to include the greenery. Take your time and put each flower exactly where you want it. Sometimes I even practice painting a certain bloom a few times on some scrap paper.

Once you have finished, add some details with markers or pens to give the piece more depth. You can even jump right in and paint it all again. Test out alternative arrangements and the results will be different every time.

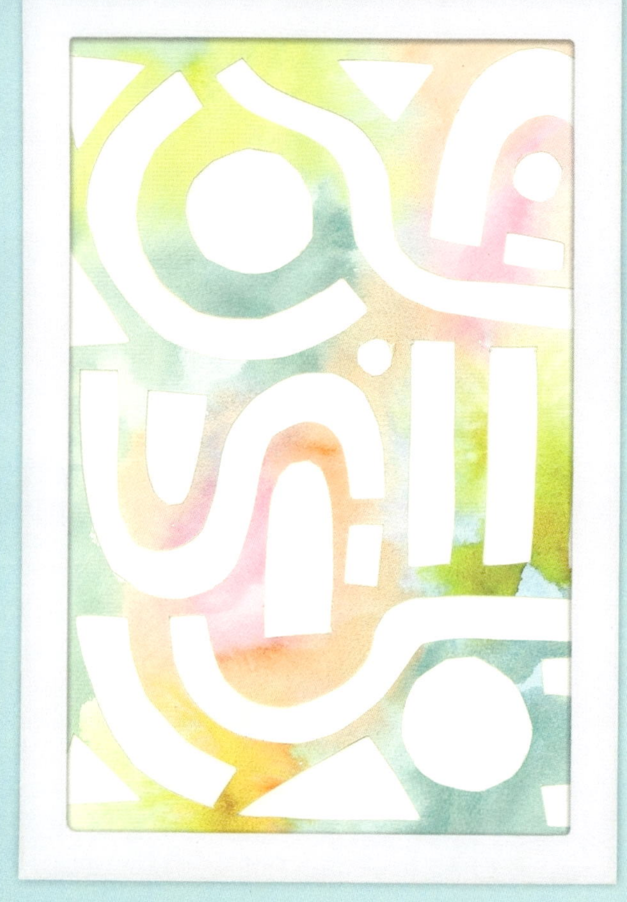

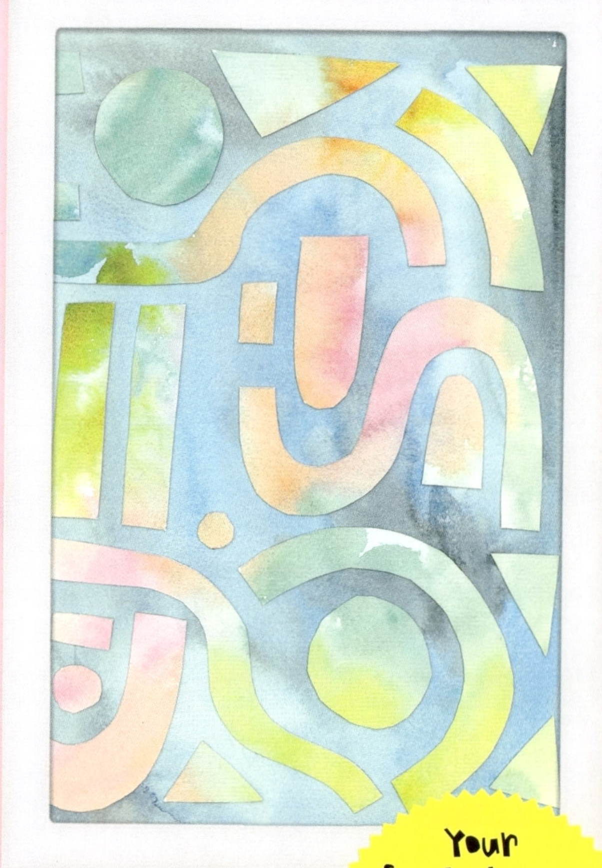

Your finished piece

This project makes a lovely pair of paintings, so be sure to hang the pieces next to each other. Or give one away to your best friend!

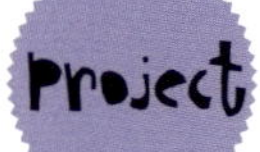

Geometric collage cut-out

When I first tested out this project, I was planning on using only the shape cut-outs, but I ended up loving how the background of the page looked, too. A happy accident led to two matching pieces of art that look beautiful next to each other.

YOU WILL NEED

- Watercolor paper
- Watercolor paint
- Large paintbrush
- Pencil
- Craft knife
- Glue

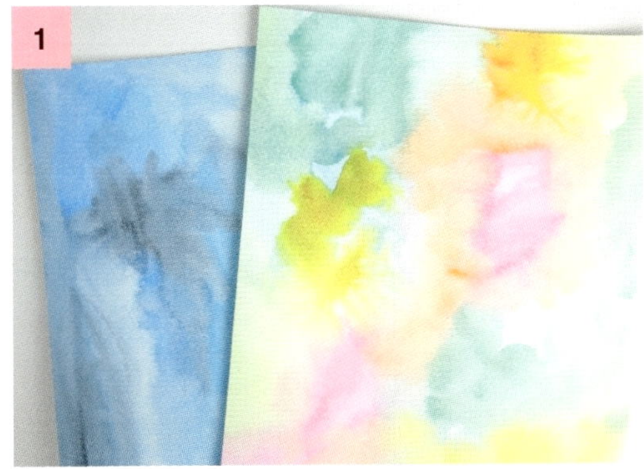

Start by filling two sheets of paper with color. I chose to do one sheet with light pastels and the other much darker. Having some contrast is good, but the color choice is up to you.

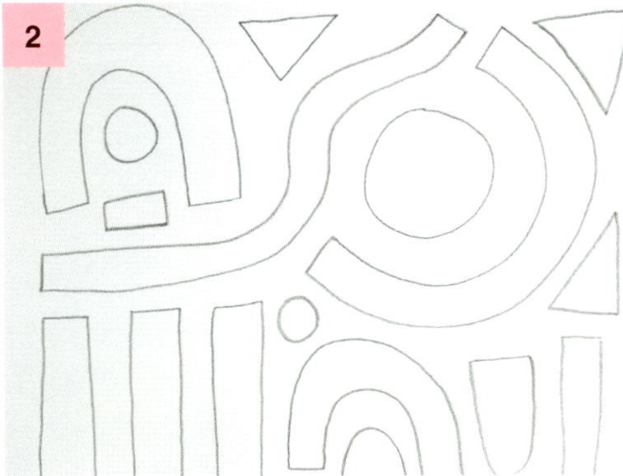

Flip one sheet over and start drawing a geometric design on the back with a pencil. Keep the shapes fairly simple because you will be cutting them out in the next step.

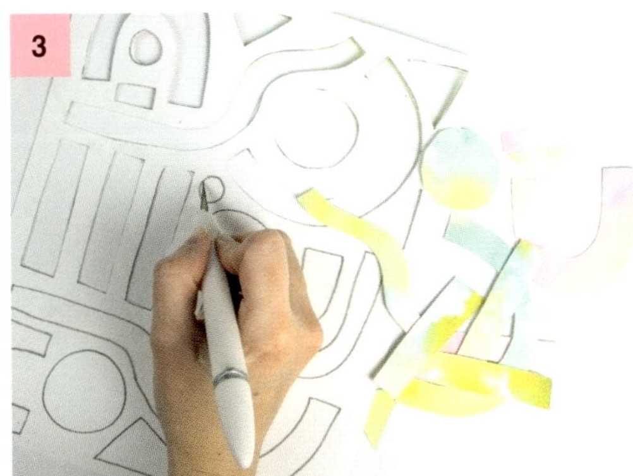

Using a craft knife, carefully cut out each shape from the page. Take care to preserve not only the shapes but the background too.

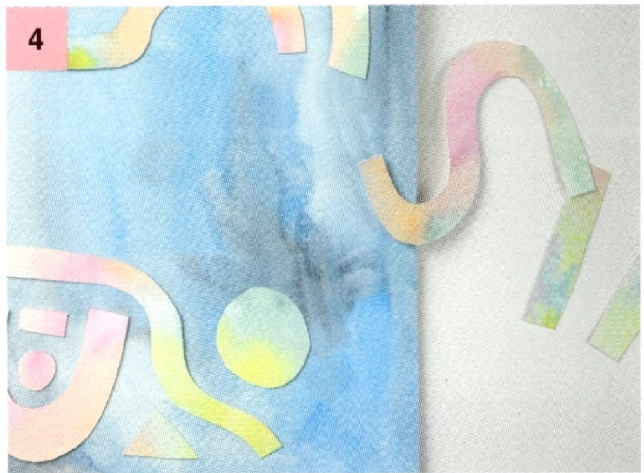

Grab the other sheet of paper and start assembling the pattern on it using the background as a guide. Once it is all put together, glue each shape down.

Project Watercolor quilt

YOU WILL NEED

- Watercolor paper
- Watercolor paint
- Pencil
- Ruler
- Small round brush
- Scissors

I really admire people who have the patience to sew—I much prefer the instant gratification of painting. For this project, we are going to take our inspiration from quilts. If you are not a quilter, you can begin by browsing for a quilt pattern to replicate on paper.

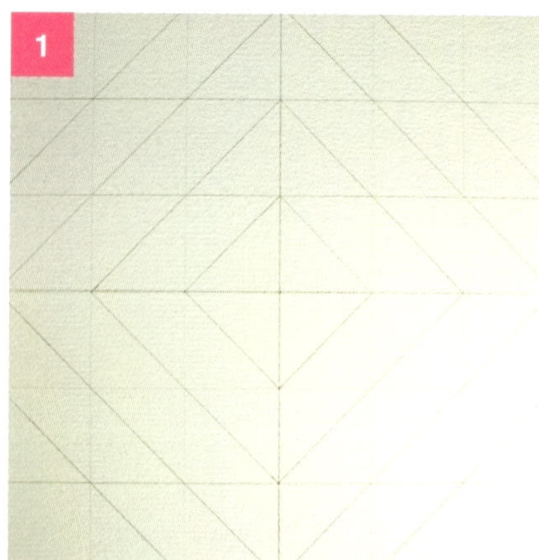

Start by drawing out your quilt pattern with a pencil and ruler. Find the center of your page first and then work out from there.

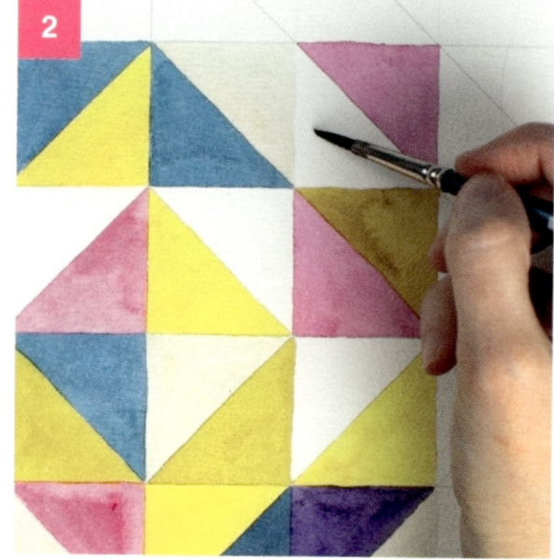

Once your pattern is laid out, begin carefully filling each section with color using a small round brush. If you don't want bleeding colors, be sure to let each part dry before painting its neighbor.

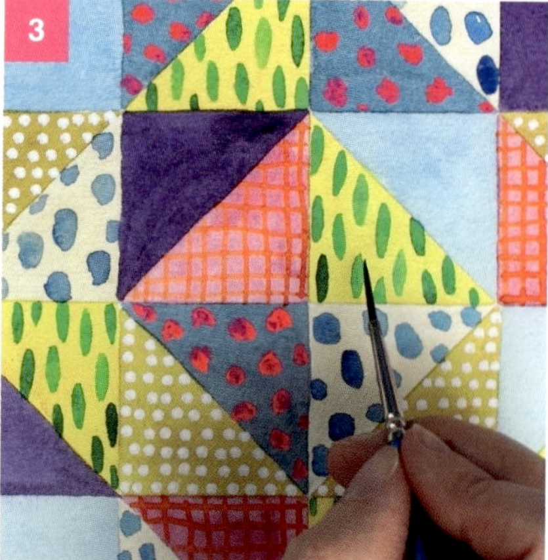

When the base colors are dry, add some pattern. You can even bring in other mediums here, such as markers, gouache, or pen. After letting your quilt square dry, add the last few details and trim the paper down to a square.

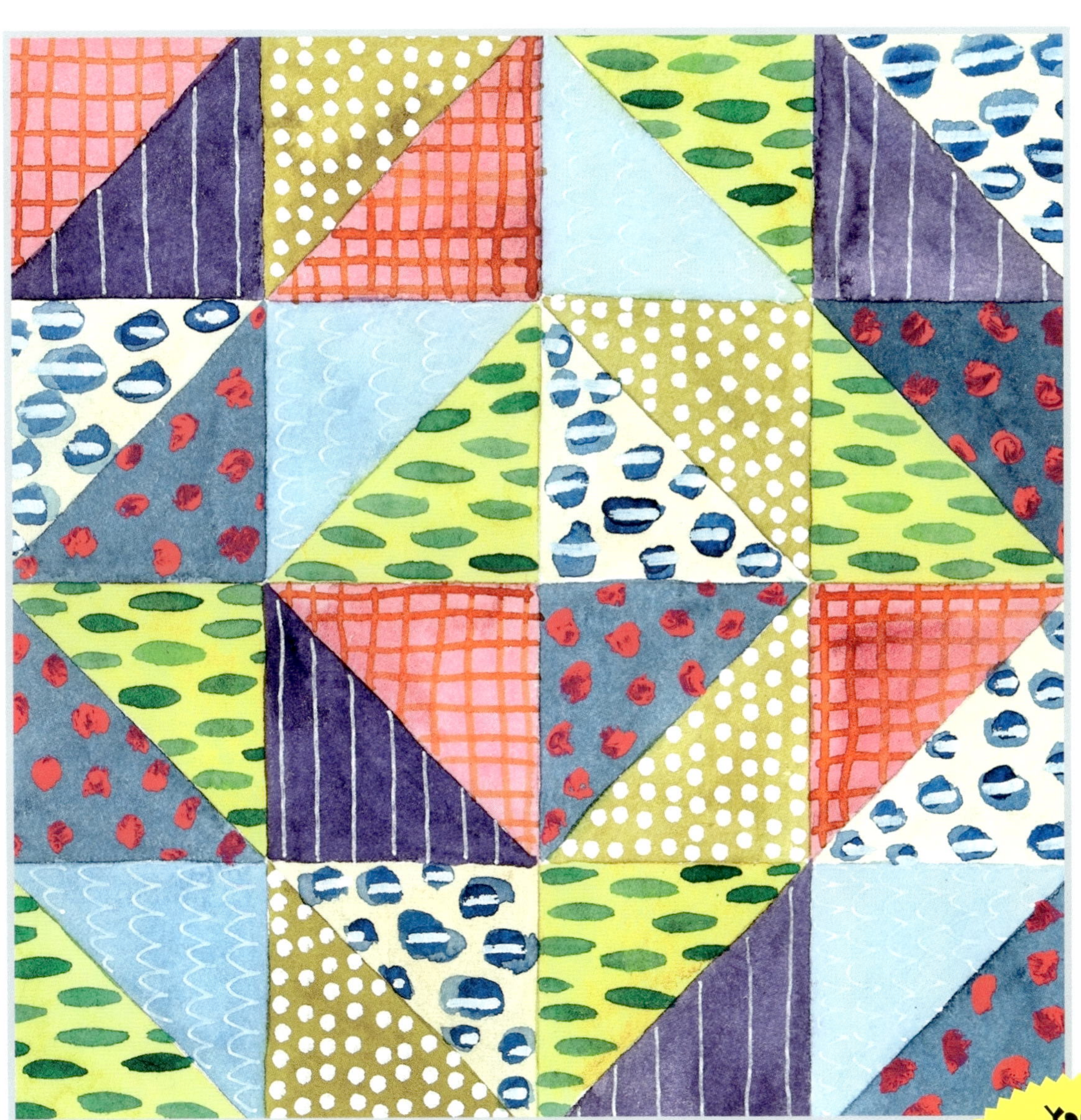

Your finished piece

This is like a mini exercise in designing your own fabric collection. Geometric, floral, or large-scale—there are so many styles to consider.

Index

Illustrations are in *italic*, projects are in **bold**.

Credits

To my husband, Ryan, for always supporting my crazy ideas, and to my son, Stanley, for being the cutest distraction. Now, please, take a nap.